CW00501629

CHICHESTER
Then and Now

Chichester
OBSERVER
www.chichester.co.uk Established 1887 1501 - 2001

CHICHESTER
Then and Now

Phil Hewitt

breedon books
PUBLISHING

First published in Great Britain in 2009 by
The Breedon Books Publishing Company Limited
Breedon House, 3 The Parker Centre,
Derby, DE21 4SZ.

© Philip Hewitt, 2009

All Rights Reserved. No part of this publication may be reproduced, stored in a retrieval system, or transmitted in any form, or by any means, electronic, mechanical, photocopying, recording or otherwise without the prior permission in writing of the copyright holders, nor be otherwise circulated in any form or binding or cover other than in which it is published and without a similar condition being imposed on the subsequent publisher.

A catalogue record for this book is available from the British Library.

ISBN 978-1-85983-701-6

Printed and bound by TJ International Ltd, Padstow, Cornwall.

Contents

Introduction

Chichester's Rich Heritage

Something very reassuring happened to me time and time again during the preparation of this book.

Put on a suit, carry a folder of papers under your arm, stand in front of a historic part of Chichester, whip out a camera – and very soon you will be accosted.

Within seconds someone will be at your elbow and, with a slightly forced friendliness, they will challenge you: 'You're not going to knock that down, are you?'

Tempting as it was to say 'Yes, the bulldozers arrive on Monday', it was far more enjoyable to stand and chat about just what a great city we are privileged to live and work in.

Chichester people are fiercely proud of Chichester – and that is why the city has managed to preserve so much of its past. Chichester is a city worth protecting, and the people of Chichester have preserved it to their utmost.

The result is that we now enjoy a unique historical patchwork. The Market Cross, a vestige of a thriving mediaeval market town, stands at the intersection of two Roman roads which house a wealth of superb Georgian buildings. Victorian chapels add to the mix, while the main streets are lined with a rich array of modern shops.

These days, the stores do not seem to stay for long, but always others take their place, all part of the constant change which ensures the city's commercial viability.

This book is about that change, but it is also about the deep underlying continuity which ensures Chichester remains the city we all know and love.

With the help of the West Sussex Record Office in Orchard Street and Chichester District Museum in Little London, I have chosen a range of archive images and then tried to replicate each photograph by standing where the earlier photographer once stood.

Street signs clutter the pavements, cars seem to be parked anywhere and everywhere, and at times I took my life in my hands as I tried to get the angle just right while not getting flattened by the oncoming traffic.

But the results have opened my eyes, just as I hope they will open yours. The past is all around us in Chichester if only we stop and look. In many cases this simply means looking up.

North Street, South Street, West Street and East Street offer a range of shops you could find pretty much anywhere, but look above the shop fronts and you start to appreciate buildings genuinely unique to Chichester.

For this photographic tour of Chichester, the Market Cross seemed the best place to begin before moving out to the site of the old West Gate and re-entering the city centre from there.

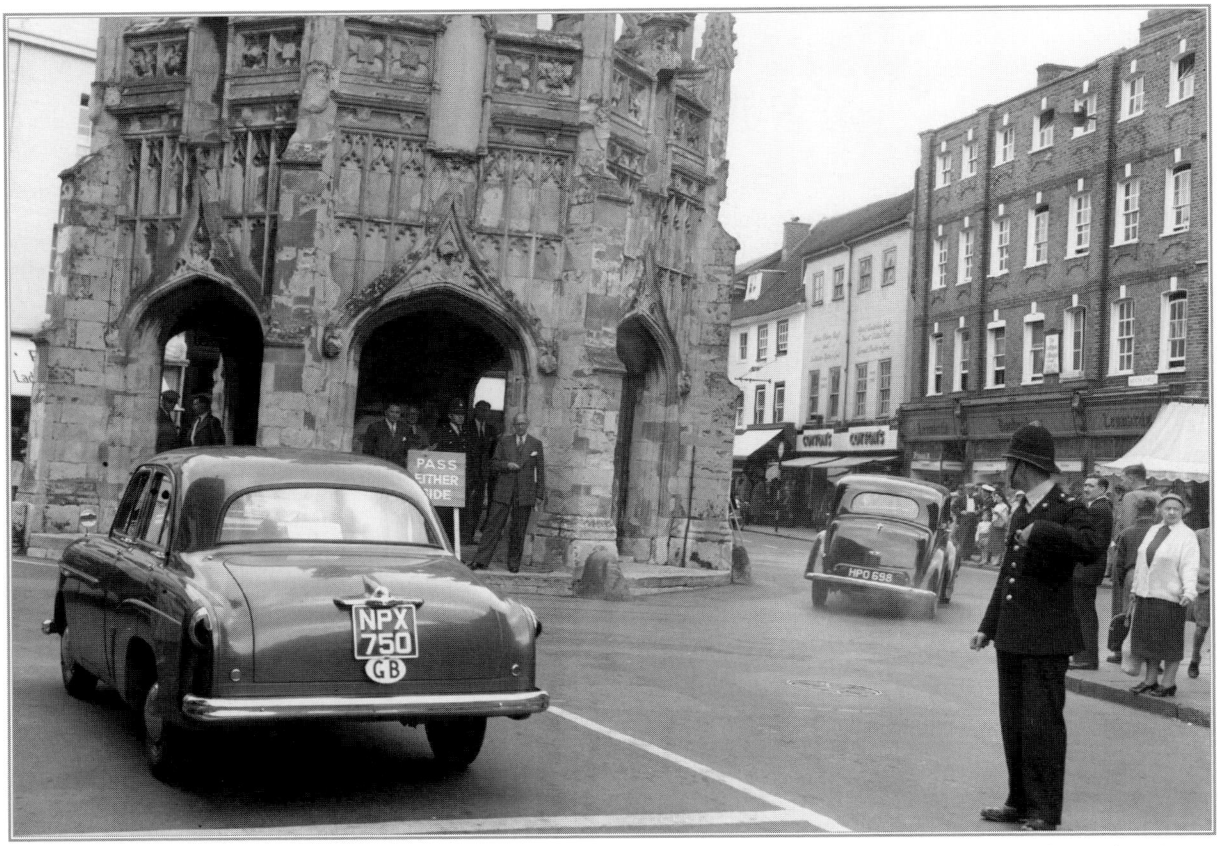

Above: A policeman anxiously watches the results of an experiment in traffic control at Chichester's Market Cross on 12 August 1955 – the day cars could drive in both directions around the Cross. *Below:* The Cross today.

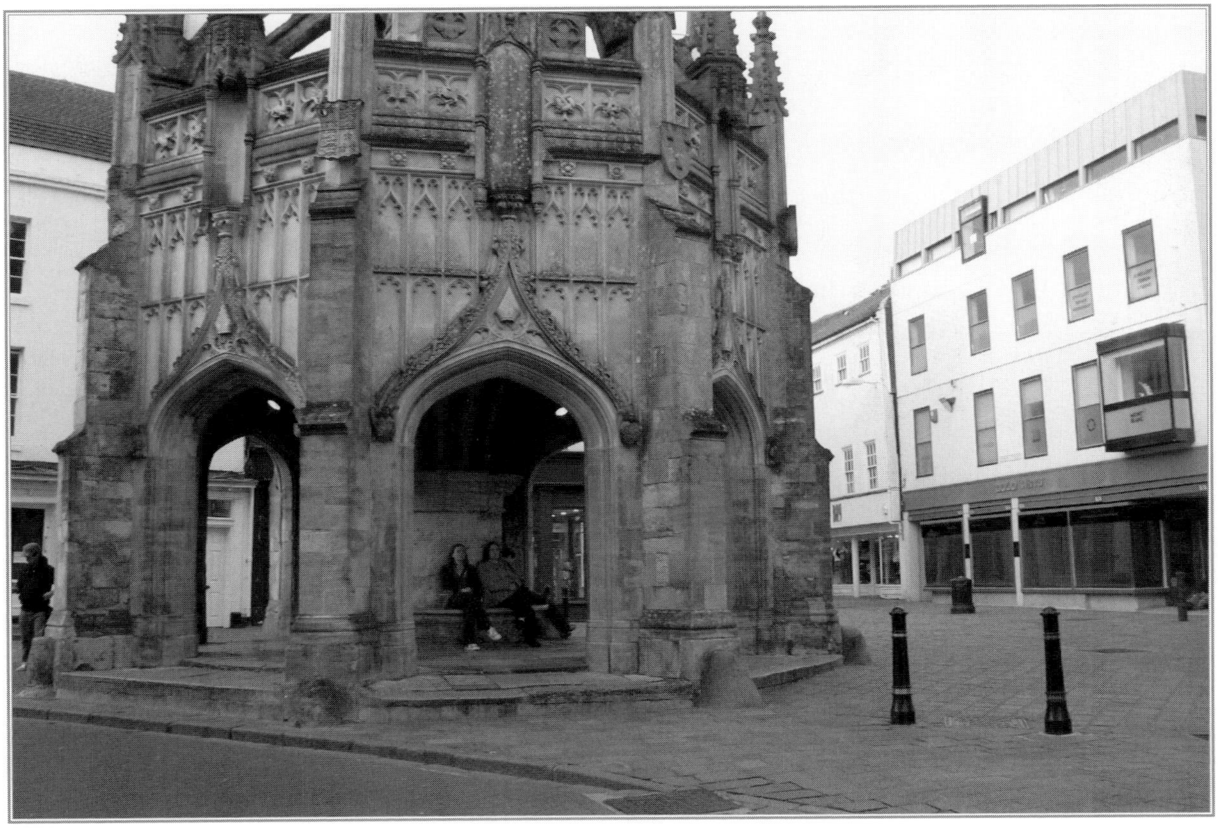

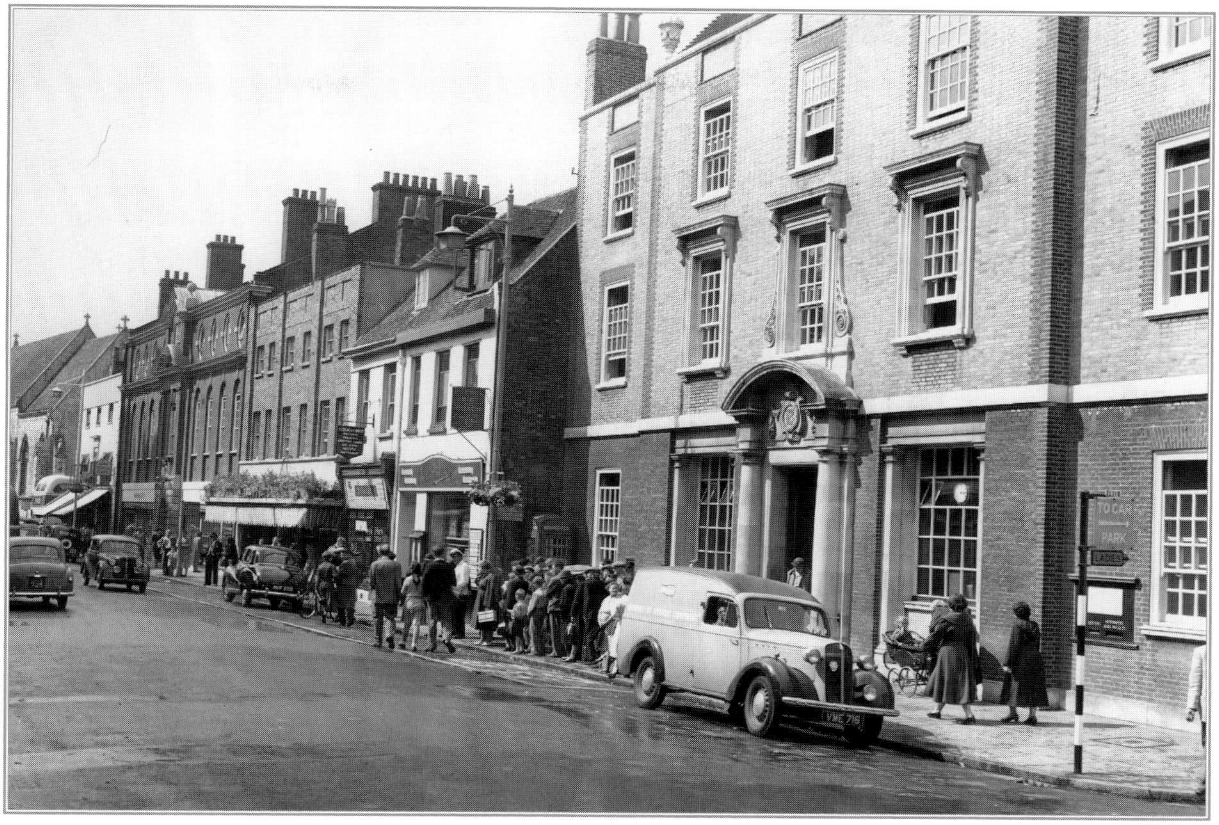

Just to the left of the Post Office in this 1950s view of West Street is the Southdown Motor Services ticket office. To its left are Gough Brothers, fine art dealers, and then Morants drapers store.

The same view today.

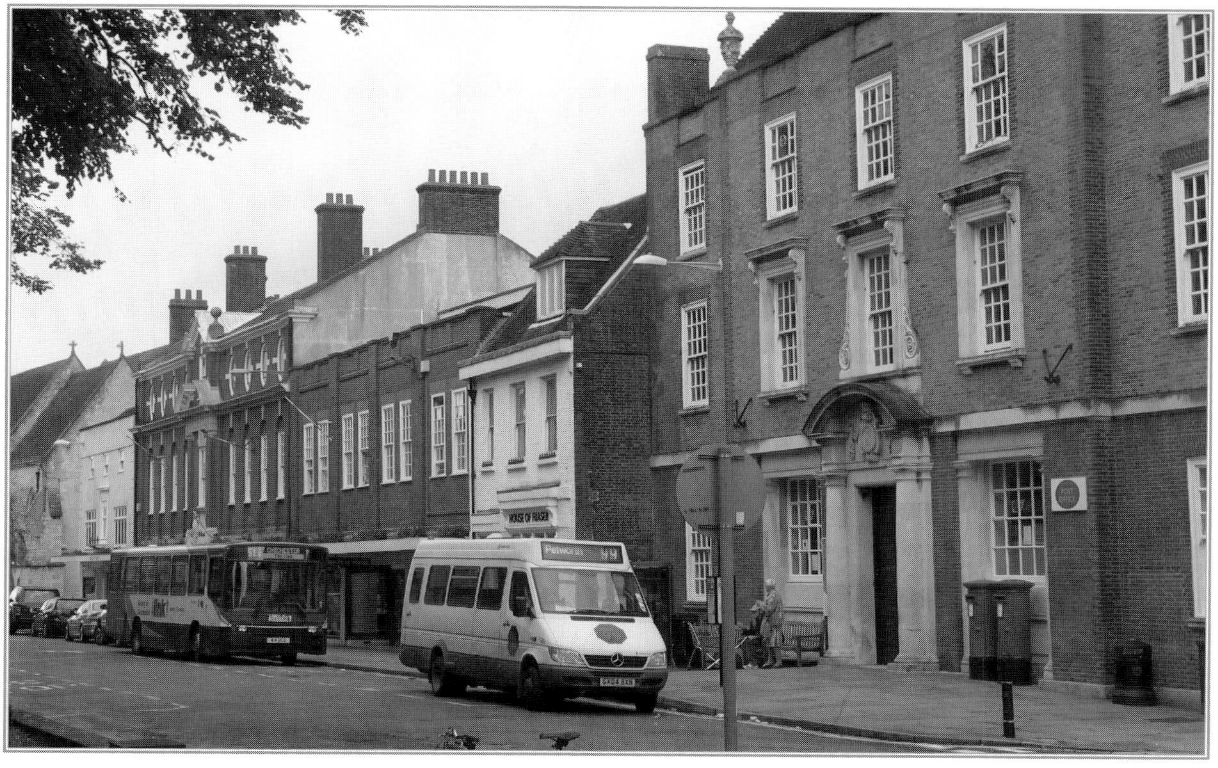

The book continues with glimpses into North Street, South Street and East Street before looking at the other 'gates' – East, North and South.

The final chapters take a themed approach, beginning by looking at the fate of the city's first four cinemas, part of the city's cinema-going heyday. It is a remarkable thought that three cinemas were once running simultaneously within several hundred yards of each other.

The next chapter looks at what I think is the most fascinating aspect of Chichester, the fates of its ancient churches. Two have been demolished, a third has become an arts centre, a fourth awaits further development, a fifth is a pub and a sixth a bookshop.

The book concludes with a look at some of the city's pubs before acknowledging the important place the County Record Office and the District Museum occupy in the city. They conserve and they preserve, but not in an arid, hideaway sense. They are there to serve anyone with an interest in Chichester history and they do so with a superb blend of professionalism, knowledge and enthusiasm. Both have been invaluable in the preparation of this book. My thanks to Alan Readman and Simon Kitchin in particular.

And so, let the tour begin…

Phil Hewitt
March 2009

CHAPTER 1
THE CROSS

A Symbol of the City

Standing at the intersection of the Roman roads which run north to south and east to west through the city, the Market Cross is one of the great symbols of Chichester.

Just as the cathedral has been a constant presence throughout successive centuries of worship, so the Cross epitomises successive centuries of trade – a daily reminder that Chichester was shaped above all by its importance as a market town.

Mediaeval Chichester was characterised by a wealth of different industries which flourished simultaneously. Needle-making thrived just outside the city; leather-making, concentrated in the Pallants, was also important and, in 1314, Chichester was one of only 12 cities in England given a charter to trade wool.

Most important of all was the trade in livestock, as the image below records. Dating from the late 1800s, the photograph shows a trader at the Cross and sheep being driven to market, summing up the city's commercial origins.

Every second Wednesday animal markets were held in the streets. For centuries sheep, cows, horses, bullocks, donkeys and goats would be sold in East Street, calves in North Street, and sheep and pigs up at Northgate.

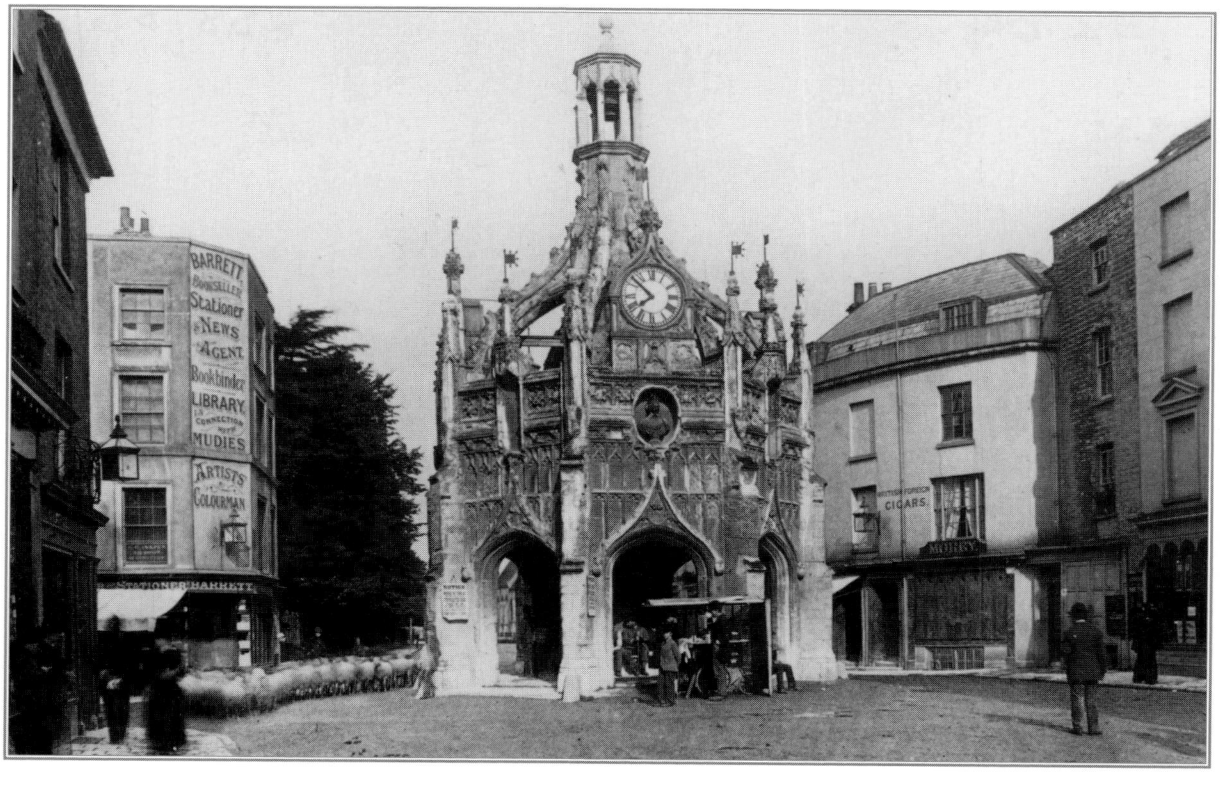

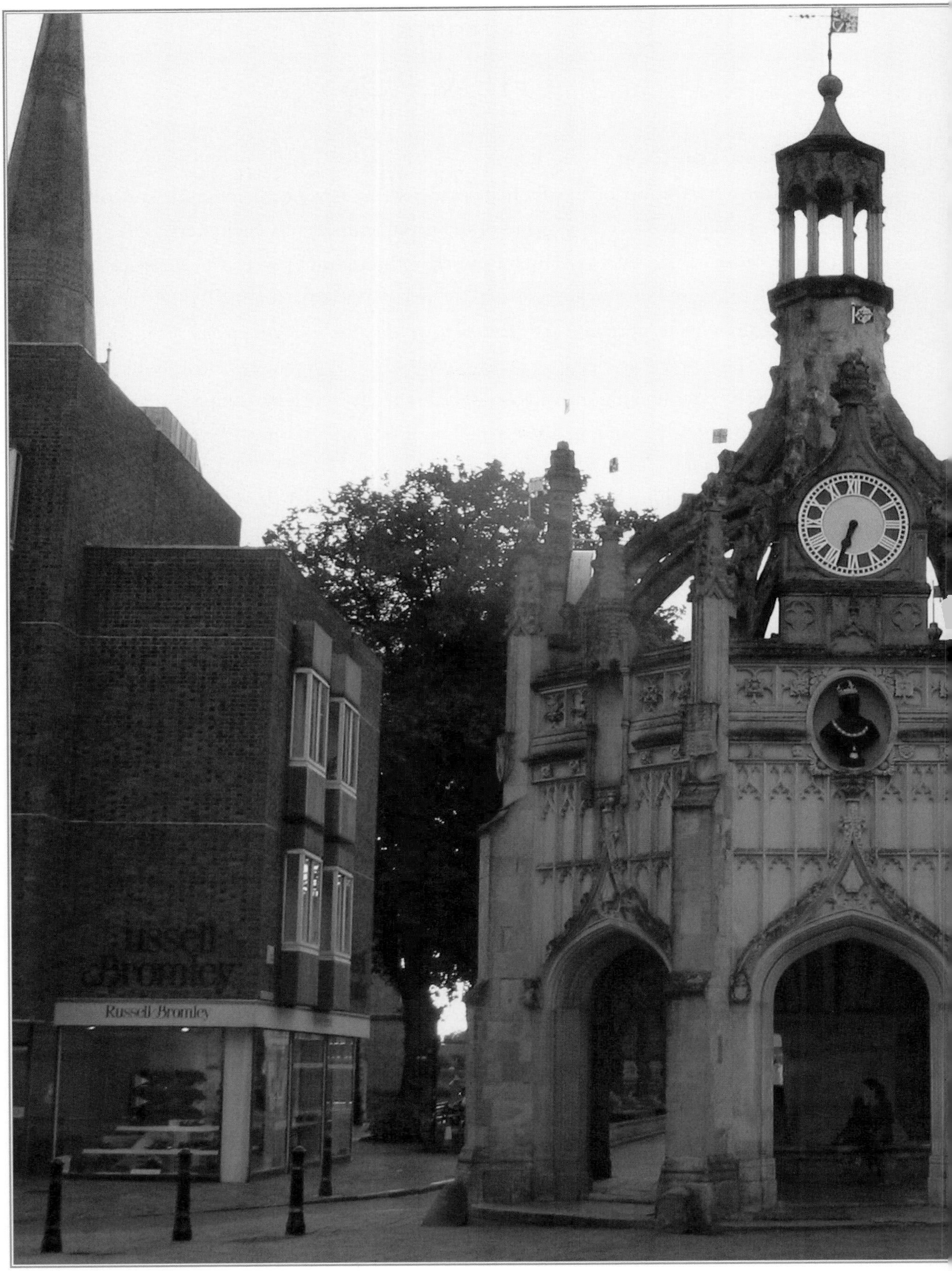
Russell Bromley
Russell Bromley

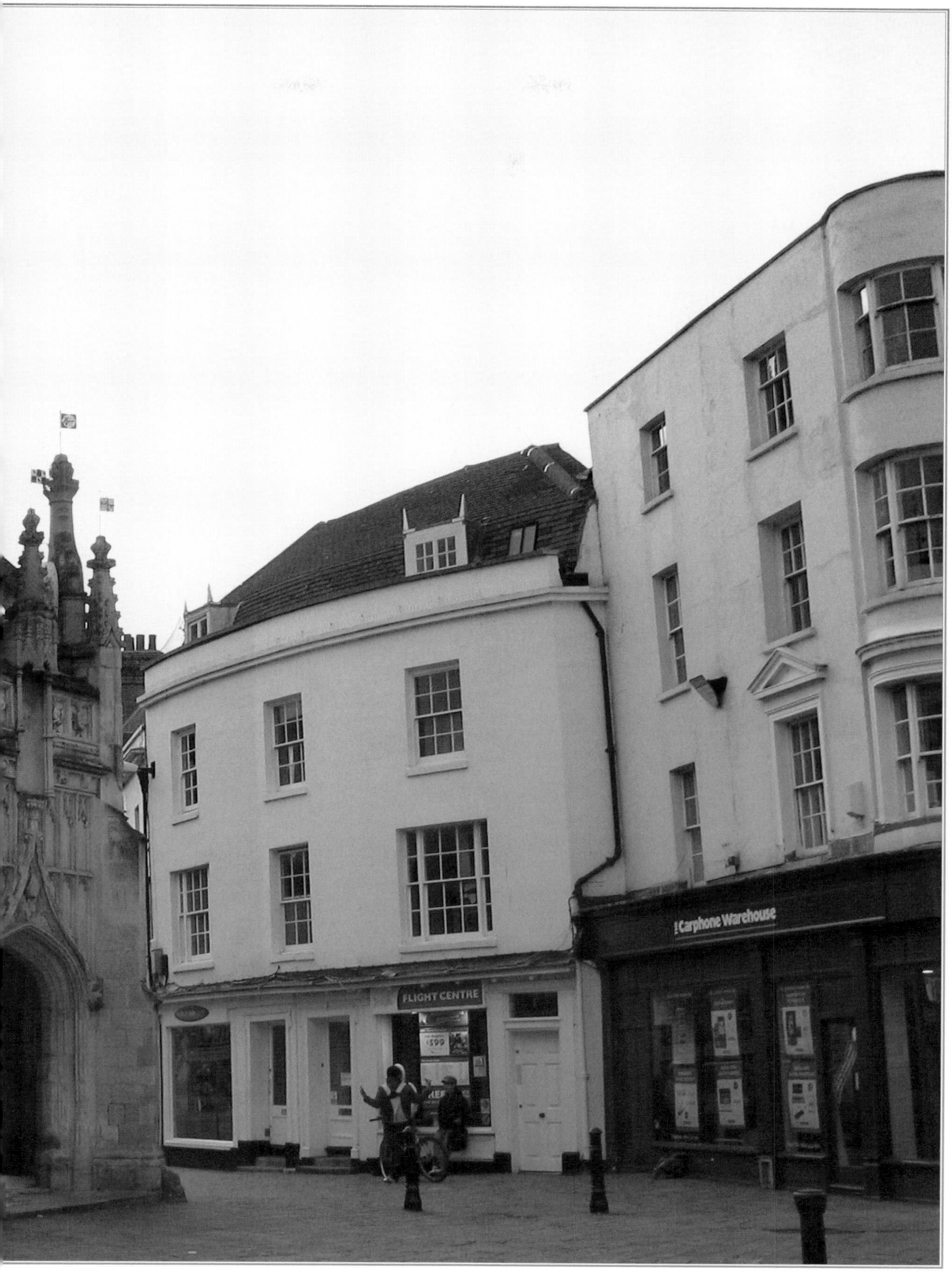
FLIGHT CENTRE
Carphone Warehouse

Chichester was also home to a thriving corn market and was a key centre for the wine trade. Also to be found in the city were curriers, saddlers, carpenters, brick-makers and maltsters – a rich mix of businesses which were all part of Chichester's trading tapestry.

It is therefore in this context that we should view the Market Cross. One of the finest in England, it serves as a reminder of Chichester's early commercial importance. Although the streets around it now hum to the sounds of different kinds of trade, the Cross itself stands remarkably unaltered as the image on pages 12–13 shows.

Bishop Story's Legacy

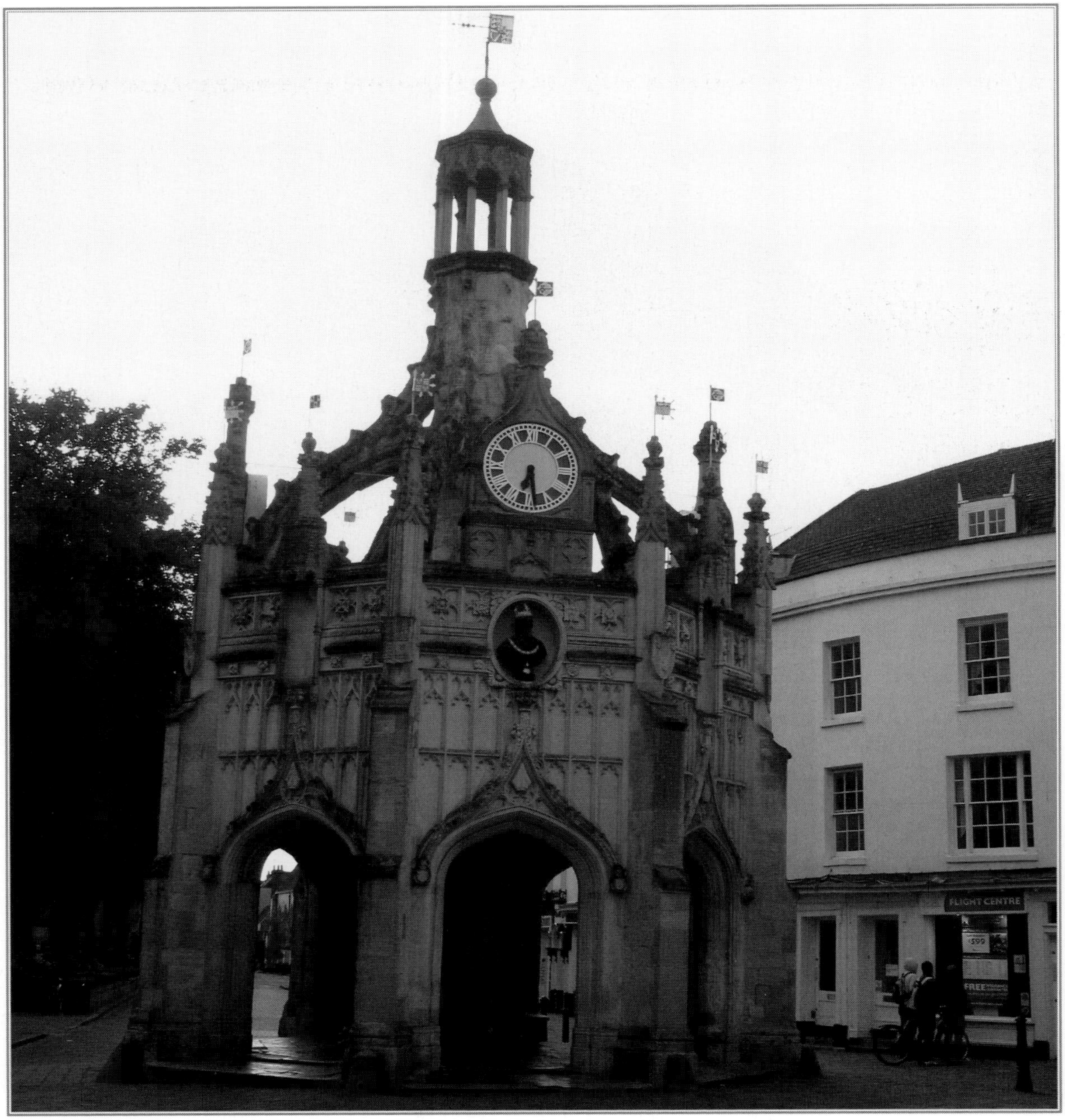

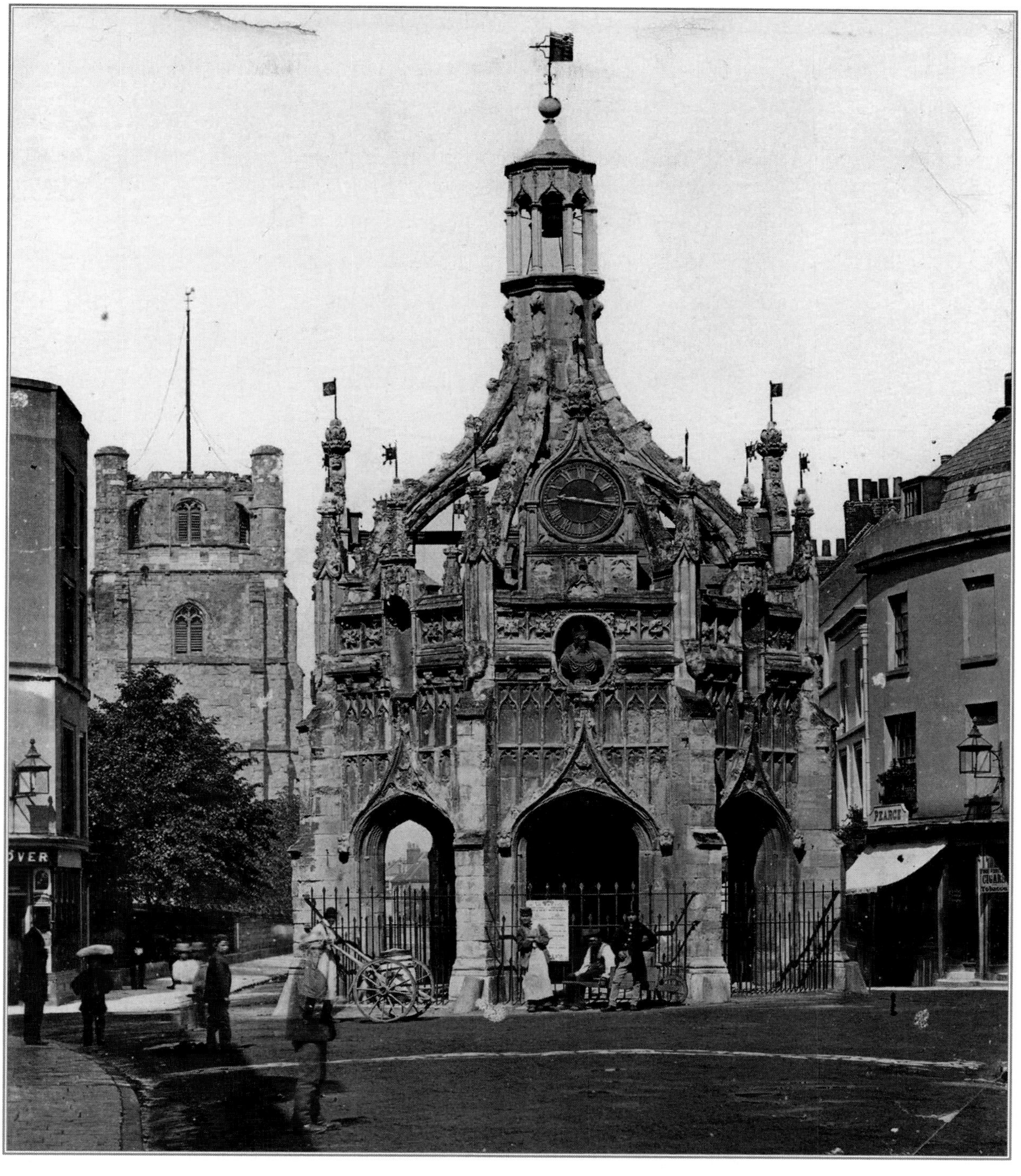

The man who gave Chichester its Market Cross was Bishop Edward Story (or Storey), a former Bishop of Carlisle who served as Bishop of Chichester from 1478 until his death in 1503.

Bishop Story was granted a charter for the building of the Cross in 1501 to provide somewhere for the poor to sell their wares. It fulfilled this role until 1808 when the present Butter Market was opened in North Street.

Trading ceased at the Cross at that date and railings – which can be seen in the older photograph, above – were installed, remaining there until about 1872.

Although Bishop Story died two years after commissioning the Cross he continued to do his bit to ensure its future, leaving £25 a year for its upkeep. Story also instructed his executors to give property in North Kingsham to the cathedral's dean and chapter in compensation for the cathedral land they had lost when the Cross was erected.

Story's other great Chichester legacy is the Prebendal School which he refounded in 1497. The oldest school in Sussex, it probably dates back to the foundation of Chichester Cathedral when it would have been a song school responsible for teaching and housing the choristers – a function it fulfils to this day. Story attached it to the Prebend of Highleigh in Chichester Cathedral, hence its present name.

Story was educated at Pembroke Hall, Cambridge, where he was elected a fellow in about 1444. He was consecrated Bishop of Carlisle on 2 October 1468 and also served as Chancellor of Cambridge University.

In 21st-century Chichester the Market Cross now seems fairly hemmed in, but when it was commissioned it would have enjoyed a wide, open setting. Modern-day encroachments certainly make it difficult to appreciate its full glory.

An Architectural Gem

Ogee-arched hoods, cusped infillings, bosses of demi-angels, quatrefoil compartments, crocketed and panelled pinnacles and open ogee arches...they are all there.

However, the technicalities do not even remotely do justice to the sheer beauty of Chichester's Market Cross, an elegant, intricately decorated structure with a charm all its own.

The Cross is built of Caen stone, with eight sides around a central shaft upon which sits a cupola, supported by eight flying buttresses. Internally, the ribbed vaulting springs from the massive central shaft to small pillars at the outer wall.

Around the base of the central column is a low stone seat which is still popular today. The stone-paved floor is raised on steps, and externally each side has a heavily moulded arched opening.

The east side of the Cross contains a bronze bust of Charles I in a specially formed niche, replacing a statue of the founder which formerly stood there. The bust of the executed king was added by Charles II in tribute to his father, perhaps rather pointedly given that Chichester was home to the regicide William Cawley (1602–67), one of the signatories of Charles I's death warrant.

The Duke of Richmond made extensive renovations and alterations in 1746, among them the addition of the weathervane on top. Since then the Cross has remained unaltered. In 1930 it was carefully repaired and treated with a stone preservative.

In the first of the two images seen here, alongside the policeman stands city pie-man Joe Faro. Faro had an oven behind his house at No. 50 George Street, Chichester. He was well known at the Cross, at the market and at Chichester's Sloe Fair between 1863 and 1913. His portable pie oven stands beside him in this photograph.

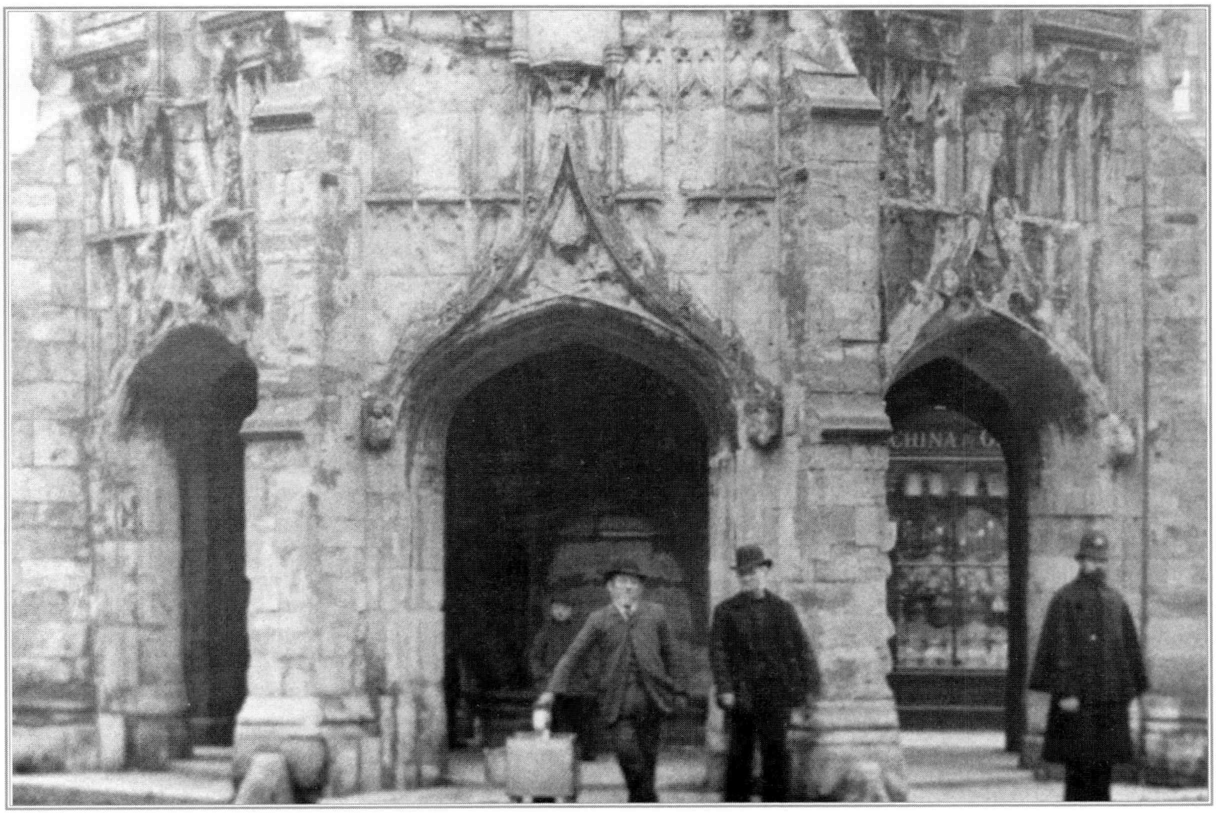
CHINA

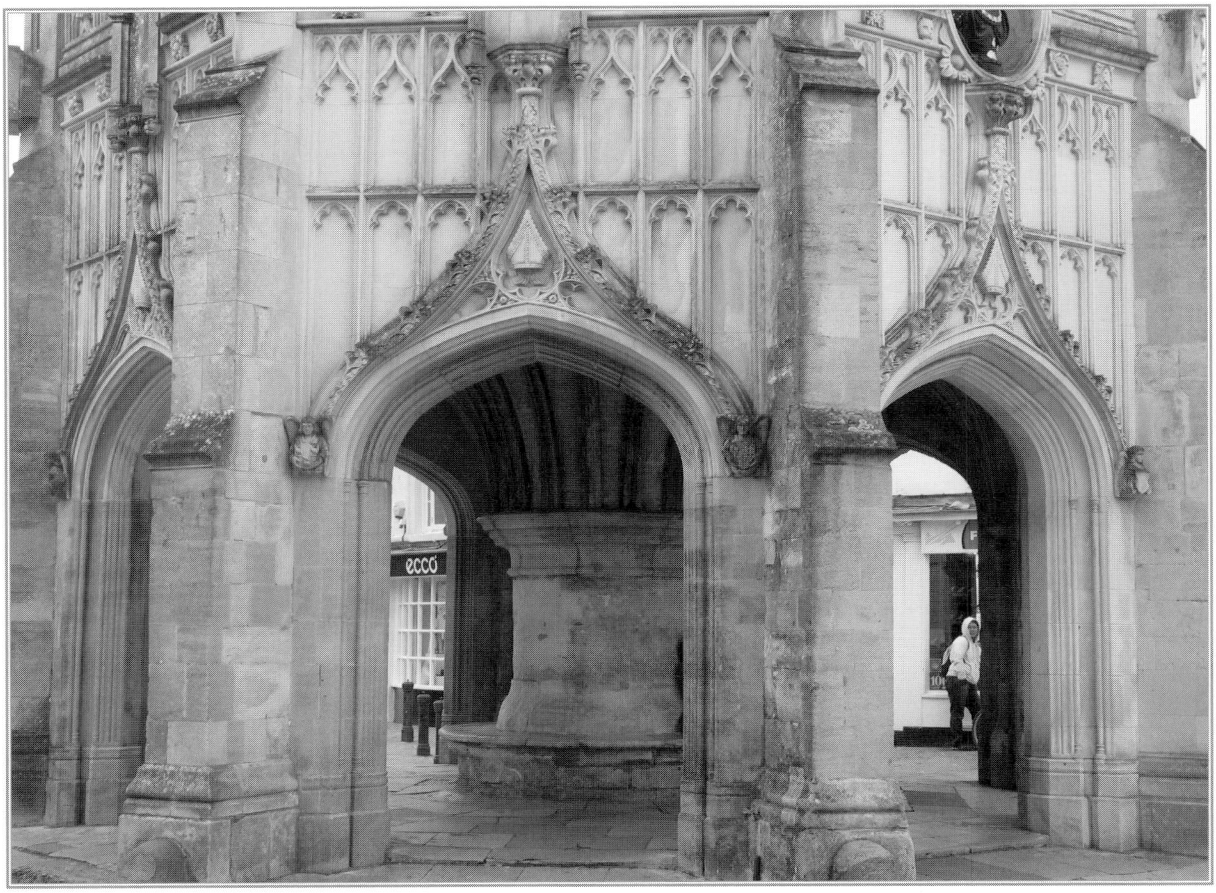
ecco

Where Chichester Likes to Gather

As trading moved away from the Market Cross, so it emerged as a different kind of focal point – an emblem of Chichester solidarity at important events.

Gathering at the Cross has long been the Chichester way to see in the New Year, and down the decades it has also been the place for various proclamations, most notably that of Queen Elizabeth II's accession to the throne.

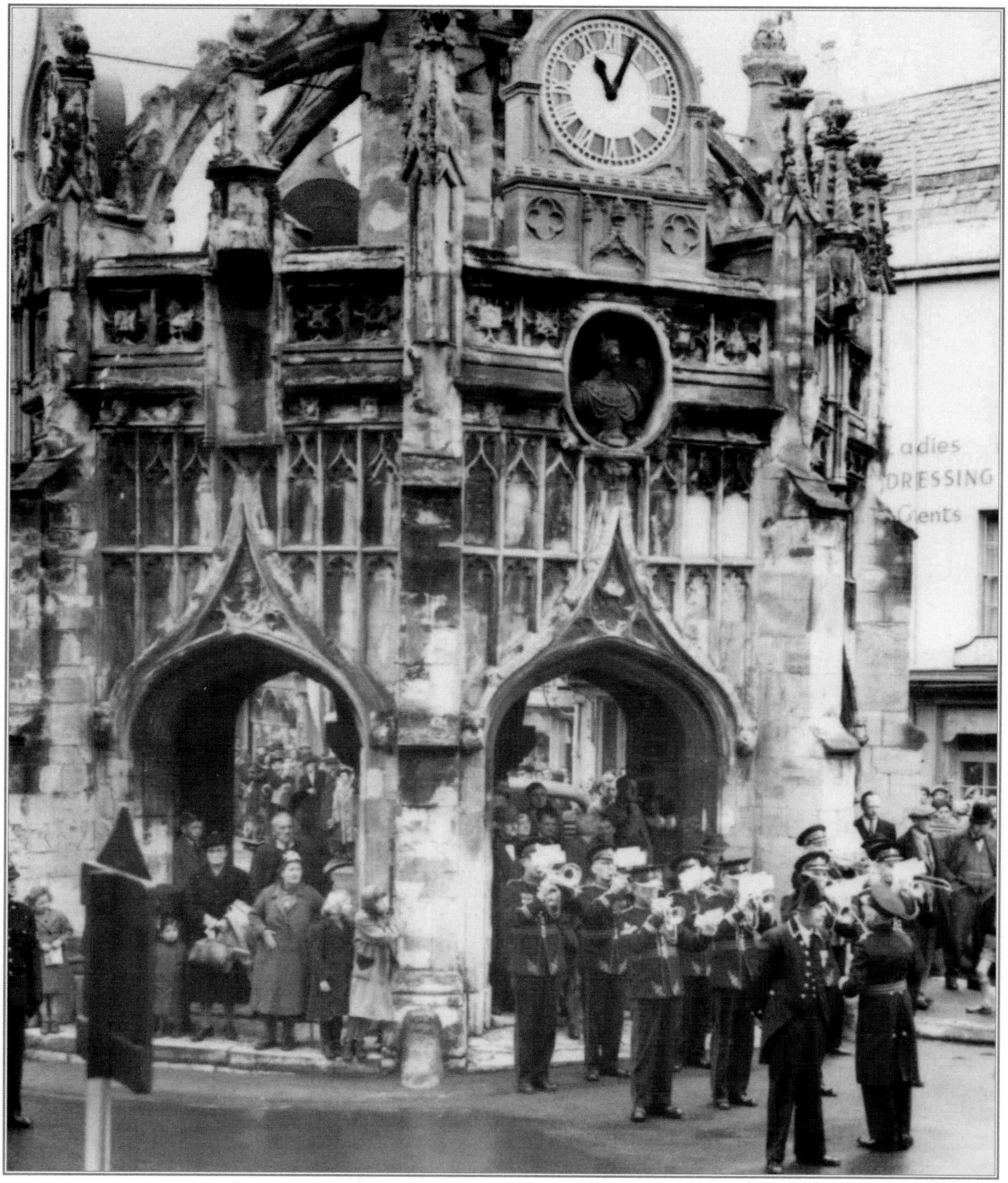

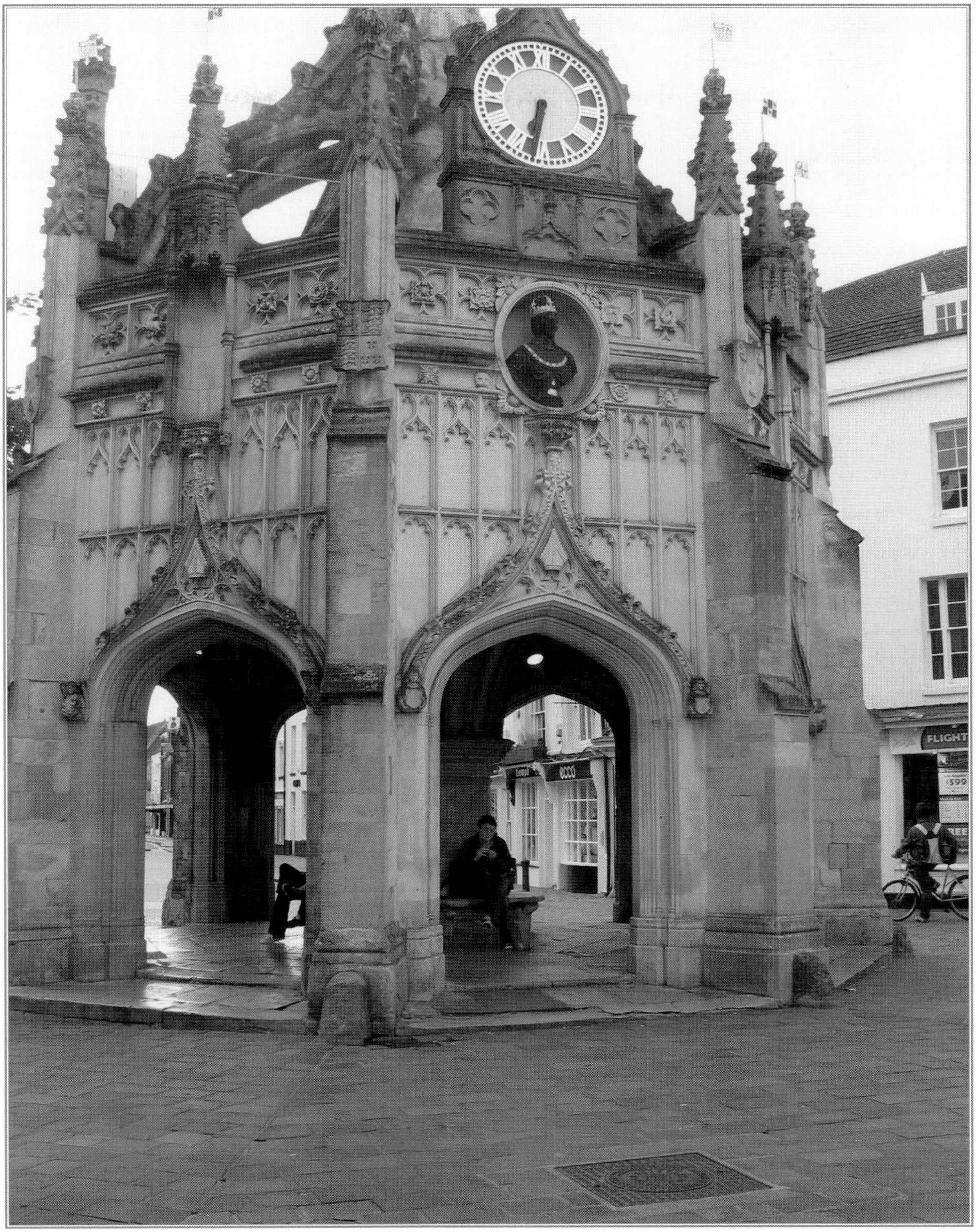

It was also towards the Cross that people instinctively gravitated when peace broke out in Europe in May 1945.

The image on the previous page, showing a band playing at the Cross, illustrates the Cross's ability to draw the crowds. The event is unknown. The date is probably between 1950 and 1960.

By then the sale of livestock near the Cross had long since ended, business having transferred to the Cattle Market in the early 1870s. Sheep farming declined in West Sussex in the early 20th century, but in the 1950s and 1960s pig farming increased, Chichester hosting one of the largest pig markets in the south.

As the century entered its final decades, however, Chichester's future as a livestock centre became ever more uncertain. The final cattle market was held on 24 October 1990.

A few years later there was marked consternation when *The Chichester Observer* announced that trading would soon be returning to the Market Cross – trading of a distinctly 20th-century kind.

The Observer disclosed plans for the Market Cross to be relaunched as a burger bar, plans which apparently already had significant local authority backing. It was just a matter of time before hamburgers, cheeseburgers, veggie burgers and the like would be cooked on the premises, behind the Cross's newly re-railed archways.

The howls of protest were already starting to rise when the good burghers of Chichester noticed the date: 1 April.

Chapter 2
West Street

God Save the King!

Here is a sight which would have inflamed the parliamentarians who so destructively besieged and attacked Chichester's royalist centre during the English Civil War.

Their attack did little long-term damage to royalist fervour. Three centuries later in 1937, at pretty much the point at which General Sir William Waller launched his assault in 1642, we see a celebratory arch marking the coronation of King George VI.

Chichester boasts a proud tradition of royal visitors and a great willingness to celebrate events of royal importance. The photograph below shows an archway decoration at Westgate – a celebration typical of Chichester, a city which liked to show its loyalty by invoking its mediaeval gates.

Like most Roman walled towns Chichester was divided into four quarters by two main roads crossing approximately in the middle of the town, thus creating North Street, South Street, West Street and East Street. Each had its own gate and this is roughly where the city's West Gate would have stood.

This is an appropriate point from which to begin our exploration. The imitation West Gate below leads the eye towards the city centre along West Street, always the most residential of the four main streets.

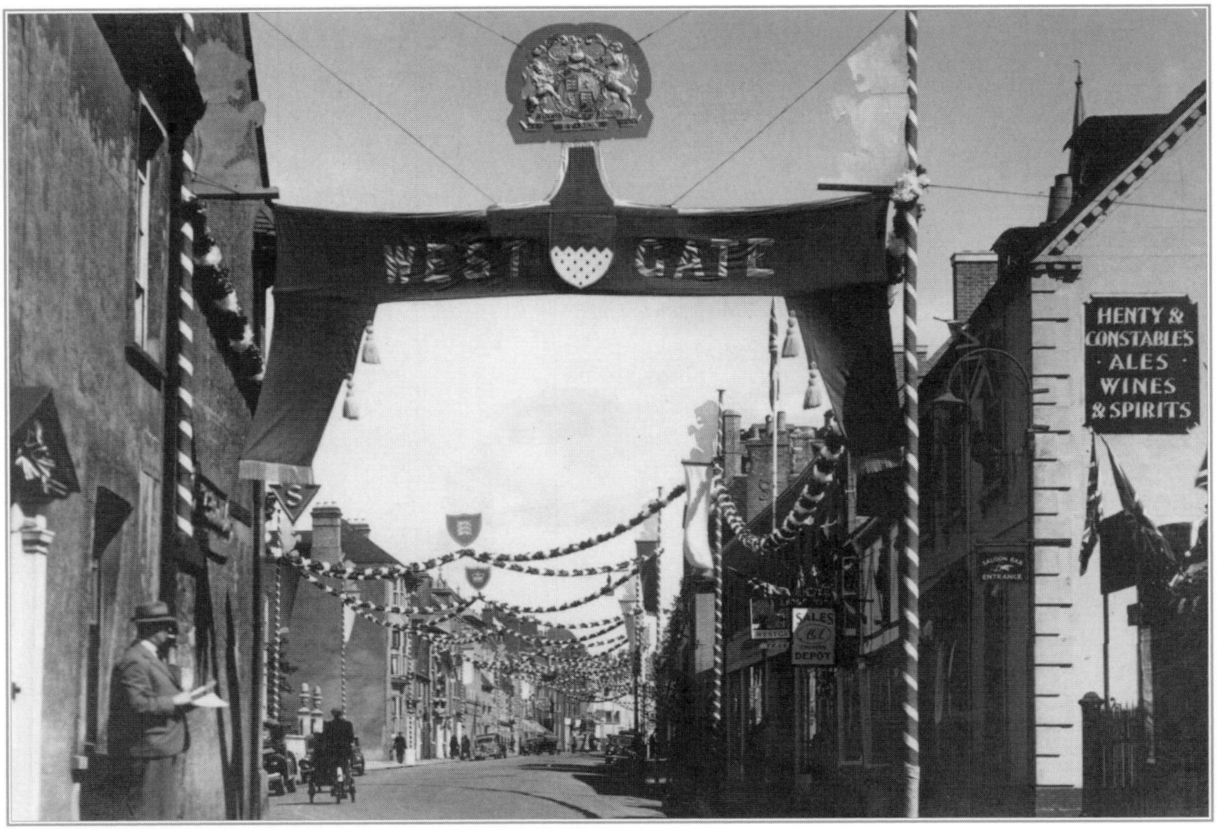

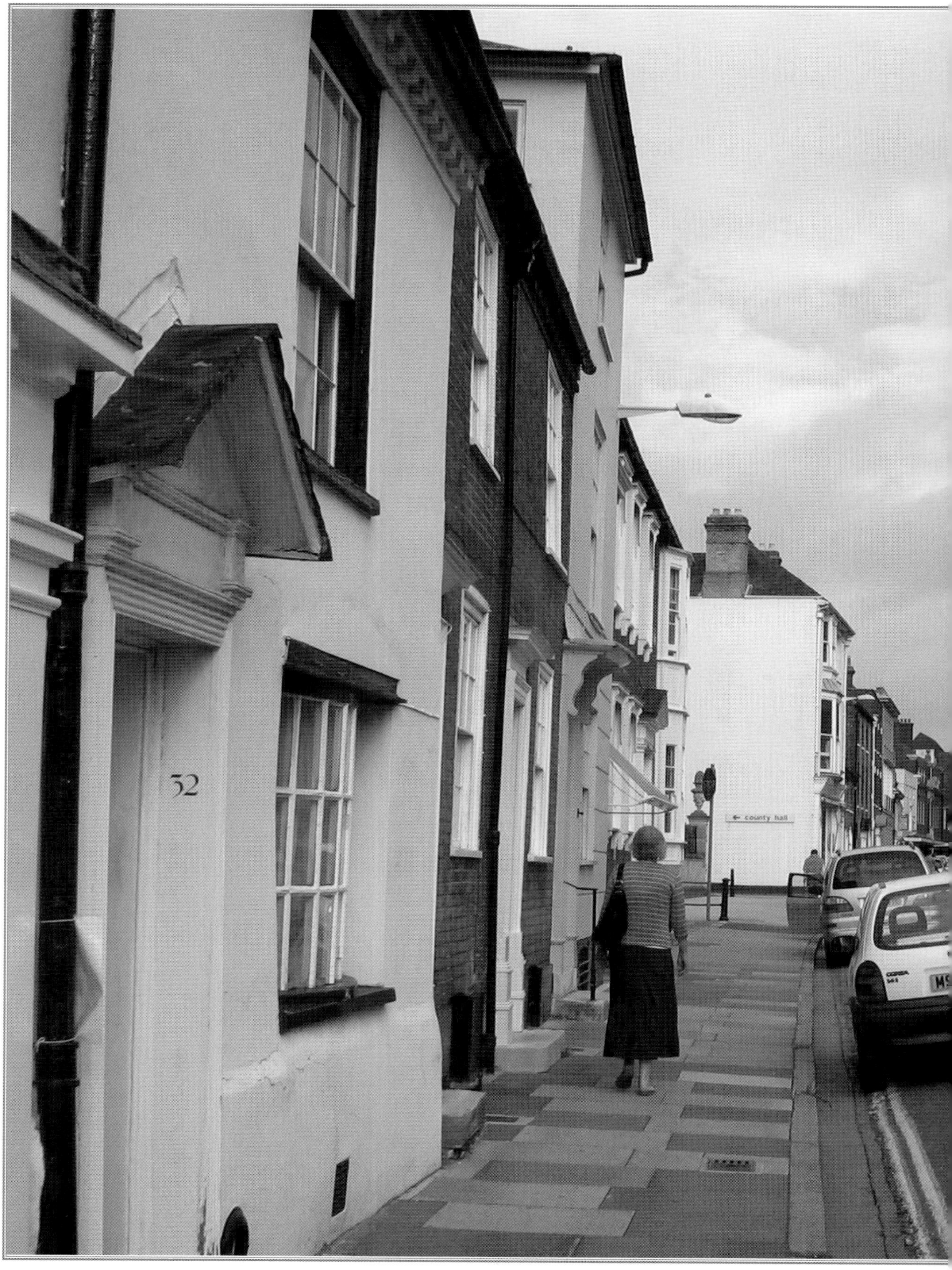
32
county hall

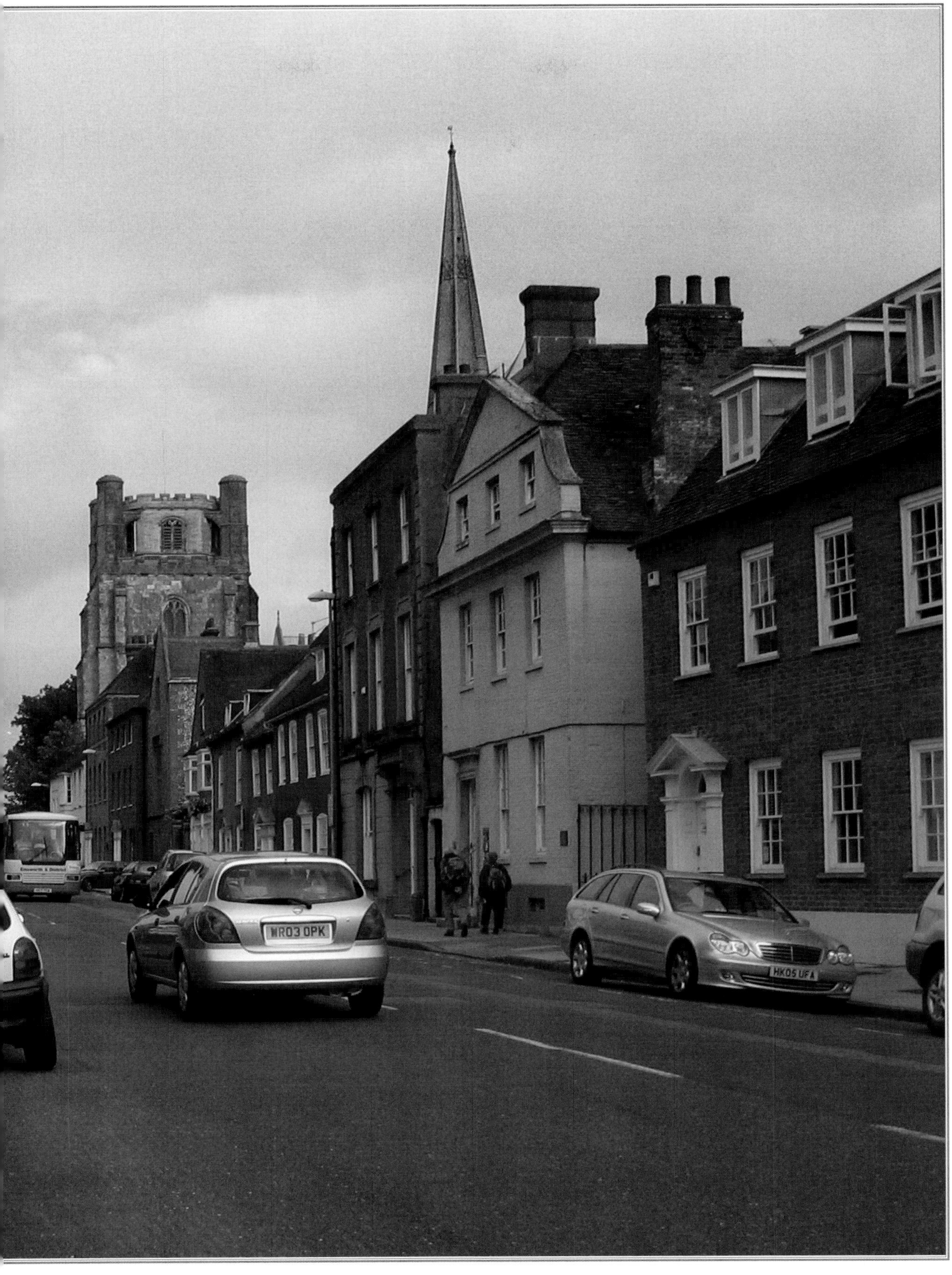
WR03 OPK
HK05 UFA

To the left in the picture on pages 22–23 you can just glimpse the entrance to the historic Edes House; to the right the cathedral spire is visible above the rooftops. This is an area which has consistently attracted wealthy occupants – generally the professional classes who so flourished during Chichester's Georgian heyday, a period which greatly shaped the city.

The country saw enormous economic advances and these were reflected in Chichester, most particularly in its architecture. Chichester was a thriving market town with the emphasis on agriculture – a fact which meant it was well placed to flourish under the successive King Georges.

Edes House – A Georgian Treasure

The cars clutter around it now but there is no denying the elegance of Chichester's Edes House, a beautifully proportioned brick house which in recent years has carried the name of John and Hannah Edes for whom it was built in 1696.

Photographs contrasting past and present in the city's main shopping streets show time and again the way beautiful brickwork has been painted over for no obvious reason.

Fortunately, Edes House has suffered no such desecration. Its red brick and Portland stone remains untouched. Over the door is the Edes family coat of arms, a chevron between three leopards' faces.

John Edes, a maltster, moved to Chidham shortly before 1688. He was the elder son of John Edes of Dedham, Essex, and the nephew of Henry Edes, Canon Residentiary of Chichester. Edes

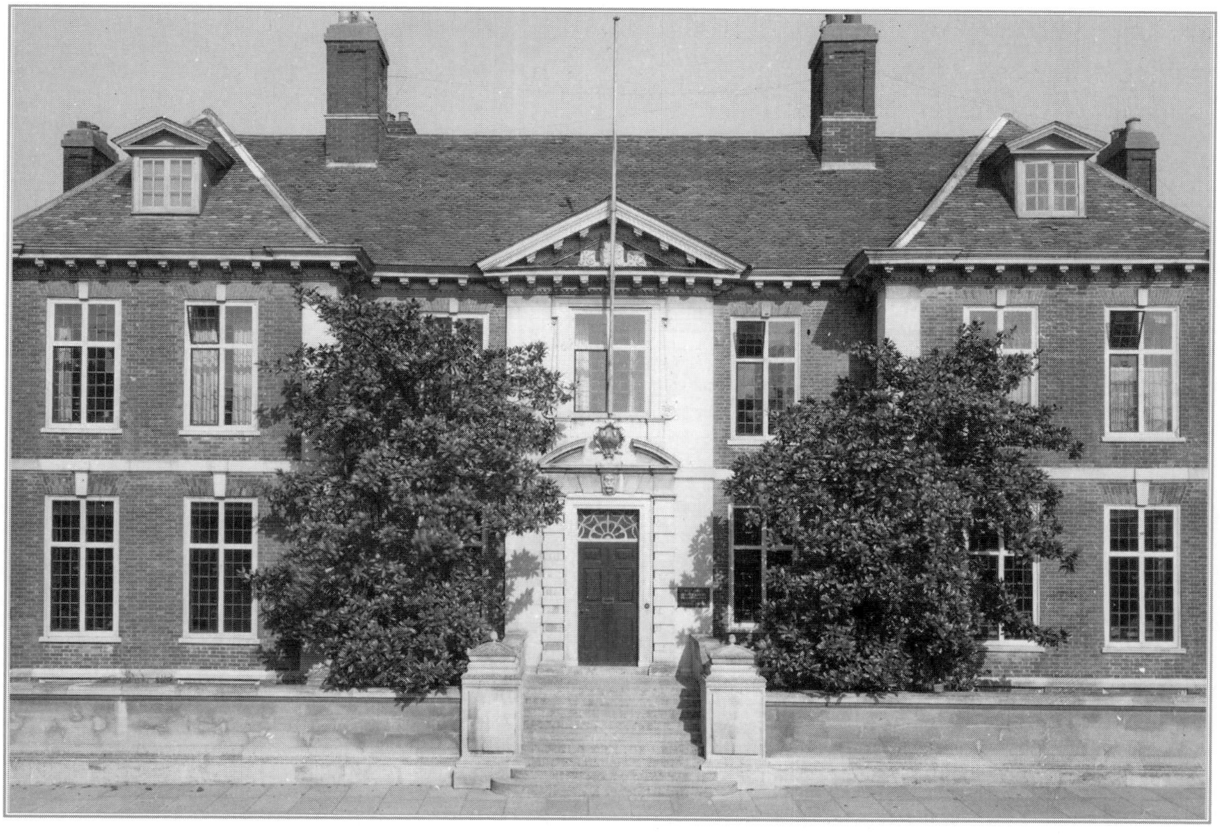

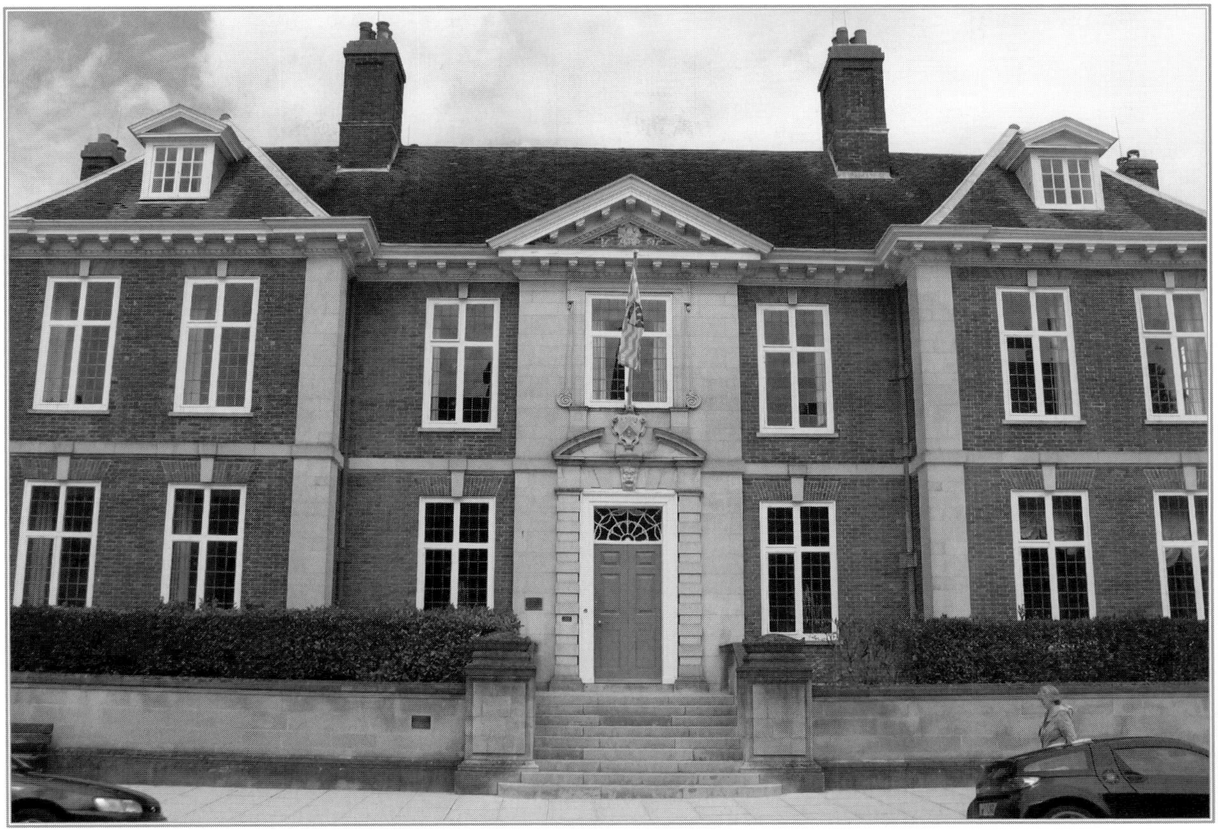

married Hannah, daughter of Thomas Aylwyn of Chichester, in 1693 and soon began to plan a residence to match his standing.

Edes House was the result, though sadly he died a year before its completion, leaving his widow Hannah to oversee the finishing stages.

It seems that the house was nameless until the mid-19th century when it was described in a will as Westgate House, a name which continued until 1905 when it became known, rather prosaically, as West Street House.

Six years later it became Wren's House, a name simplified to Wren House in 1967. The building finally became Edes House in 1993, in recognition of the fact that Sir Christopher Wren almost certainly was not its architect.

Edes House – Changing Times, Changing Uses

The two images of the back of Edes House on pages 26 to 28 offer a good challenge for the spot-the-difference aficionados.

A large lower window has been replaced by a small round one, the newer mortar still contrasting with the old; the rear entrance has been completely redesigned, and a bulky first-floor centrepiece has been – thank goodness – removed.

Not even Edes House has been immune to change, as these photographs of the back of the building amply show. However, fortunately some of the changes have been for the better.

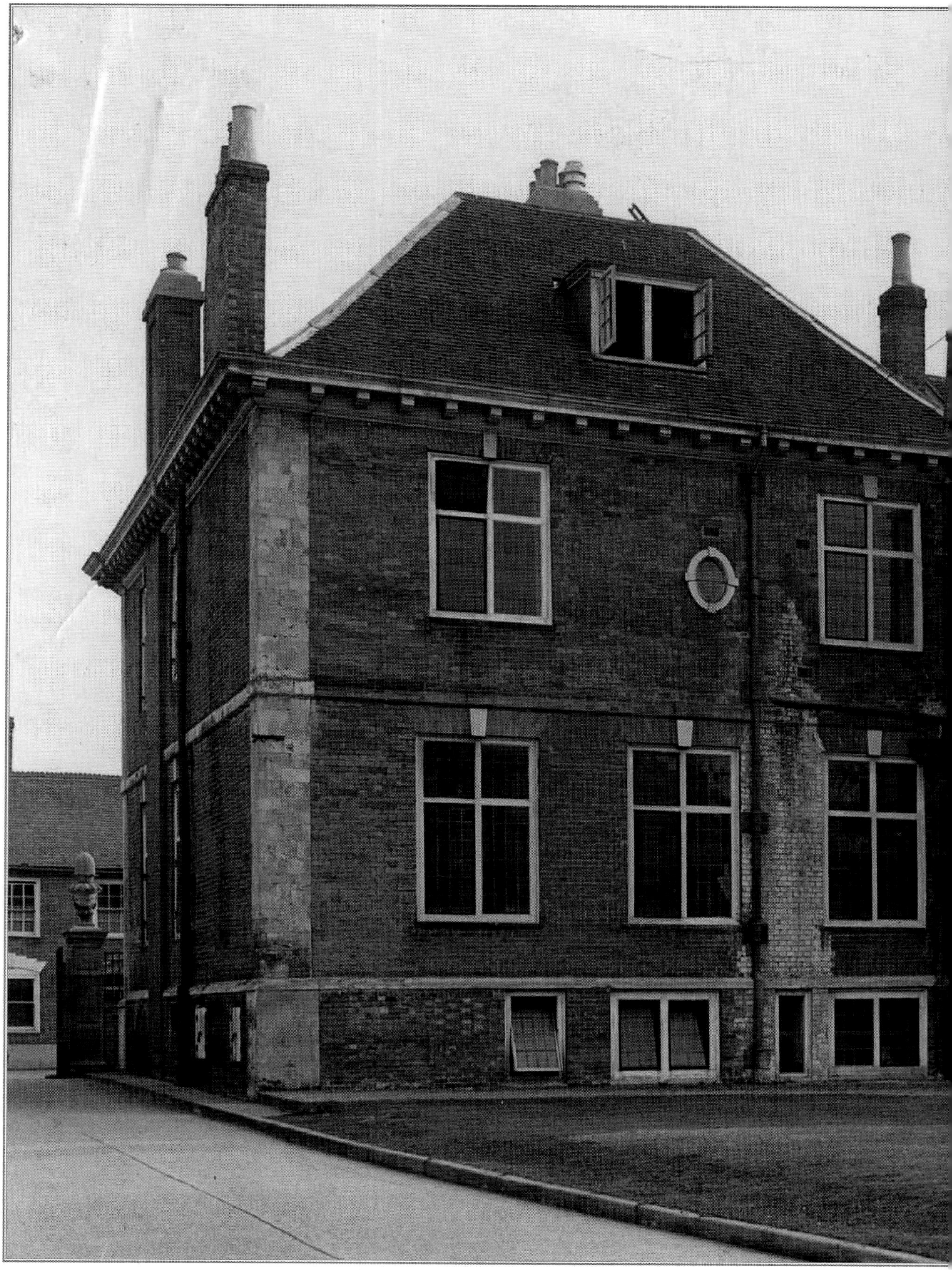

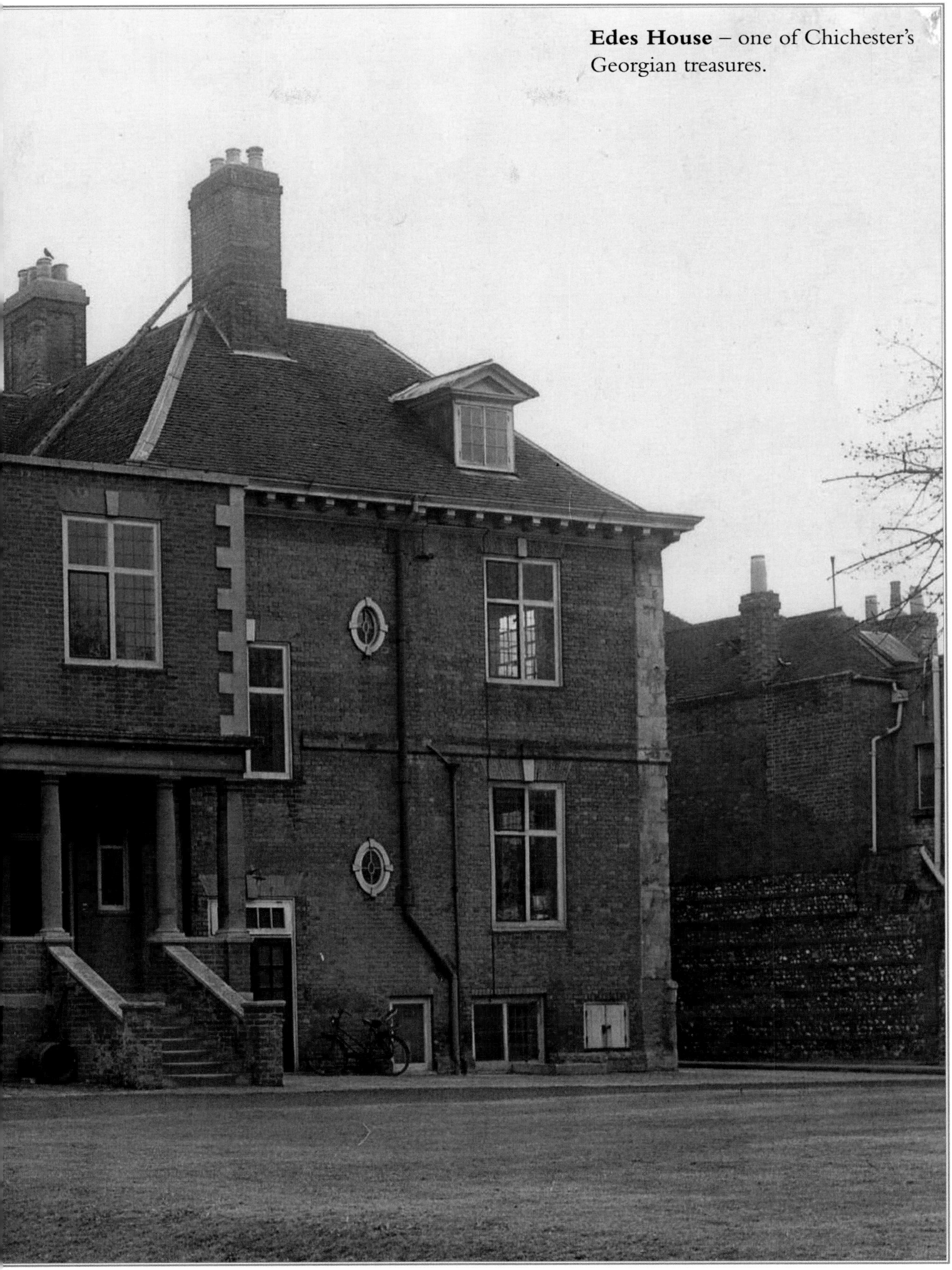

Edes House – one of Chichester's Georgian treasures.

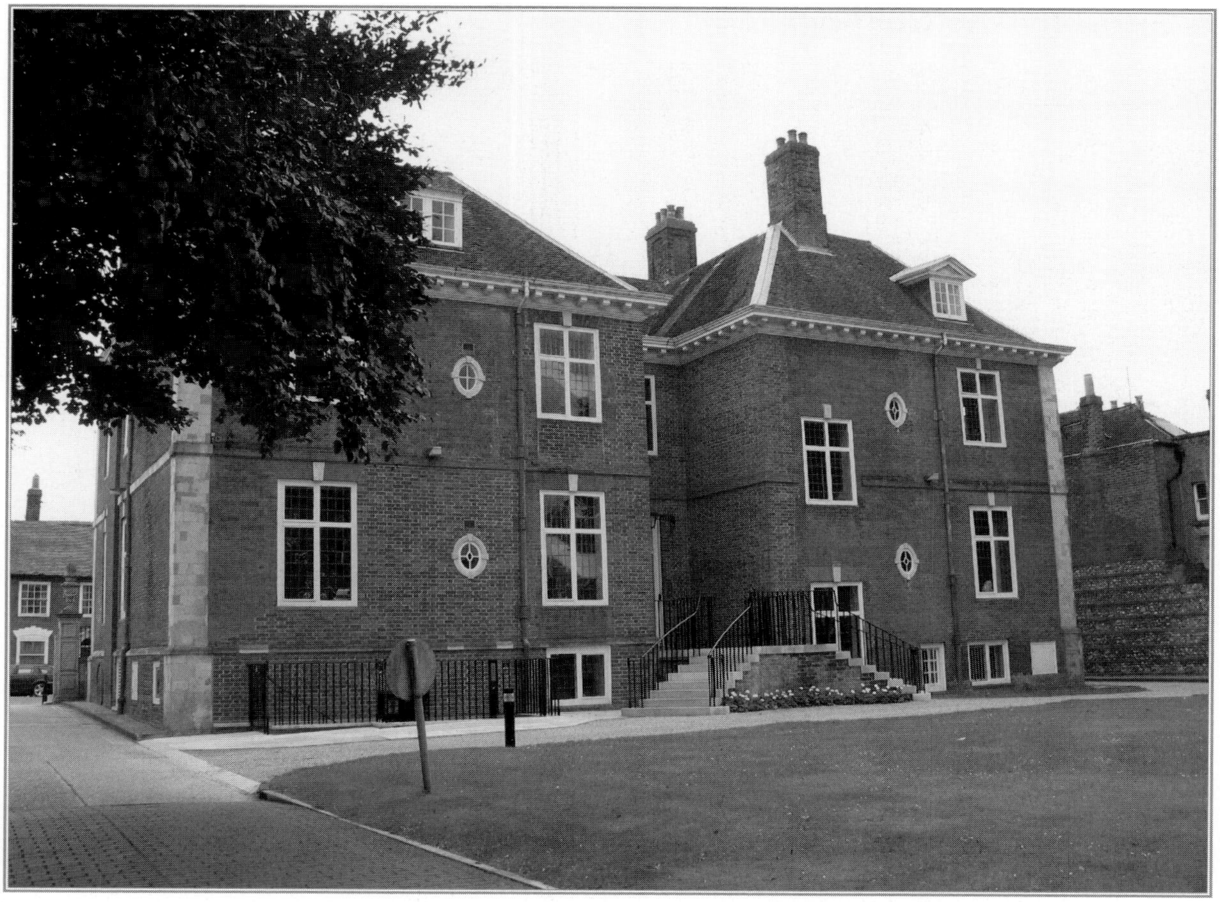

Also subject to change has been the use to which the building has been put to down the decades.

West Sussex County Council bought Wren's House, as it was then known, in 1916, and until the building of the present County Hall just opposite in 1936, Edes House was used as offices by the council.

After the opening of County Hall, the house served as the County Library headquarters before being converted in 1967 to provide accommodation for the County and Diocesan Record Offices.

When the new County Record Office opened nearby in Orchard Street in 1989, the opportunity arose to restore Edes House for county council and community use.

The Edwardian extension was demolished on the north elevation and the new rear entrance and external steps – evident in the newer photograph – were constructed. Inside, partitions were removed to restore the original feel of the house, and decorations and furnishing were chosen to reflect the building's rich character.

These days you can even get married here – provided you do not throw confetti in the house or on the steps. It is also occasionally used for musical evenings.

A Focus for the County

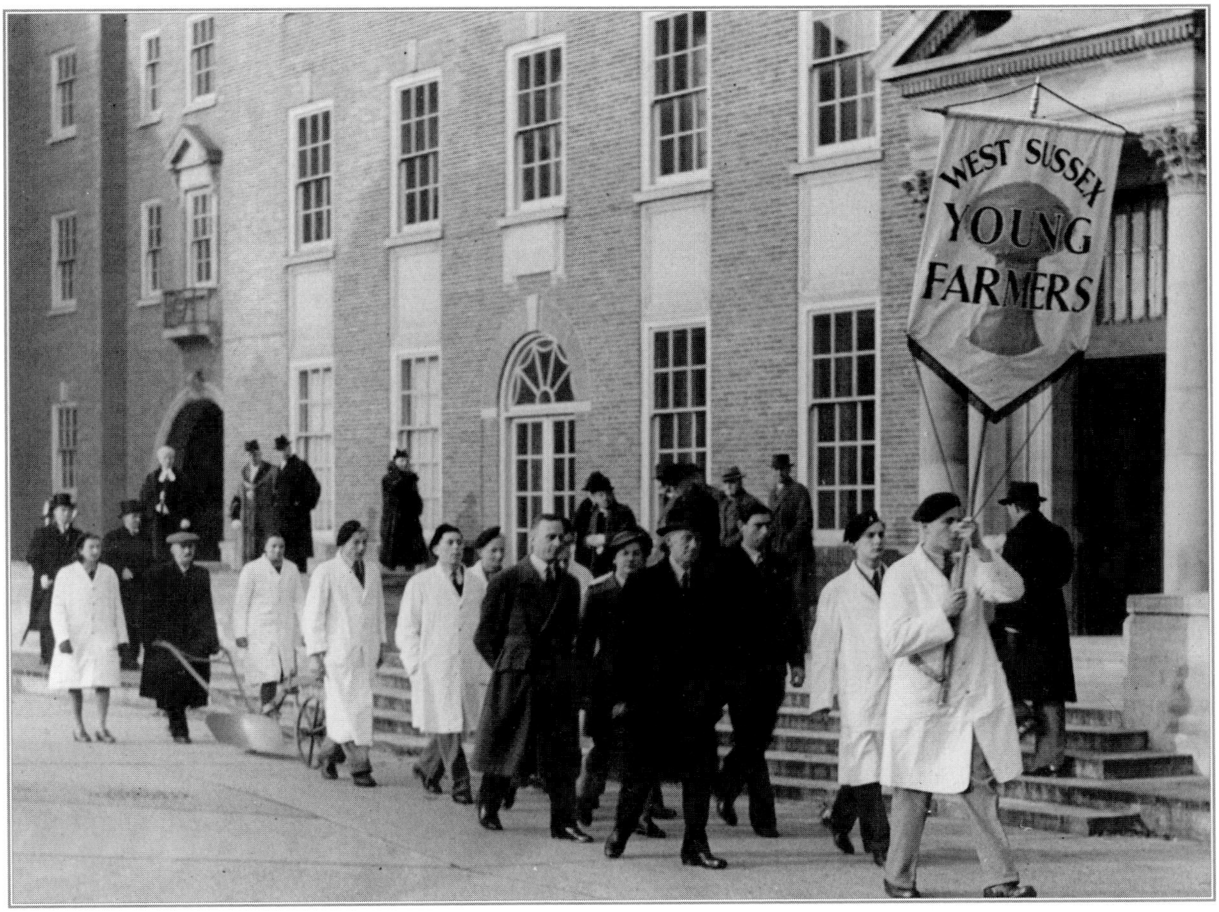

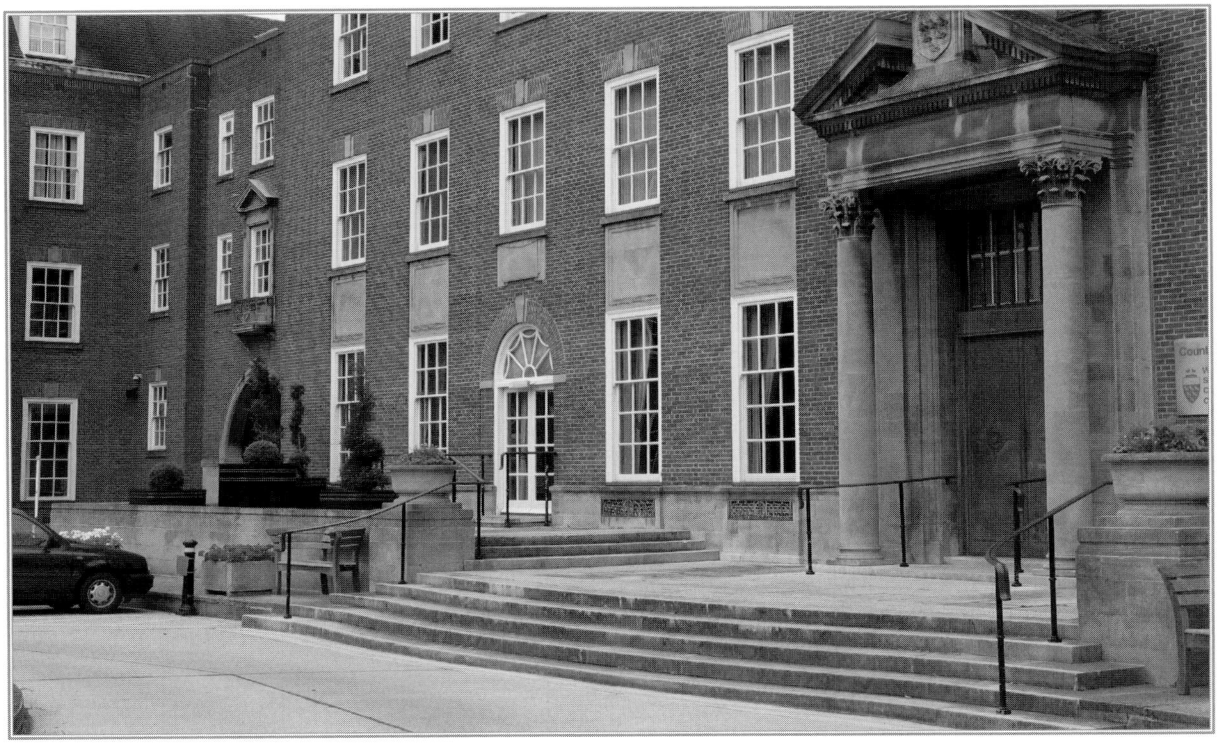

Edes House ceased to be the County Hall for West Sussex when the new County Hall was built behind it, part of the significant expansion which Chichester underwent in the 1930s.

The decade began with the development of Whyke Building Estate, with Cambrai Avenue followed by Velyn Avenue. The 1930s also saw the opening of the new police headquarters in Southgate and the opening of the Lancastrian infant school.

Chichester's first council houses had been built in the 1920s. By 1939 they numbered nearly 500.

The 1930s were also the decade which gave the city St Richard's Hospital, and, in 1937, Chichester opened its fourth cinema, the Gaumont, in Eastgate Square, in a building later to become the town's swimming baths.

The images on page 29 show the main entrance to County Hall. In the older image the West Sussex Young Farmers are processing on Plough Sunday in January 1945. The parade was an important event, reflecting Chichester's market origins and the strength of its farming population.

Groups of young farmers from across the district would converge on Chichester on Plough Sunday, a traditional celebration of the beginning of the agricultural year. A ploughshare would be brought into church with prayers for the blessing of the land.

Scarcely seen now – though apparently it is enjoying a slight revival in some places – Plough Sunday was traditionally held on the Sunday after Epiphany, between 7 and 13 January. Work in the fields traditionally began the next day, Plough Monday.

A Side Street Steeped in History

Somewhere between 1880 and 1914 would seem to be the best guess for dating this beautiful image of Chichester Cathedral from Tower Street (page 31), a side street leading north from West Street.

Two pubs, the Fighting Cocks Inn and the Ship Inn, almost face each other; a man loiters under the pub sign; and in the background the cathedral bell tower looms large.

Scroll forward a century and the two pubs have gone; trees now partially obscure the view of the cathedral spire.

Perhaps most strikingly the Lancastrian School has disappeared. Nothing remains now of the establishment which once embodied a pioneering system, seeking to make education more accessible to the working classes.

The school has become history – which is appropriate perhaps given that it stood on a site now earmarked for the building of Chichester's new District Museum. Currently a car park, the site contains the remains of the Roman baths of the city of *Noviomagus Regni*. These baths, discovered in the 1970s, will be exposed as part of displays telling the story of the Chichester district.

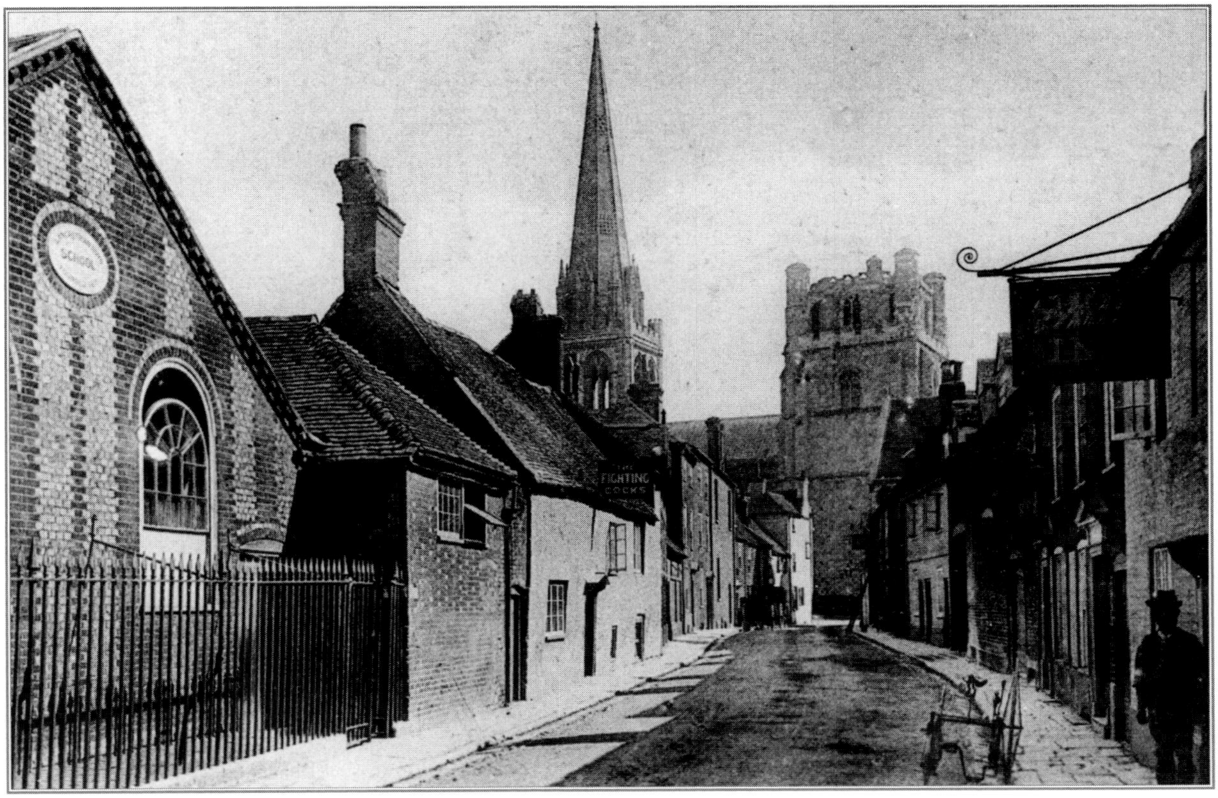
SCHOOL
FIGHTING
COCKS

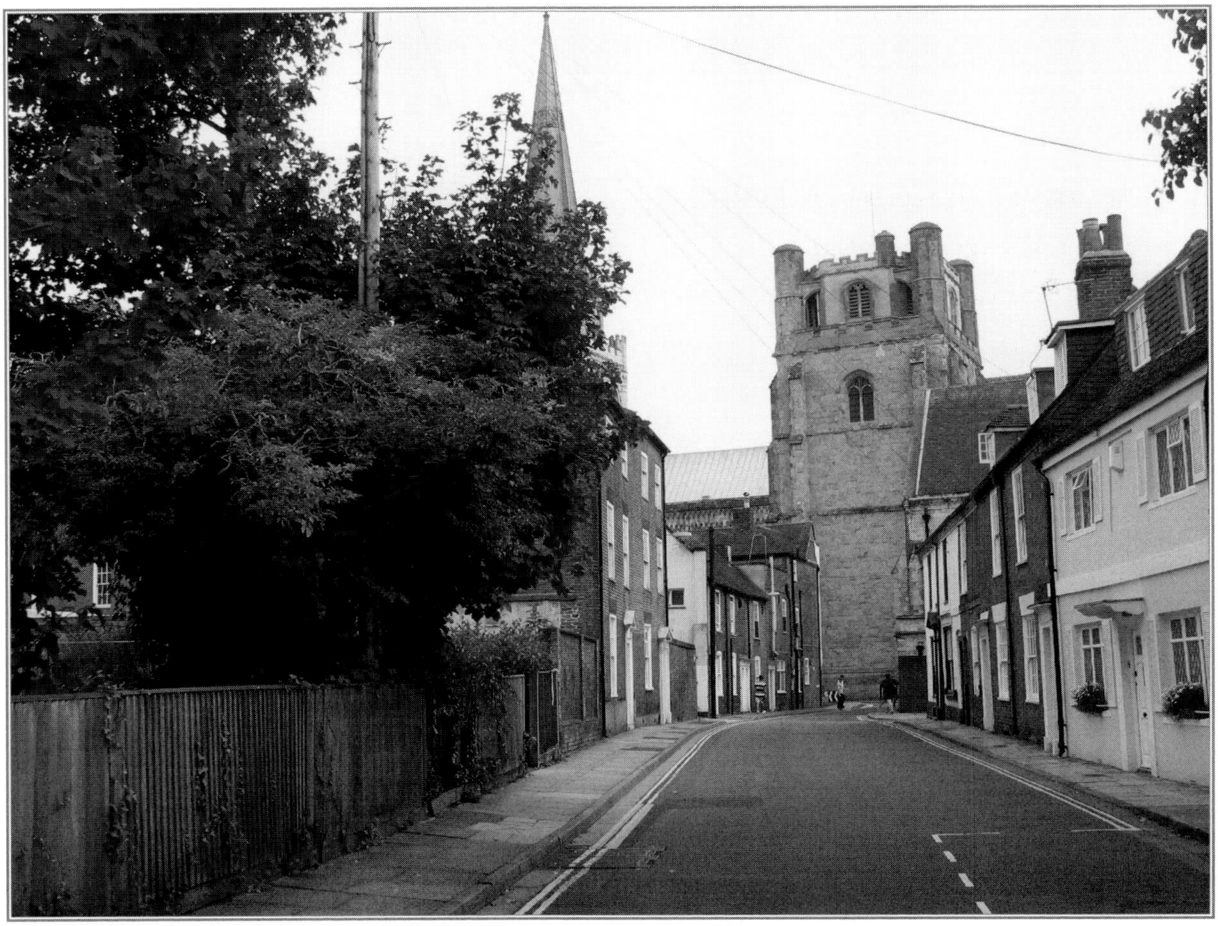

Excavations in Tower Street, formerly West Lane, have also produced items from other periods of Chichester's history, among them late Saxon pots, providing a miniature story of the district. Later, in the 12th century, people were making bells at the site, perhaps for the new cathedral just yards away.

Tower Street's houses are mostly of the late-18th and early-19th centuries. Considerably more recent in the street, and still very striking, is Chichester Library, built in 1967 to a ground-breaking circular design.

A Saint for the City

Where these West Sussex Young Farmers once walked, there now stands a striking commemoration of St Richard, the patron saint of Chichester.

St Richard (1197–1253), one-time Bishop of Chichester, was canonised in 1262. His shrine in Chichester Cathedral was a focus for pilgrims until its destruction in 1538. Since 2007 his saint's day, 16 June, has been celebrated as Sussex Day.

St Richard is perhaps best remembered today for the prayer believed to comprise the words he spoke on his deathbed. It begins 'Thanks be to Thee, my Lord Jesus Christ, for all the benefits Thou hast given me.'

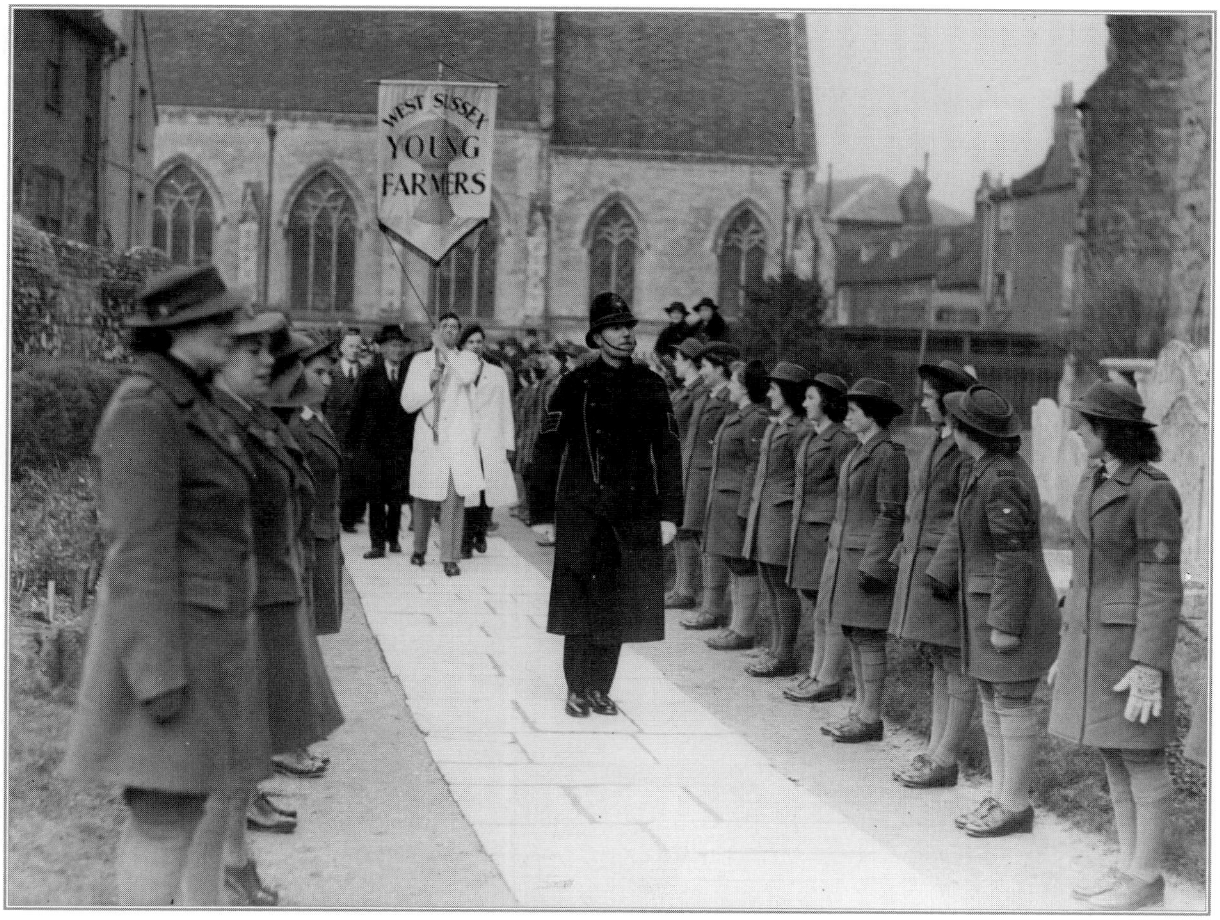

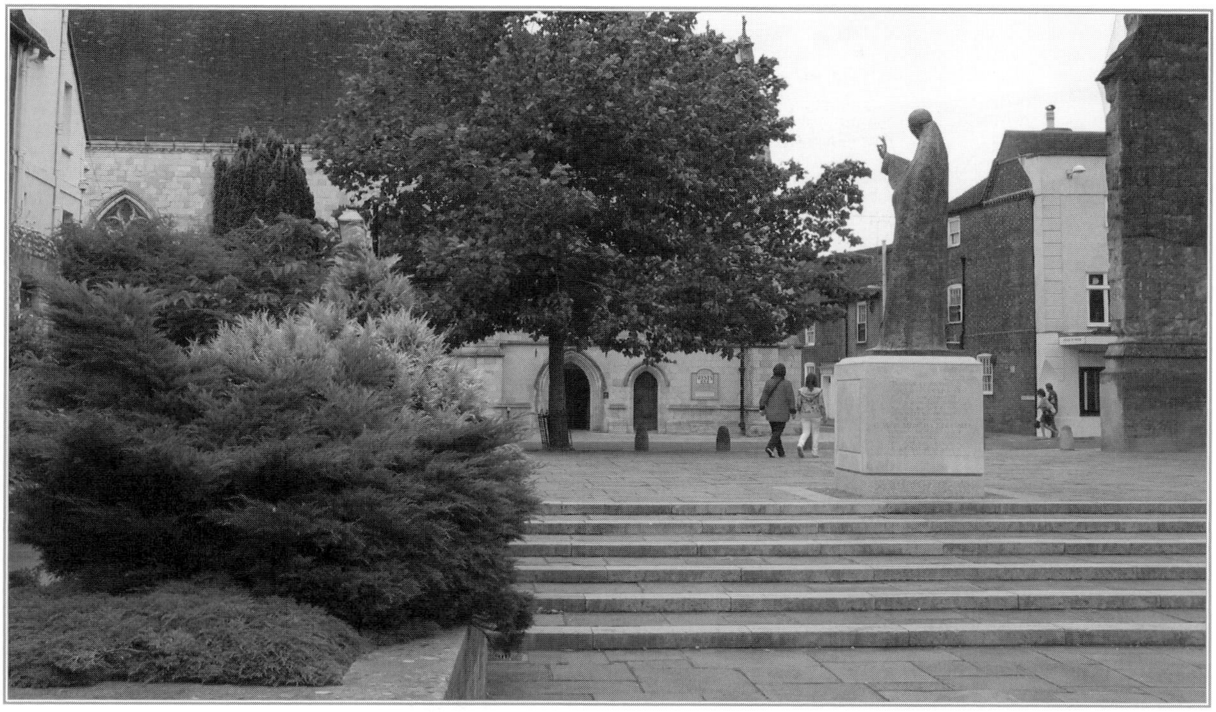

Standing at the western entrance to the cathedral, the statue of St Richard – bronze and one and a half times life-size – was commissioned by the Friends of Chichester Cathedral to celebrate the millennium.

Unveiled by the Bishop of Chichester in 2000, it is the work of Midhurst-based Philip Jackson, the man behind some of Britain's most important landmark sculptures over the past two decades.

Since 1988, when he was commissioned by Manchester City Council to create the Peace Sculpture for St Peter's Square, Manchester, Philip Jackson has been creating sculptures to commemorate significant moments, events and people.

As well as the sculpture of St Richard, Jackson is the creator of the much smaller Christ in Judgment set within the cathedral itself. The sculpture of Minerva at Chichester Festival Theatre also bears his stamp.

Chichester's Unique Bell Tower

The pace of change in Chichester these days can be just a little worrying for those concerned about its ancient heart and traditions.

However, overleaf are two pictures to offer hope to those who cling to continuity. Very little has changed in the 60 or 70 years between these two images – pictures of a structure which makes Chichester unique.

Chichester Cathedral is the country's only cathedral with a detached mediaeval bell tower. Thirty-six metres high and 11 metres square at the base, it is seen here in an image dating from the 1930s or 1940s.

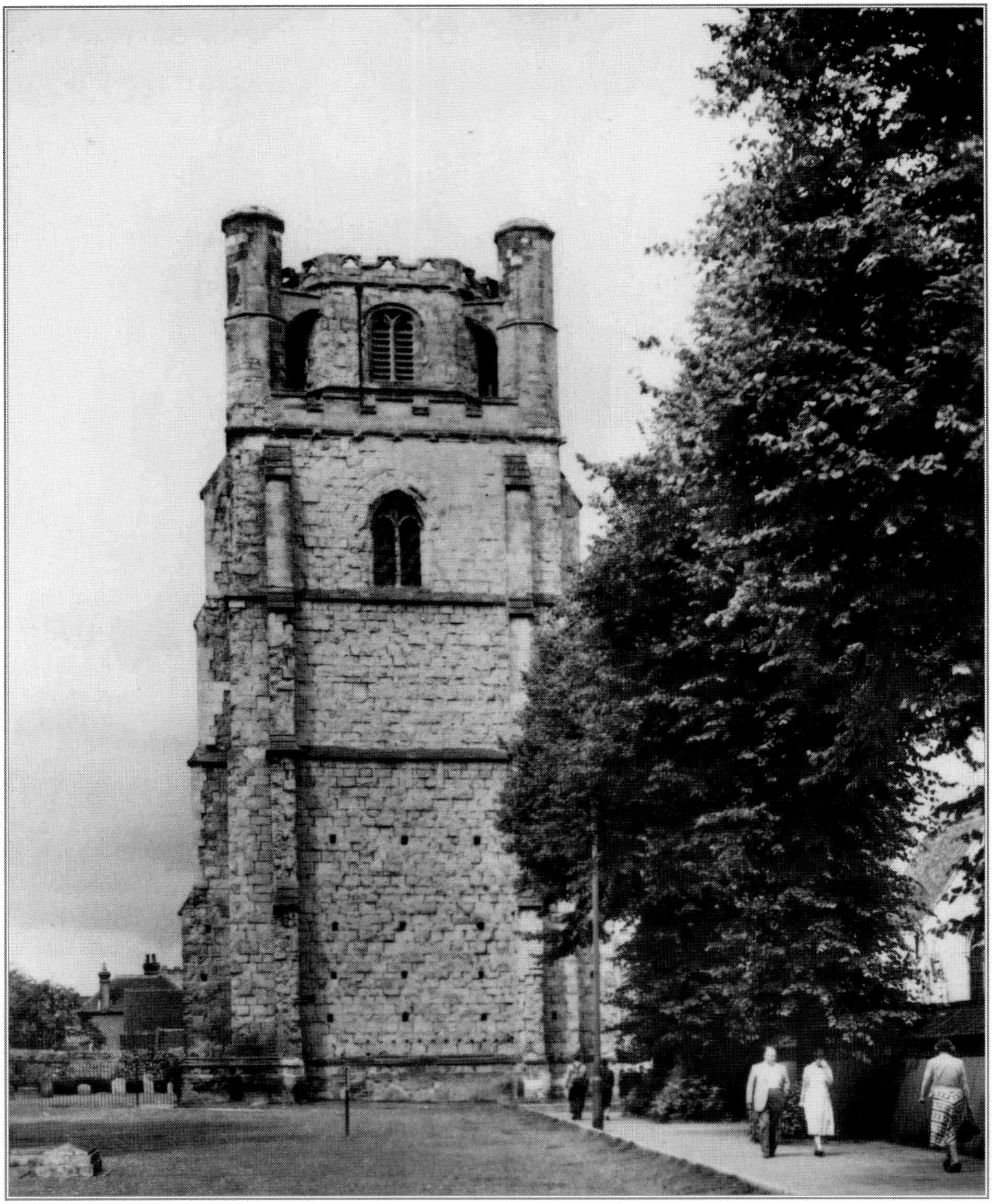

It was built when the cathedral's central tower had become too weak to carry its bells. Work was started on it in about 1375 and completed around 1440. In its early days it was known as Ryman's or Raymond's Tower. At the angles are square buttresses of four stages reaching nearly to the parapet.

Inside the tower is a board recording that the tower was restored between 1902–08 at a cost of £2,300, when the stone facing was chemically treated.

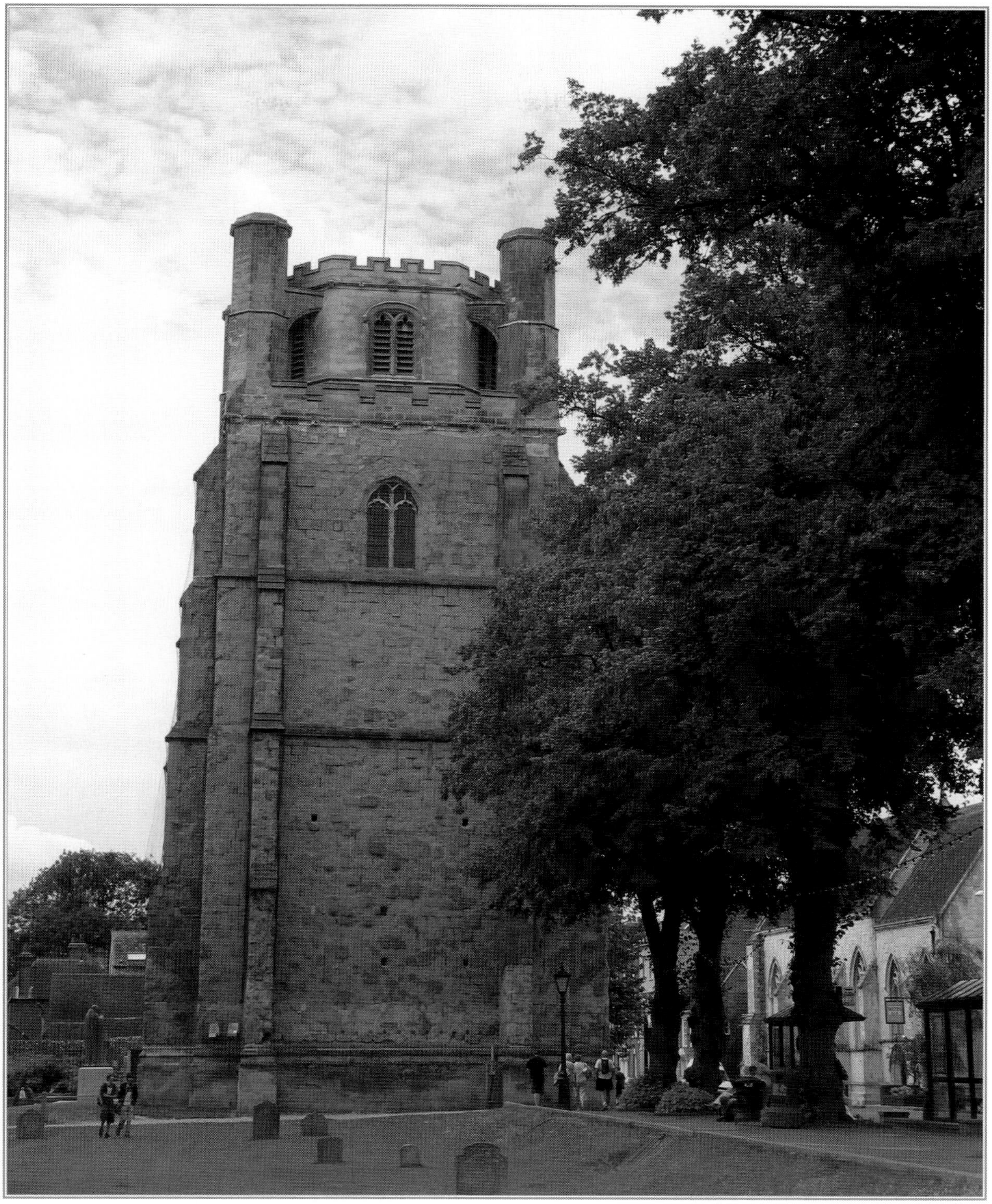

In September 2008 the tower was cleaned up again while it awaits full restoration. Around six workers on abseil ropes pulled back the netting surrounding the tower to remove vegetation growing underneath it. The seven-day-long project, costing around £9,000, was undertaken to ensure public safety until much needed restoration could begin in earnest.

Chichester Cathedral.

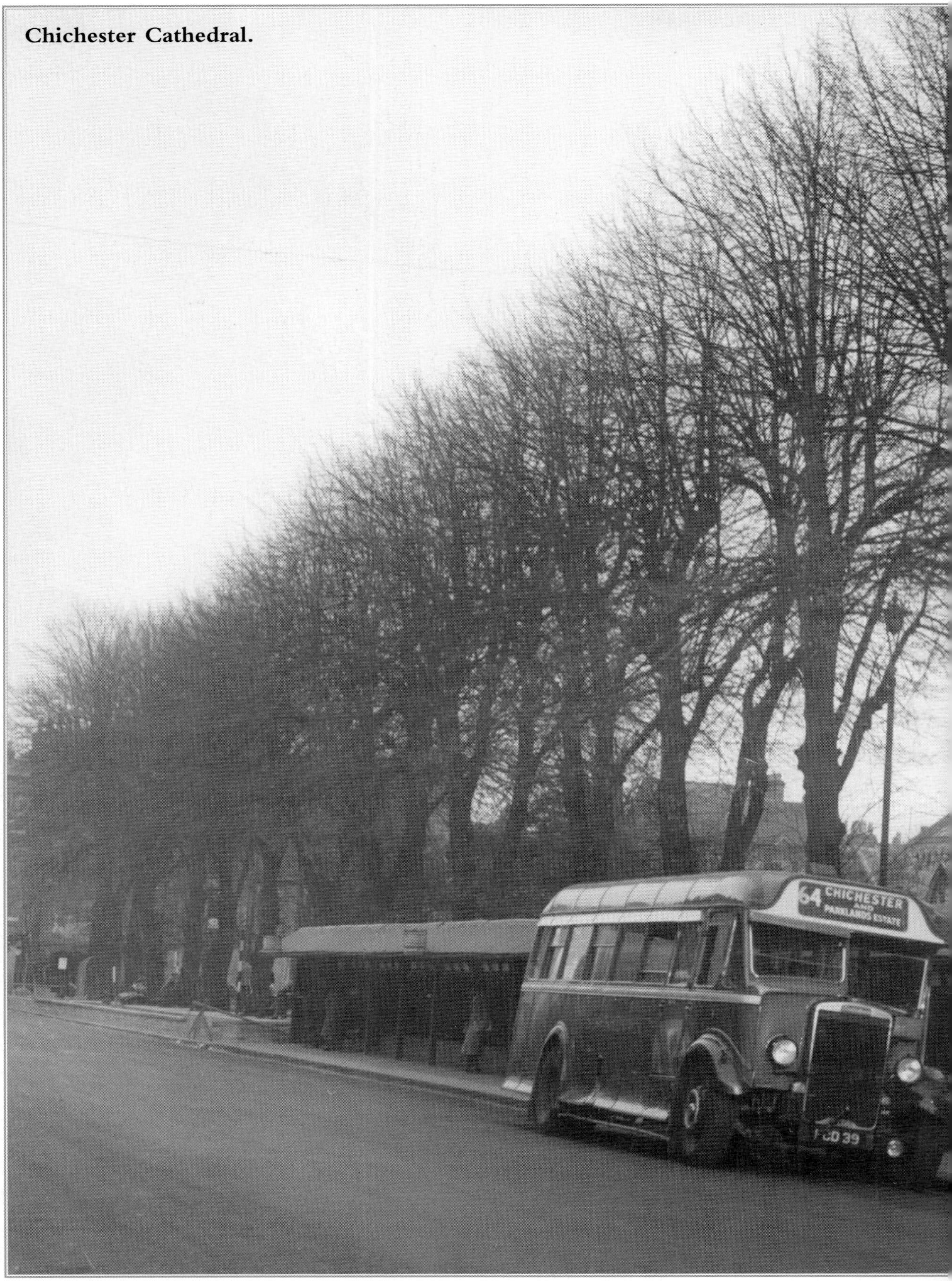

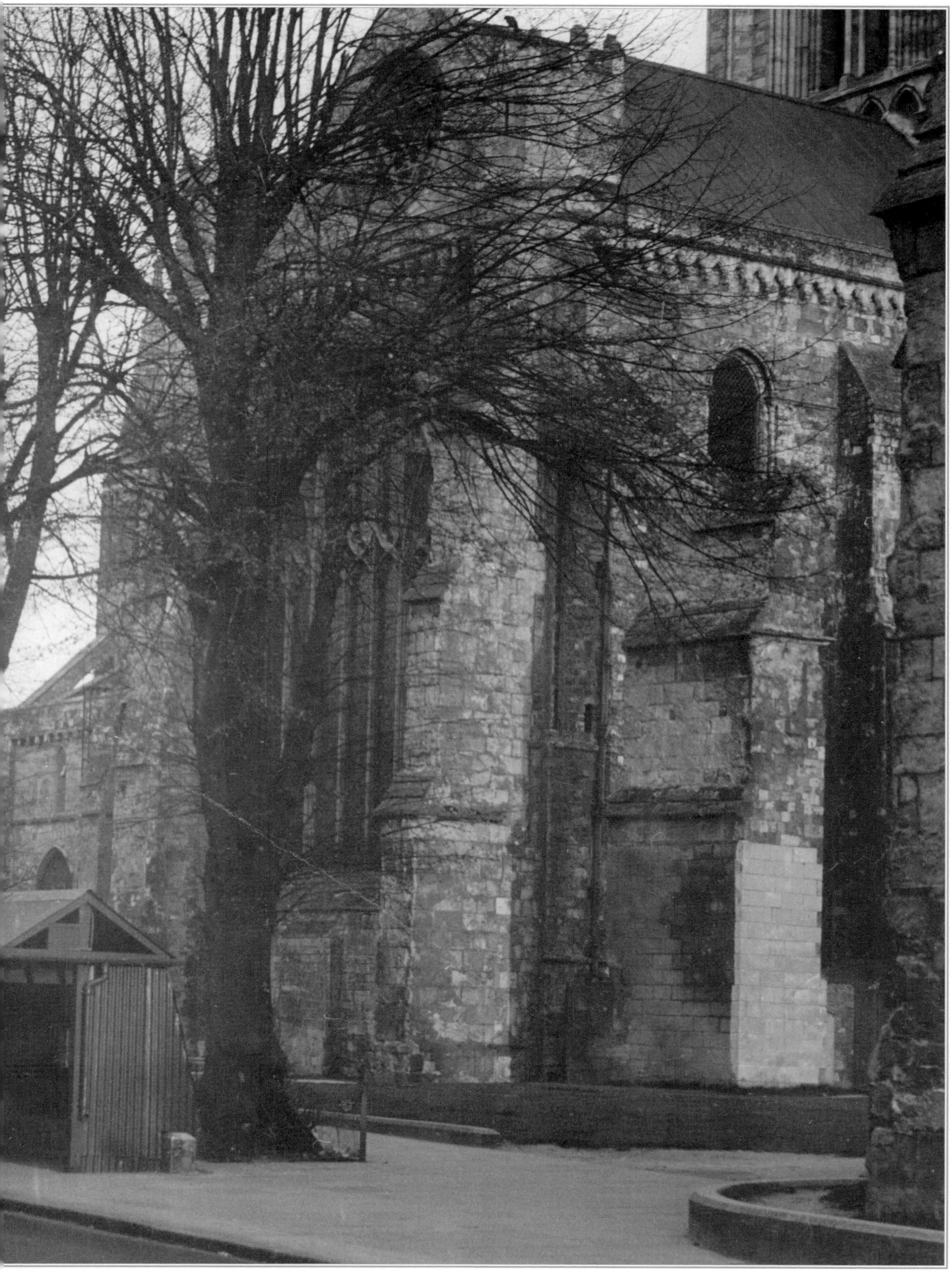

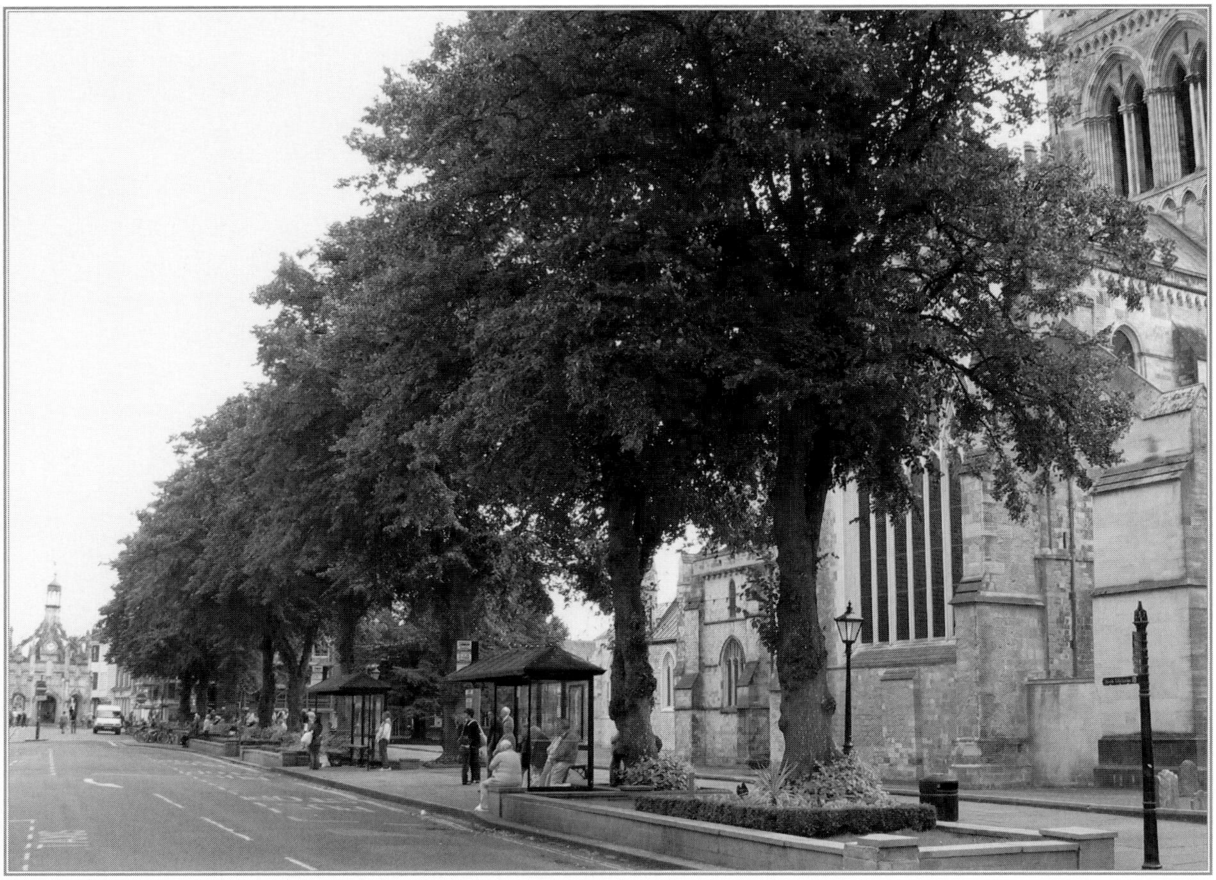

Again, little seems to have changed in this glimpse along the southern side of West Street towards the Market Cross.

To the right is the cathedral, Chichester's magnificent ecclesiastical centrepiece which celebrated the 900th anniversary of its consecration in 2008.

The original cathedral was built on the coast by the Saxons at Selsey, but in 1075 a decree from the Council of London forced a move to the existing Minster Church of St Peter in West Street, Chichester.

Work on building the present cathedral started soon after, leading to its consecration in 1108 in the time of Bishop Ralph Luffa. Six years later the cathedral was badly damaged by fire. It was completed for a second time by Bishop Luffa before his death in 1123 and reconsecrated in 1184 by Bishop Seffrid. Another fire followed soon after, with rebuilding work this time lasting from 1188 until a further reconsecration in 1199.

These photographs offer a view of the cathedral we owe to the Victorians, who reopened the cathedral churchyard to West Street. In 1205 King John gave licence to the Bishop of Chichester to build shops, 12ft in breadth, in front of the burial ground on the north side of the cathedral. Butchers, bakers, blacksmiths and the like remained there until the city decided to clear the site, works which lasted from 1848 until 1852 and ensured the open view of the cathedral we enjoy today.

A Lost City School

Chichester's civic dignitaries are on the march in this photograph, dating from around 1960. They pass along a West Street which has seen significant changes down the decades.

Towards the left in this image can be seen the church of St Peter Subdeanery, which later became a shopping arcade and is now a bar. It was the only one of the eight ancient parish churches within the walls of Chichester which was not situated in the two eastern quarters of the city.

Nearby is the site of the Oliver Whitby School, now part of the House of Fraser store. The year 2002 saw the 300th anniversary of its founding, but the school itself had long since gone, closing on 21 December 1949 after having become something of a dinosaur in the post-war era.

Oliver Whitby, son of an Archdeacon of Chichester, died at the age of 39, but in his will – written with the knowledge of approaching death – he left money for the education of 12 poor boys to be taken from Chichester, Harting and West Wittering. The terms of the will were very specific.

These three locations were places where the family owned farmland and property, and these were the places from which the funds for the school were to be generated.

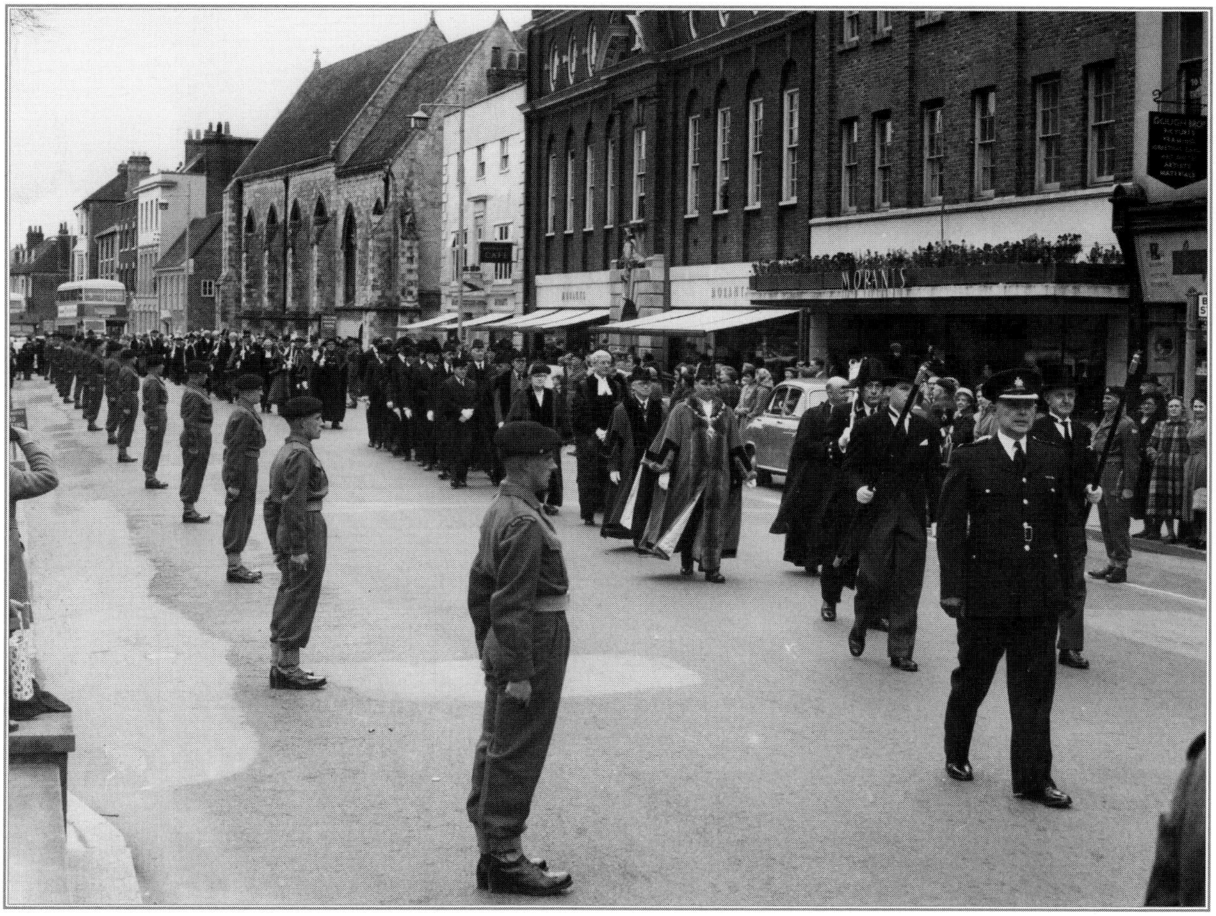

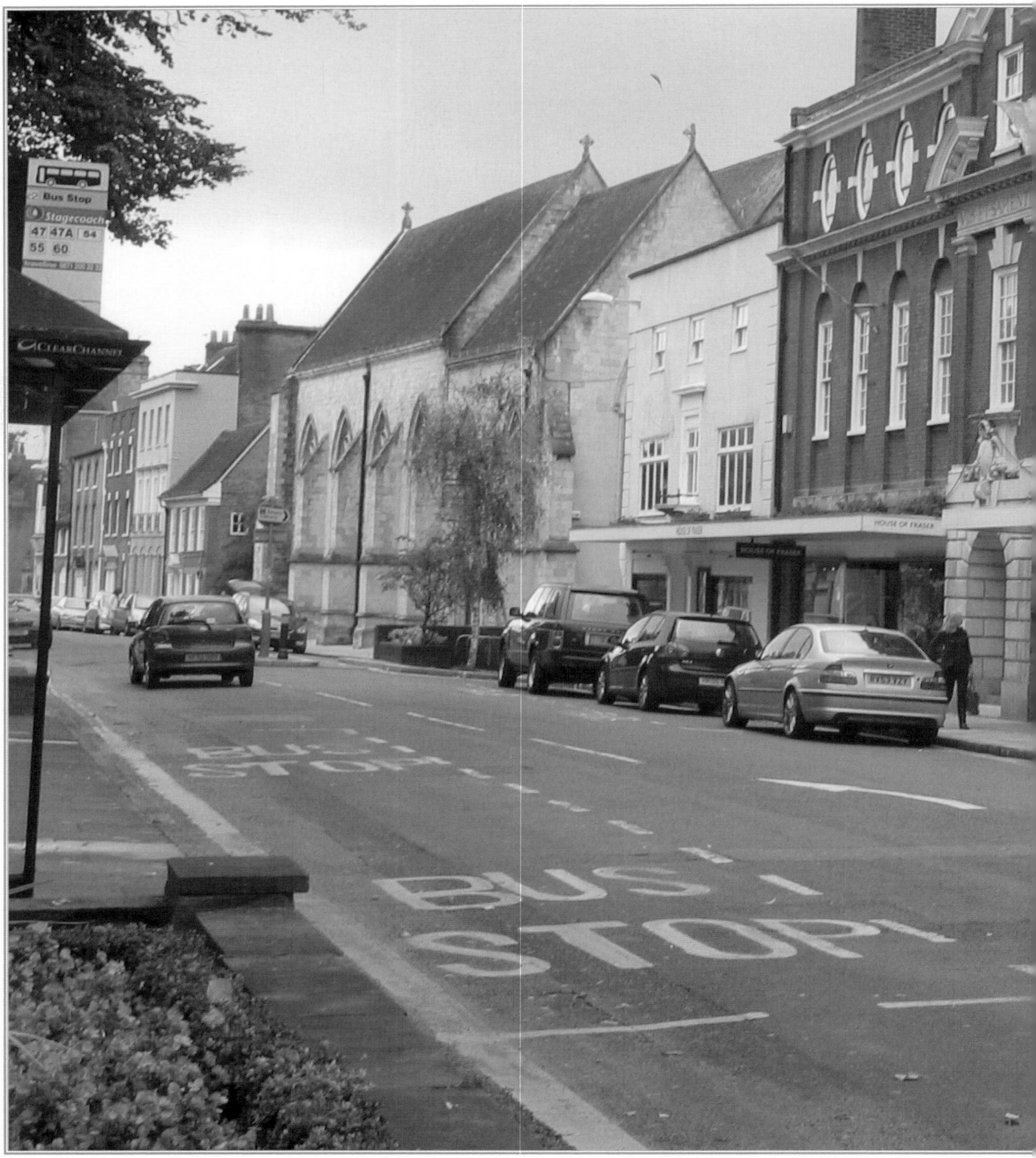

At the time of the parade on page 39, House of Fraser was still Morants. Originally a Southsea shop, Morants was bombed out of Portsmouth and the business moved to part of the old Oliver Whitby School buildings. Morants decided to remain in Chichester after the war, taking over the rest of the building when the Oliver Whitby School closed.

The area remains today an important part of Chichester's shopping centre, but the school motto can still be seen written in the stonework above the main entrance to the building.

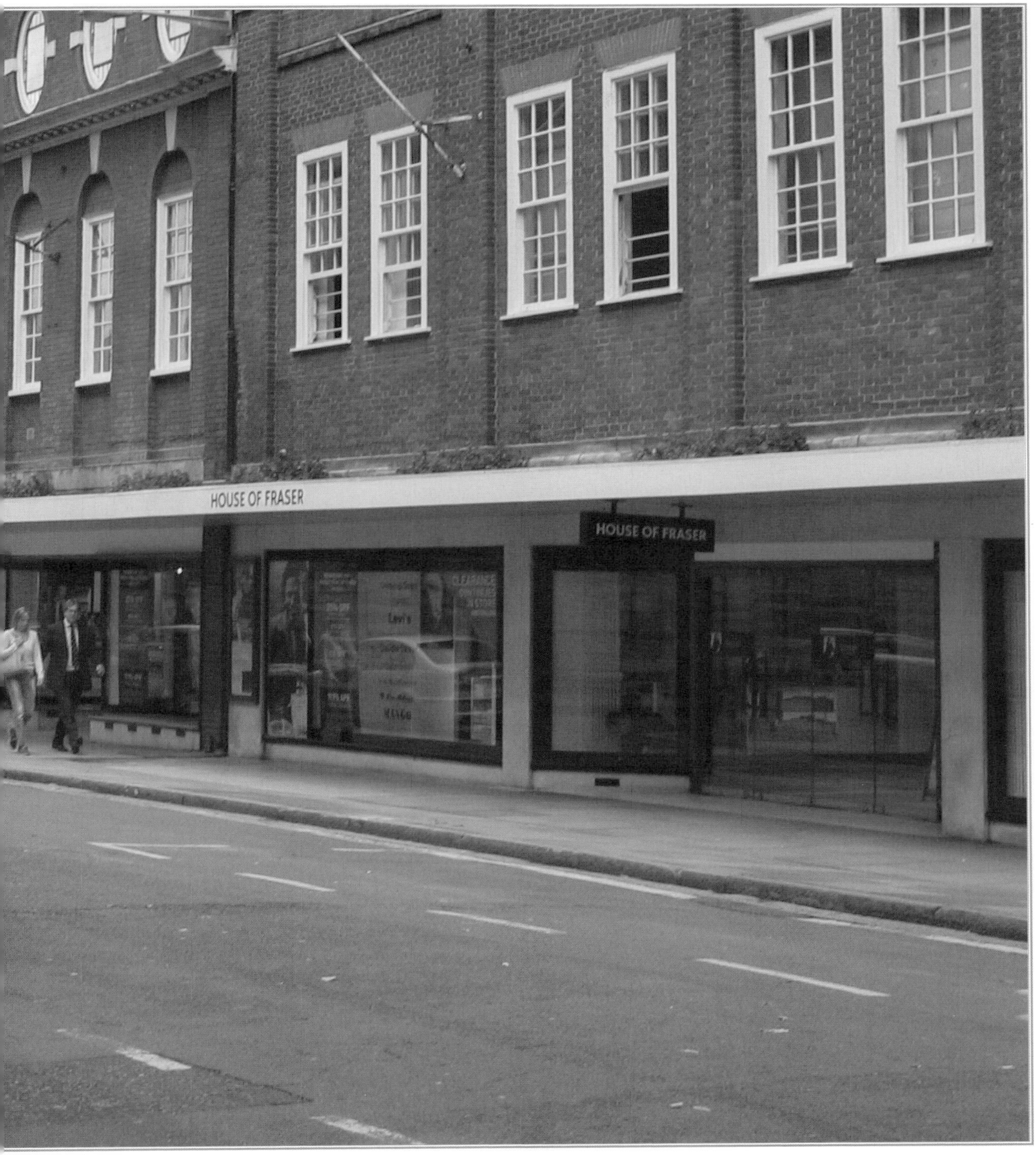

The Dolphin & Anchor

The disappearance of Chichester's city centre hotels in recent years has been one of the city's minor tragedies, with none more regretted perhaps than the Dolphin & Anchor, a hotel which really was part of the Chichester townscape, superbly set in West Street and looking across towards the cathedral.

All is not lost however. The modern-day scaffolding in the photograph overleaf masks the

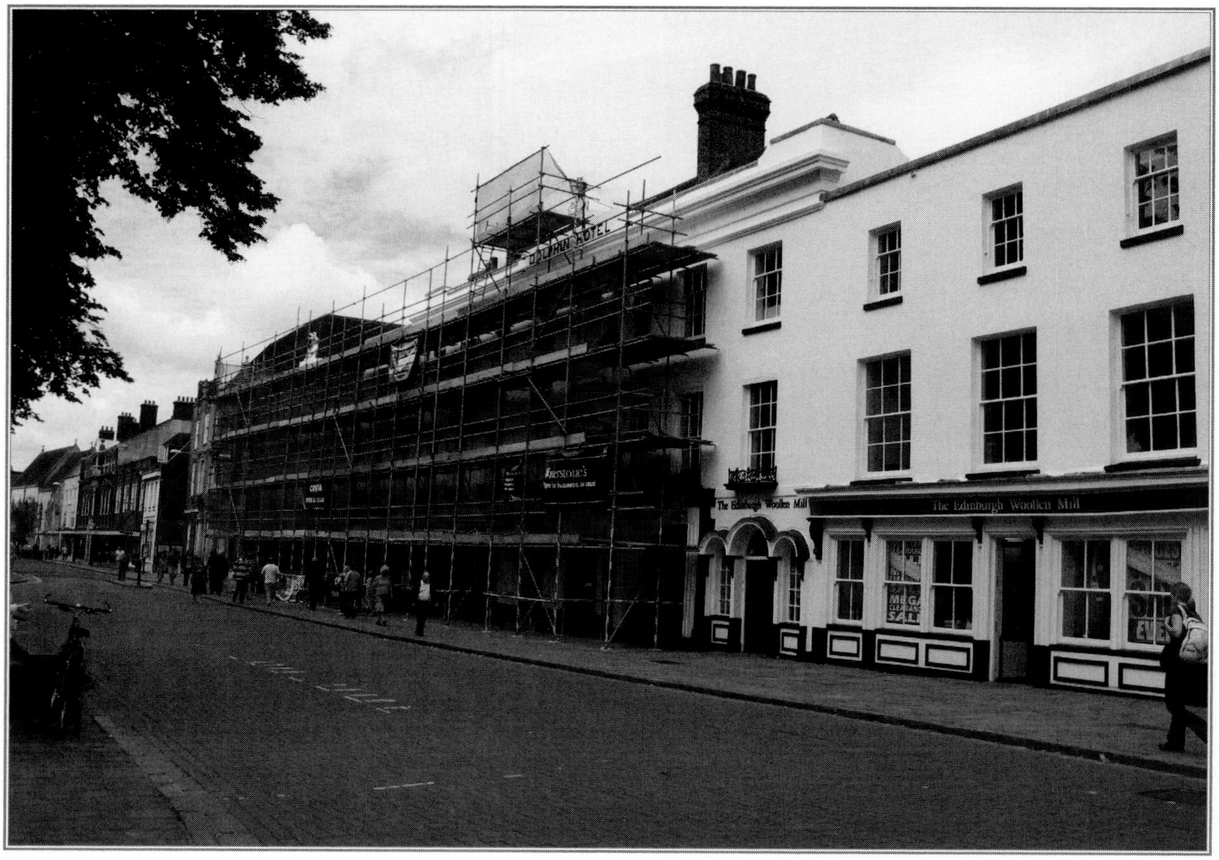
The Edinburgh Woollen Mill
The Edinburgh Woollen Mill

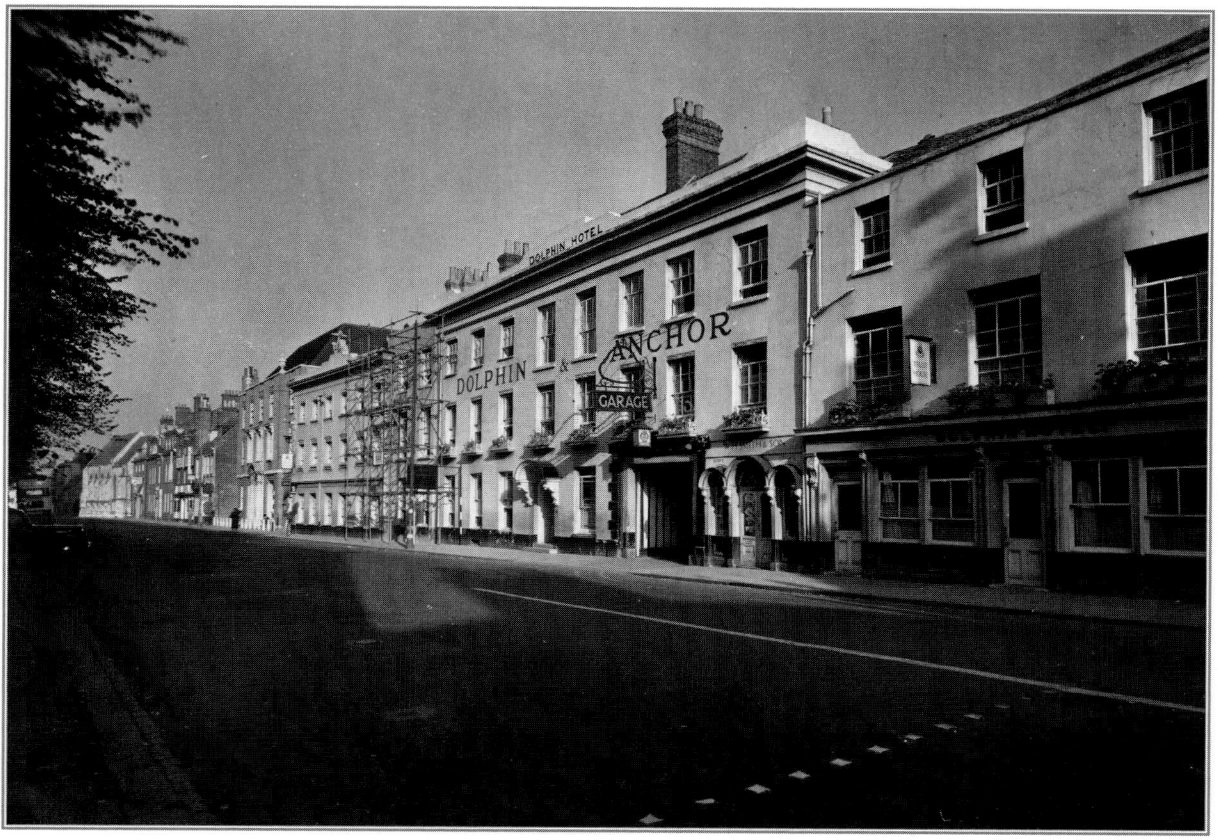
DOLPHIN HOTEL
DOLPHIN & ANCHOR
GARAGE

fact that the hotel's façade remains largely intact. Outwardly at least, the building retains much of its charm.

Inside, the former Dolphin & Anchor now houses a Waterstone's bookshop and a Wetherspoon's pub, the latter opening its doors on 23 March 1999 – a use which takes the building back to its days as a coaching inn.

With its large lettering on the wall, The Dolphin & Anchor had been a Chichester landmark since 1910 when the neighbouring rival inns – The Anchor and The Dolphin – combined.

The Anchor, on the corner of West Street and Chapel Street, dates from the 17th century. The Dolphin is thought to date from 1649 – though some claim it was established as early as the late 15th century. It was certainly up and running by 1660 and in 1670 was listed as containing 23 hearths, a number equalled only by the Bishop's Palace.

In 1768 The Dolphin was rebuilt and was used by visitors to Chichester and also by local groups, by prize-fighters and by the militia. By 1791 it was boasting 'the best of liquors, a well furnished larder, unexceptionable stabling, neat post chaises, and a coach to and from London every day, good horses and careful drivers'.

CHAPTER 3
NORTH STREET

Pedestrianizing the City

This postcard looking north up North Street (*c.*1950–60) gives an indication just why pedestrianization was needed.

North Street had seen a good deal of rebuilding since the 1940s. With its two churches, its role as home to the city council and its wealth of shops, it was arguably the most important of the four main streets leading from the Cross – and clearly it was getting busy.

A bypass had been built to the south of the city in the 1930s, but increasingly it was the city centre which needed to be relieved. An experimental pedestrianization scheme was put in place in 1976 and soon became a permanent feature.

There can be few people who lament the days when traffic ploughed right through the centre, but there were plenty who were worried about the way pedestrianization forced delivery lorries into the much smaller back streets, damaging their character and disturbing their residents.

The pedestrianization of much of North Street and East Street covered the heart of Chichester's city centre shopping area and was generally regarded as proof that the city's civilised centre was worth preserving.

Particularly interesting in the older picture is the prevalence of shop blinds, a big part of the character of the city centre for a good part of the 20th century.

Traditionally North Street has been home to food and clothes shops. Beyond these are buildings which were once (and some still are) large private houses.

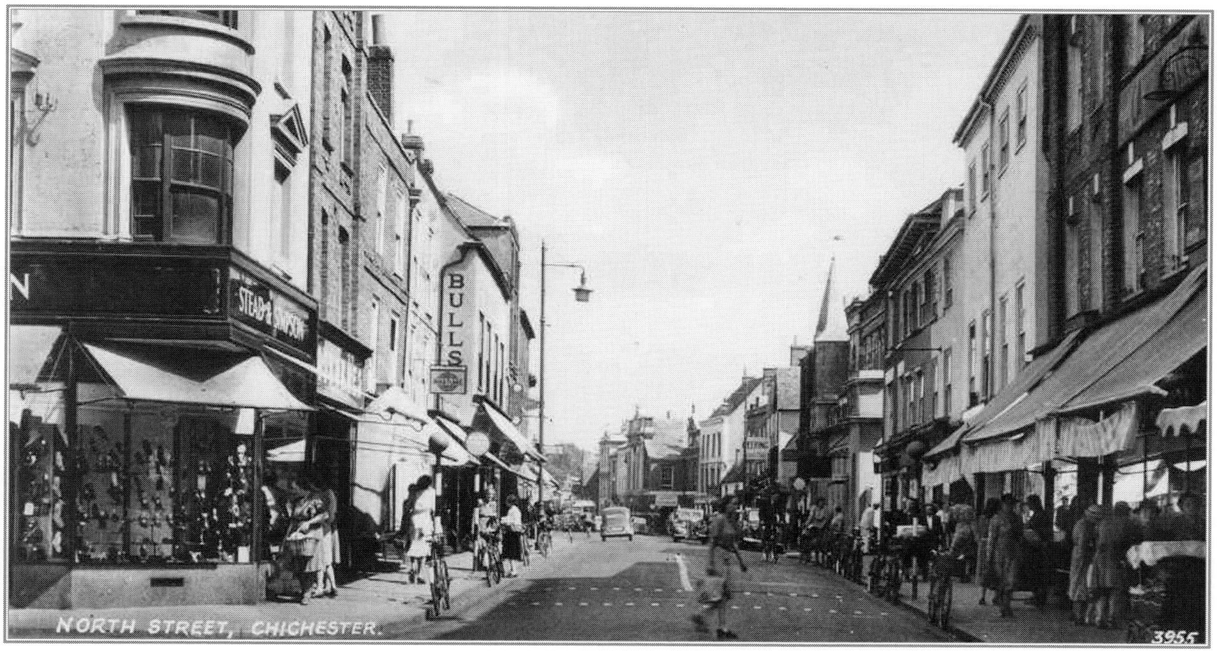

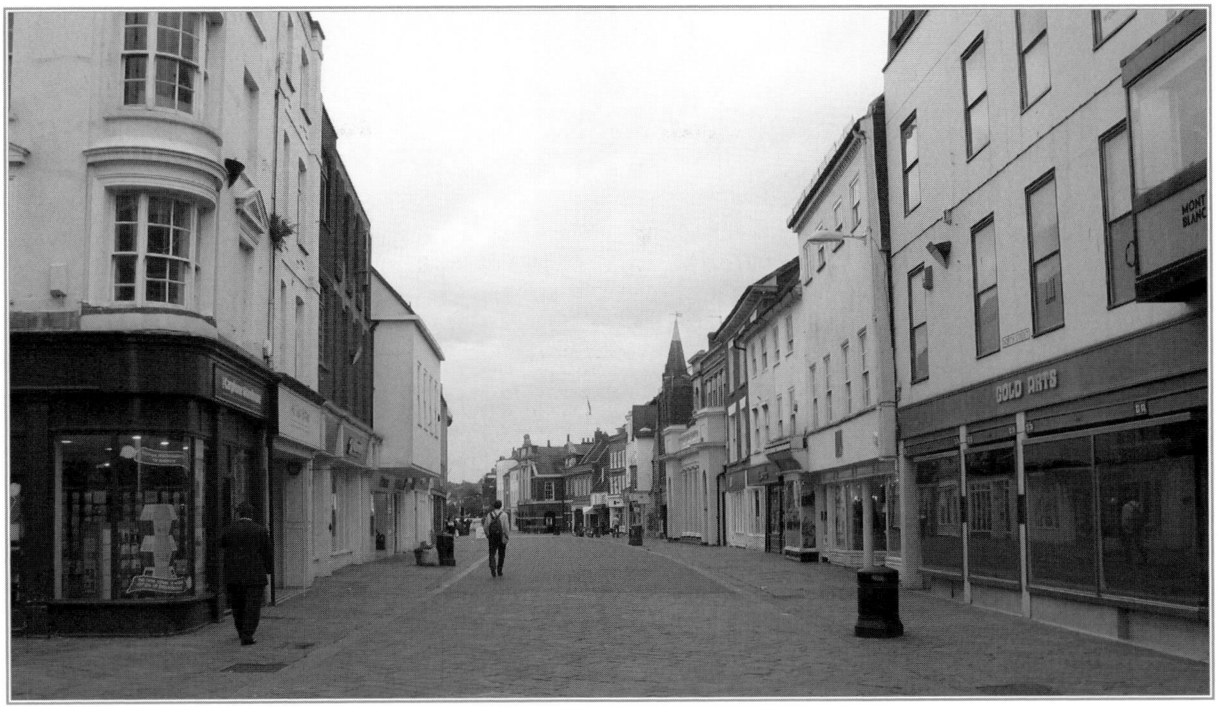

Stead & Simpson shoe shop on the left has now become The Carphone Warehouse. Gold Arts and the Nationwide Building Society are among the other stores which now greet you as you head north from the Cross.

'Happy and Fortunate'

1959–60 is the probable date for the lovely image of a snowy North Street overleaf, somehow looking much wider in the days when buses and lorries were very much part of the street scene.

The column-fronted building on the right-hand side of the street, just to the left of the centre of the photograph, is the Council House. Replacing an earlier timber-framed structure, it was built in 1731 in the Palladian style popular at the time. At the top of the façade is a Latin inscription which translated reads 'in order that the council and the people of Chichester and their posterity might be happy and fortunate, this council house was begun and completed in the year of our Lord 1731, in the reign of George II, Elector and King'.

The Council House was paid for by public subscription under the mayoralty of the Duke of Richmond. Along with the Assembly Room, it would have been a focus for the flourishing social round of the Georgian city.

The house consists of an open arcade leading to the hall, on the north side of which is the staircase leading to a square landing and off which were the various civic chambers. The Council Chamber, over the west front, is entered from the landing's west door.

Also visible in both photographs is another of Chichester's numerous disused city-centre churches. Just next to the Stanton sign is St Olave's, dating from the 11th to the 13th century, which is now a bookshop. The church consisted only of a chancel and a nave, both small.

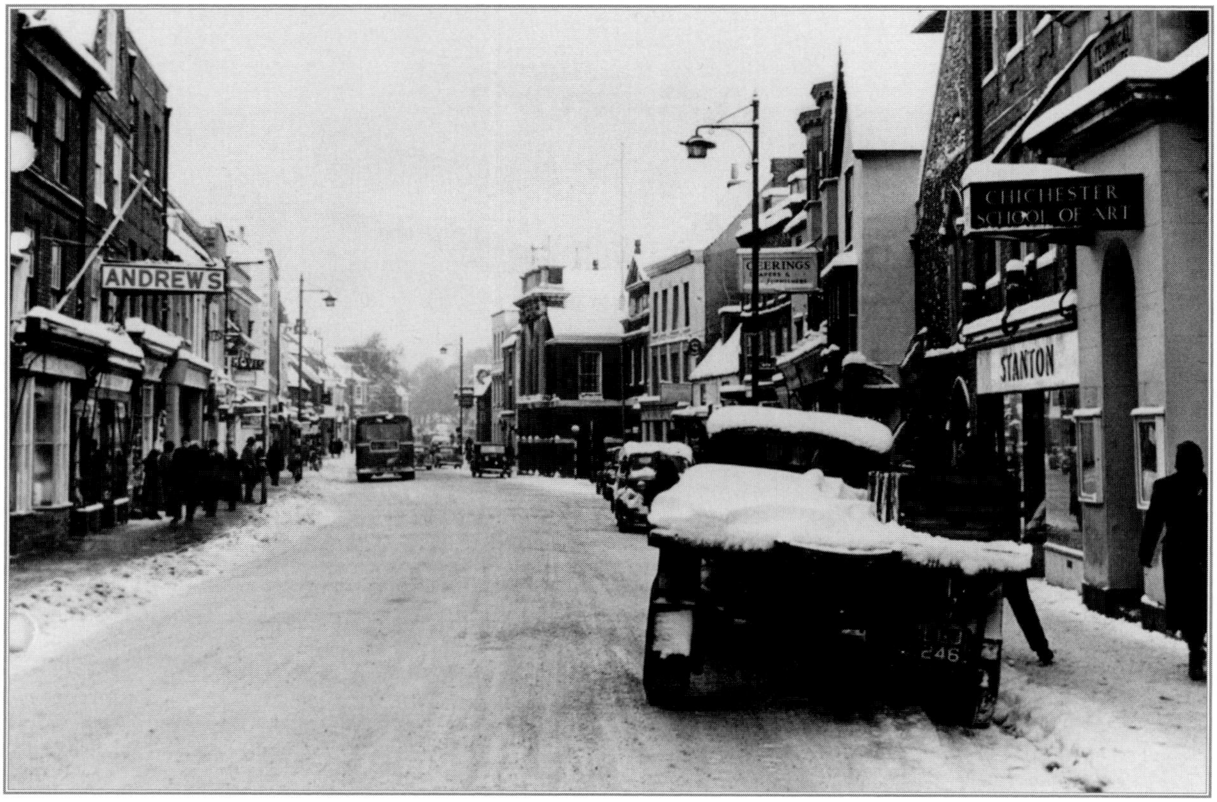

Chichester School of Art, visible in the older image, was then in the upper storey over the Butter Market.

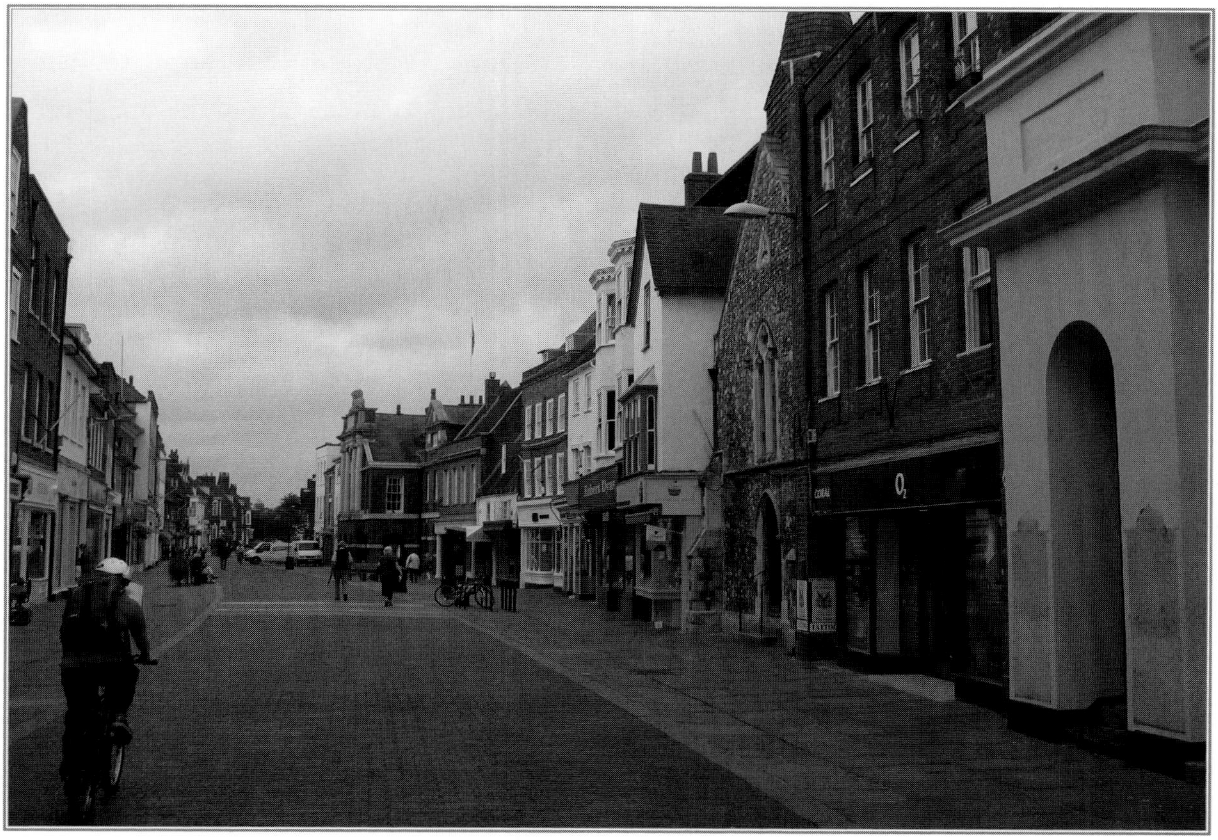

Eight Centuries of City Rule

North Street is the traditional home of the city's administrative offices. The 1958 image, overleaf, shows Chichester's civic leaders in procession, among them the mayor, an office going back in the city more than 800 years.

The city council has been based at the Council House in North Street for more than 250 years, but the roots of the council go back even further. In the Council House there is a list of the mayors of Chichester dating back to 1239 when Emery de Rouen first occupied the office.

Chichester City Council is the parish council for the city of Chichester, but other than a series of charters there are no records of its early years, although it is known to have met in a wooden building in the middle of North Street near the present-day Butter Market.

The Butter Market is another Chichester landmark steeped in history, and its columns are visible in the distance in both pictures. It was opened in 1808, and as a result the Market Cross – no longer open to traders – was enclosed within railings. With its imposing entrance through a series of columns, the Butter Market was designed by architect John Nash.

The 1958 photograph captures part of the pageantry which surrounded the enthronement of the new Bishop of Chichester, Roger Wilson, who remained in post until 1974. Wilson was the successor to Chichester's celebrated wartime bishop, George Kennedy Allen Bell (1883–1958). The 50th anniversary of Bell's death in 2008 was marked in Chichester with a series of events and lectures.

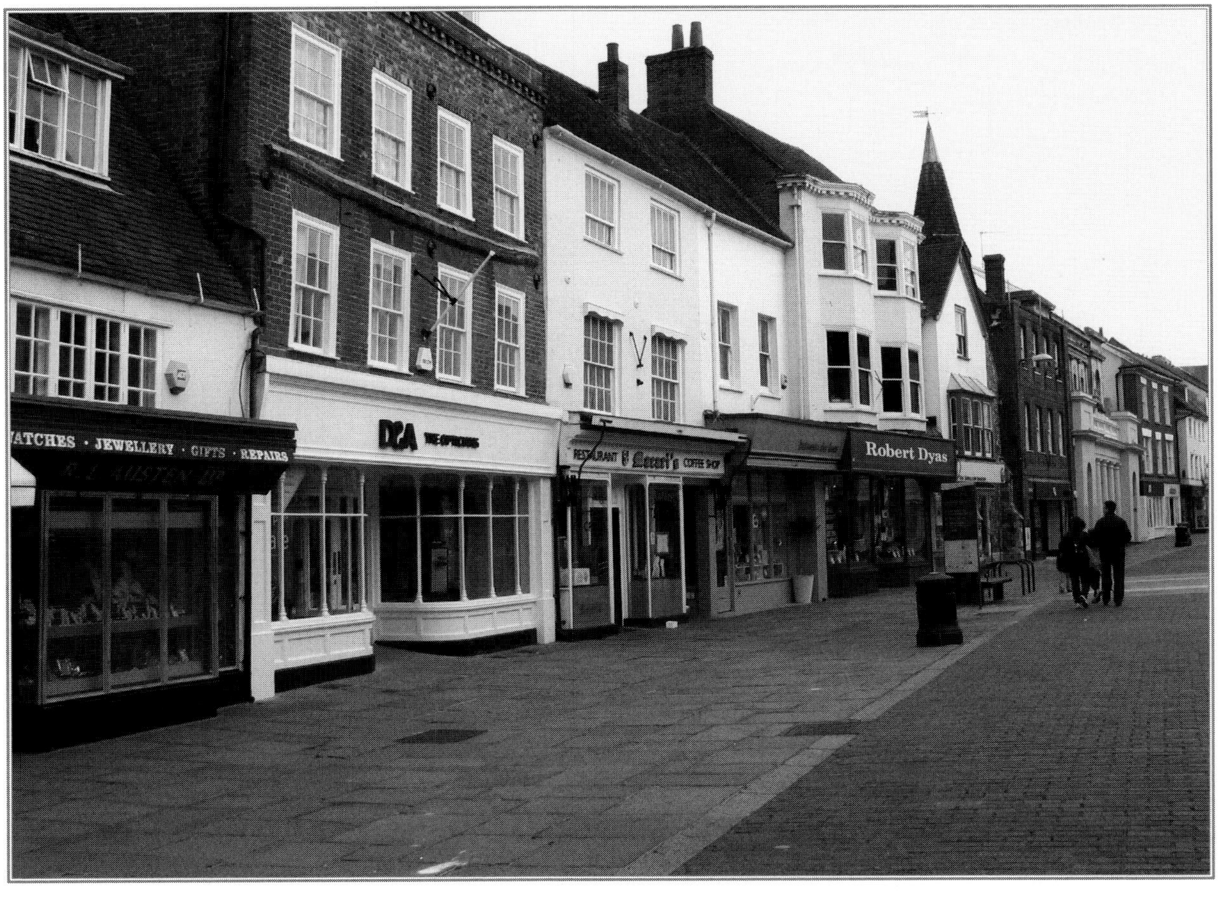

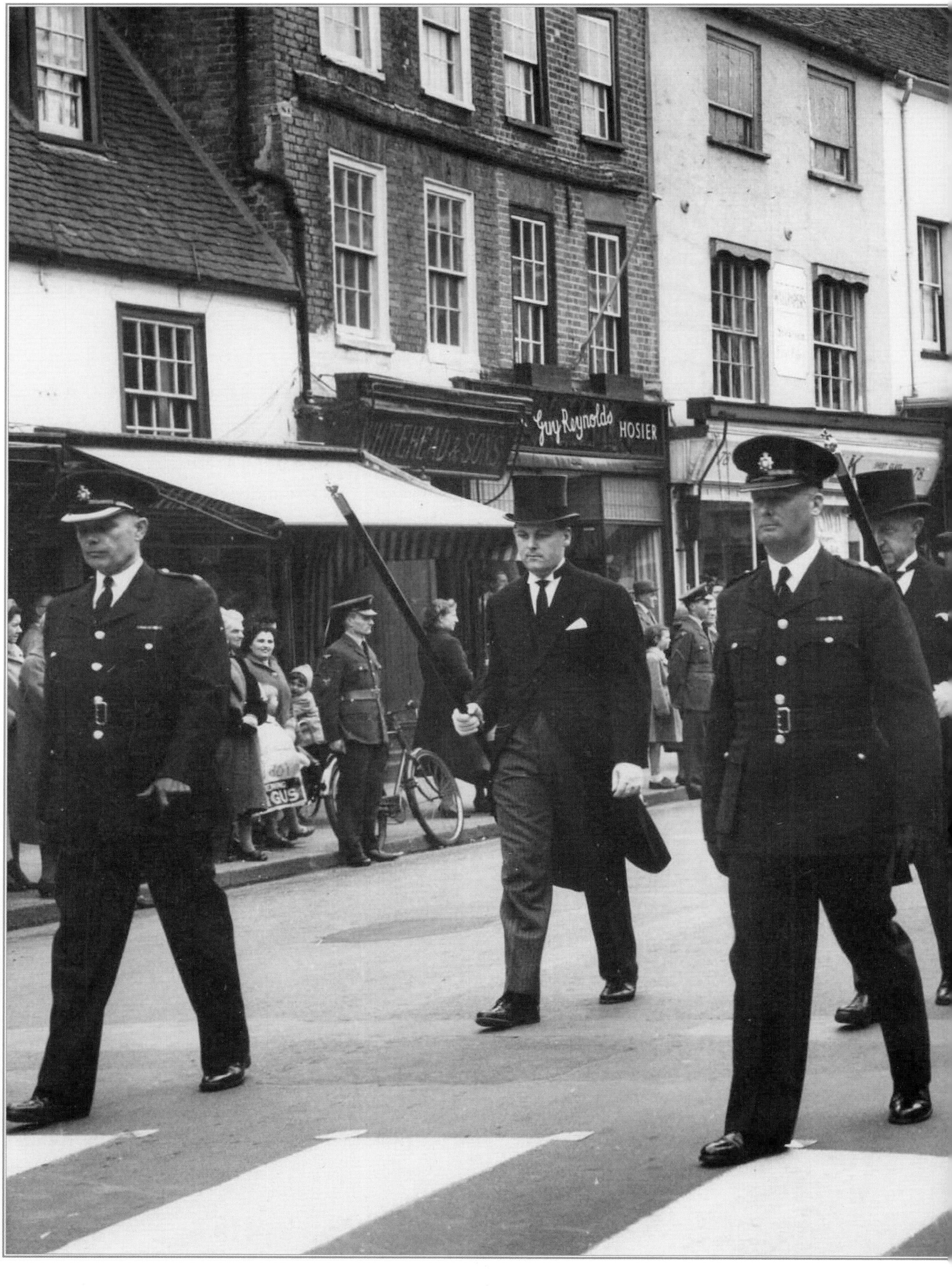
Guy Reynolds
HOSIER

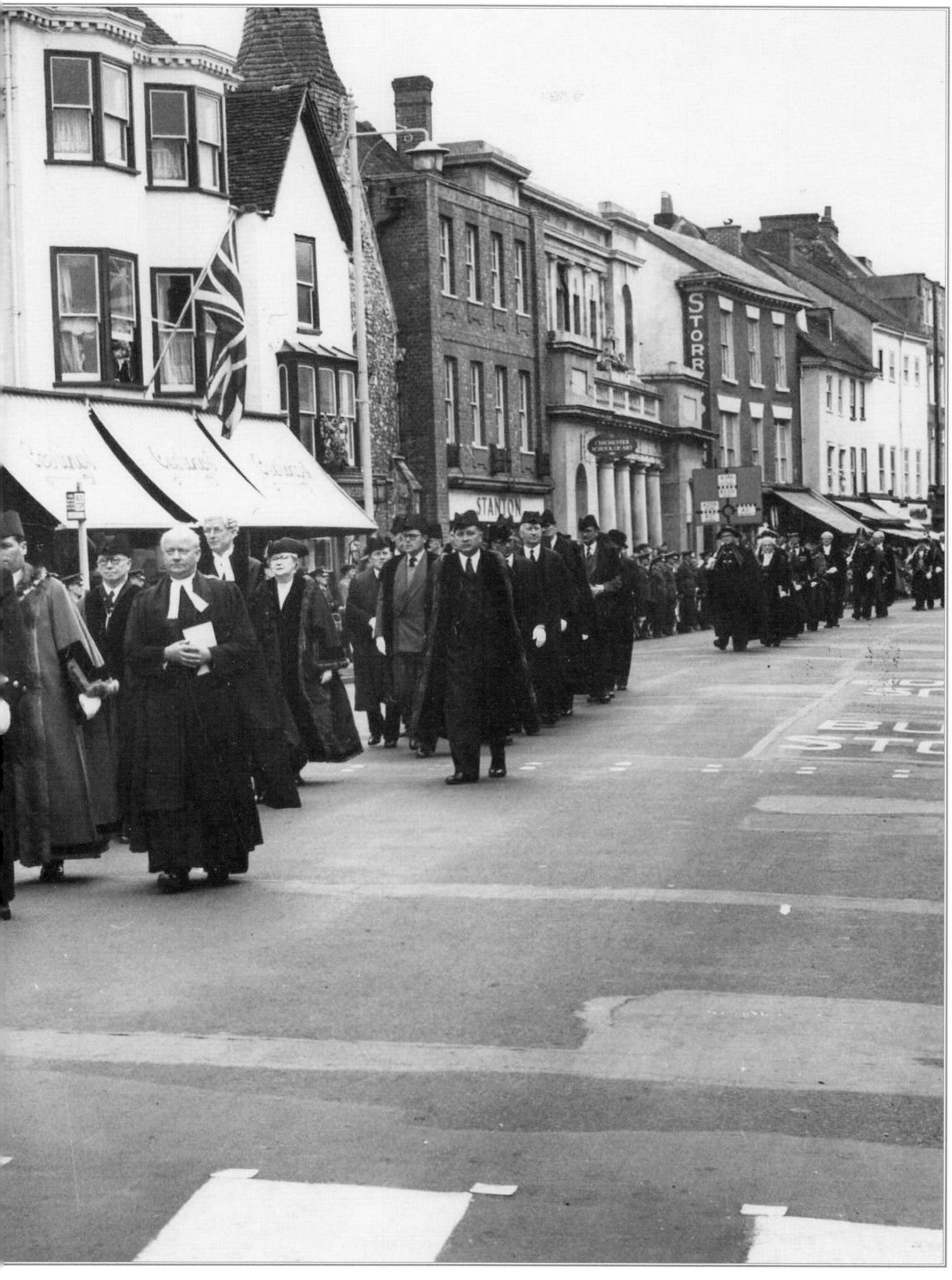
STORR
STANTON

Gutted by Fire

Do you remember the shop? Or do you remember the fire? In 1974 Shirley's in North Street was destroyed by a devastating blaze which threatened to engulf the whole heart of the city.

The Sainsbury's fire just before Christmas 1993 was a tragic spectacle, but the Shirley's fire was quite something else. Fire chiefs admitted that Sainsbury's, right on the city's edge and with a massive car park beside it, was a comparatively easy fire to fight and contain.

However, Shirley's was a night-time blaze, right in the city centre, with people living nearby and a busy hotel just yards away.

Paul White received a 2.30am wake-up call from his cashier: 'Mr White, the shop is on fire!' It was a wake-up call which effectively spelt the end of the line for one of Chichester's oldest family businesses.

Shirley Bros, formed in 1846, moved across the road within weeks of the fire but closed the following year. The blaze gutted the shop, wrecking the façade and aspects of the building going back to the 14th century.

North Street was closed for days after the blaze, which drew 120 firemen from West Sussex and Hampshire in 25 fire engines. The biggest Chichester blaze in living memory and certainly since the war, it caused damage estimated at a quarter of a million pounds.

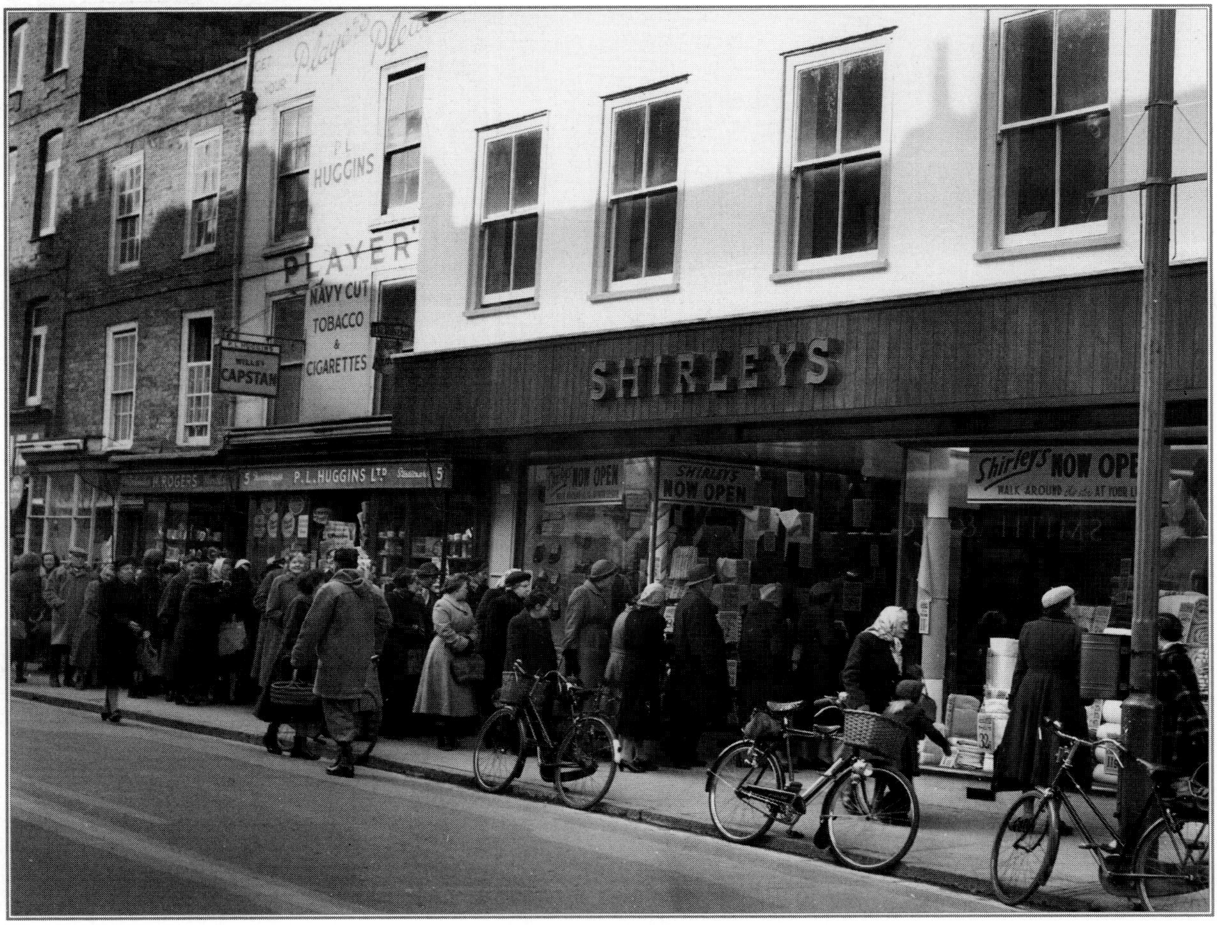

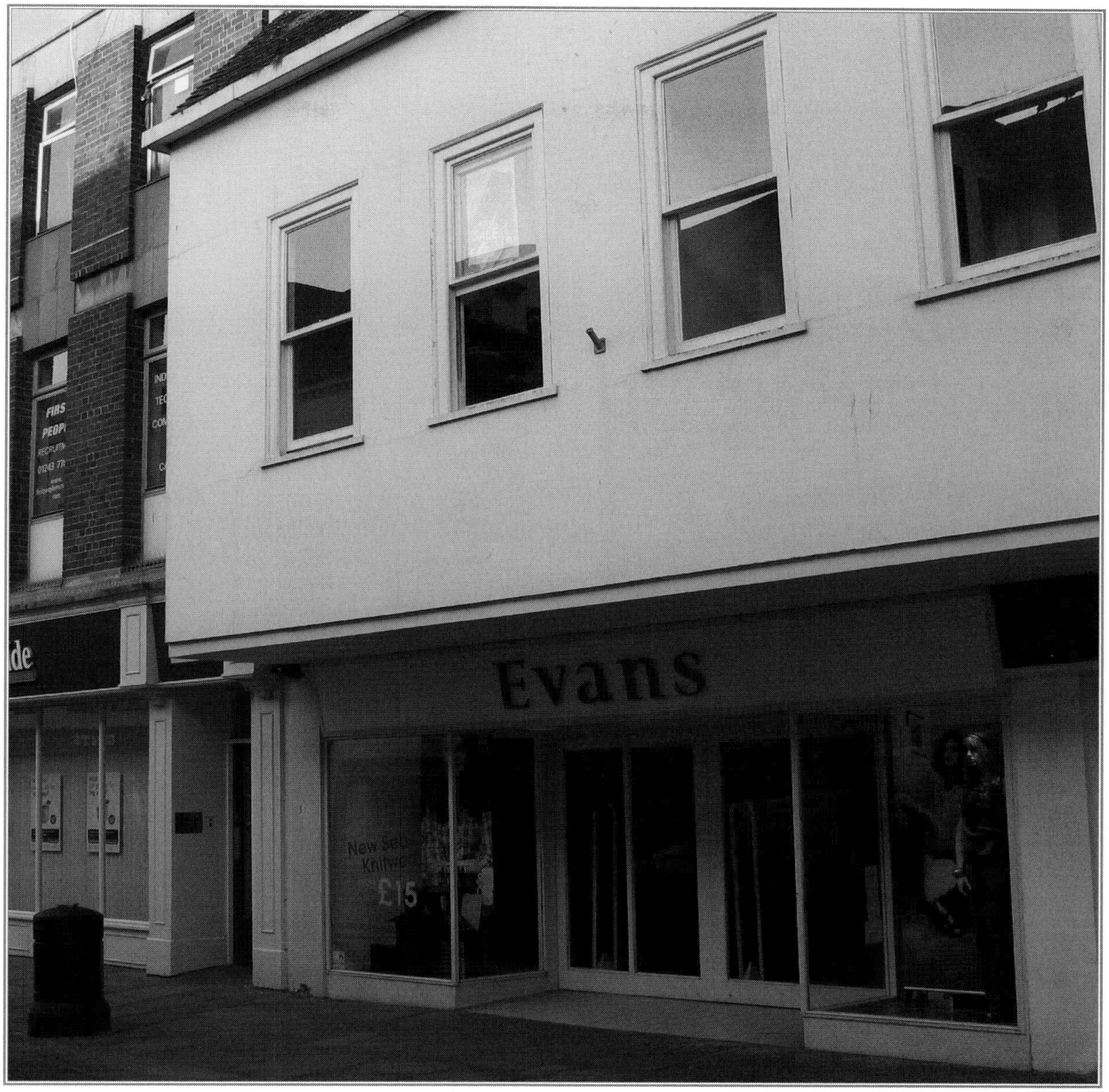

A wind from the south-west heightened fears for neighbouring buildings and the nearby Dolphin & Anchor Hotel was evacuated. Around 60 guests assembled in the main lounge before being led, some still in their night clothes, to the safety of the street.

The site is now Evans clothes shop.

'Nix over Six'

A difficult winter has seen a sad number of shops disappear from Chichester's city centre. The most lamented perhaps has been Woolworth's, for so many years so much a part of our lives.

Woolworths went into administration in November 2008 with debts of £385 million; Deloitte was unable to find a buyer and so the firm's 807 British stores launched their clearance sales, the start of a staged programme of closure.

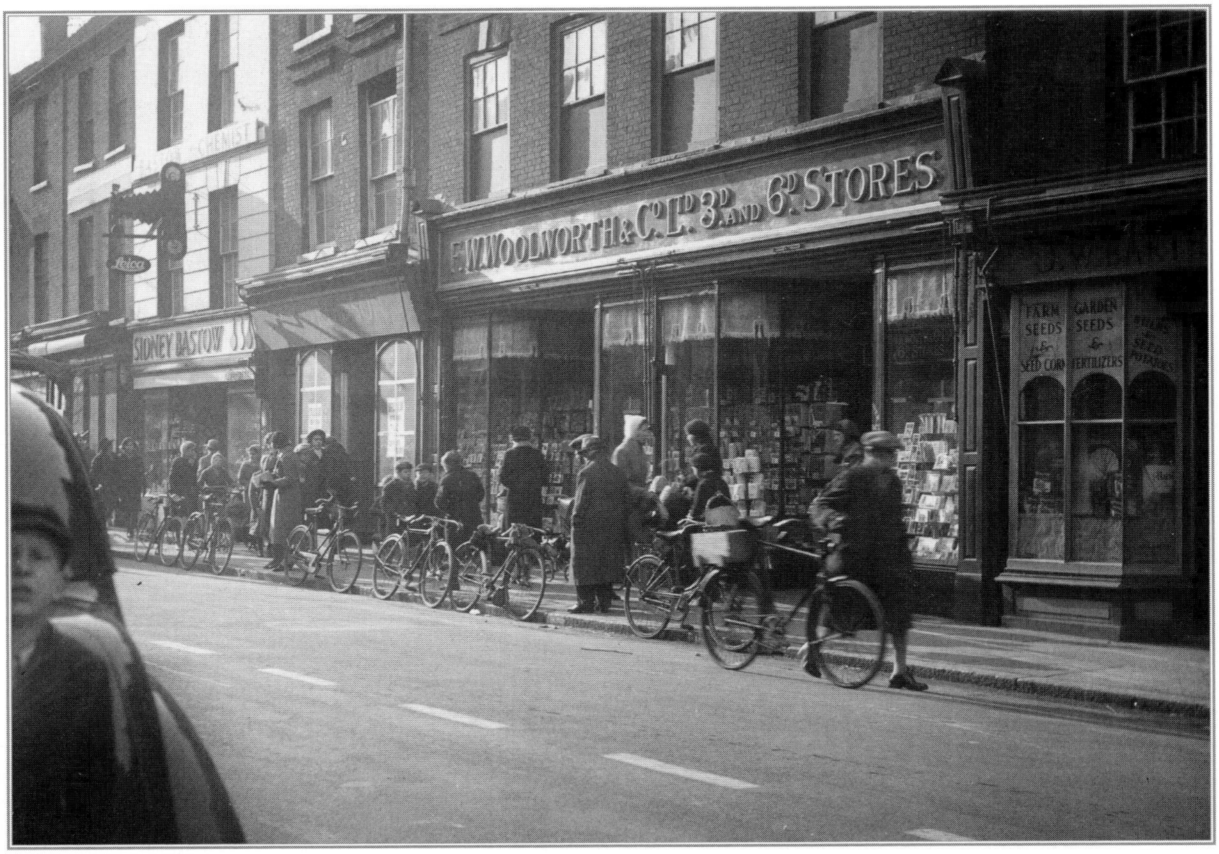
F. W. WOOLWORTH & Co. Ltd. 3d AND 6d STORES
SIDNEY BASTOW
FARM SEEDS & SEED CORN
GARDEN SEEDS & FERTILIZERS

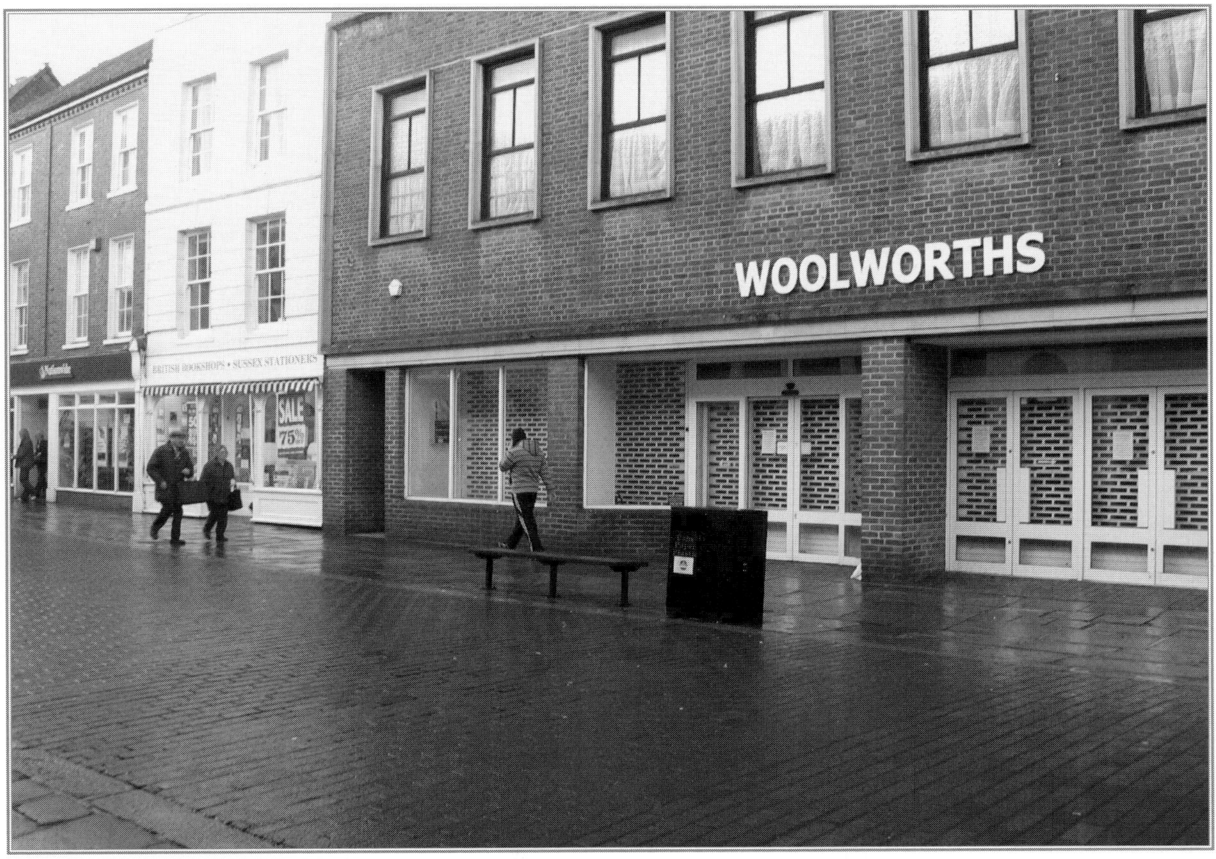
WOOLWORTHS
BRITISH BOOKSHOPS • SUSSEX STATIONERS
SALE

By the end of the first week in January 2009 Woolworth's was no more, leaving more than 27,000 people unemployed. With those jobs went a piece of history, a part of all our childhoods.

One of the original American five-and-dime stores, the F.W. Woolworth Company (or Woolworth's to the rest of us) opened its first British store in Church Street, Liverpool, on Friday 5 November 1909. In the early 1920s F.W. Woolworth was simply unbeatable, at the forefront of a retail revolution that introduced good-quality, mass-produced goods that everyone could afford. Customers loved it, and the company expanded massively.

But World War Two took its toll. The British economy saw rapid price inflation and Woolworth's bosses met in New Bond Street to make one of the toughest choices of their lives – to abandon the company's motto of more than 30 years' standing, namely 'Nothing over 6d' or 'Nix over six'. Inflation meant they could no longer offer much of their range within the sixpenny limit so they decided to abandon the limit at least for the duration of the war.

The store at Hammersmith in London was one of the first to show no reference to '3d and 6d Stores' on its fascia. In its place, to the left and right of the words F.W. Woolworth & Co Ltd, they placed Frank Woolworth's diamond 'W' motif.

Chichester's Woolworth's stood in North Street and for years it did well, expanding southwards between the taking of these two photographs.

In the older photograph, Bastow's the Chemists occupied No. 9, now Sussex Stationers. The shop to the right of Woolworth's in the earlier image belonged to Bartholomew's Corn Merchants. Advertisements for seeds and fertilisers can just be seen in the window.

CHAPTER 4
SOUTH STREET

South Street's Rich Mix

Chichester was once again in royal party mood for this appealing image of South Street, probably dating from the mid-1930s – a throwback to a time before the big multiples took over the main streets.

A Chichester directory for 1923–24 makes fascinating reading for the glimpse it gives of the mix of businesses the city's main shopping areas offered in the years between the wars.

Nos 1, 2, 3 and 4 South Street were occupied respectively by Charge & Co Drapers, W.H. Barrett, Domestic Bazaar Company and Shippam's. Also near the Cross were Griffiths Bros, the London Central Meat Company, C.C. Allen and Alfred Sykes Drapers.

No. 13 South Street was home to *The West Sussex Gazette* office while No. 54 was the Chichester office for *The Portsmouth Evening News*. These were the days before both papers came under the same ownership.

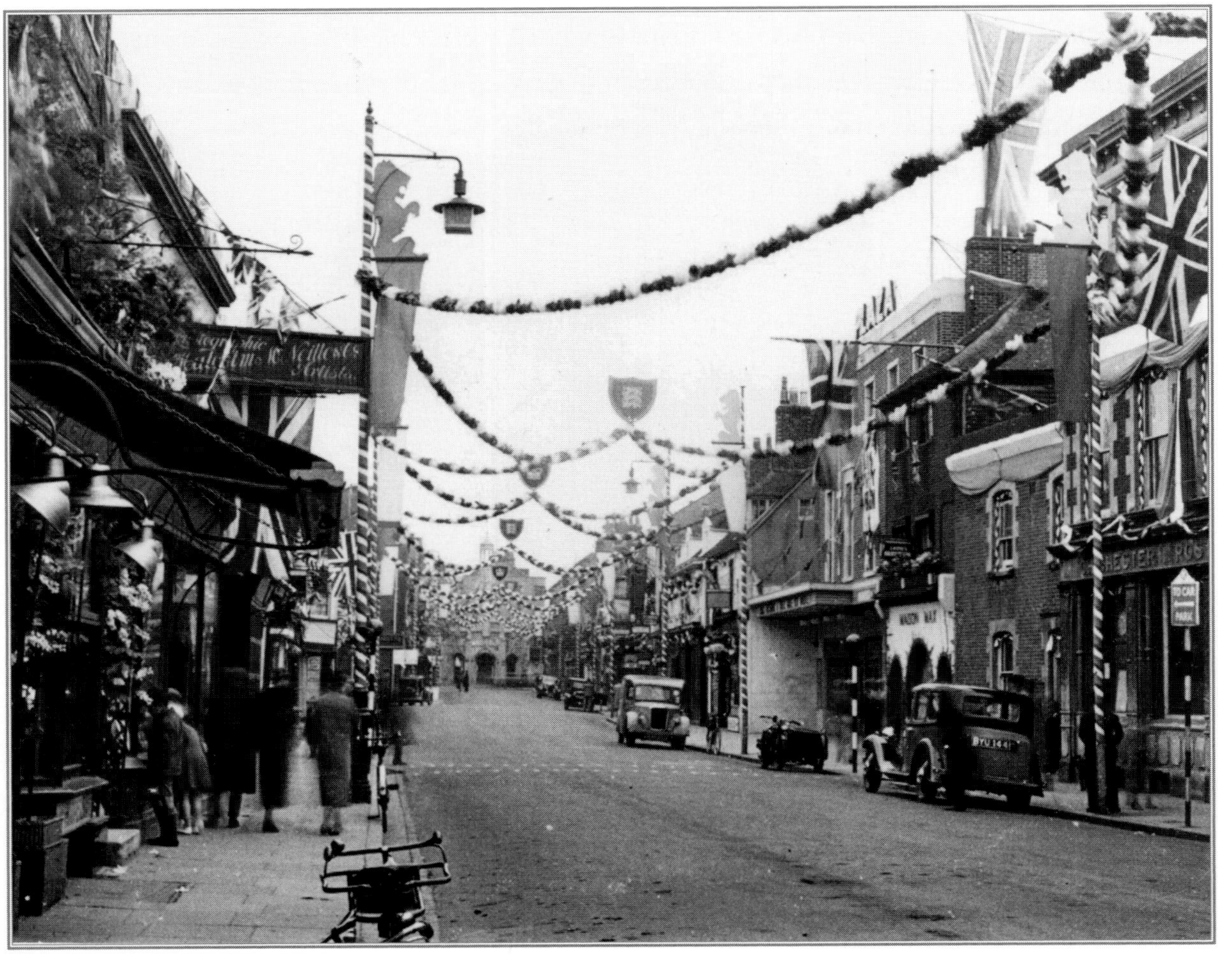

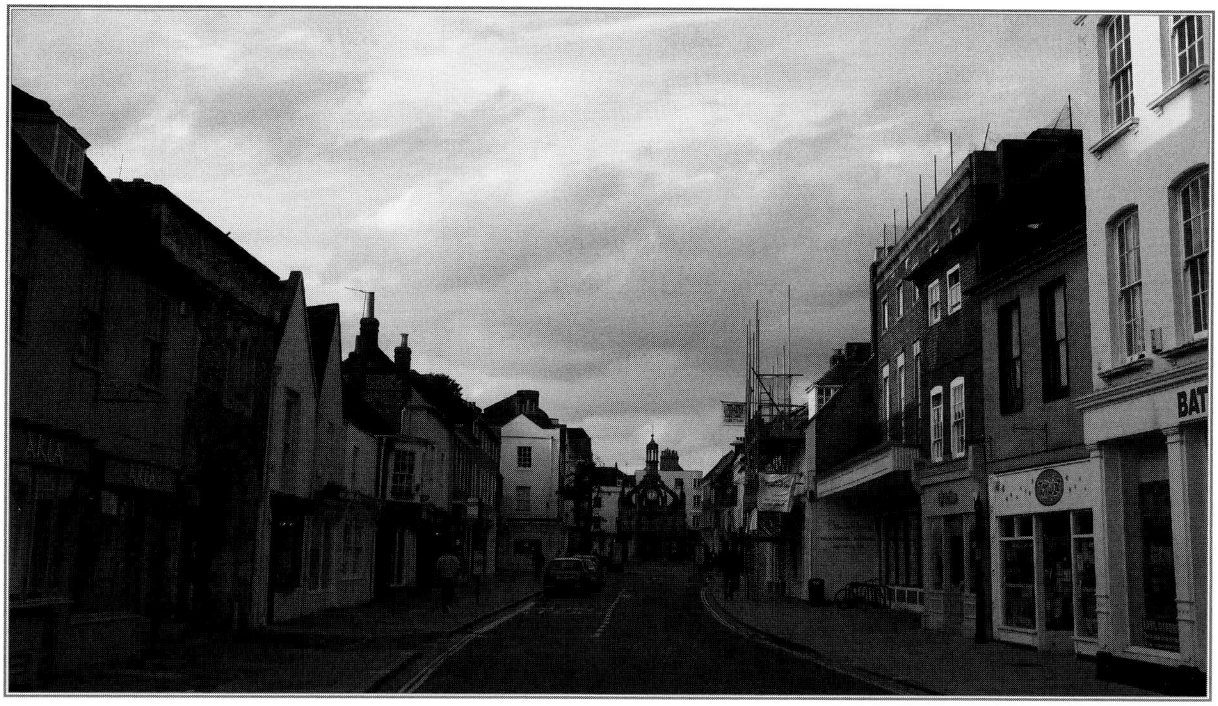

Madame H. Maye was a South Street costumiere, while R. Hillsdon's gun-maker and sports goods shop is still remembered in the city. No. 45 hosted the Assessor and Collector of King's Taxes for Chichester, Aldingbourne and Apuldram District. No. 46 was the Royal Café and No. 52, seen on the right in the older photograph, was the post office. Turnbull's outfitters, the Chichester Gas Showroom, Bushby's high class tobacconists and Bishop Bros were other familiar South Street traders.

Nowadays the names on the shopfronts may have changed but South Street still remains a busy shopping street. Businesses now include Bath Travel, Oxfam, Toywizz toy shop and the Maison Blanc patisserie.

'Read All About It!'

It used to be Bishops Bros shoe shop; now it is Steamer Trading Cookshop. Other occupants down the ages have included a maltster, a butcher, a watchmaker and a couple of grocers, but for many years until 1994, No. 69 South Street was base camp for the city's newspaper.

The Chichester Observer began life as *The Chichester Observer and West Sussex Recorder* on 15 June 1887. In its early days it was published by Acford's at No. 19 South Street, with the Acford family becoming hugely important in the history of the paper.

The paper progressed and prospered under the editorship of Mr Acford and then later under that of his daughter Marjorie.

In March 1914 the printing of the paper changed to premises in Little London. Then in January 1968 production of *The Observer* moved to new headquarters at Hilsea in Portsmouth, where it enjoyed all the very latest technologies of the electronic revolution.

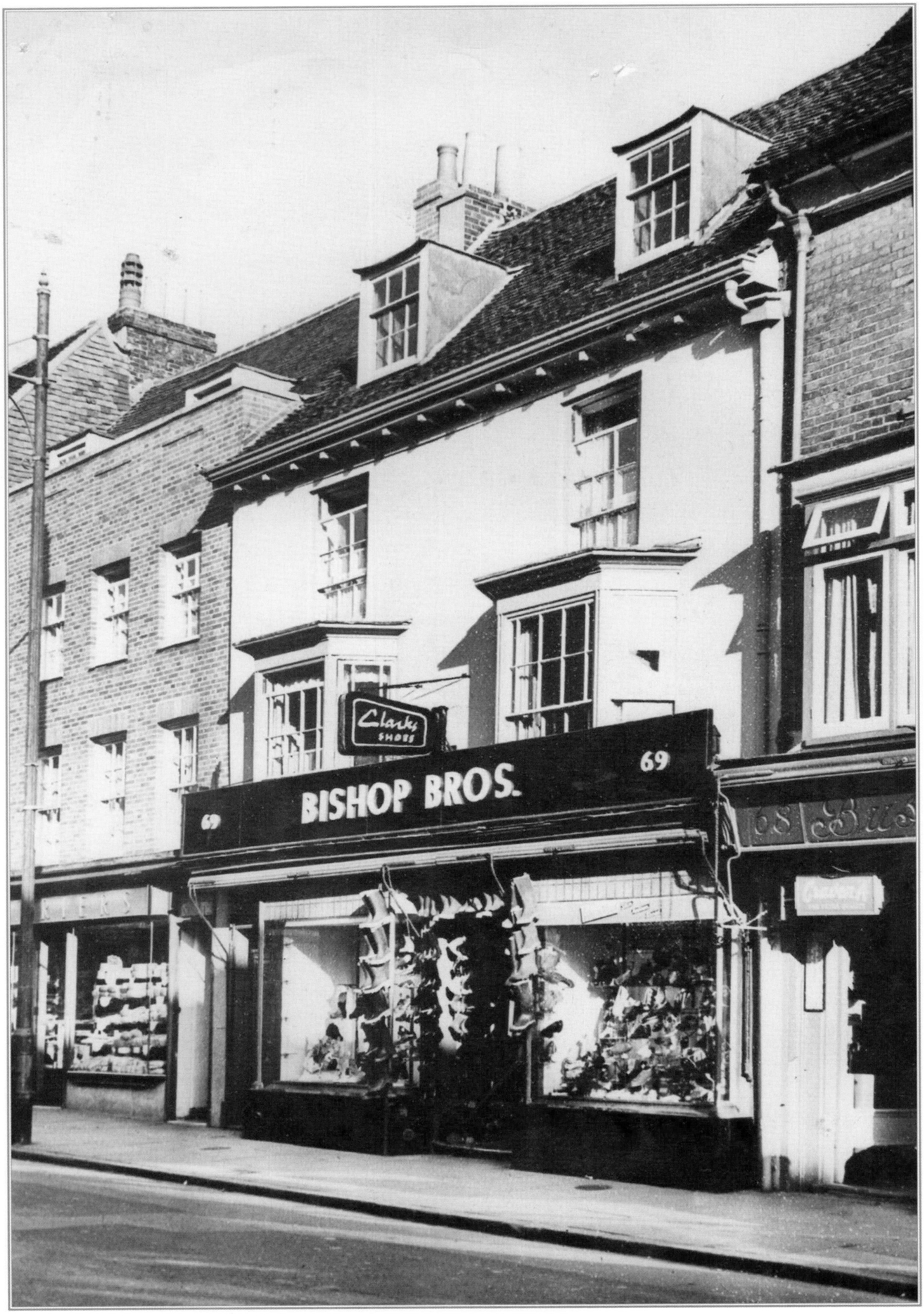
Clarks
SHOES
69
BISHOP BROS.
69
68

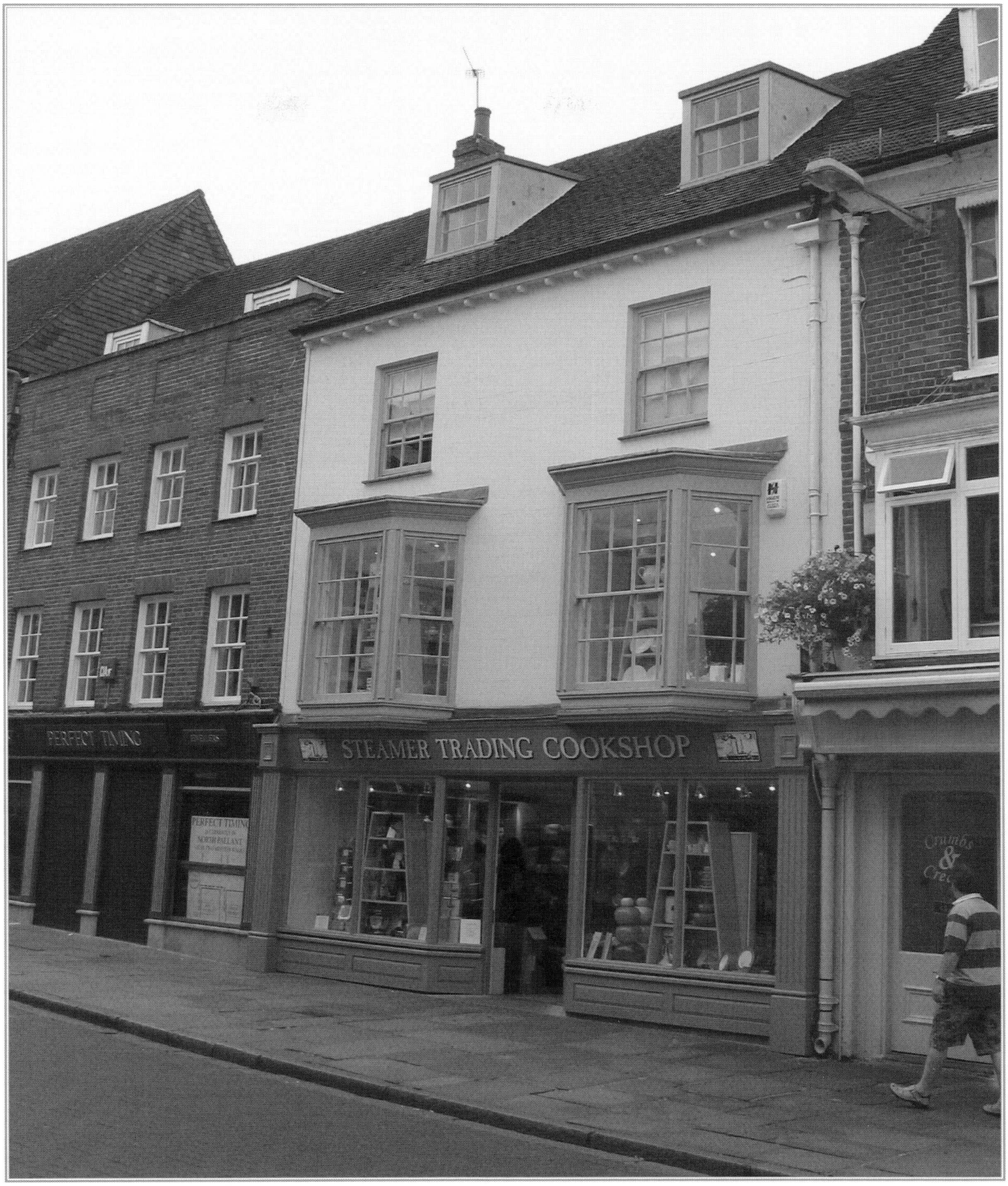

In 1950 the new editor of *The Observer* was H. Stote, who was succeeded in 1956 by J.A. Neal. Mr Neal was succeeded by Graham Brooks, who retired in 1992.

By now *The Chichester Observer* was sited at the offices at No. 69 South Street, where it remained until its move in 1994 to Unicorn House, Eastgate Square, under the editorship of Keith Newbery. On Keith's retirement Colin Channon took over. In 1999 Portsmouth & Sunderland Newspapers was acquired by Johnston Press.

Changing Face of South Street

'Didn't that used to be such-and-such?' is a game that is very easy to play in Chichester city centre where shops come and go with great regularity.

Southgate used to be home to Waitrose; South Street used to be home to Texas. Very little has stayed the same.

Take this stretch of shops on the upper-eastern side of East Street, part of a stretch of 17th and 18th century buildings.

Where once there was Bishop Bros, Bushby's, Emile's and Curry's, now – nearly 50 years later – there is the Steamer Trading Cookshop, Crumbs & Creams, Nation and Barnardo's, all part of the changing face of a street with its trading roots going back to the 13th century.

Eight hundred years ago there was a row of little shops running south from the Market Cross on both sides of the street as far as West Pallant. As the years passed, the shops extended further south on the western side, while on the eastern side mansions appeared.

North Street boasted the city's administrative centre, its market and two churches; East Street had the banks and the biggest inns. South Street could not really rival either in importance but it did boast two early post offices and was home to the city's first theatre.

Opening in 1791, the theatre was part of a circuit which included Southampton, Winchester, Portsmouth and Newport on the Isle of Wight. After its closure in 1850 the building was sold at

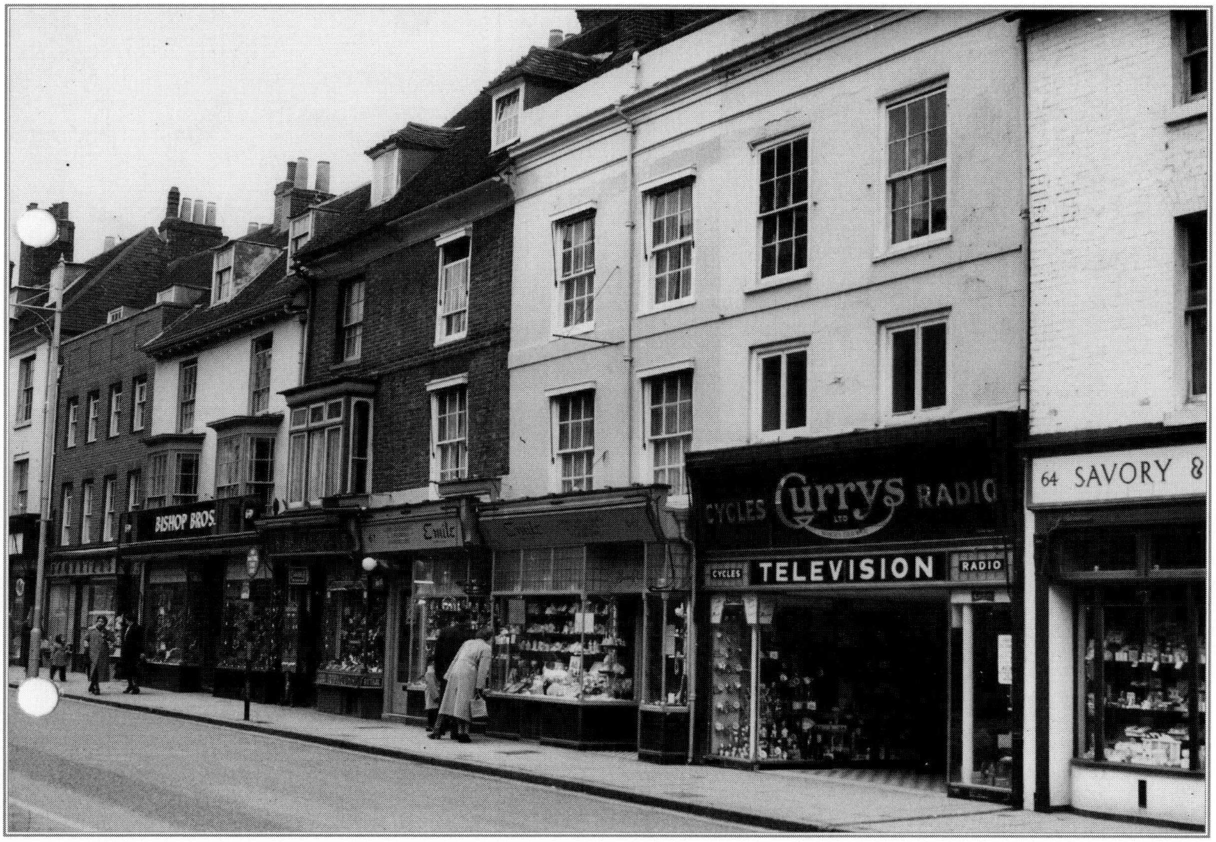

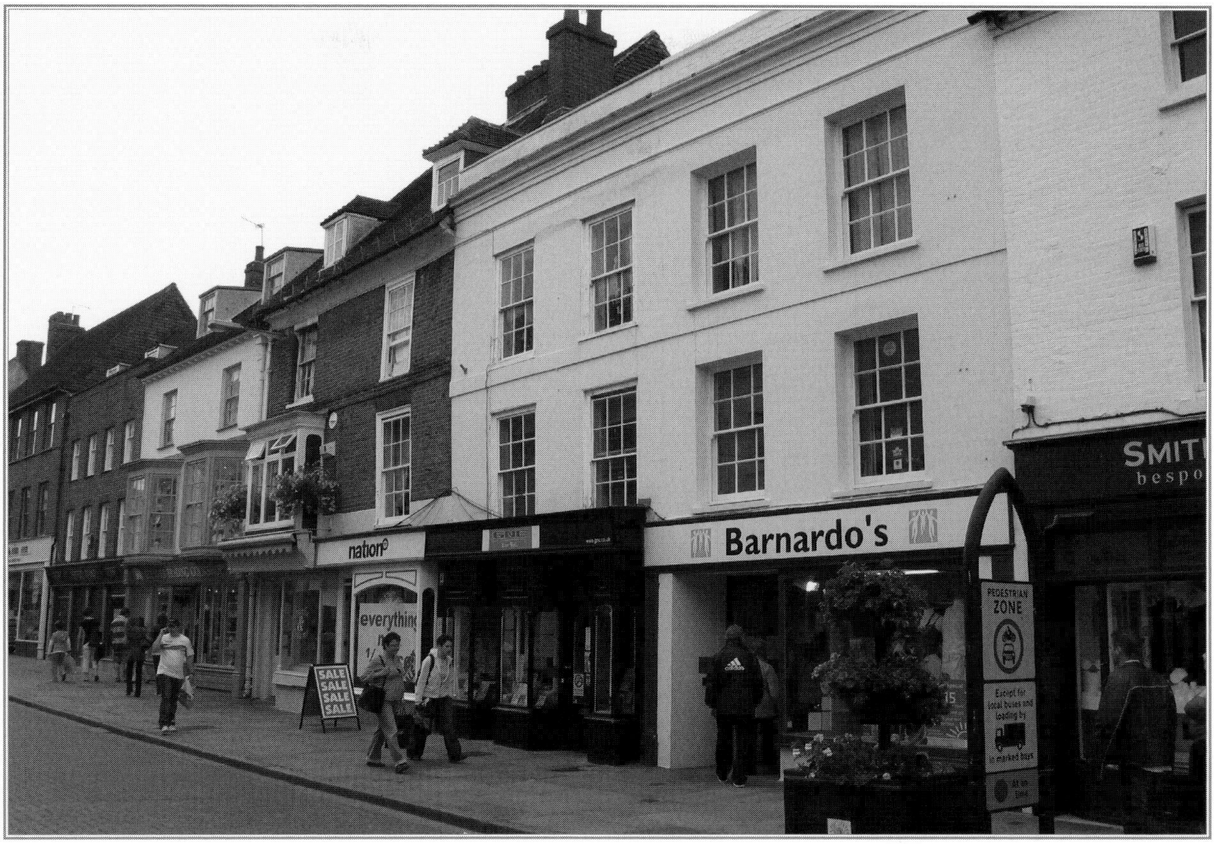

auction to become variously a brewhouse, gymnasium, library, furnishers, a box office for Chichester Festival Theatre and, more recently, shops. It is now the pizza restaurant Zizzi.

Canon Gate

Canon Gate, situated on the west side of South Street, remains largely unaltered in the century which separates the two images seen on the following pages.

Canon Gate, pictured on the left of both of the photographs, today houses the offices of the Chichester Festivities, the popular arts festival which offers two weeks of music and speakers in various venues across the city every summer.

The earlier image probably dates from somewhere between 1890 and 1910, a period which saw an upturn in fortunes for the mediaeval gatehouse in Canon Lane.

It seems likely that Canon Gate was constructed in the late 1520s. It is possible that it is a more recent construction than the buildings to its right. Behind their frontages they conceal 15th-century work.

The gatehouse is built of flints with stone dressings and is two storeys high. In the 19th century it fell into disrepair and for a time the space between the smaller arches was used as a stable. In 1894 it was restored by Ewan Christian and the upper storey was reconstructed.

Canon Gate leads into Canon Lane where the main residences of the cathedral clergy are sited. At the end of Canon Lane is the Bishop's Palace and to the left is the entrance into the Bishop's Palace Gardens.

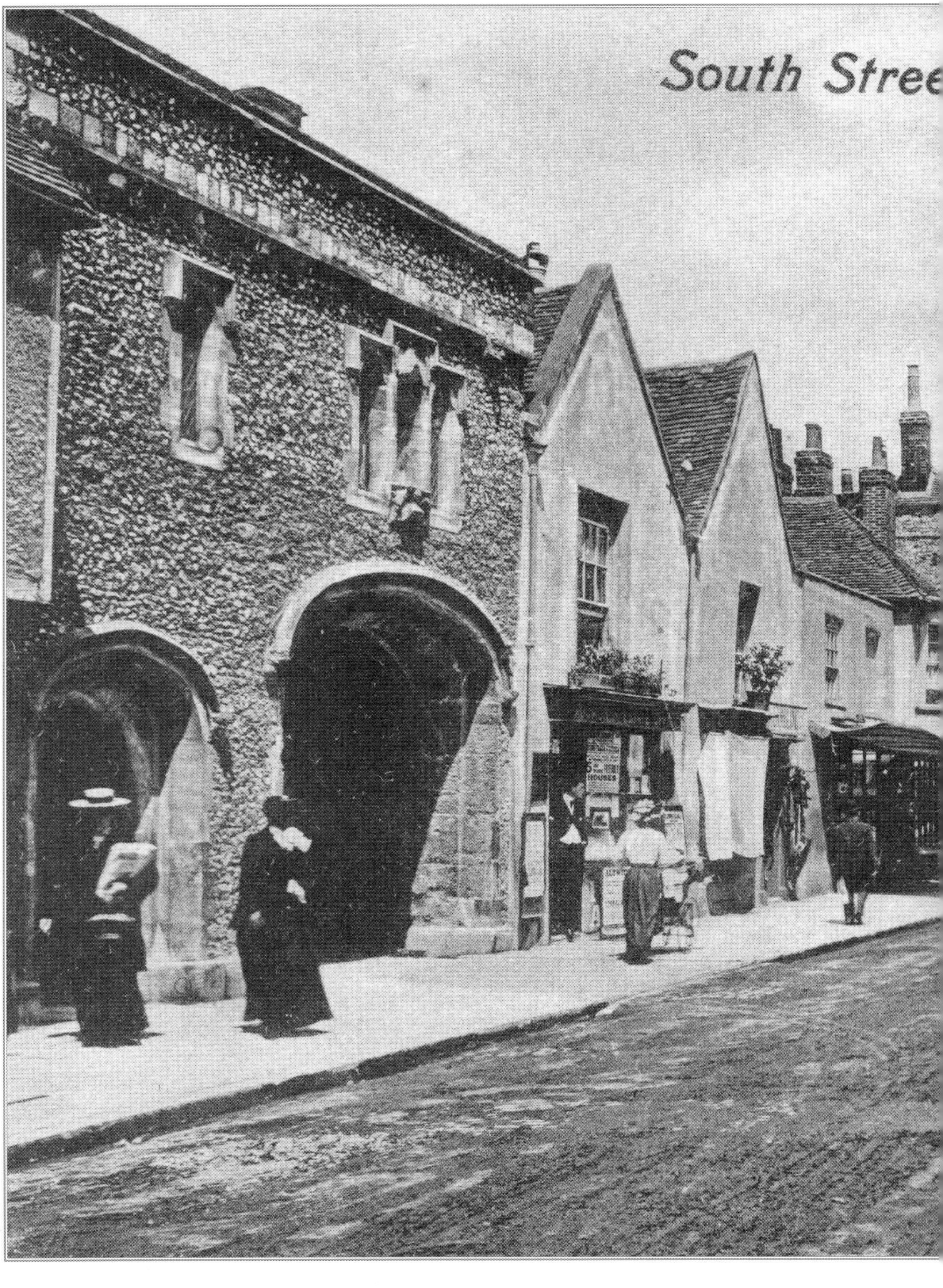
South Stree

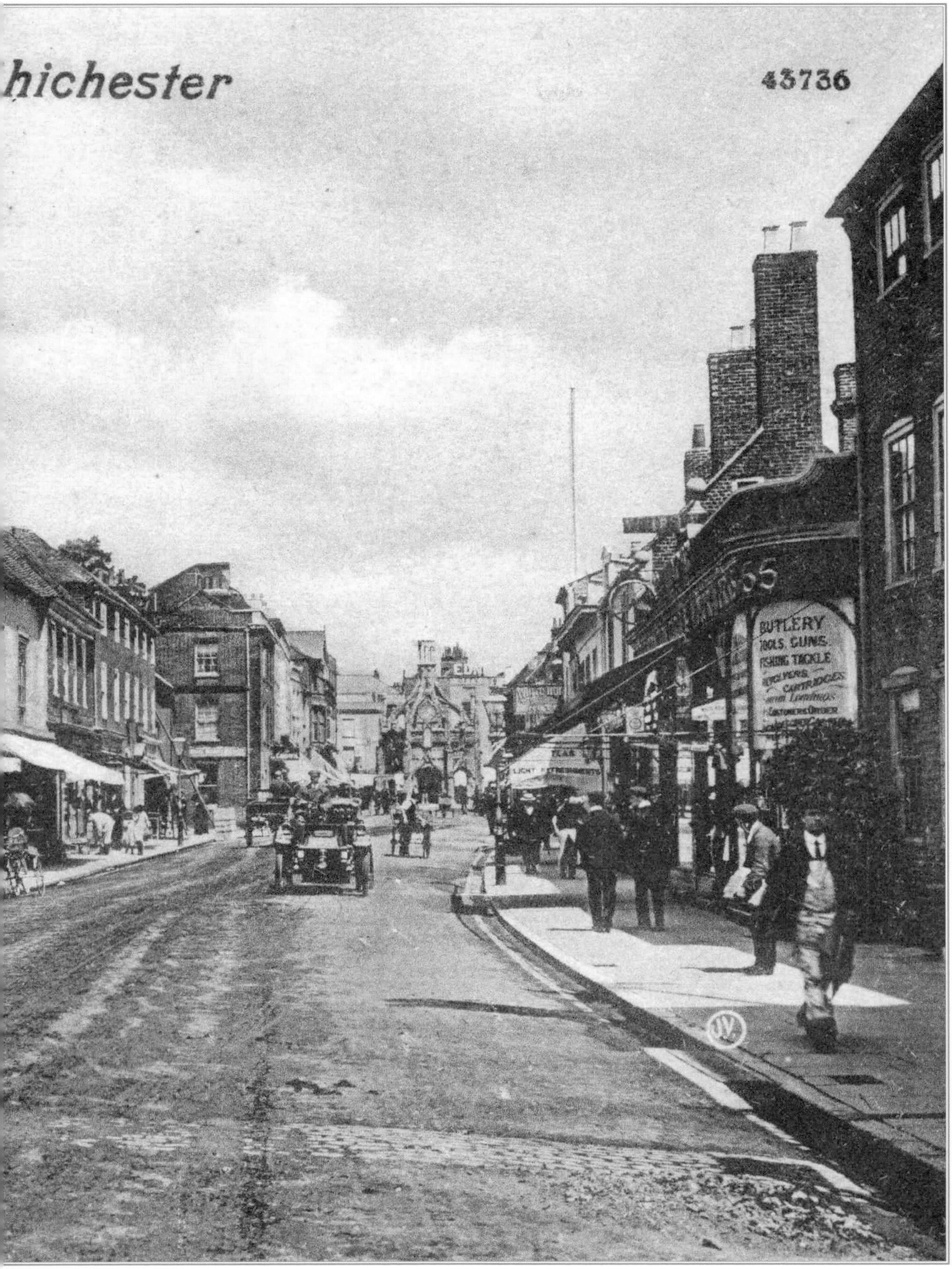
hichester
43736
TOOLS, GUNS
FISHING TACKLE
CARTRIDGES

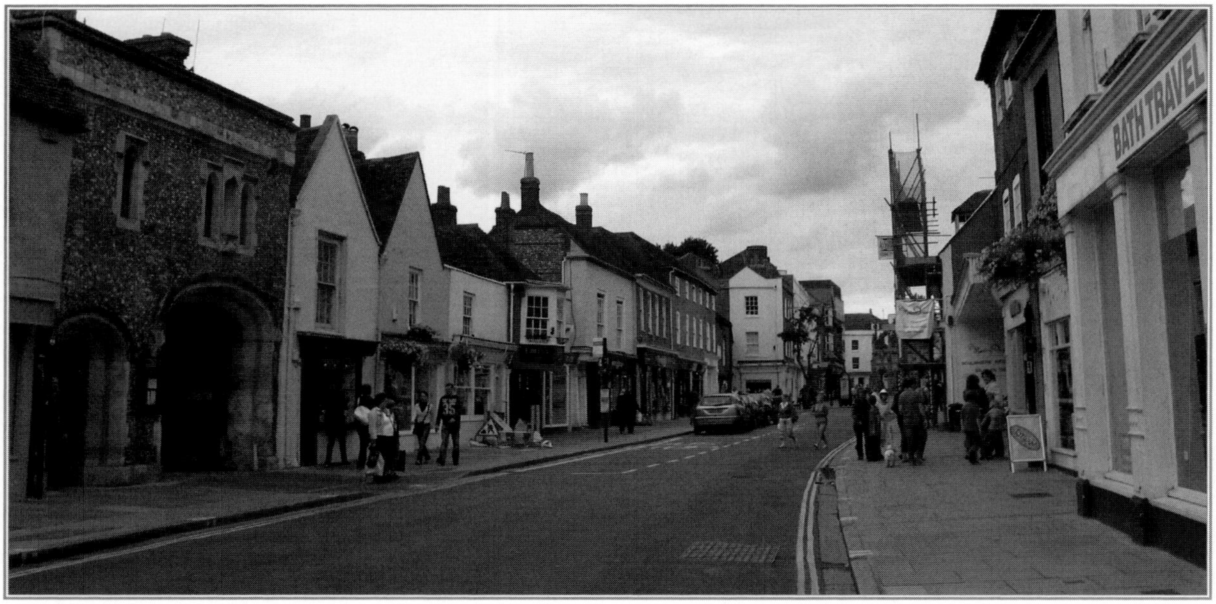

Bounded on the south by the city walls, Bishop's Palace Gardens offers a formal garden with meandering paths, a popular lunchtime retreat away from all the hassles of modern office life. The garden includes an ornamental fish pond, herbaceous borders, annual bedding, shrub beds, a rockery and rose borders.

Heading back out onto South Street, it is interesting to note that the buildings at the top left originally faced westwards into Vicar's Close with their back walls to South Street. In 1825 they were made to face eastwards and converted for shop use.

South Street's Old Post Office

Chichester's first postmaster was appointed in 1796 when the Postmaster General in London took control of all postal services in the country.

The city's earliest post office was in West Pallant. By 1856 the post office was next to the Vicars' Hall. There have also been post offices in East Street and North Pallant.

The city's first purpose-built post office was in South Street, seen here (right) in an image superb in its detail. The building is still there, attractive enough as the home of Bath Travel (see photograph on page 64), but it is impossible not to feel nostalgia for the way this site once looked.

This is yet another image where the more you look at it, the more you see, from the face in the window to the lovely lamps on the van.

The building dates from around 1891 and included a sorting office – functions which are now separated. The current post office is in West Street, opposite the cathedral, and was erected in 1937. The sorting office is in Basin Road.

At a time when we are losing so many of our post offices, not least the rural ones, there is something very appealing about the grandeur of this photograph which dates from somewhere between 1900–14. You can almost sense the men's pride in their building and their new motor vehicle.

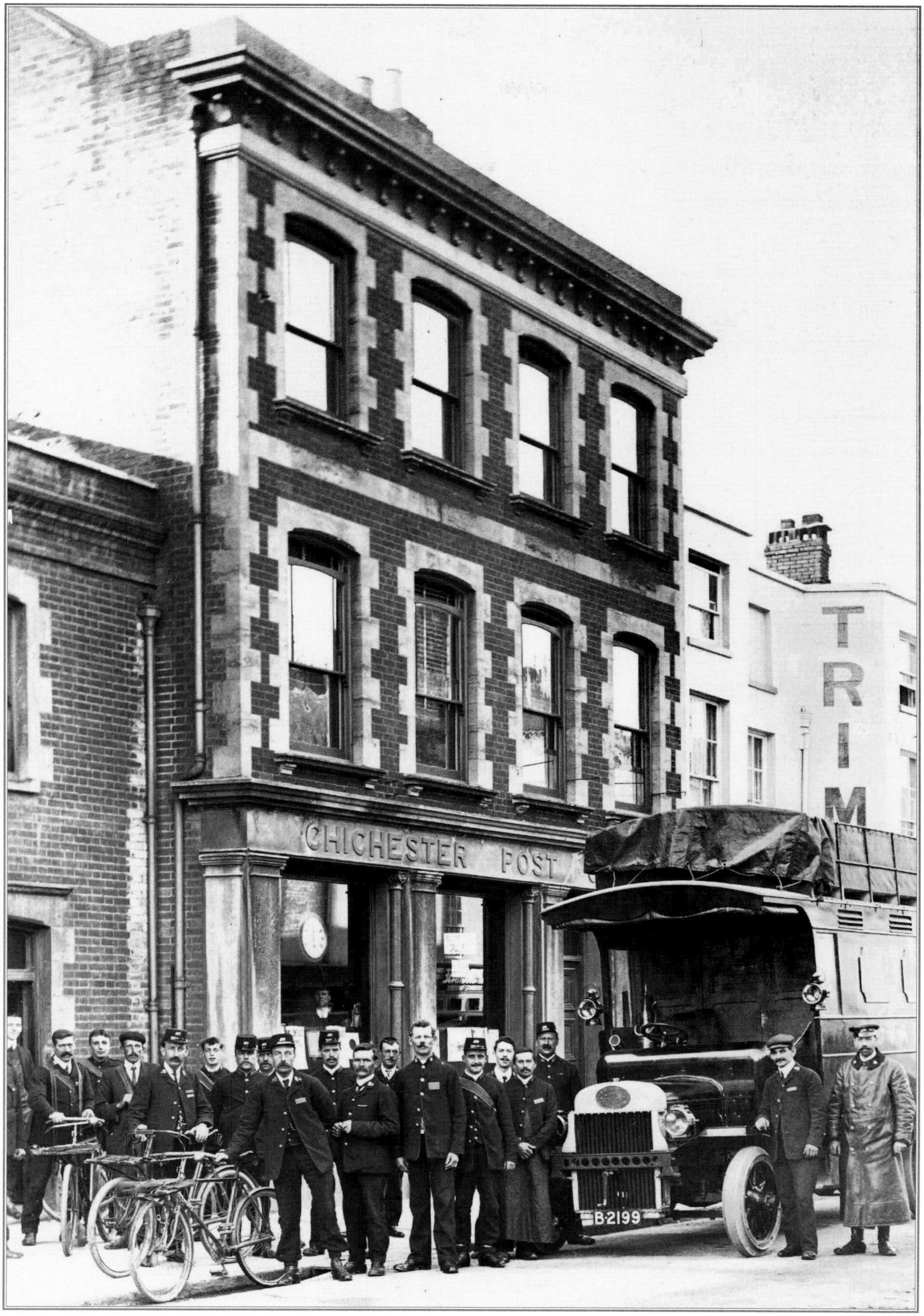
CHICHESTER POST
B-2199
TRIM

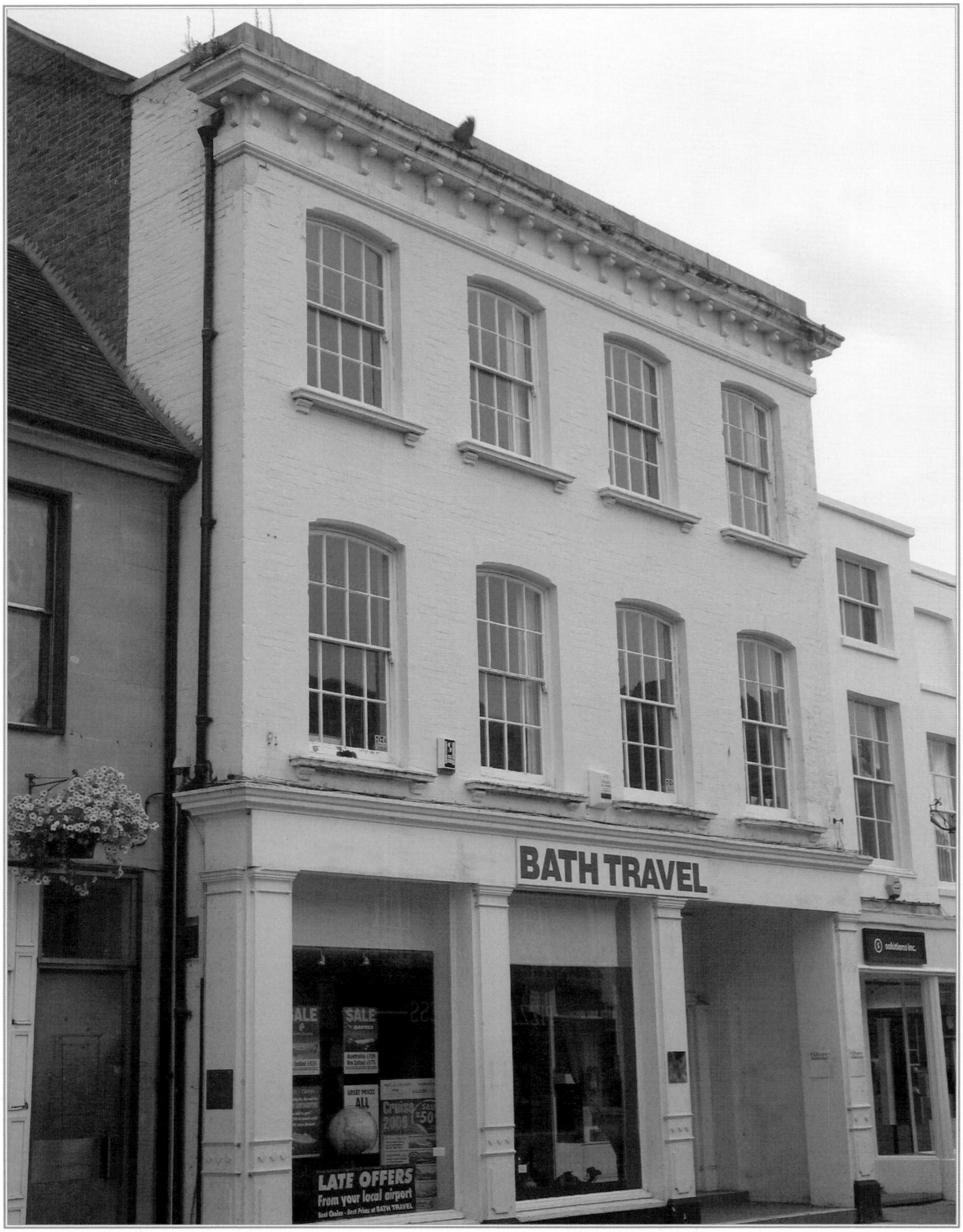
BATH TRAVEL
LATE OFFERS
From your local airport

Chapter 5
East Street

Animals Everywhere

The eastern half of Chichester city centre has historically been its busier, more populated side. Away from North Street's administrative duties and West Street's role as home to the cathedral, East Street, which bisects the city's two eastern quarters, has generally been its hectic trading street.

Life is still unfurling at a leisurely pace though in this enchanting image which looks eastwards from the Market Cross. The upper storeys of the buildings are largely unaltered today, but this was Chichester in the days before the chain stores and when bikes and carts ruled supreme.

The only main street with no churches opening directly onto it, East Street was in some ways the financial quarter. The early banks in the city were all in East Street, among them local banks like the Sussex and Chichester Bank and the Chichester Bank. It is a role which East Street retains to this day as home to Lloyds, HSBC, Barclays and NatWest.

East Street was also home to the city's market – a fact which made it a good deal less pleasant on some days than it looks in this image.

In the early 1800s the cattle market held at Chichester was reckoned to be second only in size to Smithfield in London. Livestock was sold from the streets, and if you did not like the smell,

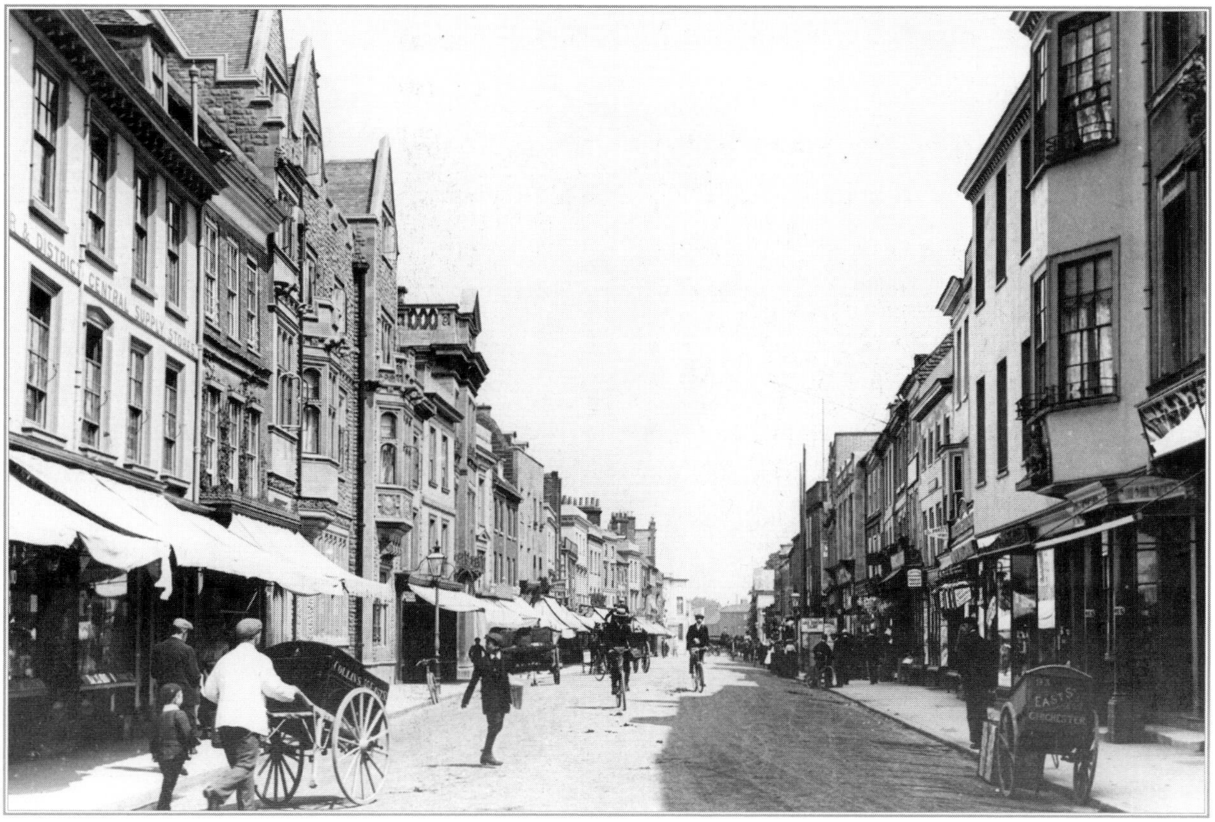

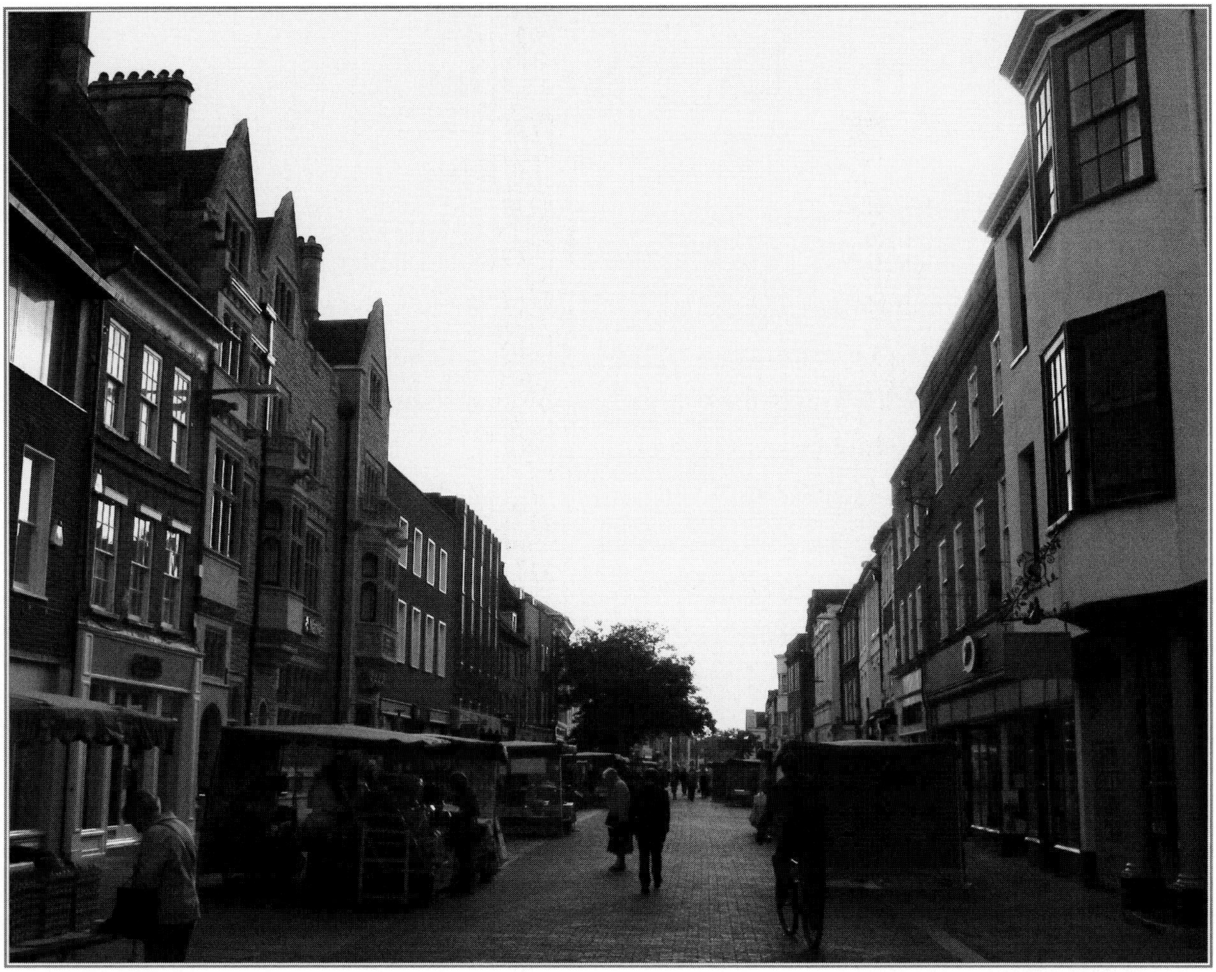

the chances are you would not be too keen on the language the traders used either. Both were said to be pretty ripe.

Not surprisingly, pressure mounted for a proper cattle market which would take the pens away from the city's streets. There were many tales of animals wandering into shops. The market even came to within a few yards of the cathedral. Something had to be done – not least because the cleaning up was often woeful.

So on 7 May 1870 the first sod was turned on the new market just south of Eastgate Square. It opened a year later but even as recently as the late 1940s cattle were still being driven through the city centre.

Above, in this recent early morning image, traders are setting up Chichester's regular farmers market – a market which most definitely does not offer livestock.

Familiar Names from the City's Past

Three well remembered Chichester businesses can be seen in this image (above right), probably dating from the 1960s.

From the 1880s chain stores started to arrive in the city. The International Stores were among the first, initially near the Market Cross in East Street and then moving to where Superdrug is now.

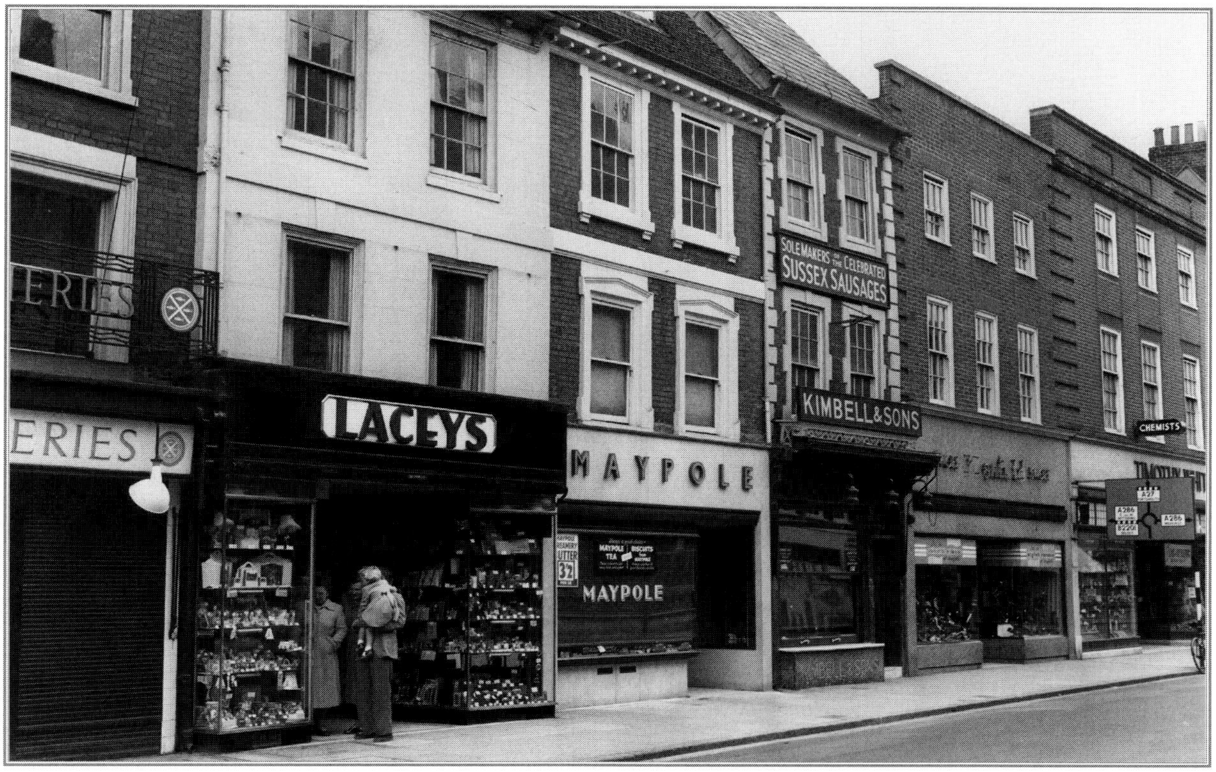
ERIES
ERIES
LACEYS
MAYPOLE
SOLE MAKERS OF THE CELEBRATED
SUSSEX SAUSAGES
KIMBELL & SONS
CHEMISTS
MAYPOLE

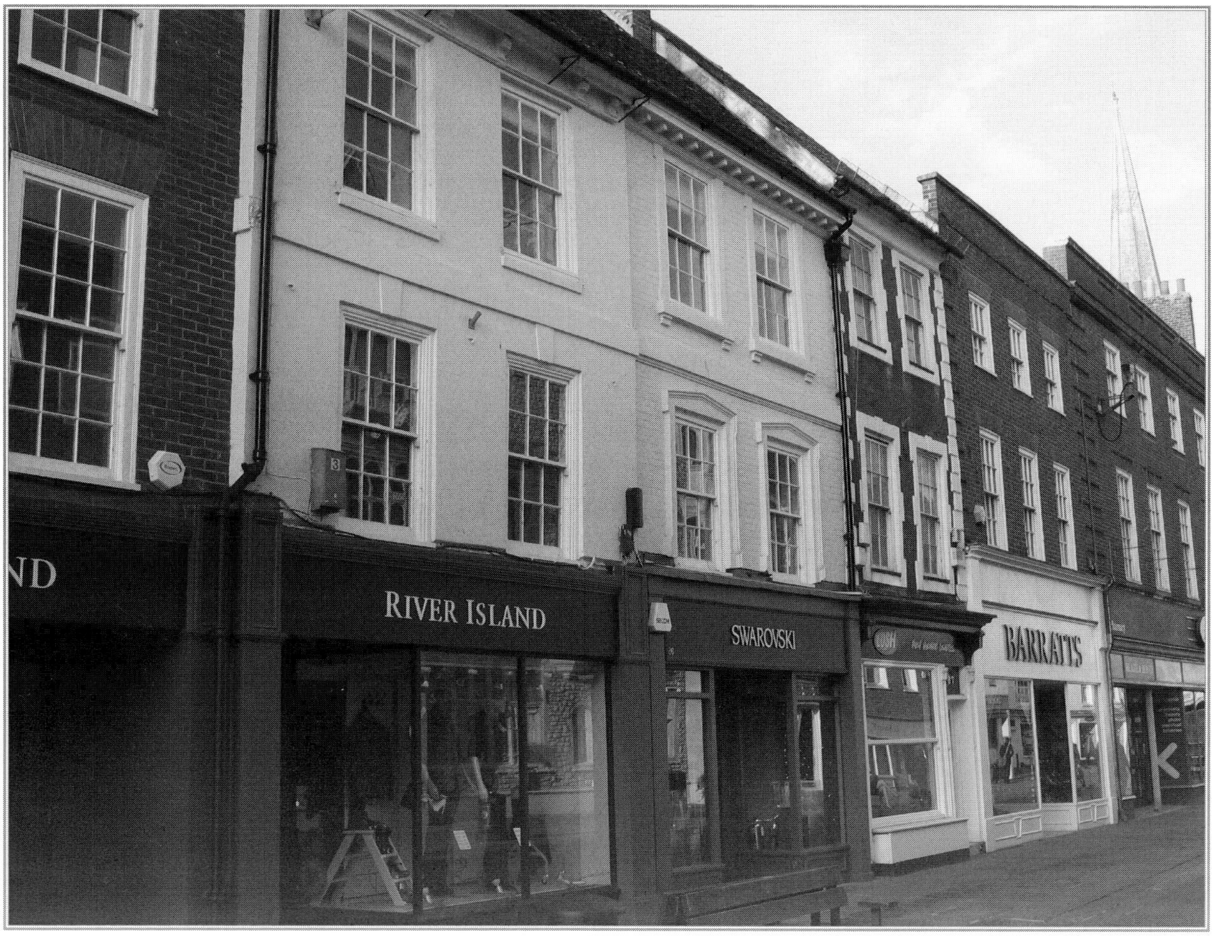
ND
RIVER ISLAND
SWAROVSKI
BARRATTS

Maypole Dairy, seen in the middle of the older photograph, was another early chain in Chichester, dating from much the same era. A store with its roots in the family provision business, Maypole specialised in dairy produce such as butter and lard and, importantly, in the development of the use of margarine.

George Watson set up the business in 1887 and opened the first shop of the Maypole Dairy Company at No. 67 Queen Street, Wolverhampton. Maypole quickly became a household name and there were soon 105 Maypole shops. Large cities such as Manchester, Glasgow and Edinburgh had several.

The number of Maypole branches had reached 985 by 1915, and the 1,000th shop opened in 1926, a success largely due to the growing popularity of margarine.

However, they did sell other goods besides. Chichester District Museum has in its collection a stoneware jar, dating probably from the 1920s to the 1950s, marked 'Orange marmalade' and 'Sold only by Maypole Dairy Co. Ltd'. Unusually, the label survives intact.

Maypole was at No. 86 East Street. Next door at No. 85 was Laceys, a stationer's owned by Sydney Lacey with branches in Bognor Regis and Worthing.

On the other side at No. 87 is Kimbell & Sons' butcher's shop. The Kimbells were an important Chichester business family with a number of grocer's and a butcher's in the city centre at different times.

Today, Nos 85, 86 and 87 East Street are respectively River Island, Swarovski and Lush.

Halsted's Ironmongers

You miss so much if you do not take the time to look up occasionally as you hurry through Chichester's main shopping streets.

The clue to this particular building's past is the key emblem which can still be seen over the middle of the upper storey (right).

Today No. 81–82 East Street comprises the jewellery shop Pia on the left and the clothes store CC on the right, but up until 1936 it was Halsted's ironmongers.

Like so many lost Chichester businesses, this was a business in which all parts of the process were carried out in the city. The shop was served by a large iron foundry on the site of the present Baffins Lane car park, and from its East Street outlet Halsted's sold steam engines, street furniture, kitchen ranges, agricultural implements and a huge range of iron products. All of them really were made in Chichester.

Again, like so many other lost businesses Halsted's was a genuine family affair, started in 1843 by Charles Townsend Halsted (1823–1891) when he and his brothers Henry and John inherited their father's plumbing, glazing and ironmongery business in East Street.

C.T. Halsted was active in the community, being a justice of the peace and twice mayor. He was also the driving force as the business expanded. A key part of its success was the East Street showroom pictured here. Look through the upper-floor windows and you will see an absolute jumble of iron goods.

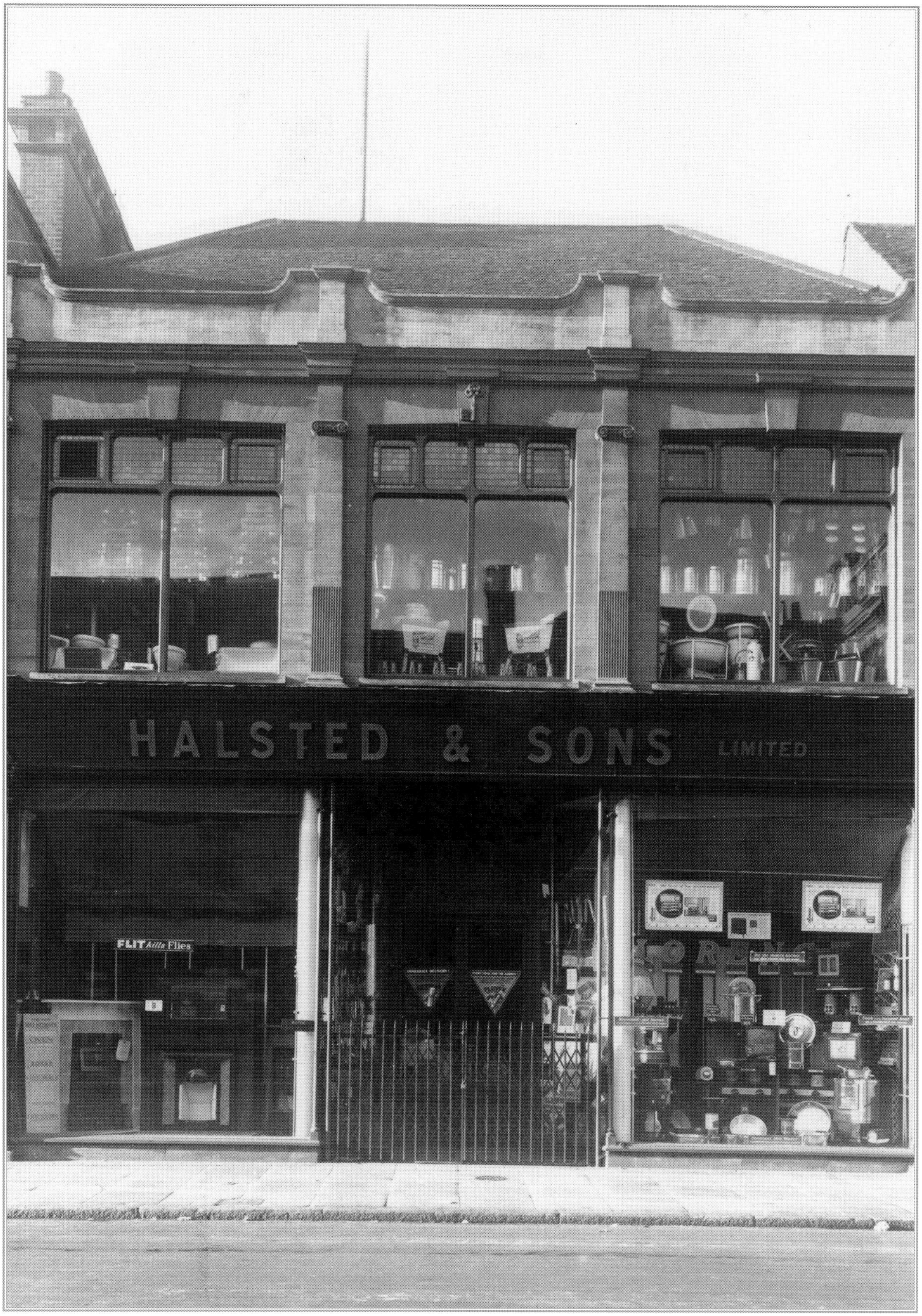
HALSTED & SONS LIMITED
FLIT kills Flies

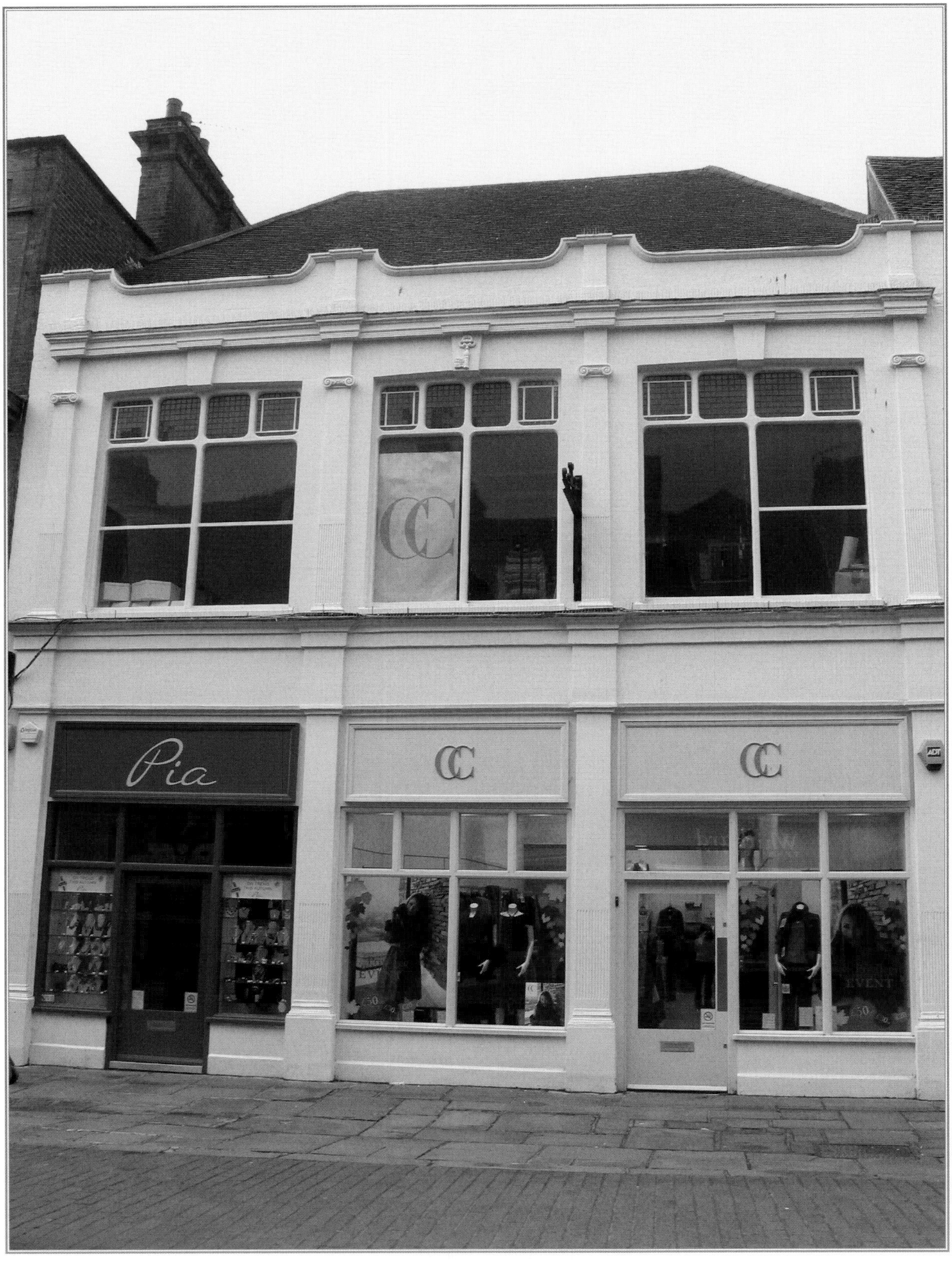

After C.T. Halsted's death, his sons and brother Henry continued the business until the 1930s. The foundry ceased production in 1932 and four years later the East Street shop closed down.

Cars Come and Go

A horse-drawn carriage pulls away from the cross; a lady pushes her bike; dogs play in the street and a boy slouches against the lamppost.

However, look along the left-hand side of this image – probably dated about 1907 – and you will see the forces gathering which will wreck the tranquillity.

It is fascinating to see that the city's first garages were in the city centre and that there is a whole row of them waiting to pounce. The West Sussex Motor Company, Motor Spirit and Motor Works all hint at things to come, though it is a fair bet no one would have predicted just how dramatically this street scene would change.

Seventy years later, Chichester reclaimed some, at least, of its lost peace when East Street and North Street were transformed into today's pedestrian precincts.

The pros and cons were thrashed out in the 1970s when a pedestrianization scheme was introduced by West Sussex County Council as the highway authority.

Businesses and residents alike had their reservations. Many traders feared people would be discouraged from coming into the city. There were also strong concerns among people living in

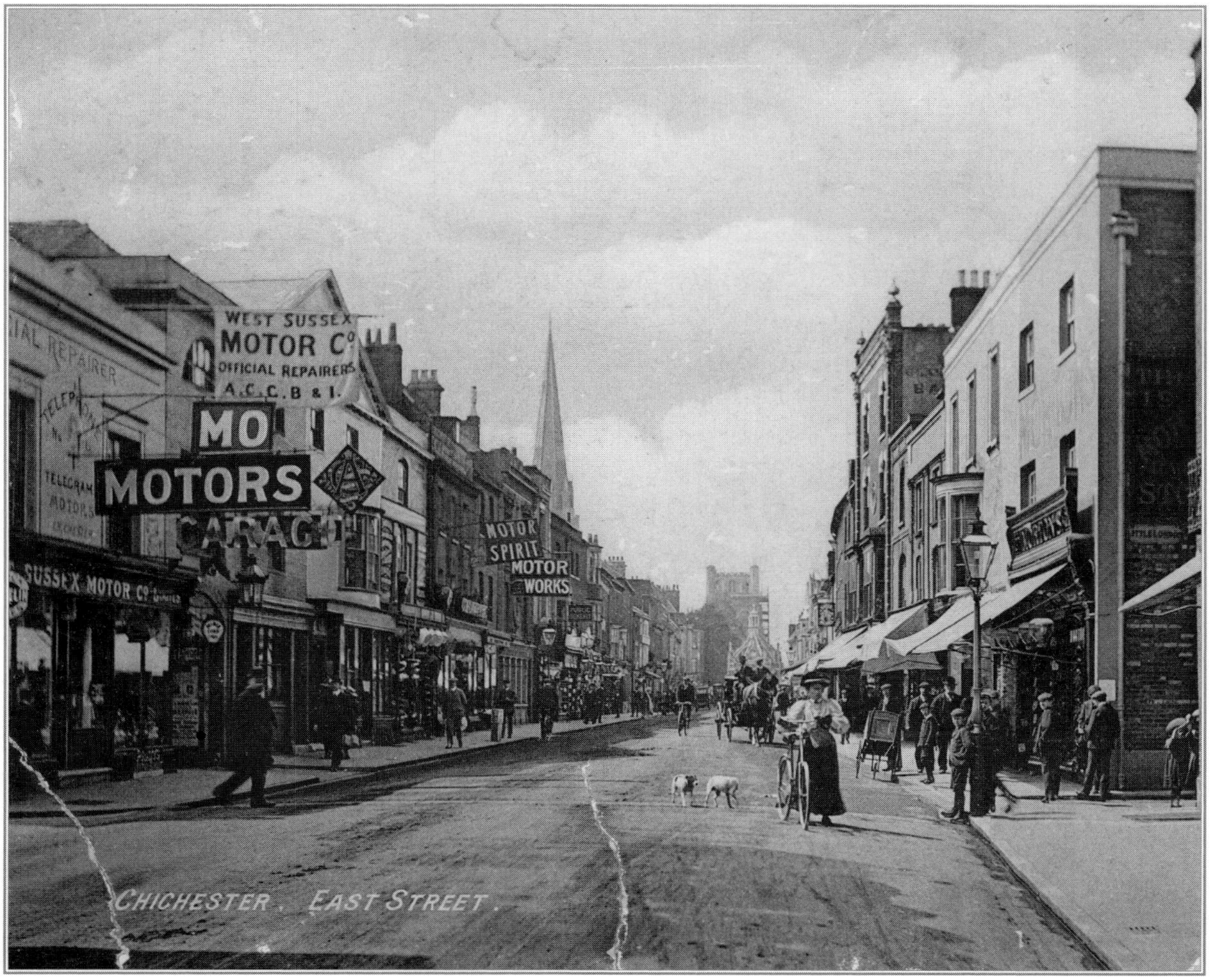

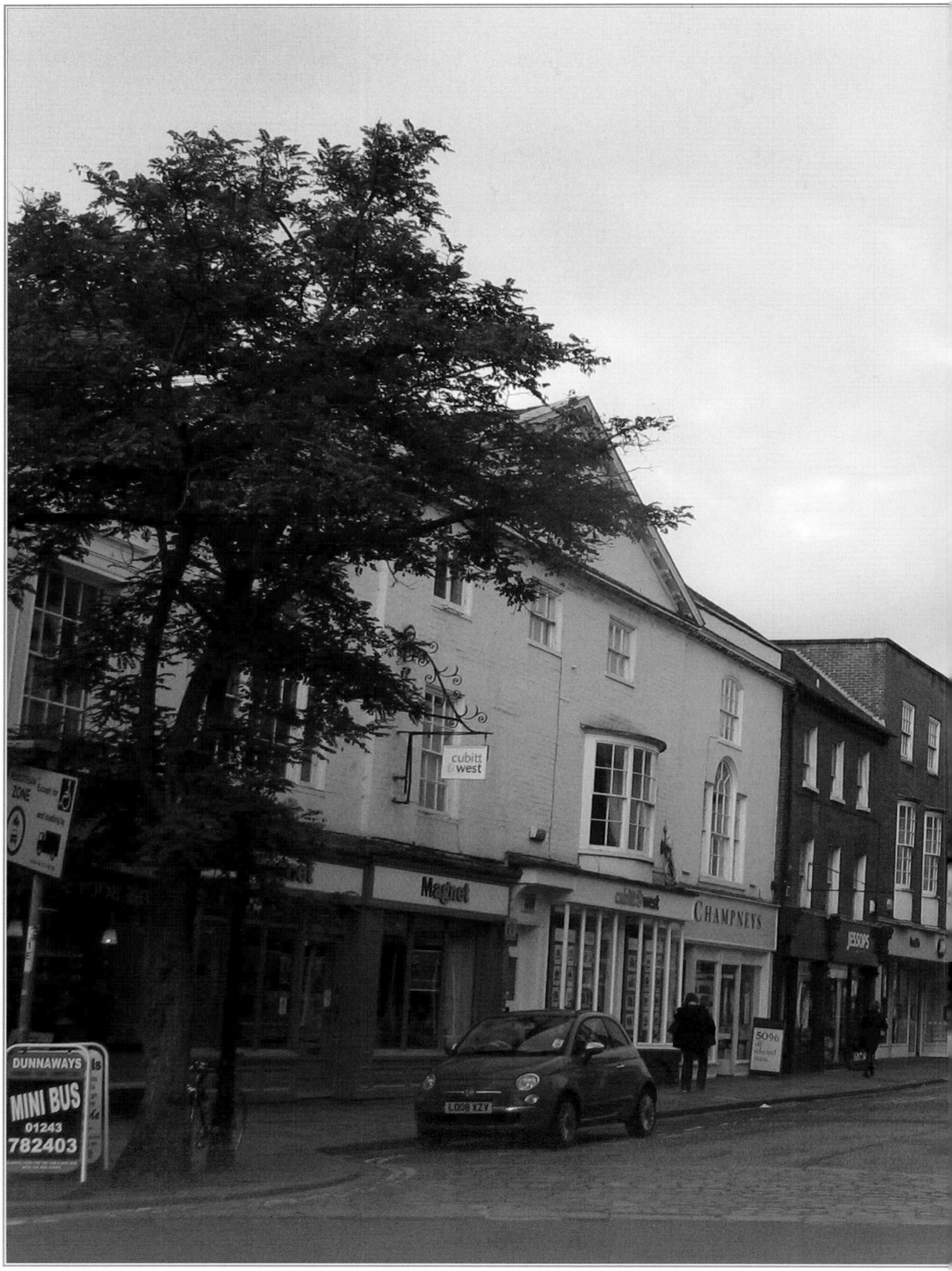
cubitt & west
Magnet
CHAMPNEYS
JESSOPS
DUNNAWAYS
MINI BUS
01243
782403
LO08 XZV

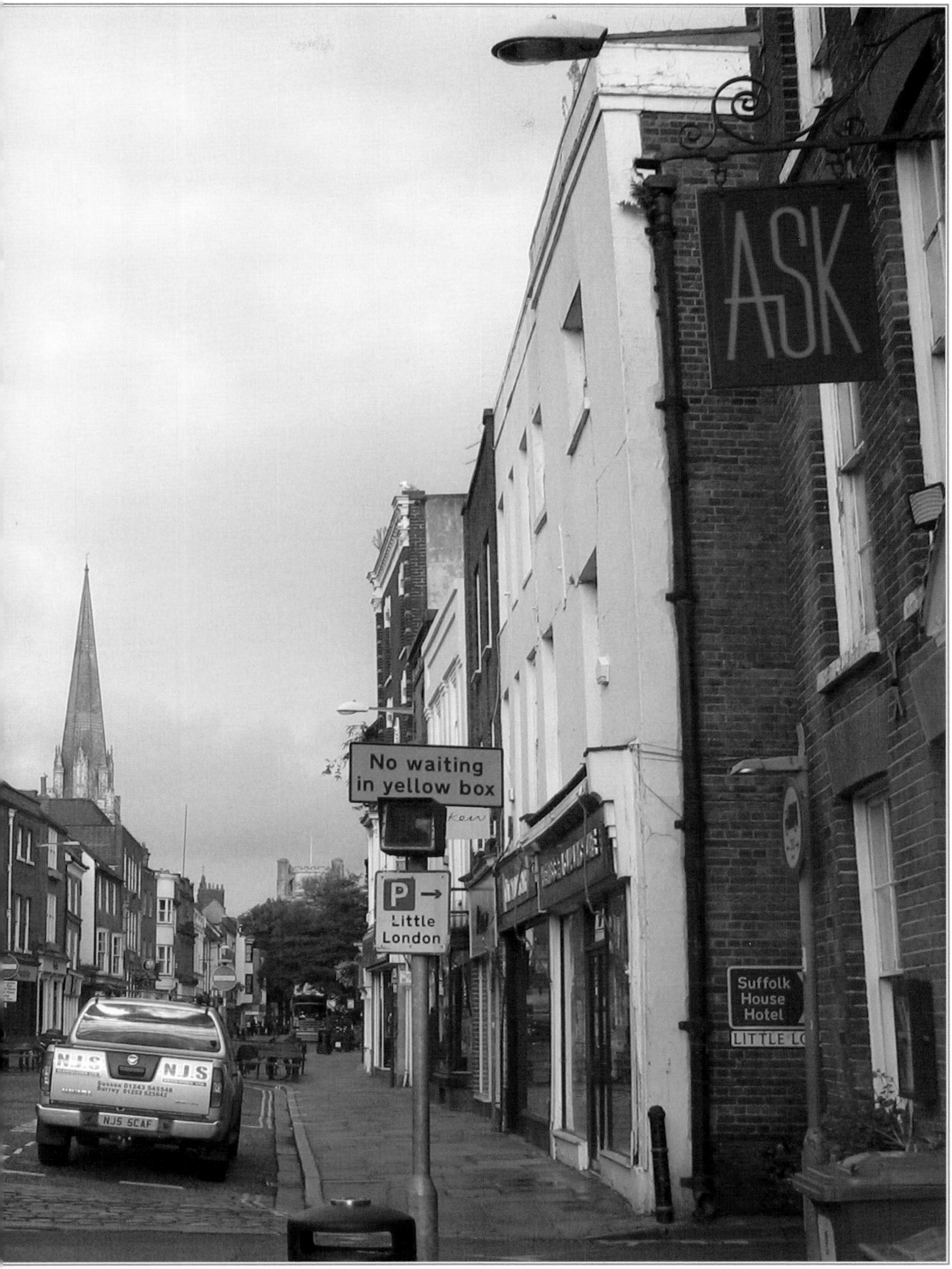
ASK
No waiting
in yellow box
P
Little
London
Suffolk
House
Hotel
LITTLE LO
NJS
NJ5 5CAF

the small streets just outside the main centre, such as the Pallants, Little London and St Martin's Square. Their worries centred on the impact of large delivery vehicles servicing shops from the rear.

However, the arguments focusing on the growing impact of traffic on the city centre won the day. Think of all the weekend traffic which pours down to the Witterings. Imagine it heading for the Market Cross – a building increasingly suffering from vibration and occasional collisions.

Most people would agree: pedestrianization was inevitable.

Sunday Best

There is so much to study in this glorious image of Chichester celebrating Queen Victoria's jubilee in 1897. The more you look, the more you see.

Chichester had put on its Sunday best in honour of the queen. There is scarcely a bare head on view if you look closely. Indeed, if you look even more closely, you start to wonder whether that is not Her Majesty in person, standing just to the left of the three girls in white blouses on the right of the picture. It is a nice thought, at the very least.

To the left of the picture is the superb Corn Exchange, a building so easy to overlook, not least during the grim years when it was a fast-food restaurant – an indignity for a building so grand and temple-like, with its six giant fluted Doric columns and its towering pediment.

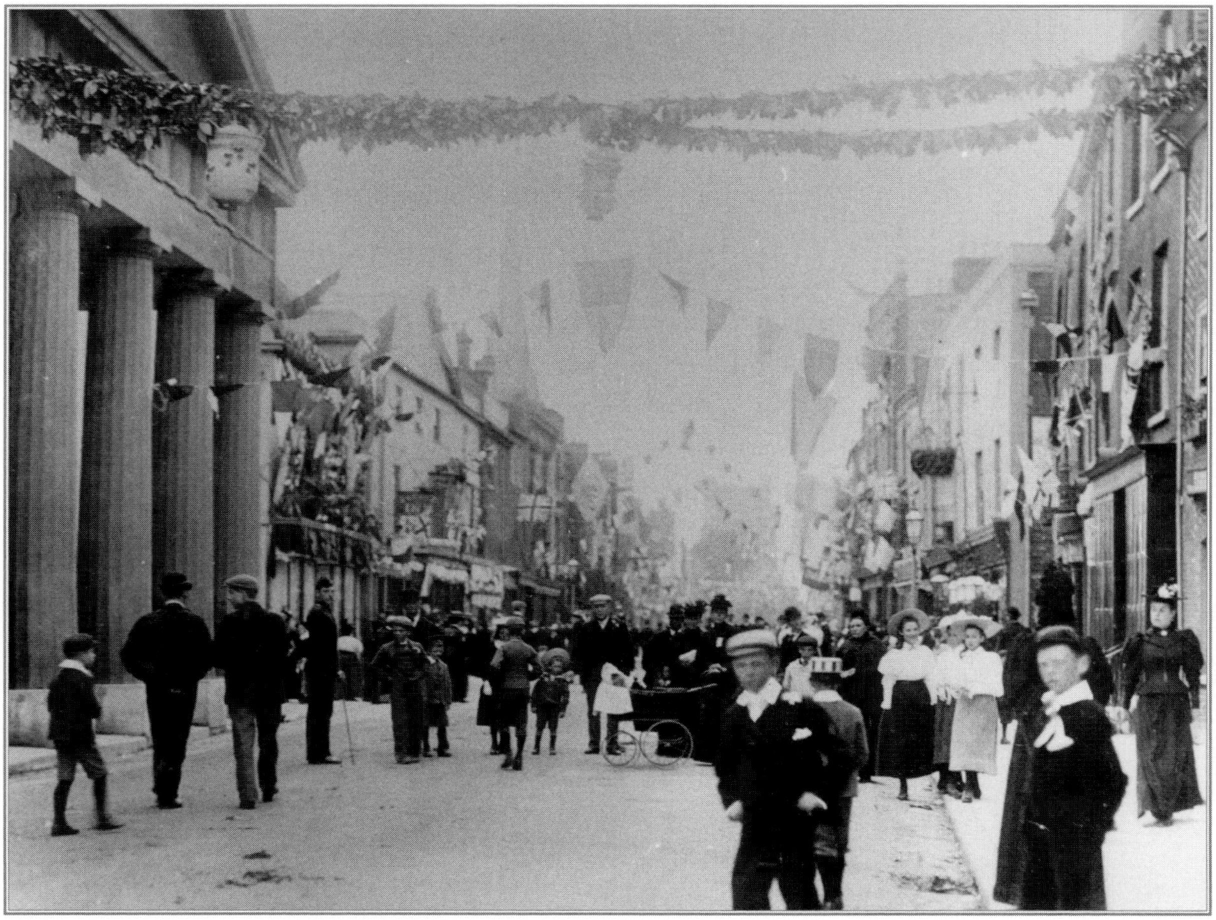

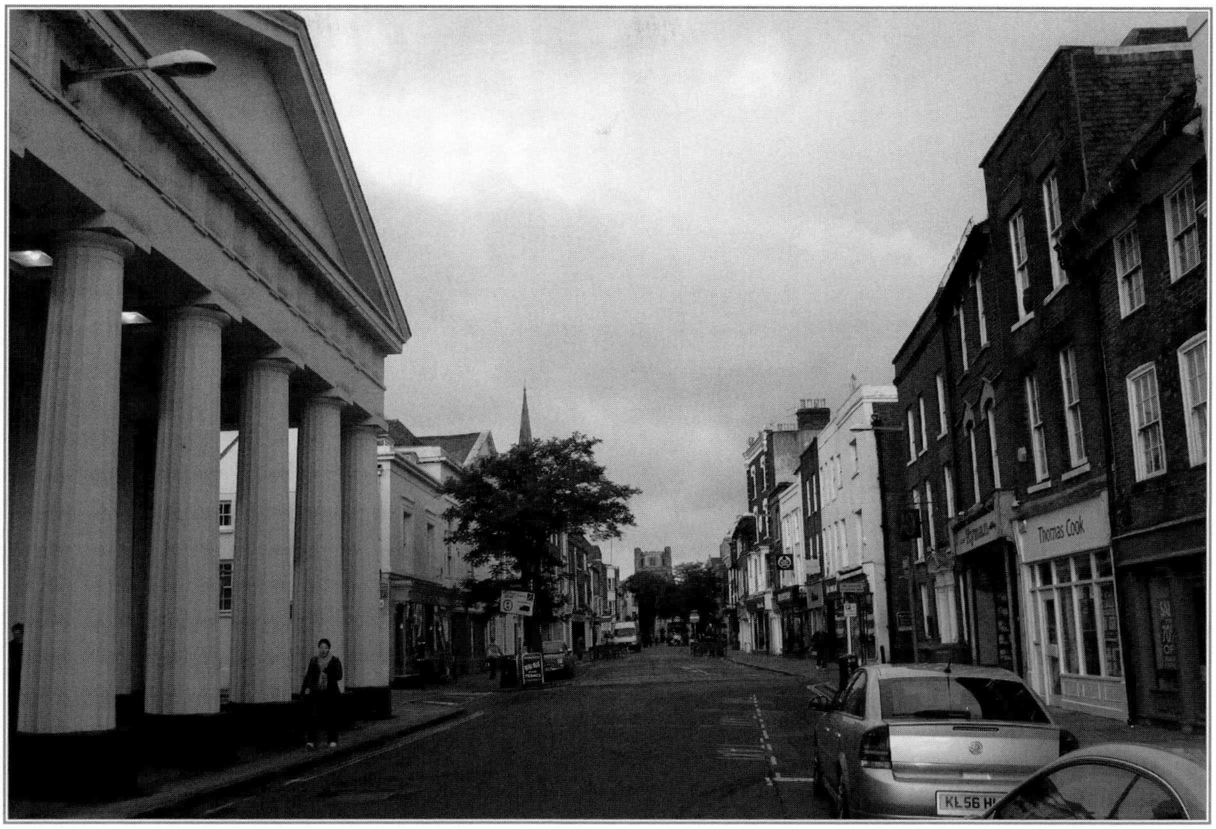

For a long time it was the city's Granada cinema, a fate rather more fitting. At least it allowed it to mingle with the gods. The screen gods, that is.

A grand example of the Greek revivalist school, the Corn Exchange was built in order to deal with the growing trade in wheat and barley for which the city had become noted. Its columns span the pavement to form a narthex. How sad it was to see it littered with McDonald's detritus.

The Corn Exchange was built in the early 1830s and its whole point was its ostentatiousness. It was a 'Look at me! I'm important!' type of building, a creation of a thriving city. Whether the clothes store Next is an appropriate occupant now is, at the very least, open to debate.

Mind your Head!

A disappointingly prosaic reason lies behind the delightful photograph on the following page, which probably dates from around 1950.

Sadly, it was not taken to record Chichester as a busy, bustling place full of life, youth and a little bit of glamour.

Instead, the image comes from the local authority's Building Services Collection, now in the possession of Chichester District Museum. The most likely explanation for the photograph is that it was posed to show the problems caused by overhanging shop blinds at a time when East Street was the main traffic route.

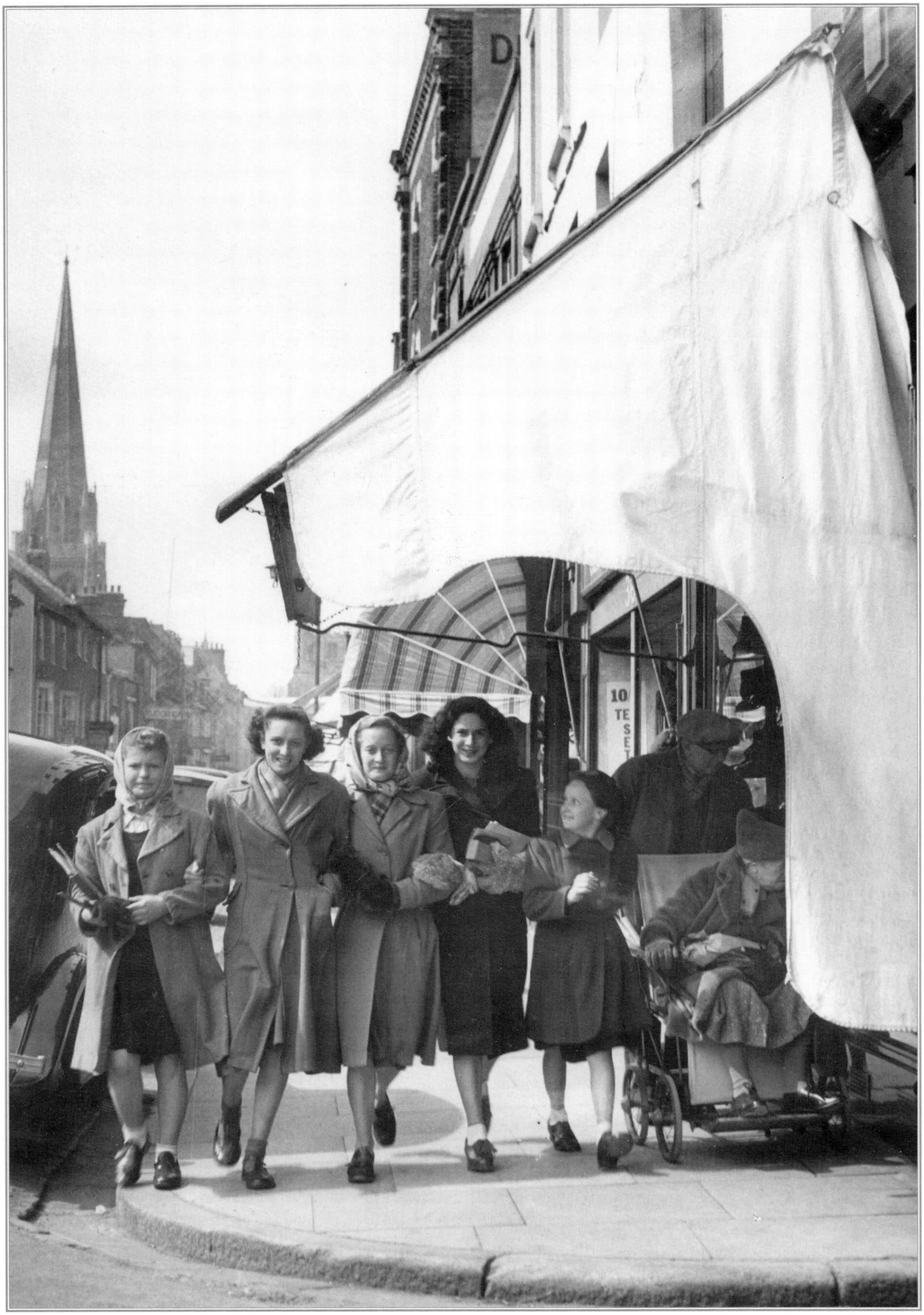

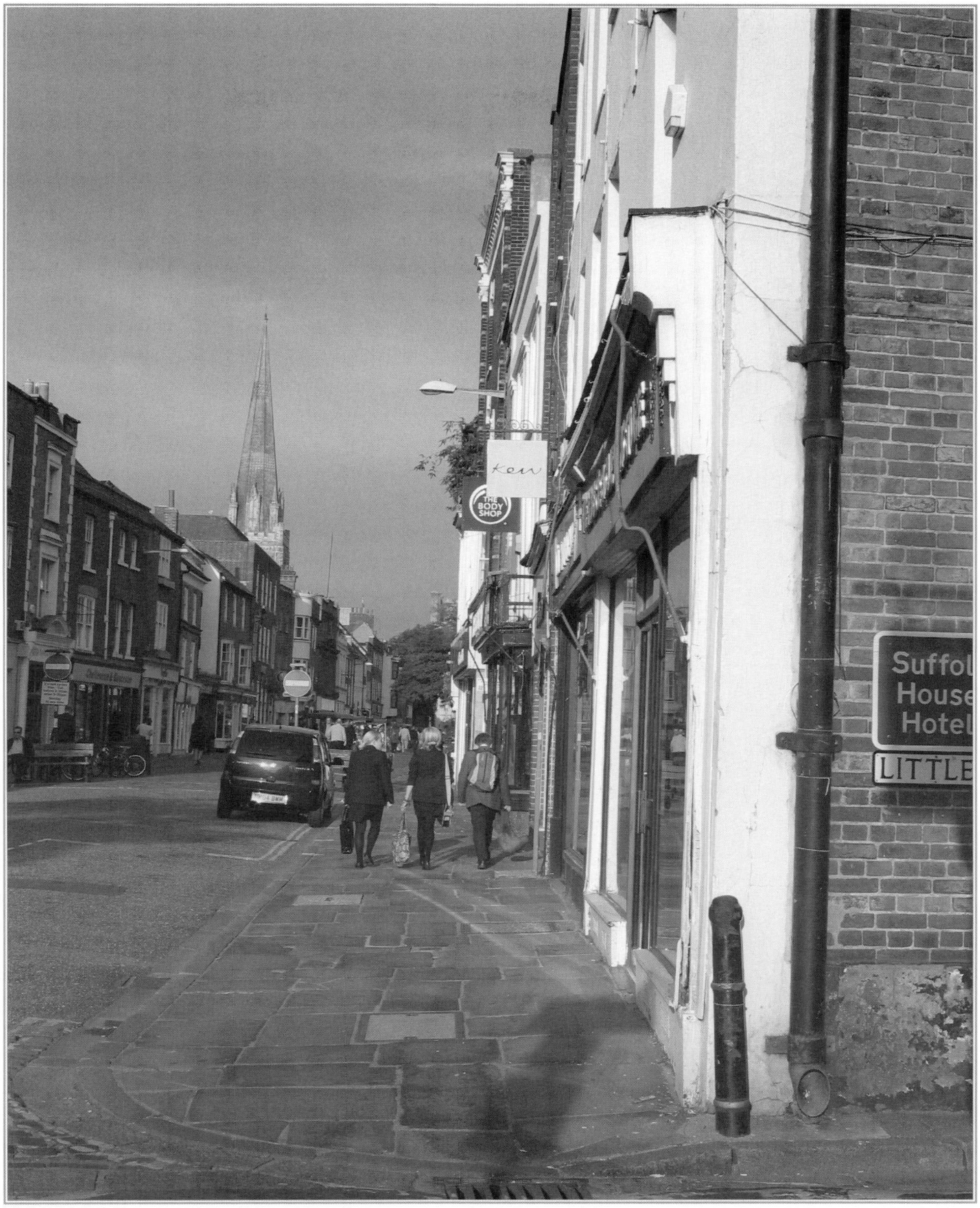

Best now simply to look at it as a glimpse back to smarter, perhaps more smiling, times. Interesting too is the rather substantial wheelchair and the flat cap of the gentleman pushing it. Between them, they were certainly making full use of the pavement space available.

The picture was taken – or, more likely, posed – on the corner of East Street and Little London.

Little London

To the north of East Street runs Little London, another area of Chichester rich in history, though sadly some of it rather dodgy in origin.

The story goes that Little London, now largely residential, got its name when the visiting Queen Elizabeth I said 'Verily, 'tis a little London'. Given that the name probably goes back three centuries before Elizabeth's reign, the story is on shaky ground – unless you argue that she was simply confirming that this was indeed Little London. Rather more interesting would be to know the tone of voice in which she said it...

Historians tell us that Little London was at one time known as Savary Lane. It leads to Priory Park which occupies the north-east quarter of the city's north-east quadrant.

Little London itself offers a succession of pleasant 18th-century houses. Currently home to Chichester District Museum, Little London has also housed a succession of inns including The Curriers Arms, The Prince Arthur and The King of Prussia.

Also in Little London is the Chichester Boys' Club which was originally the Lancastrian School for Girls, named after the Quaker educationalist Joseph Lancaster.

Today Little London is an attractive side street. But it was not always so.

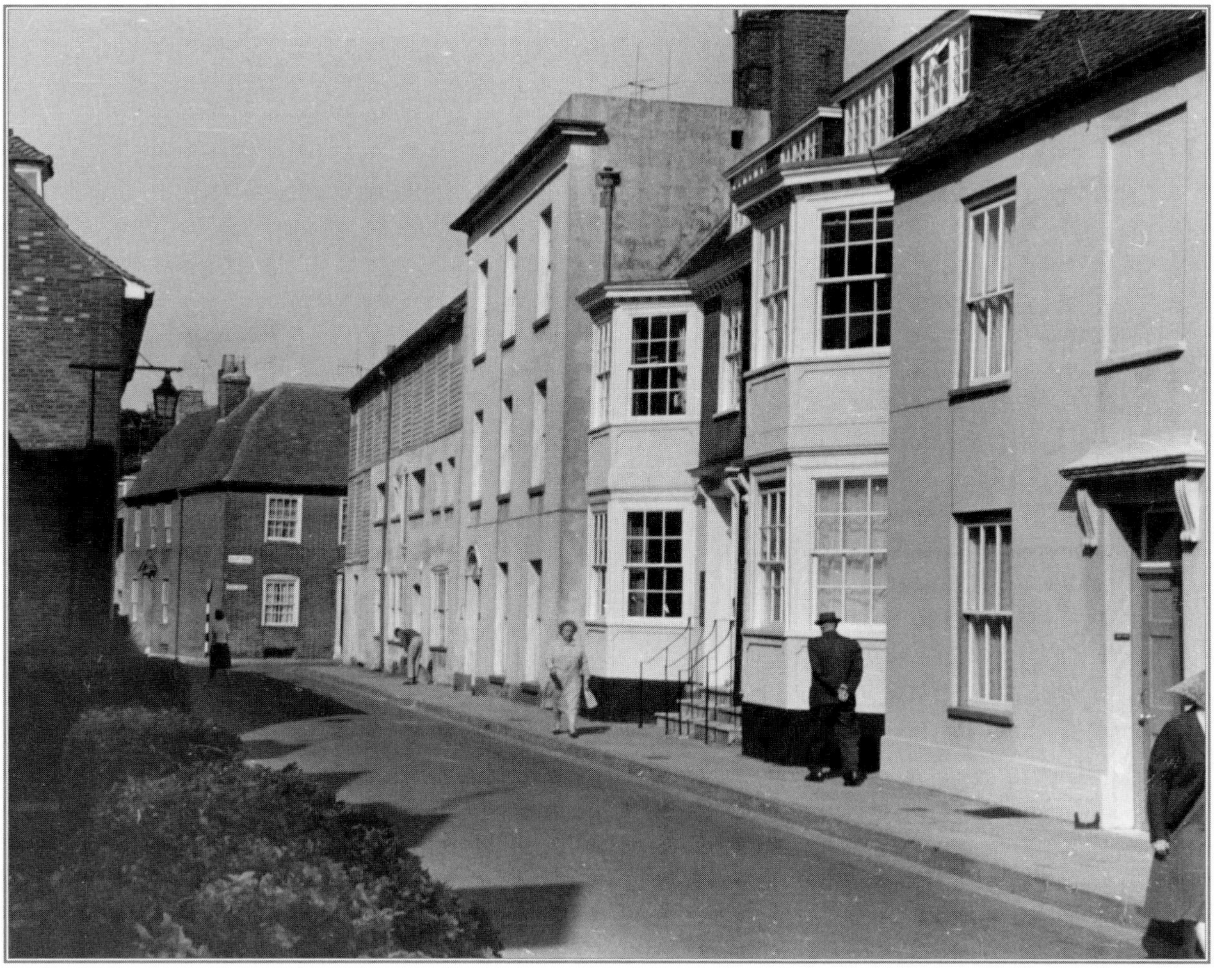

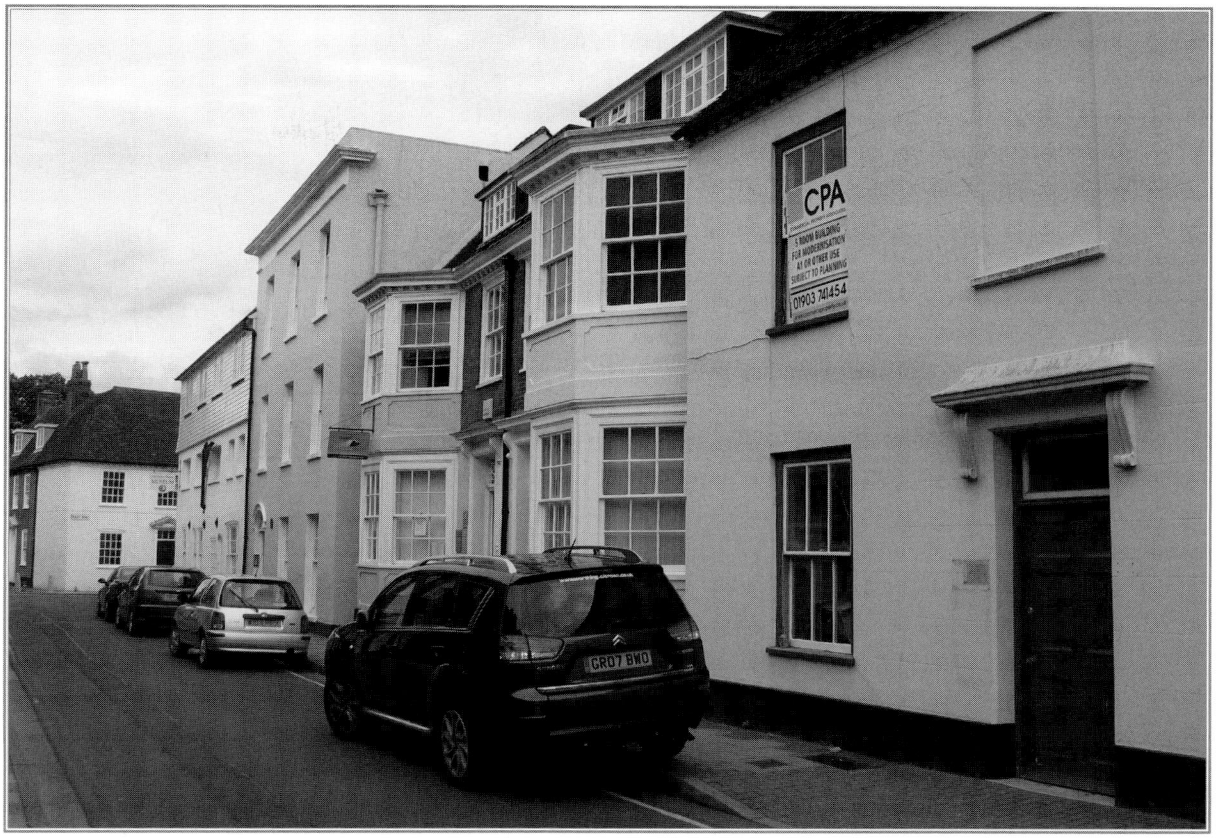

Chichester diarist James Spershott (1710–1789) recalled less pleasant days in his youth: 'The back lanes had a very mean appearance, but few houses and bad ones. The Little London in particular, which now appear(s) so gay, had only a few old houses as it were underground, the street not pitch'd but very dirty with deep cart ruts.'

CHAPTER 6

EASTGATE SQUARE

An Impressive View

East Street has probably suffered more from commercial development than any of the other main Chichester streets, but it still retains plenty of interest – and plenty of charm if you raise your eyes above first-floor level.

The view from Eastgate is still impressive, looking towards the Market Cross with the cathedral spire rising up just to the left. On the north side East Street still boasts a long run of Georgian fronts.

The older of the two images shows Chichester living up to its proud tradition of celebrating royal events, in this instance the coronation of George VI in 1937. Chichester clearly went to town that day. The entire street was decorated, and once again the mediaeval gate was fleetingly reinstated.

To the right is the entrance to the factory of the celebrated Chichester paste manufacturer Shippam's. A crown, flags and the words 'God Save The King' are part of the company's loyal salute.

A lot of people fought hard to retain the Shippam's doorway when the factory was knocked down and rebuilt as a shopping complex – a battle worth fighting. It remains a reminder of the days when factories were to be found within the city walls.

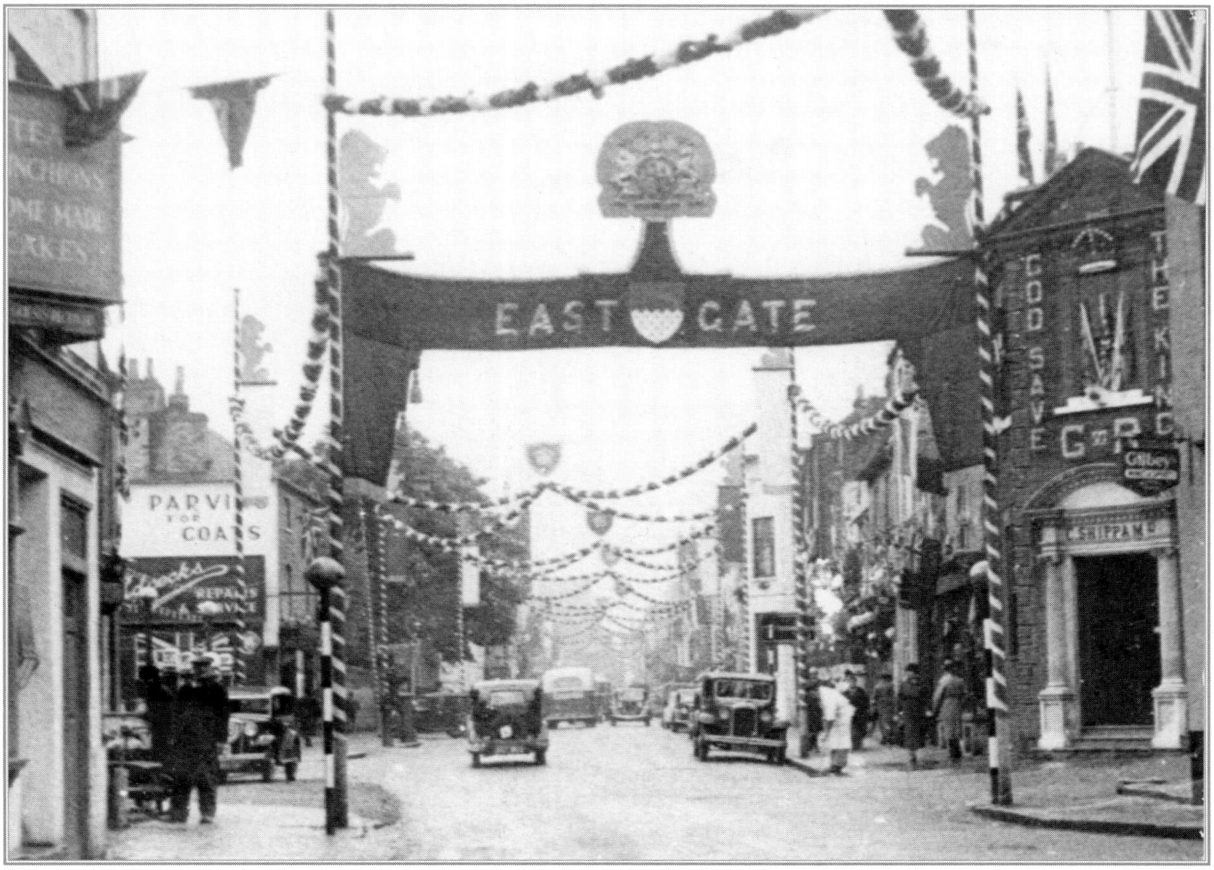

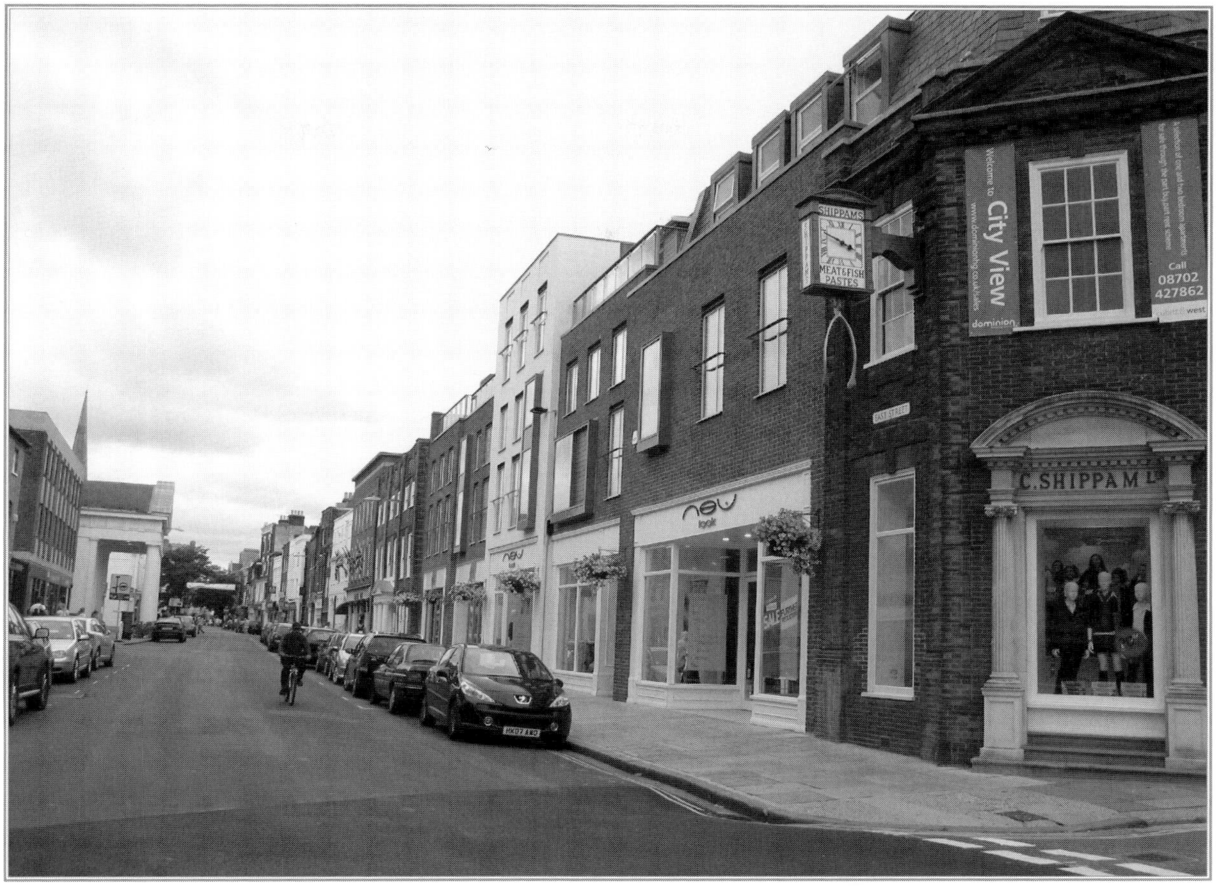

Shippam's – a Family Business

Crowds gathered to cheer Queen Mary when she graced Chichester's most famous food factory with a visit in 1924.

The splendid factory entrance had been completed earlier that year; and the city was rightly proud of a home-grown business which had shown the world the way.

Eighty years later and the entrance is still there, as indeed are the walls of Shippam's East Walls factory, but they now house clothes stores – and the Men At Work sign overleaf hints at the huge transformation this area has undergone in recent times.

When, in August 2002, the East Walls factory closed and production moved to Terminus Road, it was a landmark date in the rich history of a Chichester dynasty.

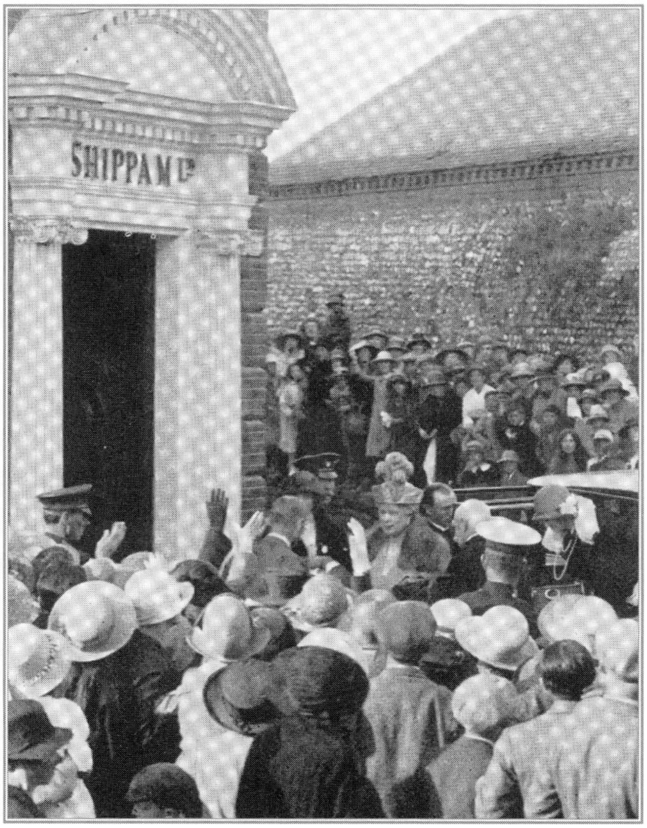

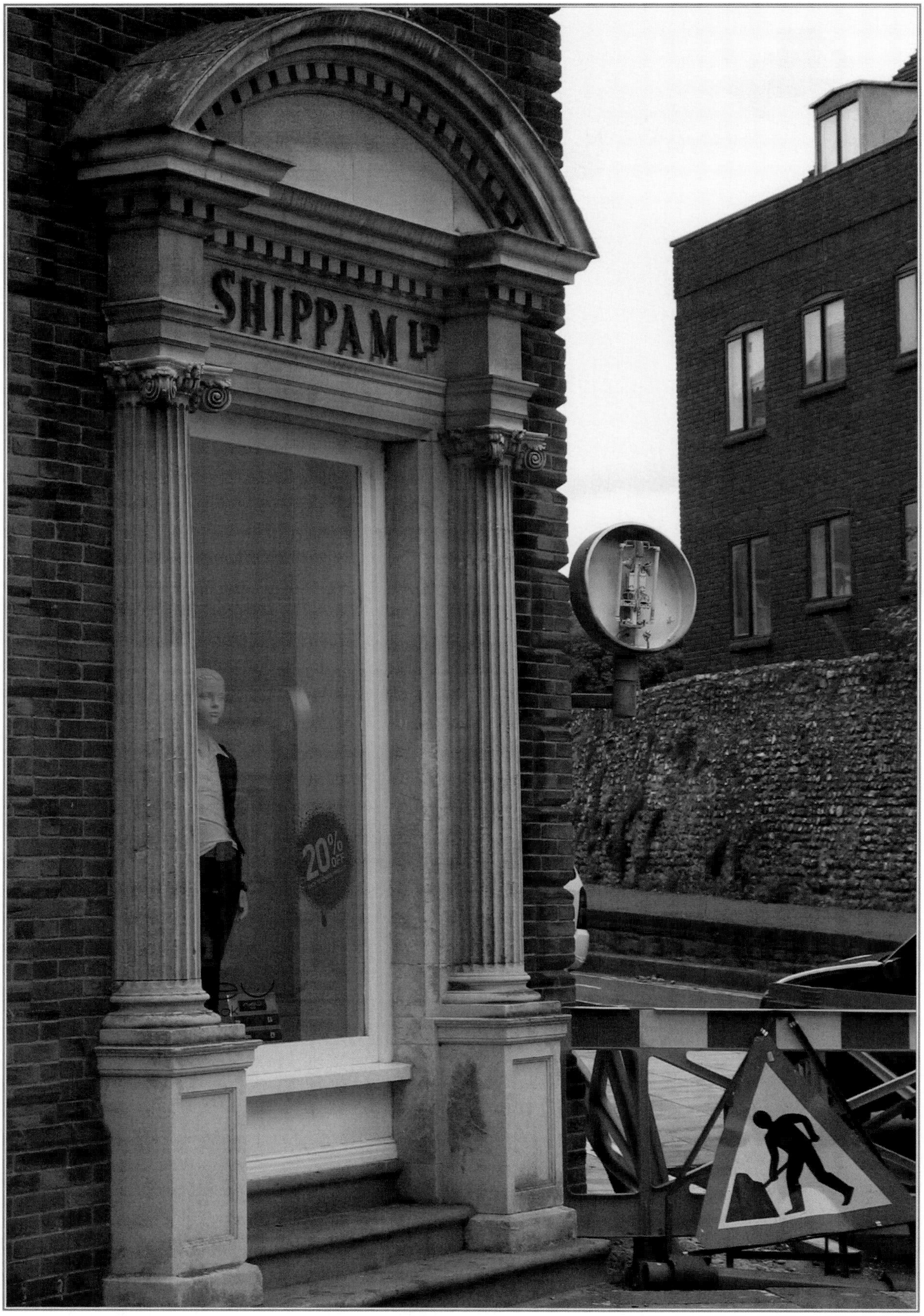
SHIPPAM LTD
20% OFF

The Shippam family was at the heart of the Chichester business community for more than two centuries. Their first venture was a grocery store which Charles Shippam I established at Westgate in 1786.

His son Charles Shippam II continued the family business; and in 1851 Charles Shippam III followed suit, opening a butchers' shop at No. 48 East Street. In 1892 a factory was built behind the shop, producing the canned goods and potted meats now synonymous with the Shippam's name.

Key to Shippam's success was a willingness to innovate and move with the times. In 1905 Shippam's first used a glass jar with a sealed metal lid and started sterilising their products for a longer shelf life. In 1955 Shippam's was among the first companies to advertise on commercial television.

Shippam's was absorbed into the Grand Metropolitan group in 1995. The last member of the Shippam family retired three years later.

Getting Away from It All

The following are another pair of images in which the present does not fare quite so well. Perhaps it is best to say that this particular part of Chichester is a work in progress just at the moment.

The older image, overleaf, tells a different story, of thriving, bustling, busy times at Shippam's East Walls factory, a building now converted to shopping. In the 1920s it was a city centre business well known for looking after its staff – a reflection of the family ethos with which it was run.

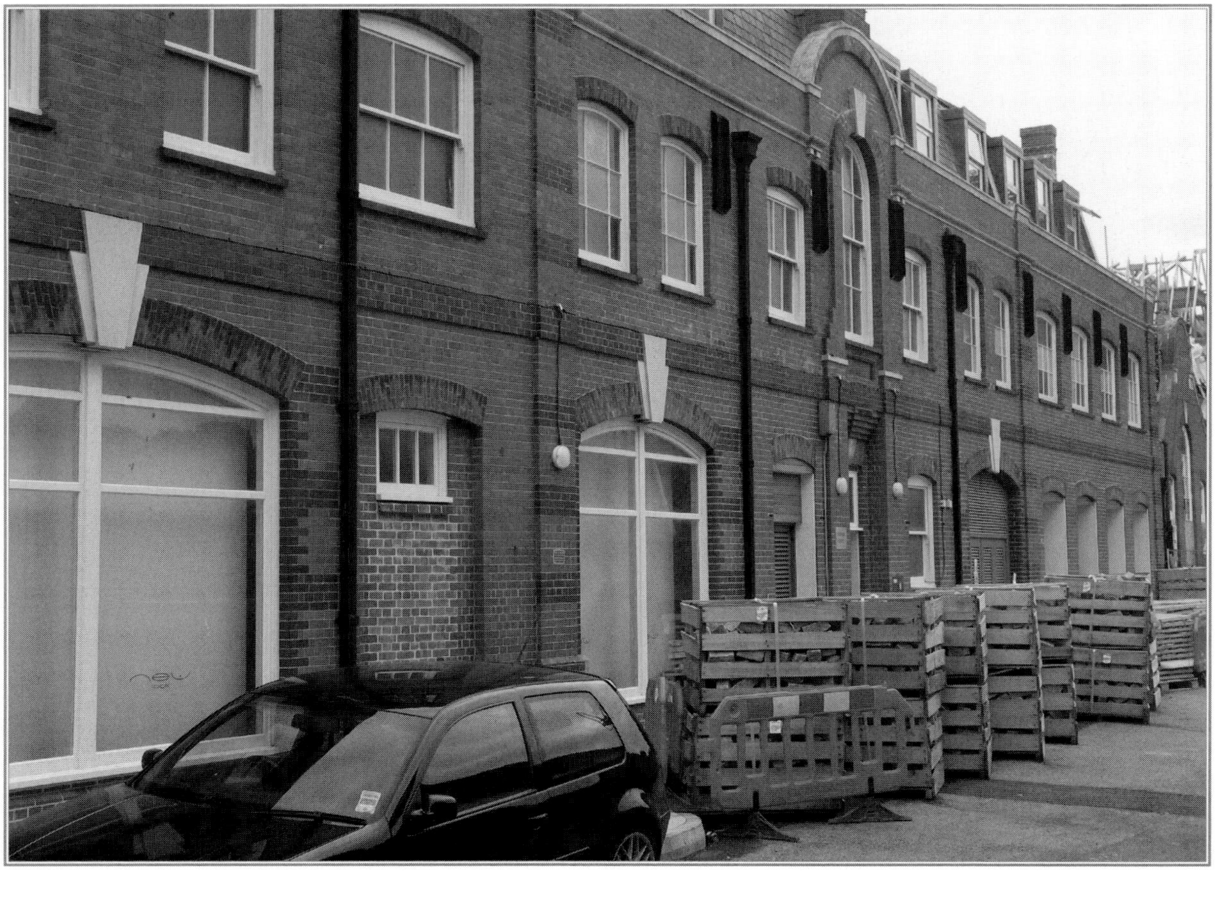

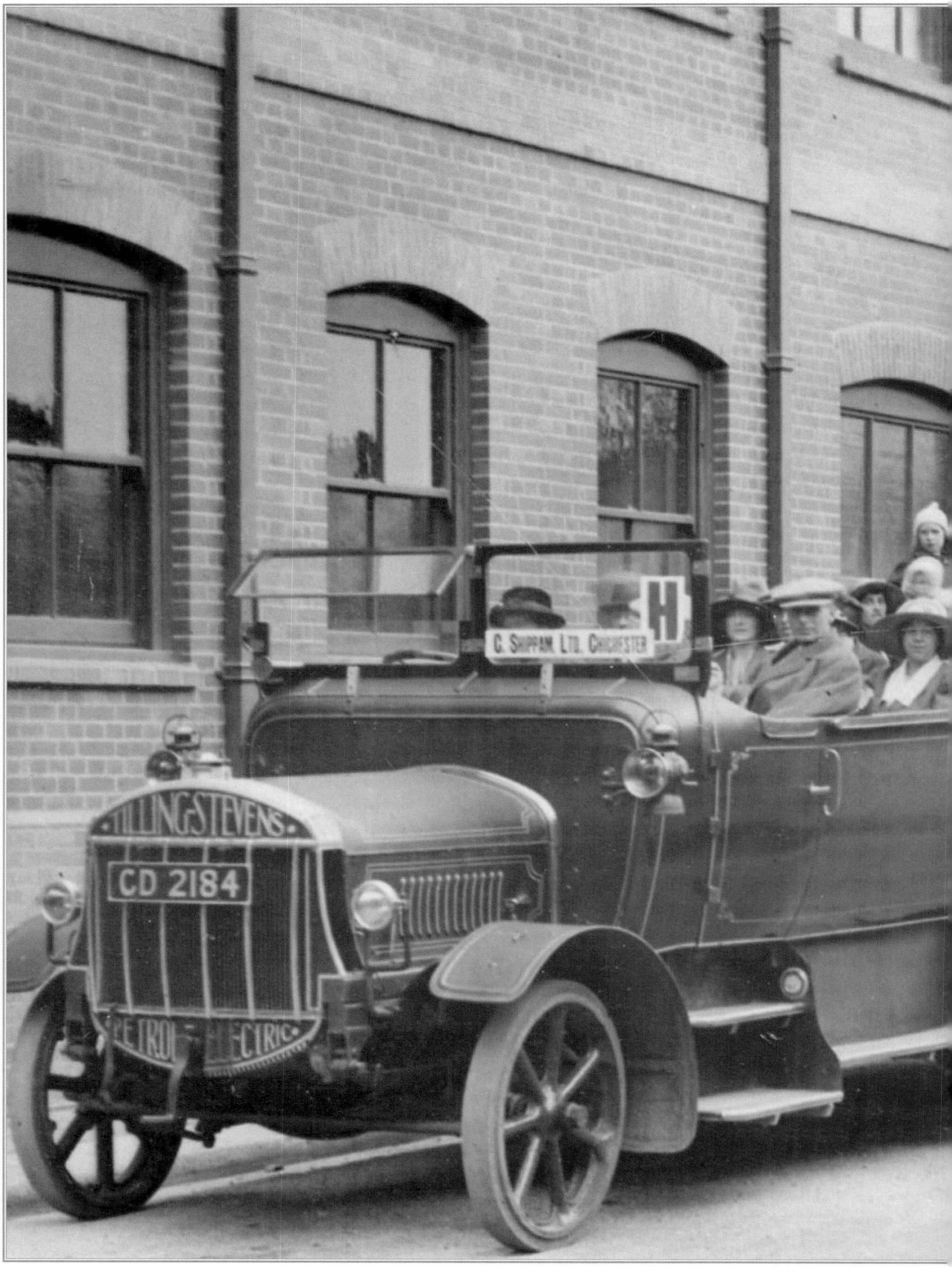
TILLING-STEVENS
CD 2184
PETROL ELECTRIC
C. SHIPPAM LTD. CHICHESTER
H

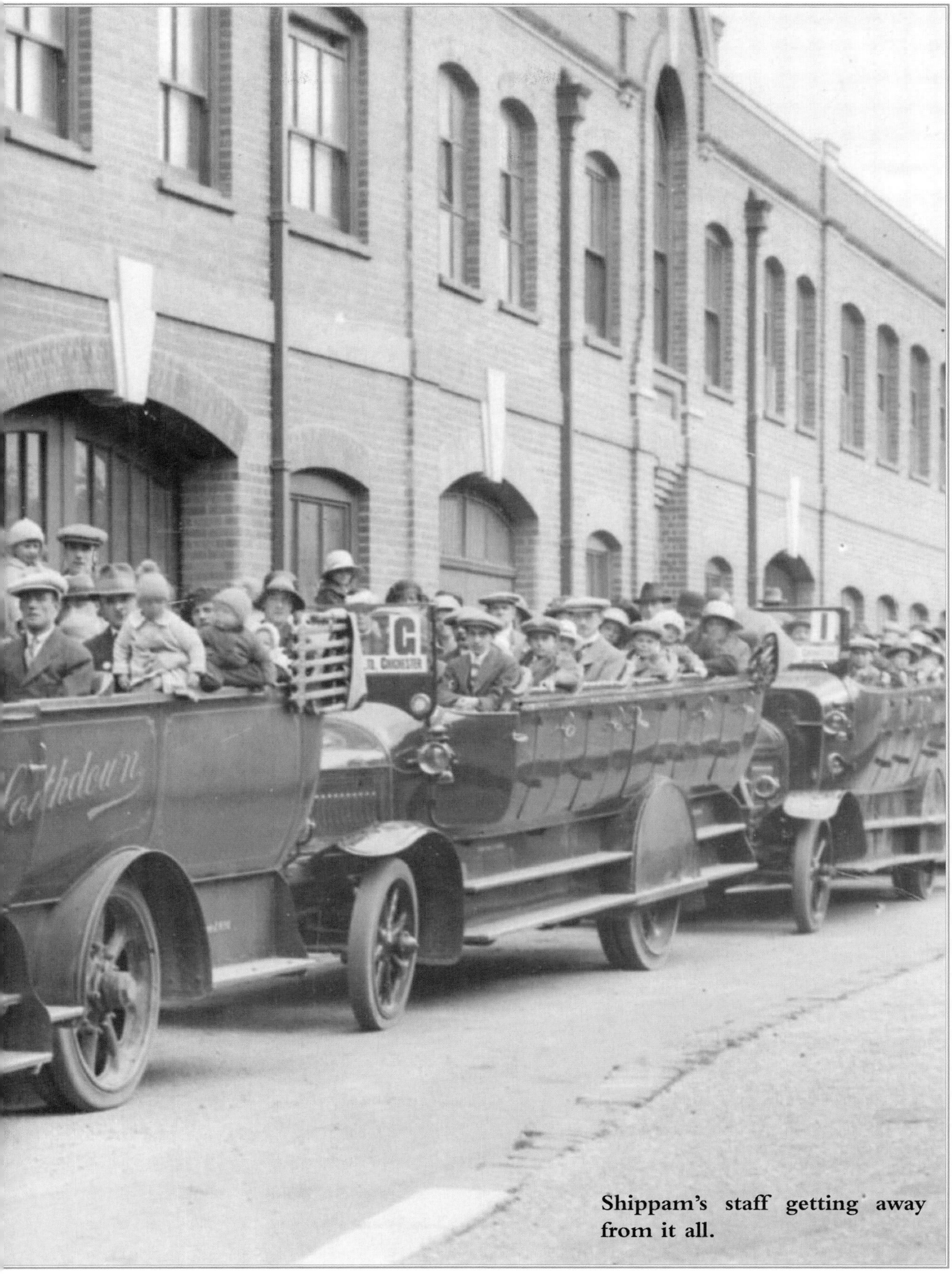

Shippam's staff getting away from it all.

A staff social club was built in 1927, and on pages 84–85 we see the business at play as the staff, behatted to a man and woman, set out on an excursion. It is typical of a number of images which still exist suggesting the paternalistic side to life at Shippam's.

The photograph on page 83 is taken just next to the city's east walls, part of those which enclose the city centre and lead from here towards Priory Park. The mediaeval walls are built on Roman foundations and offer an attractive circuit.

Sharp Garland

The smell of roast coffee still takes many Cicestrians straight back to the days when Sharp Garland's stood in Eastgate Square.

With supplies still in hessian sacks and displays which looked historic before their time, the shop – reputedly the oldest grocer in England – was a treasure trove, a cherished relic of the days before supermarkets spread their bland uniformity.

Sharp Garland's store was rich in character and also rich in history, though sadly history denied it the final year of life which would have seen it reach its 300th anniversary.

Founded in 1665, it was demolished in 1964 after a crack had appeared in its front wall. *The West Sussex Gazette* in March of that year reported that 'traffic was diverted because Sharp Garland's grocery store was in danger of collapsing into the street.' The site remained derelict for years.

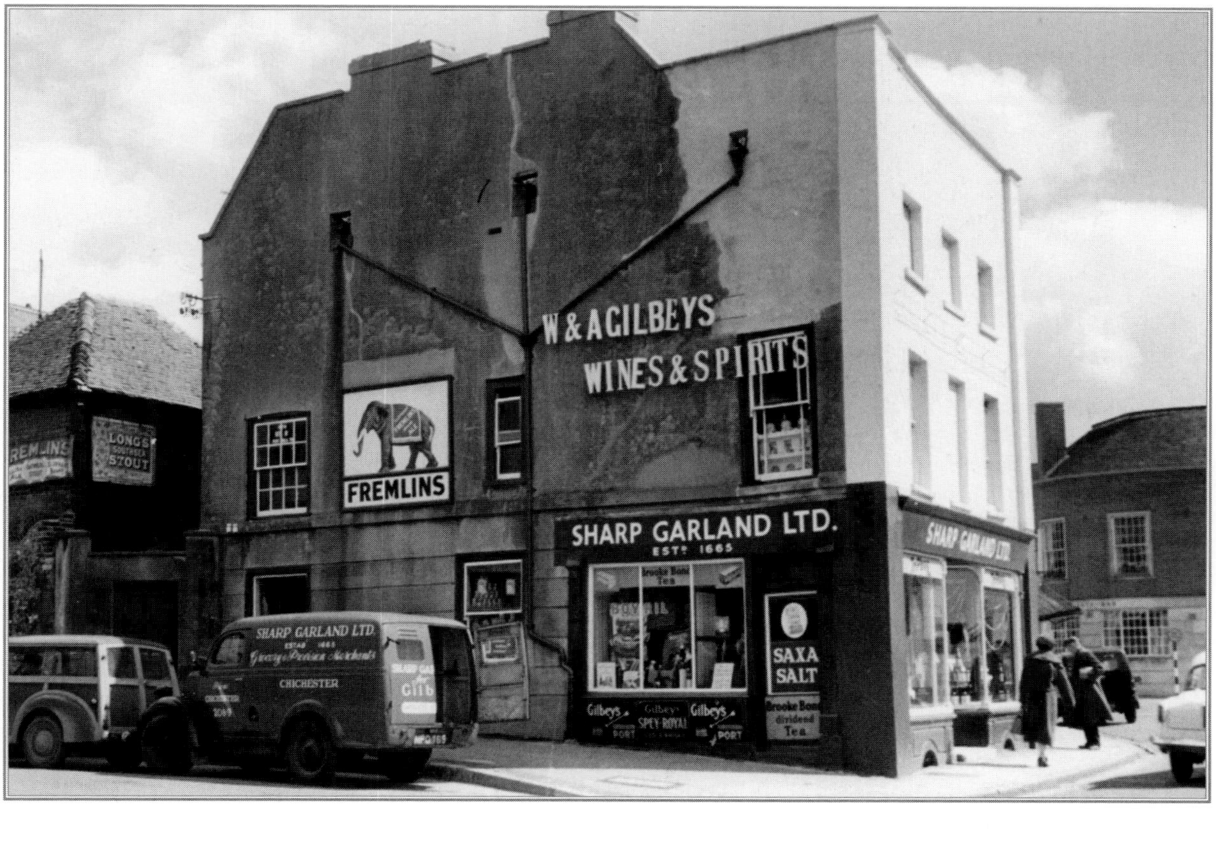

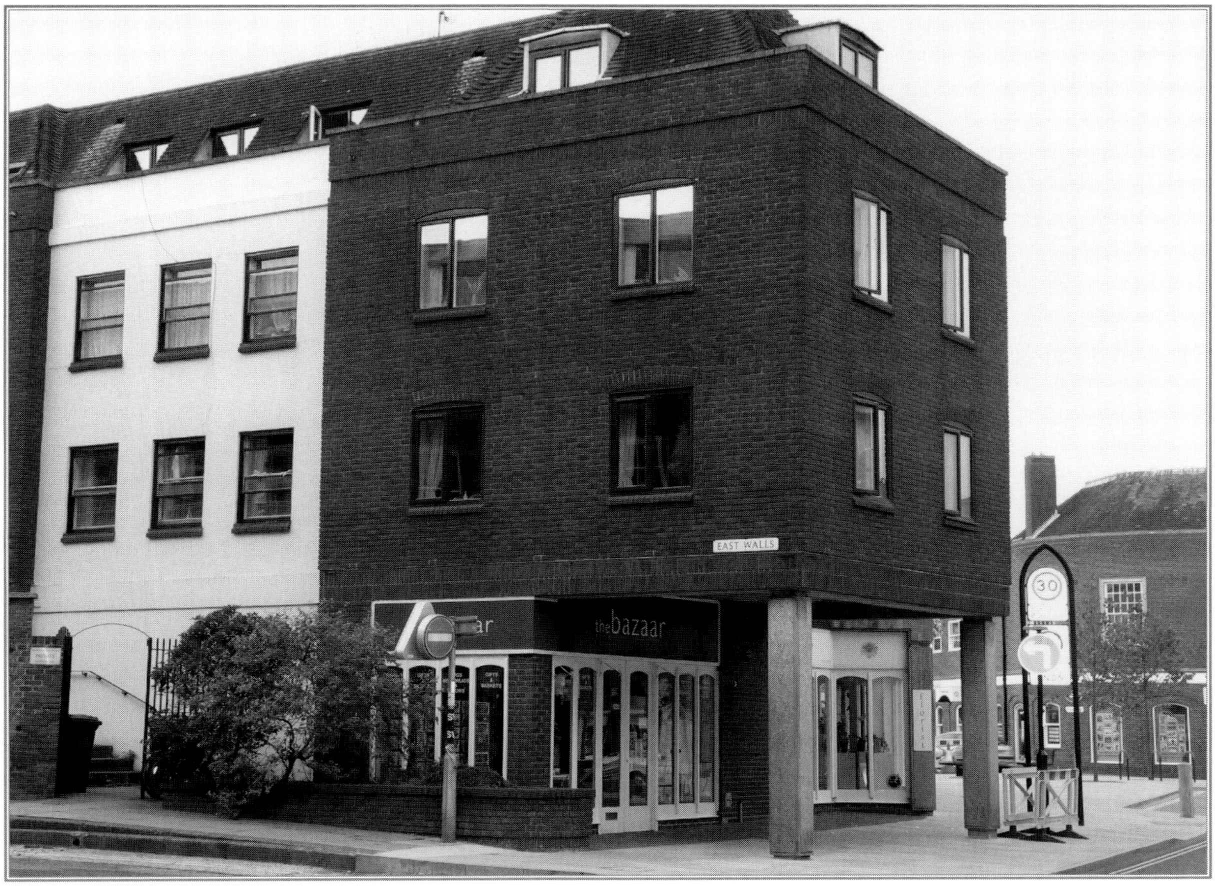

Sharp Garland and his son Sir Sharp Archibald Garland are both commemorated in nearby St Pancras Church where they were both churchwardens. Sharp Garland, who died in 1906, bought the shop in 1860. Sir Sharp Archibald Garland died in 1937. Both were mayor of Chichester several times over.

Kelly's 1909 directory gives Sir Sharp's address as No. 10 St John's Street, Chichester, and lists him as a councillor for the local authority's east ward alongside Alfred Leng, Harry Penney, William Butler, George Thomas Apps and James Albert Morris Bew.

Other shops in Eastgate Square at the time included Charles Barnes, poulterer; Baker & Son, the chemists; and Mrs Alice Jessie Brazier who had a fried fish shop.

The building which now stands on the site of Sharp Garland's shop offers accommodation above and retail units below.

Eastgate Square

Just behind you in the following image is the house in which John Keats wrote *The Eve of St Agnes*. Also just behind you is the former Unicorn Inn, now Unicorn House, home of *The Chichester Observer*.

It was a difficult place to be throughout much of 2008 because of protracted works on road-layout improvements, but despite the disturbances Eastgate Square remains one of Chichester's

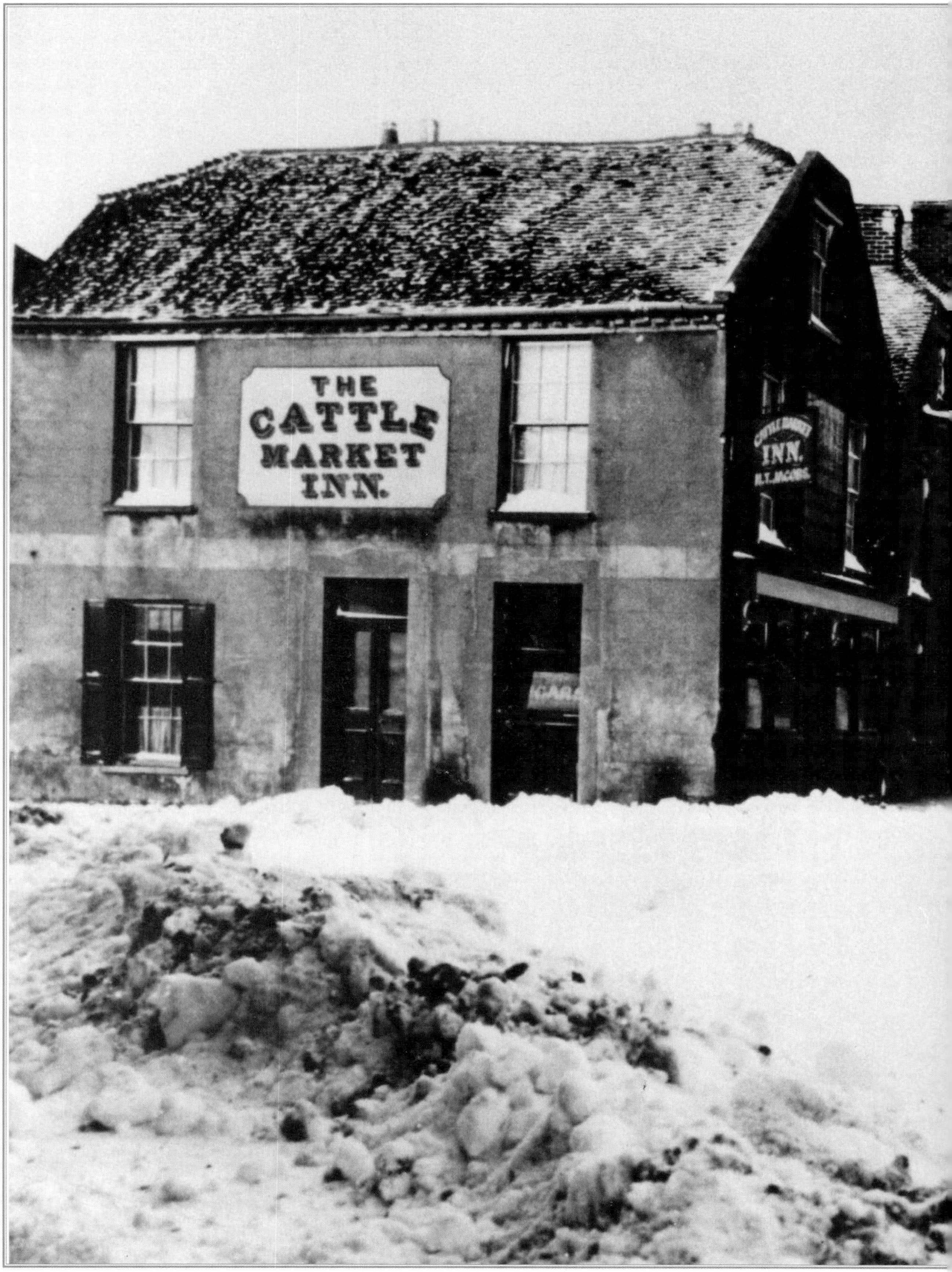
THE
CATTLE
MARKET
INN.

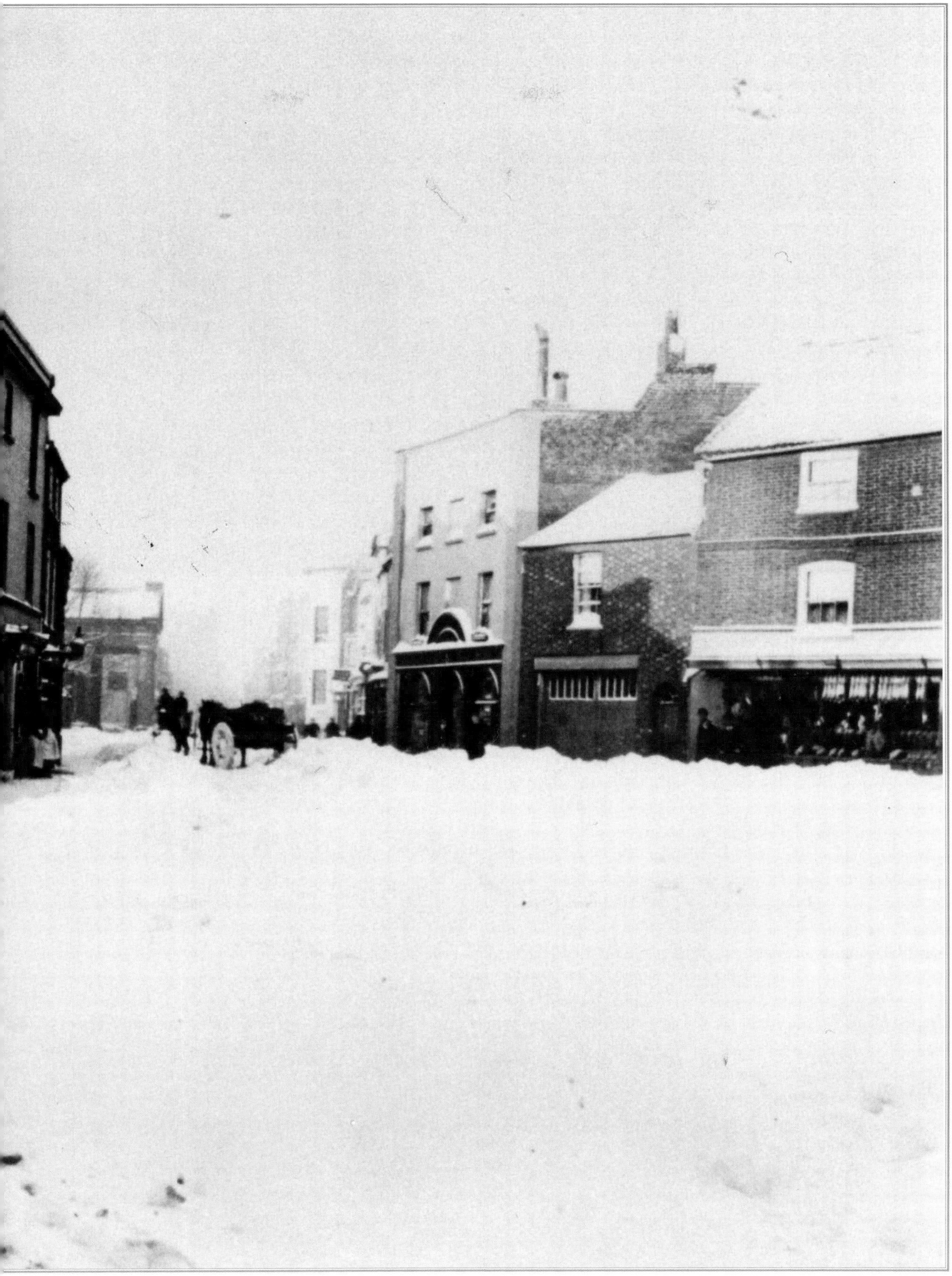

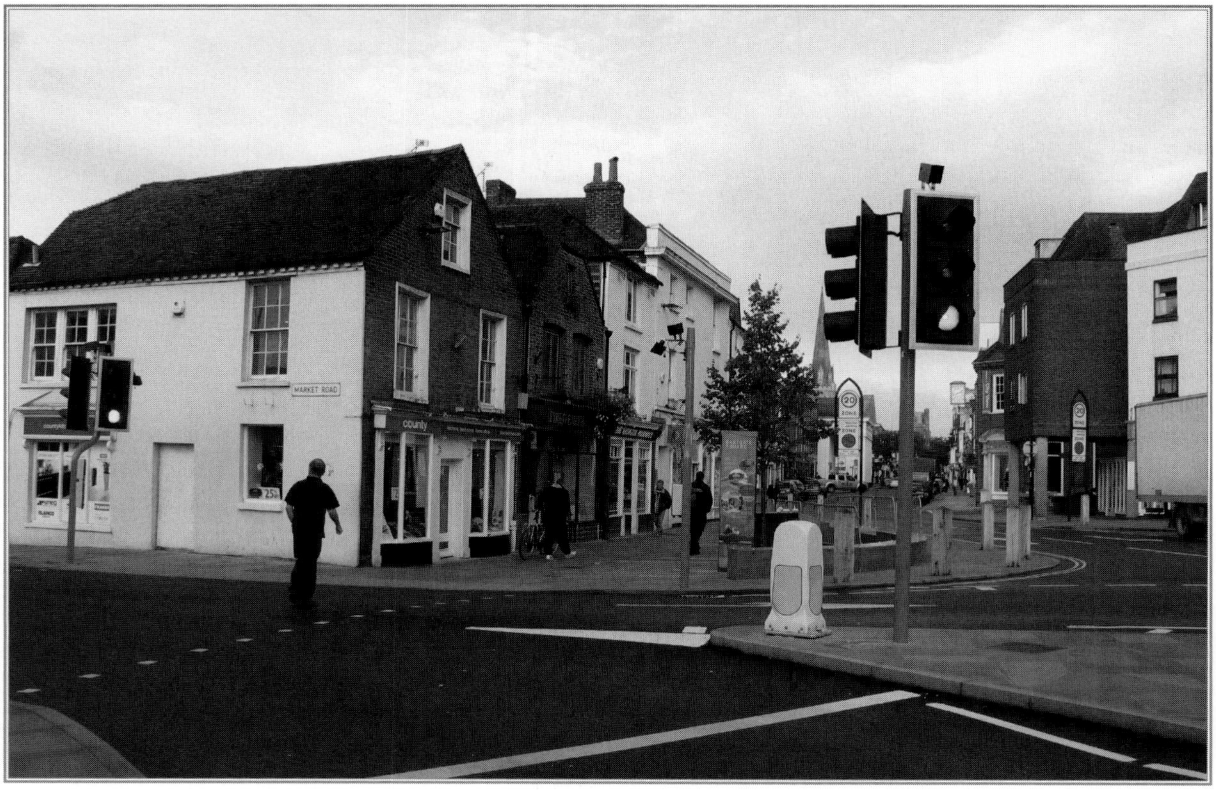

most fascinating quarters – and all the lovelier for being seen in the deep snow of 1881, a year which saw a particularly severe winter.

The Unicorn Inn dates back to at least 1670, and it was here that The Corporation of St Pancras, a charitable and social organisation, was formed in 1689. The inn was largely rebuilt in about 1760. It was then completely rebuilt in 1938 after it had been demolished to make way for a new inn at the back of the old site.

The pub shut up shop in 1960 and served as a rehearsal area for Chichester Festival Theatre for a number of years before being handed over for business use. *The Chichester Observer* moved there in 1994.

Passing through the square now is traffic on the Needlemakers one-way system, a name which conjures a lost Chichester industry. When General Sir William Waller attacked the city during the Civil War, he effectively killed the city's needle-making business. Waller attacked from the east, and it seems the locals destroyed the needlemakers' cottages in an effort to deny their attackers cover. The industry did not revive and was not helped, historians argue, by competition elsewhere, particularly in the Midlands.

The damage was certainly extensive. If you are in Eastgate Square you can be sure that nothing you can see is older than 1642. The scene above does, however, offer an interesting image of what conservationists at the Chichester Society have labelled 'pole-itis', the posts and poles plastered with signs which damage a great many Chichester street scenes with their superabundance of information.

A City Salutes its Dead

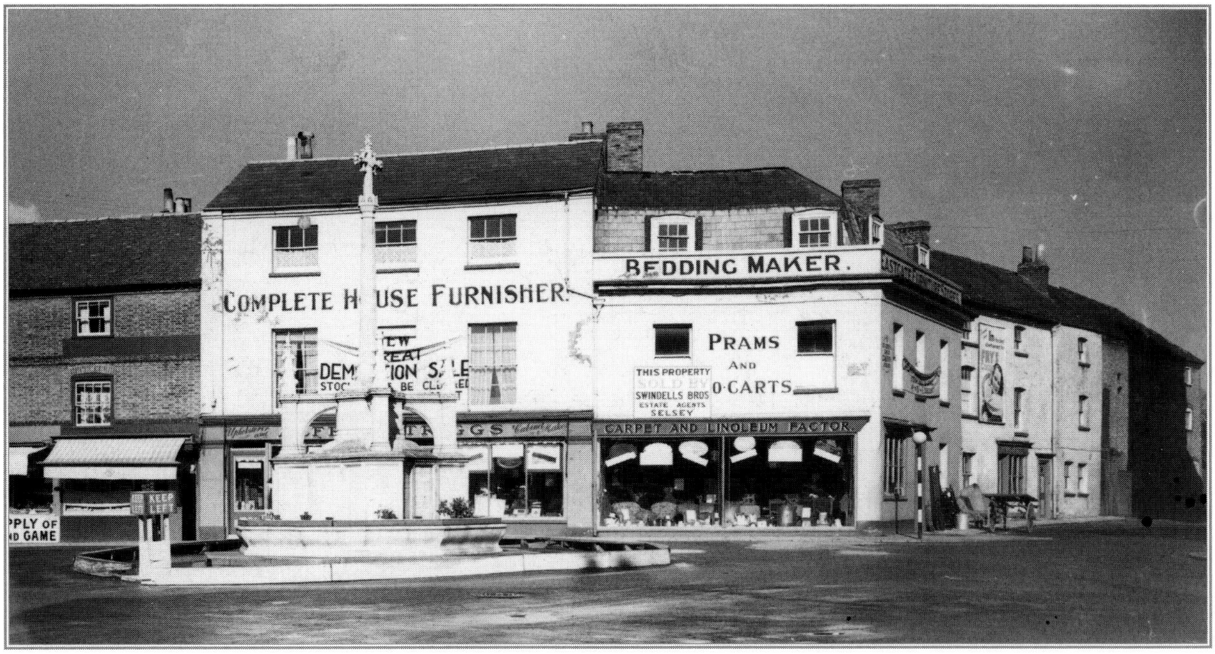

Chichester's War Memorial (seen in the image above), unveiled in Eastgate Square in July 1921, was one of the early victims of the motor car in the city.

Its position was found to be inconvenient once traffic started to grow and so the memorial was moved eastwards to Litten Gardens, where it stands today in rather more peaceful surroundings.

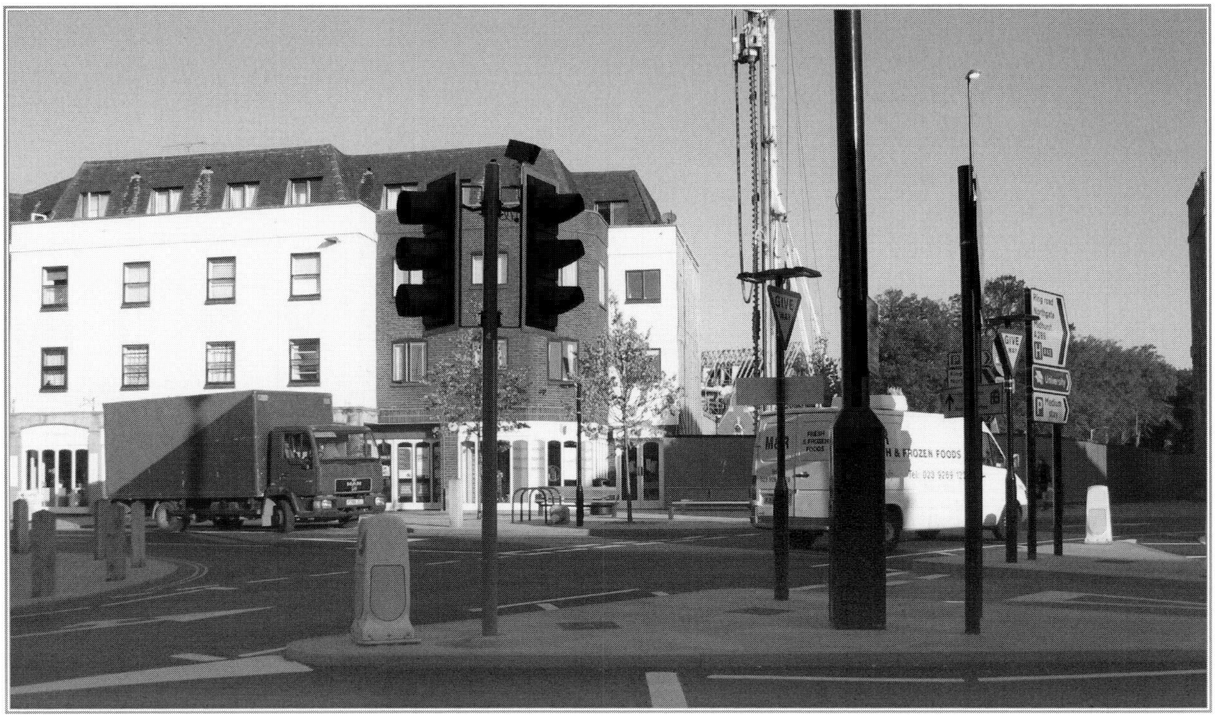

The original unveiling was clearly quite a spectacle. Contemporary accounts talk of the huge crowds which stretched back into The Hornet.

Chichester's tribute to its World War One dead was dedicated by the Very Revd Dean Hannah and was unveiled by Sir William Robertson, who entered the services as a boy soldier and ended his career as one of Field Marshal Douglas Haig's senior staff.

In January 1915 Robertson was appointed Chief of the General Staff, a position which made him the key advisor on all matters affecting British military operations on the western front. In December 1915 he was elevated to the new post of Chief of the Imperial General Staff, the most senior role the army had to offer. He remained in the post throughout the major battles of 1916 and 1917.

In 1919 Robertson was thanked by Parliament, granted £10,000 and created a Baronet of Beaconsfield in the county of Buckinghamshire. When he was appointed Field Marshal on 29 March 1920, he became the first man to have risen from the lowest to the most senior rank in the British Army.

The war memorial was moved to its new position soon after World War Two – safe from the traffic which now so dominates Eastgate Square.

Things That Go Bump in the Night

Although an improved Eastgate Square has emerged from the months of roadworks which dogged 2008, it is still a world away from the easy charm this Victorian image exudes, a real delight with its horse-drawn carts and cobbled streets and its air of bustle without hassle.

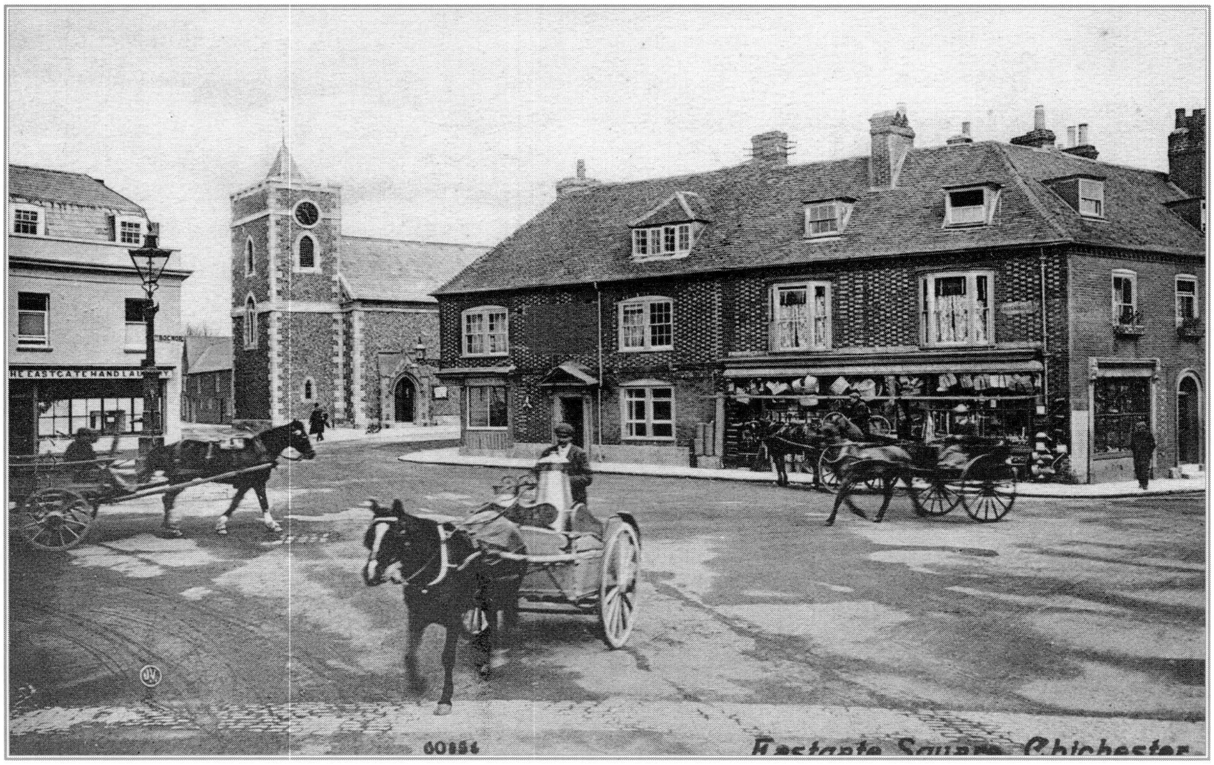

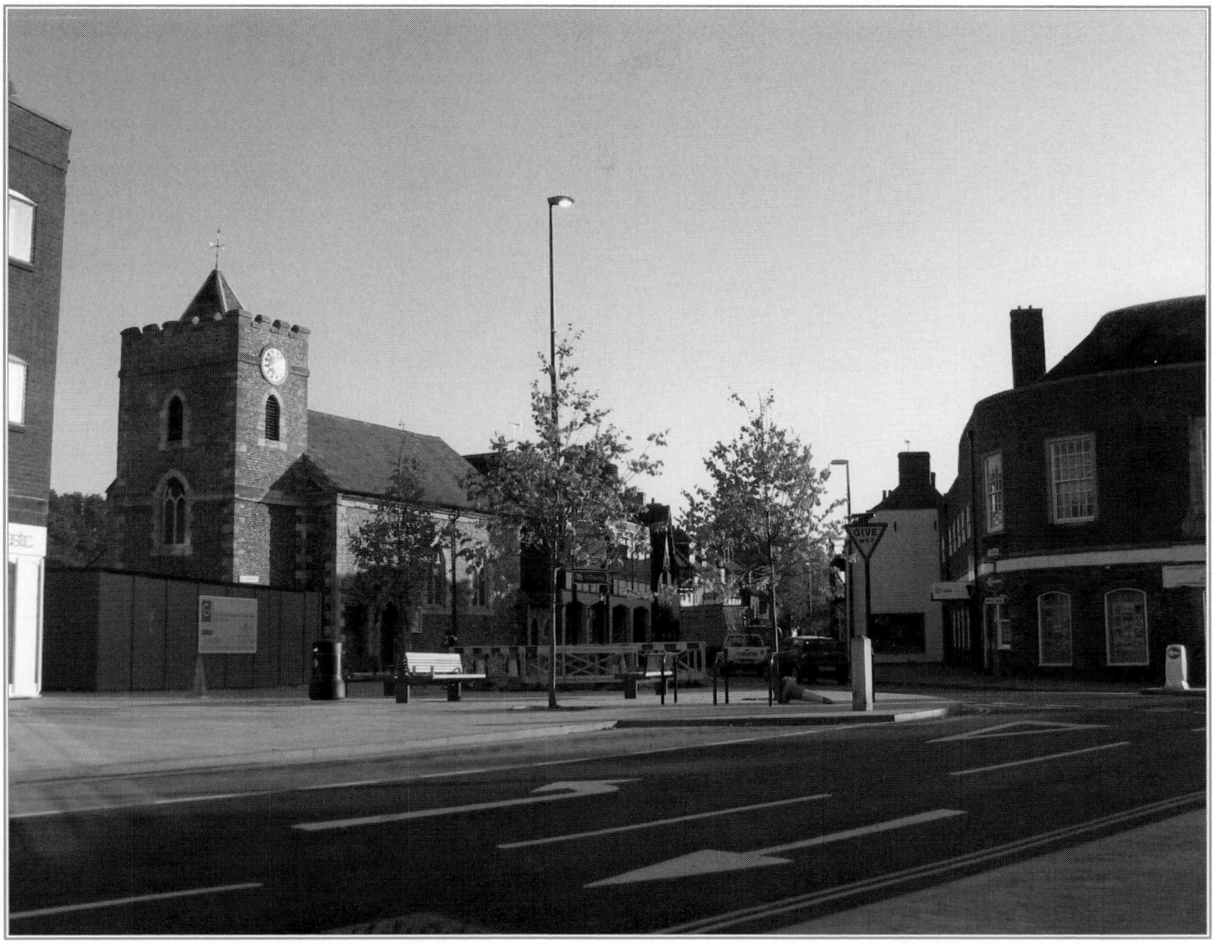

On the left in the older image is the Eastgate Hand Laundry and in the middle is the old Unicorn Inn. The only element in this particular view which has not changed is St Pancras Church, which stands unaltered amid a street scene so very different today in every other respect.

However, it is not an area which has let go of its ghosts lightly. The Unicorn Inn is now Unicorn House, home since 1994 of *The Chichester Observer* and a building which surely ranks as one of the most haunted the city can offer.

We have had it all in the *Observer* offices. Shady figures hover in corners (and no, we do not employ ghost writers); a child is regularly heard sobbing by the stairs, and objects mysteriously move though never while you are watching. A drawer will suddenly be open when you look down. A pile of papers, neatly stacked, will no longer be on the desk. Suddenly, they will be – still neatly stacked – on the floor.

Perhaps it is worth a book all of its own. We have had Victorian murders outside the door; the disturbed spirits of long-dead Romans and the ghost of a dodgy landlord apparently running guns for the IRA.

So perhaps somewhere, somehow, those horses and carts, that man with the milk churn, that chap staring into the shop window…perhaps they are with us still.

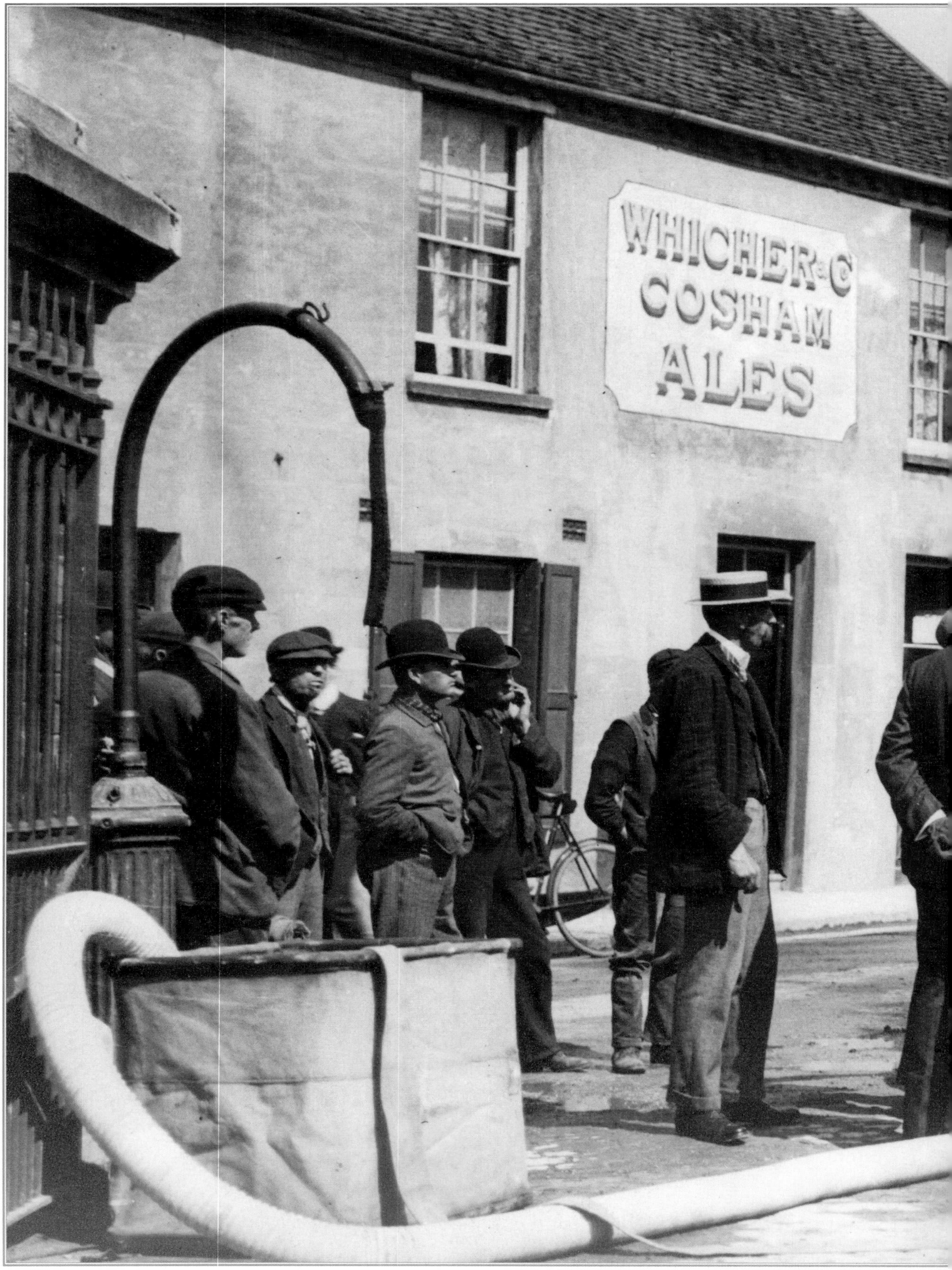
WHICHER & Co
COSHAM
ALES

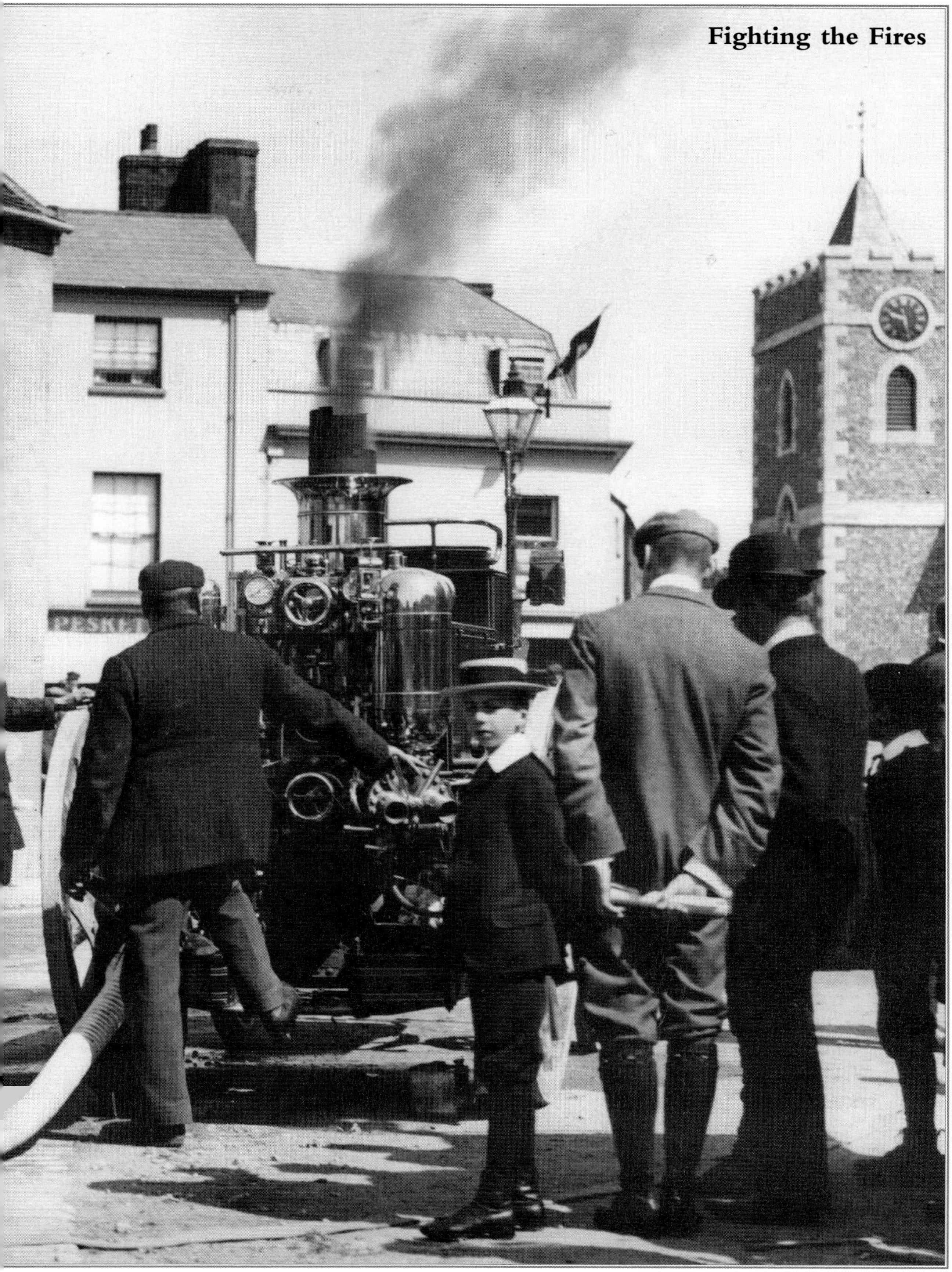
Fighting the Fires
PESKET

Another irresistible image (previous page) of Eastgate Square shows the fire brigade steam pump in action. In about 1906 payment for a new fire engine was approved by the city council. It seems likely that this photograph shows a demonstration of the new machine.

It is certainly the focus for a great deal of hands-in-pockets interest. Only the boy and one of the chaps on the left seem to have noticed that the photograph is being taken. Once again, there is not a bare head in sight.

The contrast with the modern image (below) of busy people hurrying past is striking. Note also the variation on 'pole-itis' in the more recent image. It has transformed into a rather worrying 'bendy pole-itis'.

Unchanging as ever, though, in the background is St Pancras Church, built in 1750–51 on the site of an earlier church which had been partially demolished when parliamentarians attacked Chichester in 1642. Constructed of flint with stone dressings in the style of the 15th century, it features a two-storey tower with an embattled parapet and a pyramid-shaped slate roof with an iron weathervane.

Also destroyed during the Civil War were two Eastgate Inns, The Lion and The Dolphin. On the left in the older image is The Cattle Market Inn. It became The Market Tavern in about 1874 and closed down in 1925.

To the south of Eastgate Square is the Cattle Market, which was laid out in the early 1870s and is now a car park. Beyond Eastgate to the east, the land was apparently divided into three great fields, the North Field, the Portfield and the Gildenfield. Leading away from Eastgate Square towards the Oving and Bognor roads is The Hornet, or Harnet, composed of houses and shops of the 18th and 19th centuries. The name has also been recorded as Hurnett Hill.

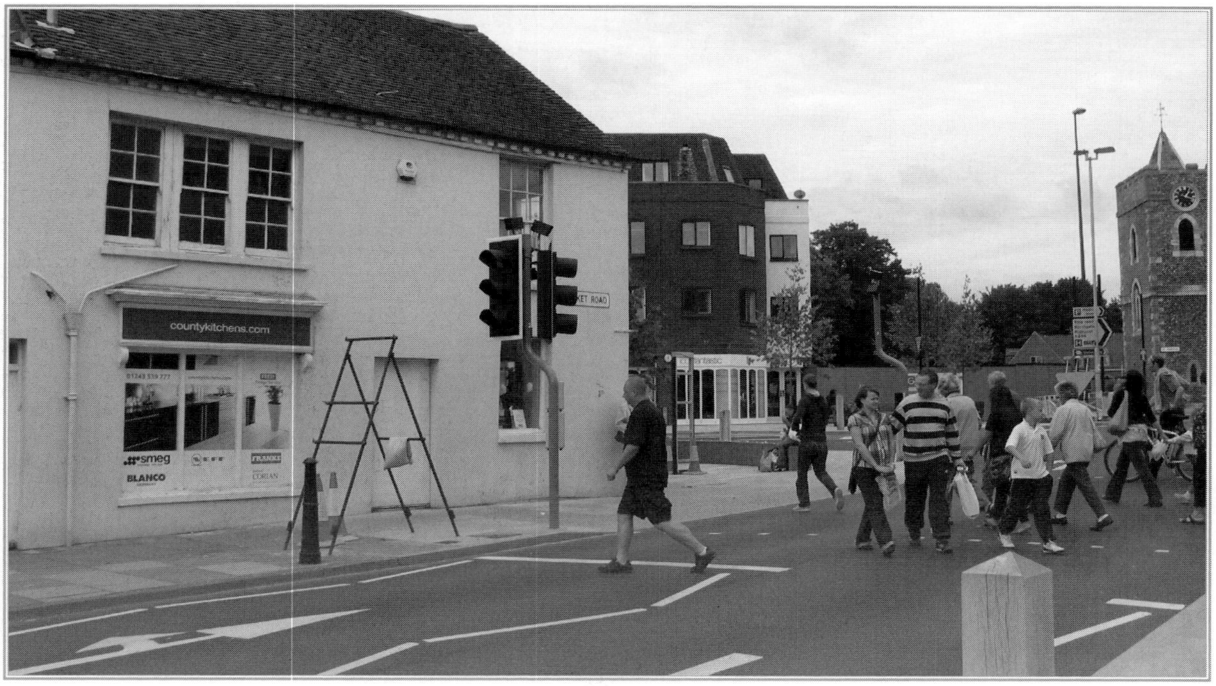

Pine's of Eastgate Square

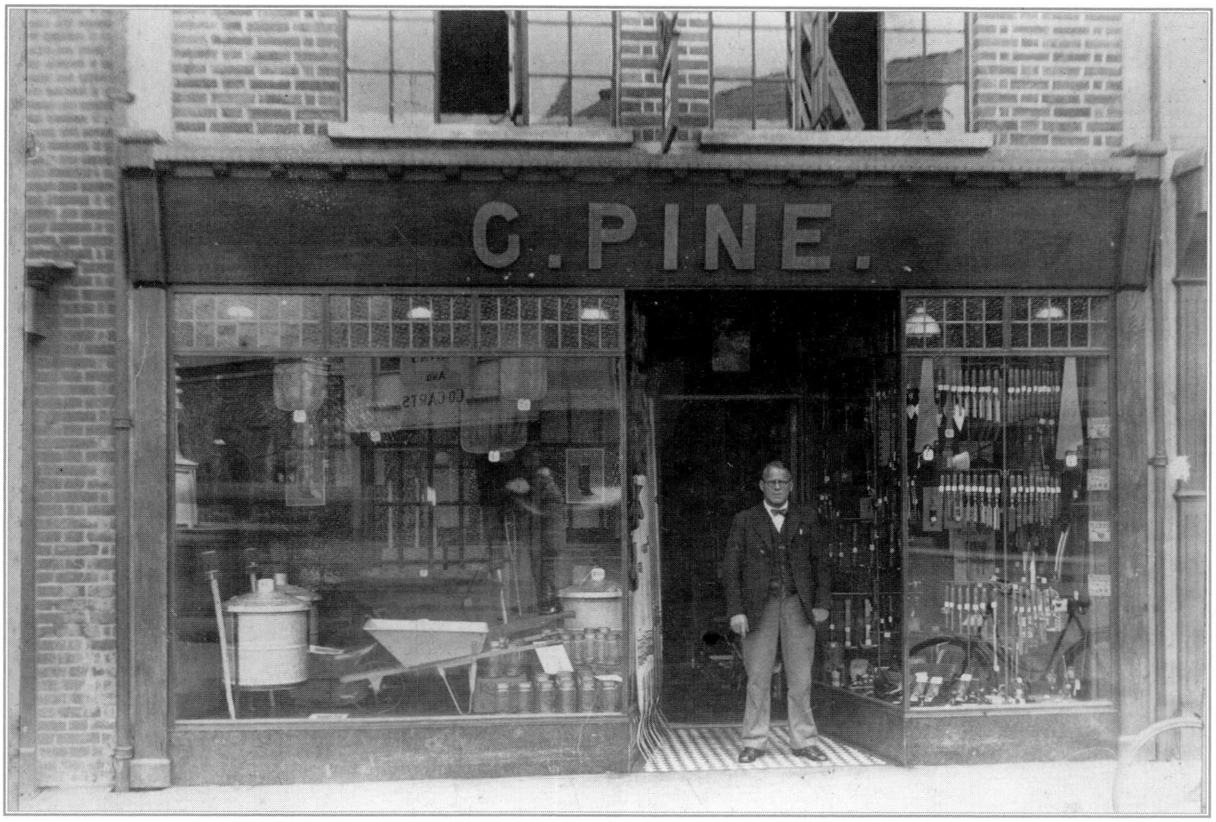

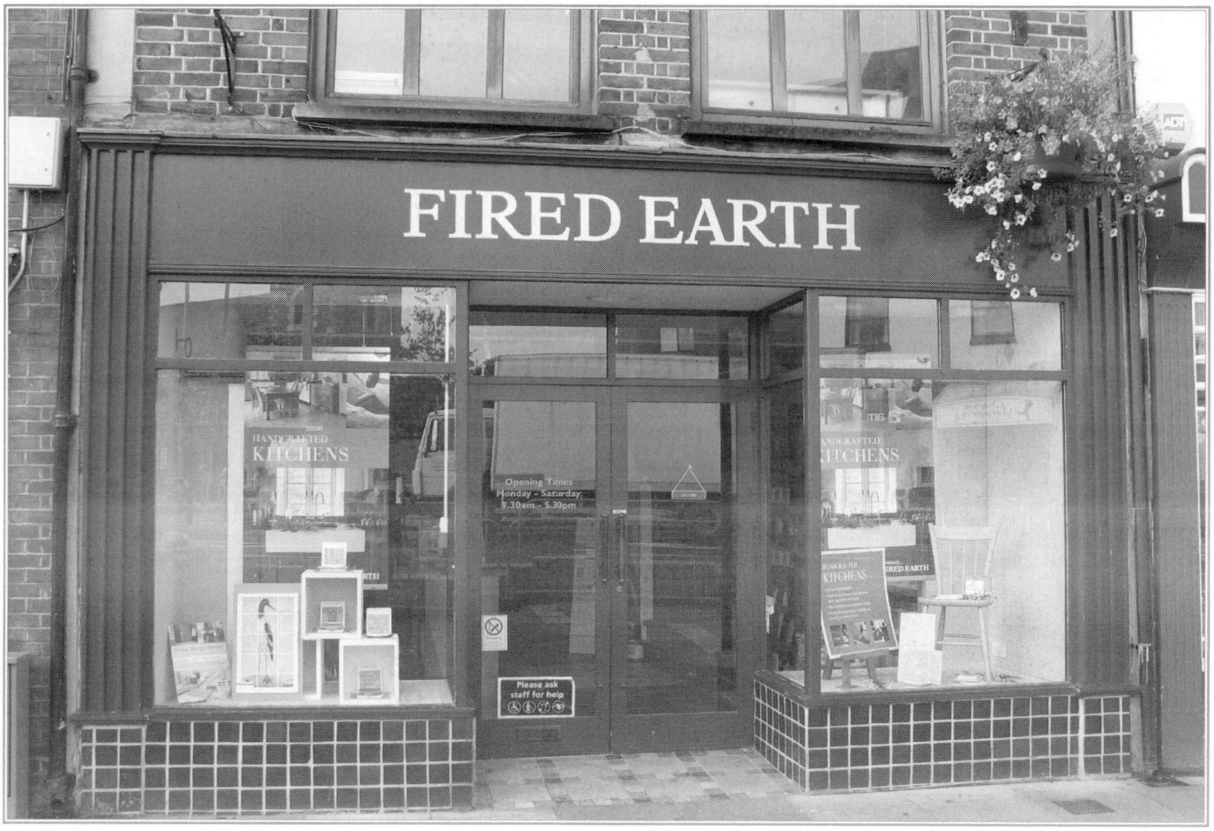

Gilbert Pine looks justly proud on the doorstep on his ironmonger's shop in Eastgate Square (page 97).

There is something beautifully old-fashioned about his thoroughly functional window display. The saws frame the neatly symmetrical array of chisels on the right; on the left are jars, shovels, brooms and a wheelbarrow.

In about 1913 Gilbert Pine bought James Light's ironmongers business next to the Unicorn Inn on the eastern side of the square. In 1928 Pine's moved across the road to the site pictured here, now Fired Earth. A probable date for the earlier photograph would be 1936.

From the 1950s to the 1980s Pine's expanded along Market Avenue. At its peak it sold tools, DIY essentials, ironmongery, garden supplies, fitted kitchens and furniture. It also had a cook shop. It even had a post office and an inside post box, all behind the shop in Eastgate Square.

When Pine's closed in 1990 26 staff were employed there. The post office transferred to Sadler's Walk, just off East Street, where it remained until 2008 when it fell victim to post office cutbacks.

In May 2008 *The Chichester Observer* reported on the emotional farewell when the post office shut its doors for the last time, along with hundreds of others as part of a nationwide reorganisation.

It was one of two planned to close in Chichester. The other, in Parklands, was saved from the axe when Post Office bosses changed their minds after feedback from the public consultation.

Sadler's Walk was Chichester's first shopping arcade, built on the site of the garden shop Sadler's which had been opened by the gardening expert Percy Thrower in the 1950s.

A City's Sacrifice

Remembrance Day 1950 is captured in this image, taken not long after Chichester's War Memorial was moved from Eastgate Square to Litten Gardens.

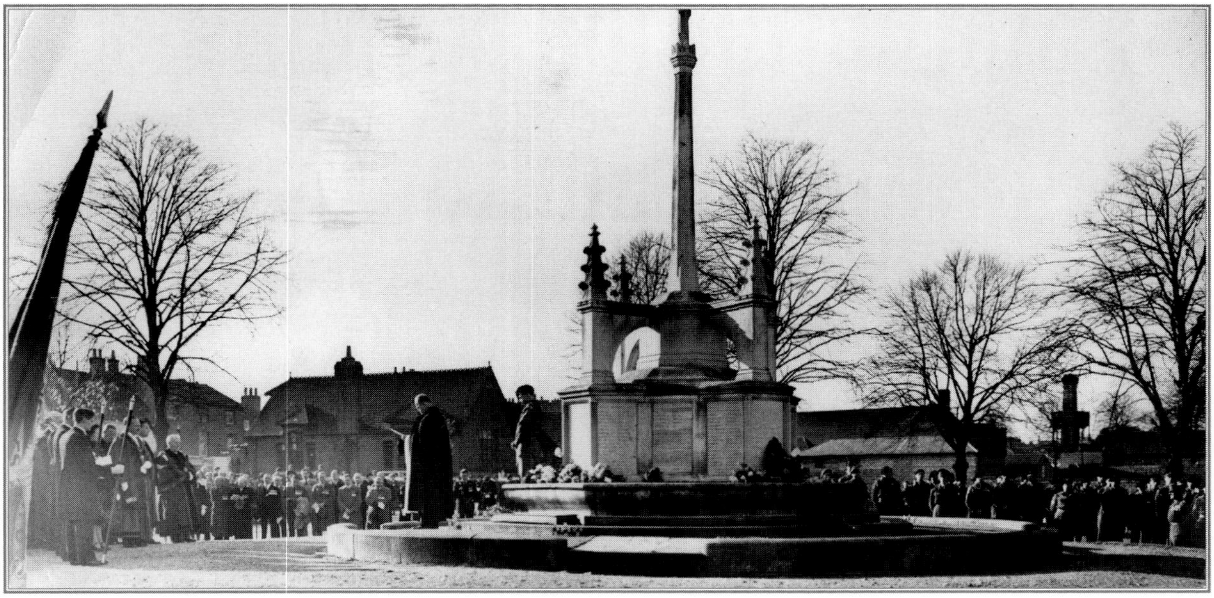

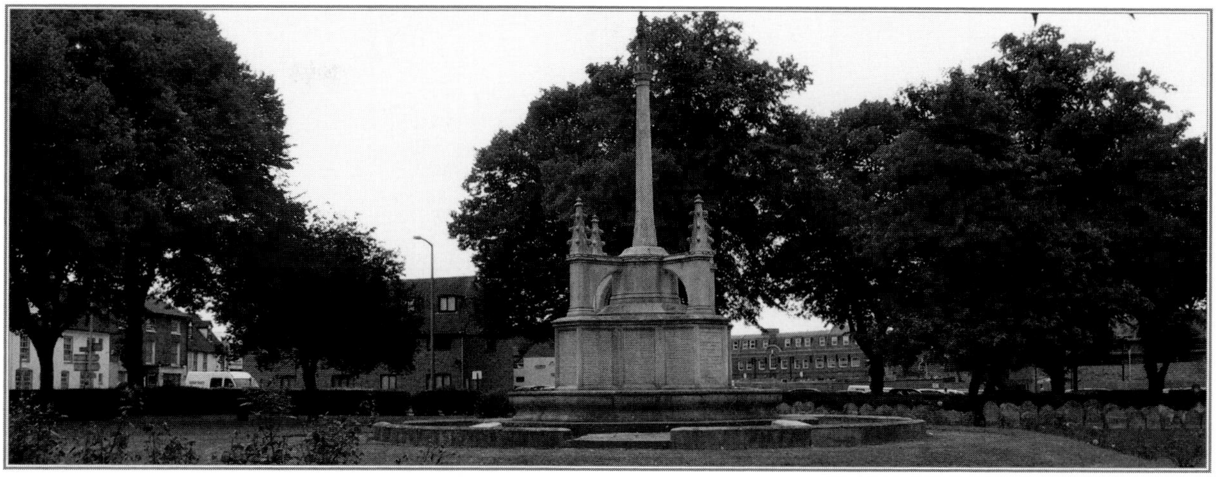

The memorial stands as a testament to Chichester's important role during World War One as home to the Royal Sussex Regiment.

Major William Lushington Osborn was the man who recruited the regiment's first Kitchener battalion, and they marched to war on 5 August 1914 from the barracks in Broyle Road. Many did not return; 323 men from the city were killed on the western front.

To their names Chichester City Council has added those of the Chichester men who perished in World War Two. Every year the mayor and city councillors along with the chairmen of Chichester District and West Sussex County Councils process to the War Memorial to attend a short Remembrance Sunday service and to observe the two minutes' silence.

In recent years Chichester's remembrance has been augmented each November by a concert of military music at Chichester Festival Theatre, in aid of the Army Benevolent Fund.

In all, the Royal Sussex Regiment lost 6,800 officers and men during World War One, a conflict which saw its second Battalion earn the nickname The Iron Regiment. During World War Two the regiment saw further service, perhaps most notably at Monte Cassino.

Post-war, the regiment saw service in Palestine, Suez, Korea and finally Aden and Radfan. On 31 December 1966 it was merged into The Queen's Regiment. The Royal Sussex vacated the barracks in Chichester in 1960.

CHAPTER 7
SOUTHGATE

And Then Came the Trains

The railways first came to Chichester in 1846 which was inevitably when the city's coaching heyday went into terminal decline. When coaching was at its peak, The Dolphin and The Anchor, then two rival establishments opposite the cathedral, would have been quite a sight as the city's two key coaching inns.

Chichester had been fairly late in developing its coaches, but it made up for lost time with regular services to London. Rather worryingly, coaches on the Midhurst road were generally armed. Robbers were ready and willing to pounce.

And then came the trains.

The London to Brighton line had a staggered opening. The Brighton to Shoreham stretch opened in 1840, followed by the Norwood Junction to Haywards Heath section in 1841, followed later in the year by the opening of the final section from Haywards Heath to Brighton.

Five years later the London, Brighton and South Coast Railway Company opened the 28-mile stretch of line from Brighton to Chichester. The following year it was extended first to Havant and then to Portsmouth. In 1881 Chichester gained a branch line to Midhurst.

Also significant in those early years was the Selsey Tram. The line was opened in 1897 from Chichester to Selsey Town and extended a further mile to Selsey Beach in 1908, although this

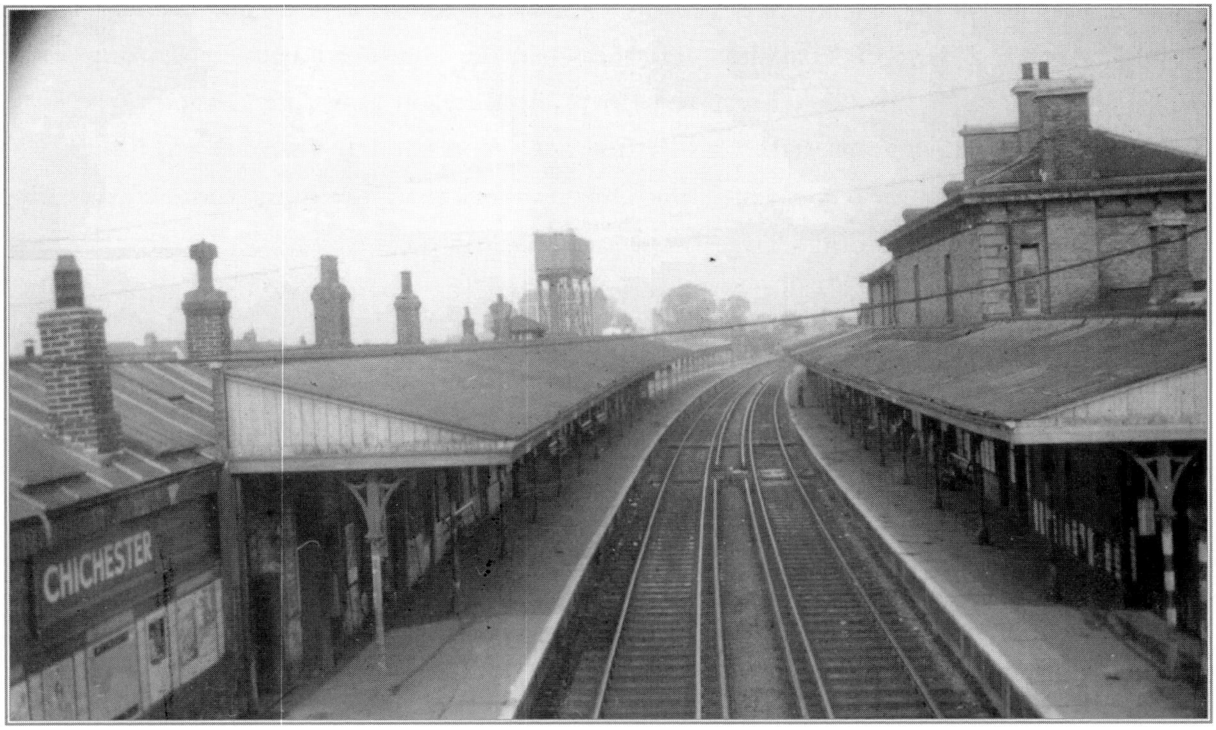

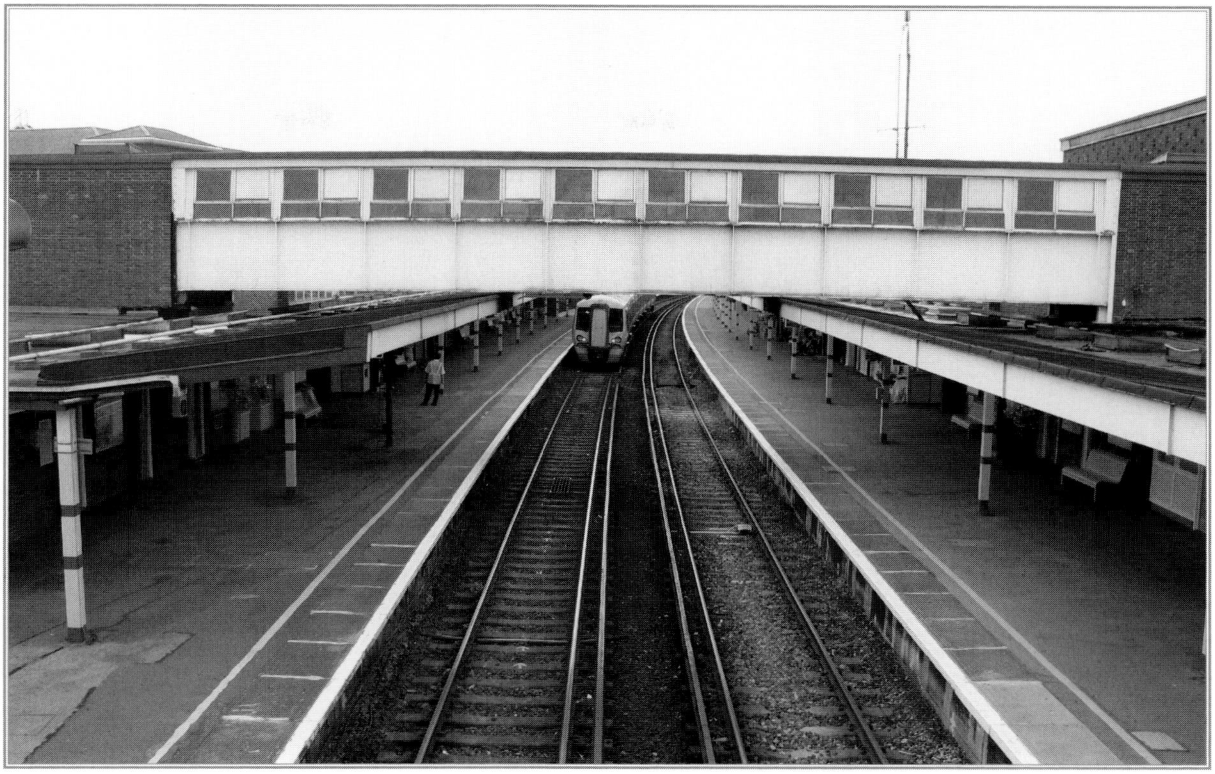

section fell out of use in 1914. After World War One the whole operation suffered greatly from road competition, and a fatal accident in 1924 was another nail in the coffin. The final nail was hammered home when bus services started up. The Selsey Tram could not compete and the line finally folded in January 1935.

The older image shows the platforms and lines at Chichester railway station before rebuilding, perhaps around 1950–57. The newer image suggests it might be time for a new makeover.

Much needed Improvements

Rail travellers to Chichester in the early post-war years had to suffer the most dismal of greetings, arriving at a railway station which did no justice to the city beyond it.

Chichester's main line station had started life in 1846 as a simple wooden affair, a structure replaced by a permanent building the following year. This then stood for more than a century without significant improvements. The deterioration was considerable.

By the 1950s the station was a miserable place, dark and thoroughly unappealing. It was rotting away before Chichester's eyes – to much indignation on the part of the locals.

However, things started to change in 1957 when long overdue reconstruction work began, clearing away a station which was the city's shame.

Facilities were considerably updated, with a spacious new booking hall the centrepiece of the rebuilt station. Contemporary accounts were wholly positive, visitors delighting in a much more positive initial impression.

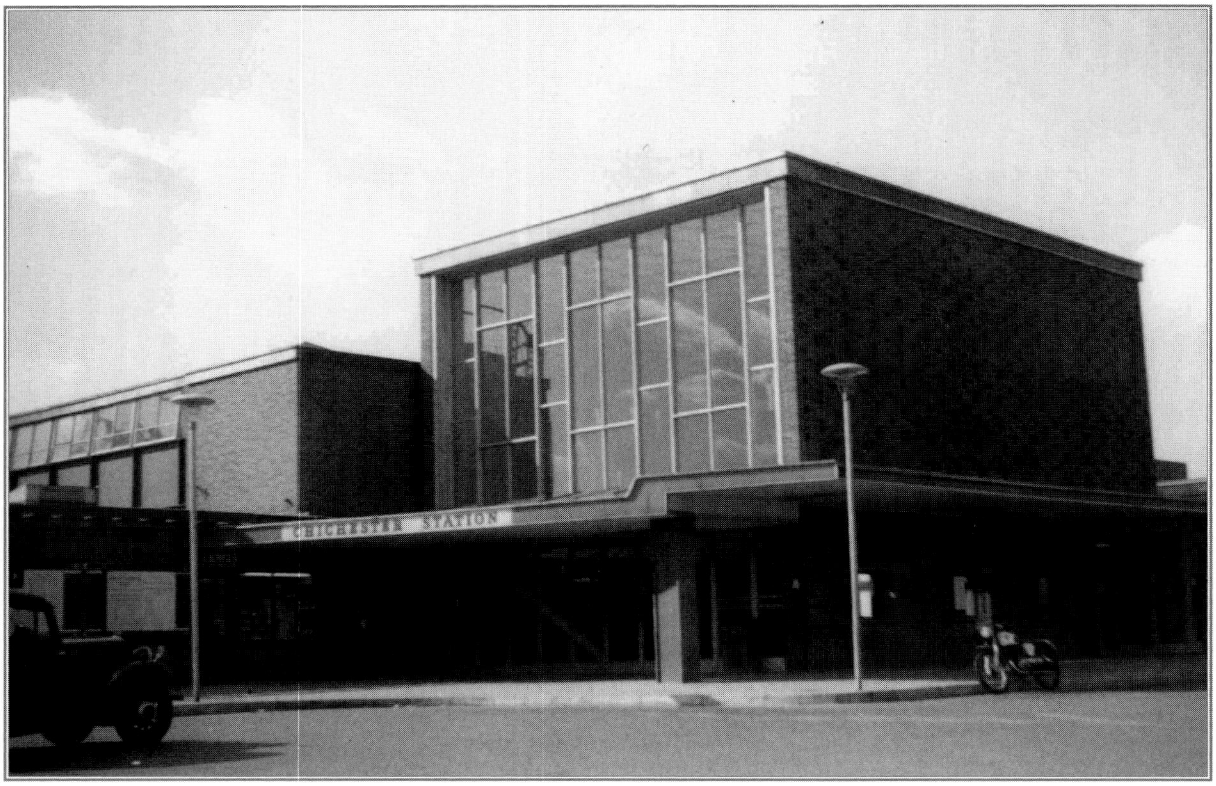

Chichester bus station was also built in the 1960s, just north of the Stockbridge Road level crossing, and confirmed the area as Chichester's public transport hub.

The older photograph shows Chichester's new railway station in about 1963. The sign saying Chichester Station is a little more discreet these days, but otherwise little has changed.

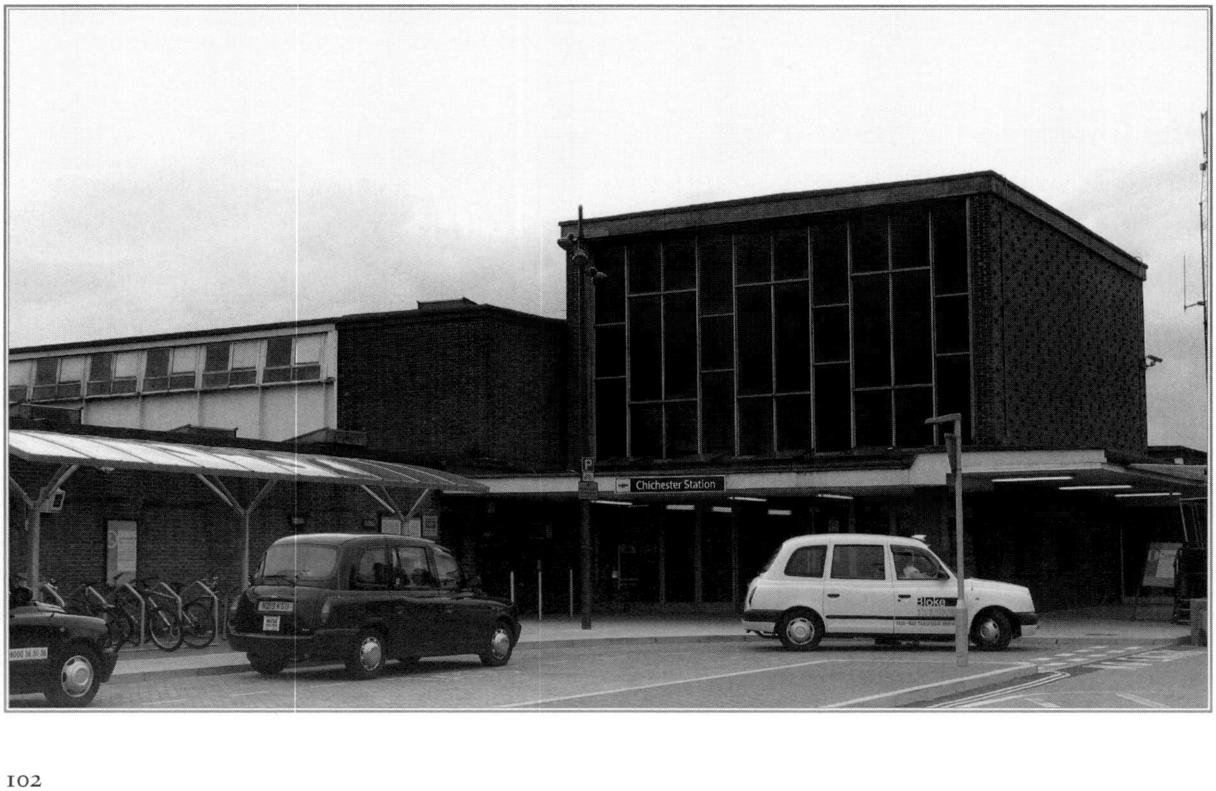

Policing the City

Where now stands Chichester's bus station once stood its police station, as these two images (below and overleaf) strikingly show.

Look closely at the picture overleaf and the words 'police station' are visible just under the roof of the rather gloomy looking but neatly symmetrical building from which the long arm of the law used to stretch.

Arguably, policing in the city goes back to the closing years of the 18th century when businessmen and respectable citizens got together a consortium aimed at prosecuting felons.

Half a century later and things were considerably more formalised, with the city boasting a superintendent and a sergeant with a constable.

The West Sussex Constabulary was founded in 1857 and worked alongside the Chichester City force. The new police station was built for them near the railway station, with the city force remaining in their Eastgate station.

Inevitably the forces were amalgamated. The combined force remained at the Southgate station from 1889 until 1935 when it moved to a modern police station in Basin Road.

It was not quite yet the end of the line for the old Victorian station which became home to the city's first mixed youth club for a while until the bus station plans reclaimed the site.

The bus station opened in the mid-1960s, a busy time for the city which also saw it gain Bishop Luffa School, the Eastgate Square swimming pool and the new city centre library.

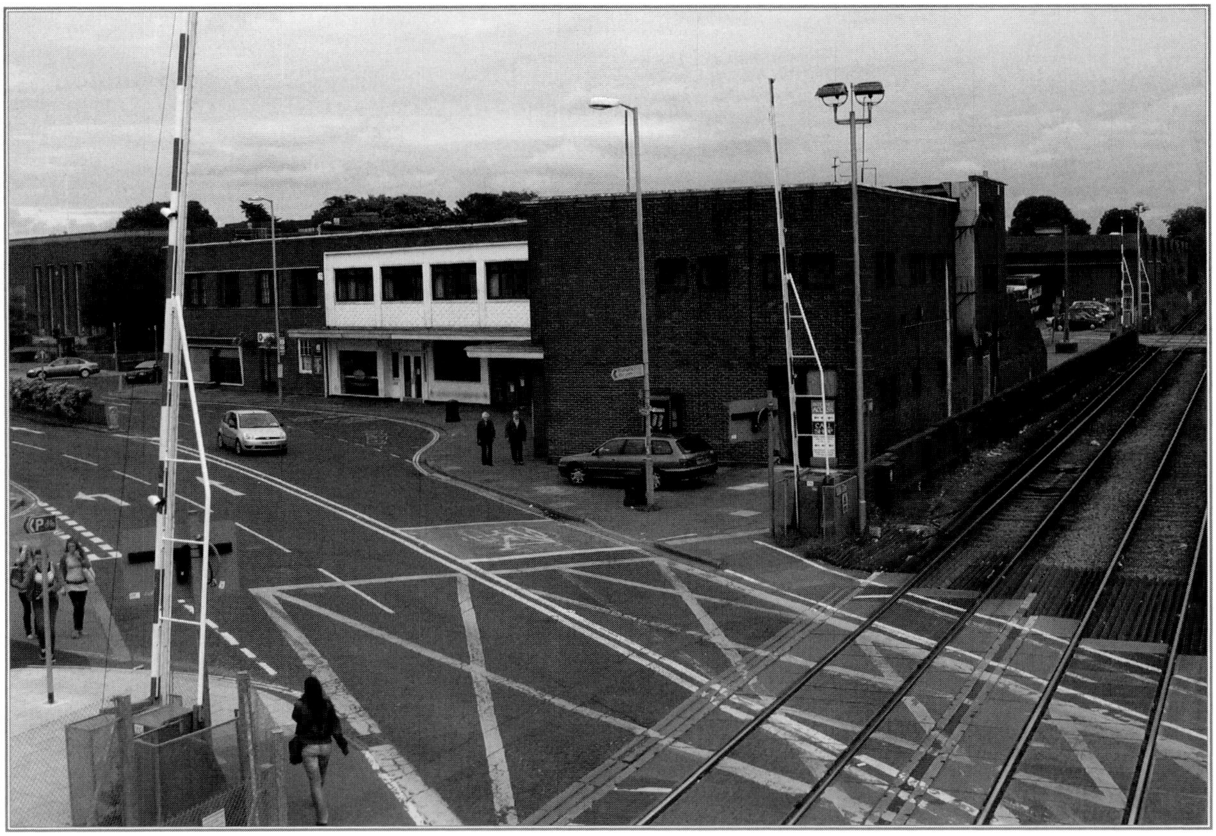

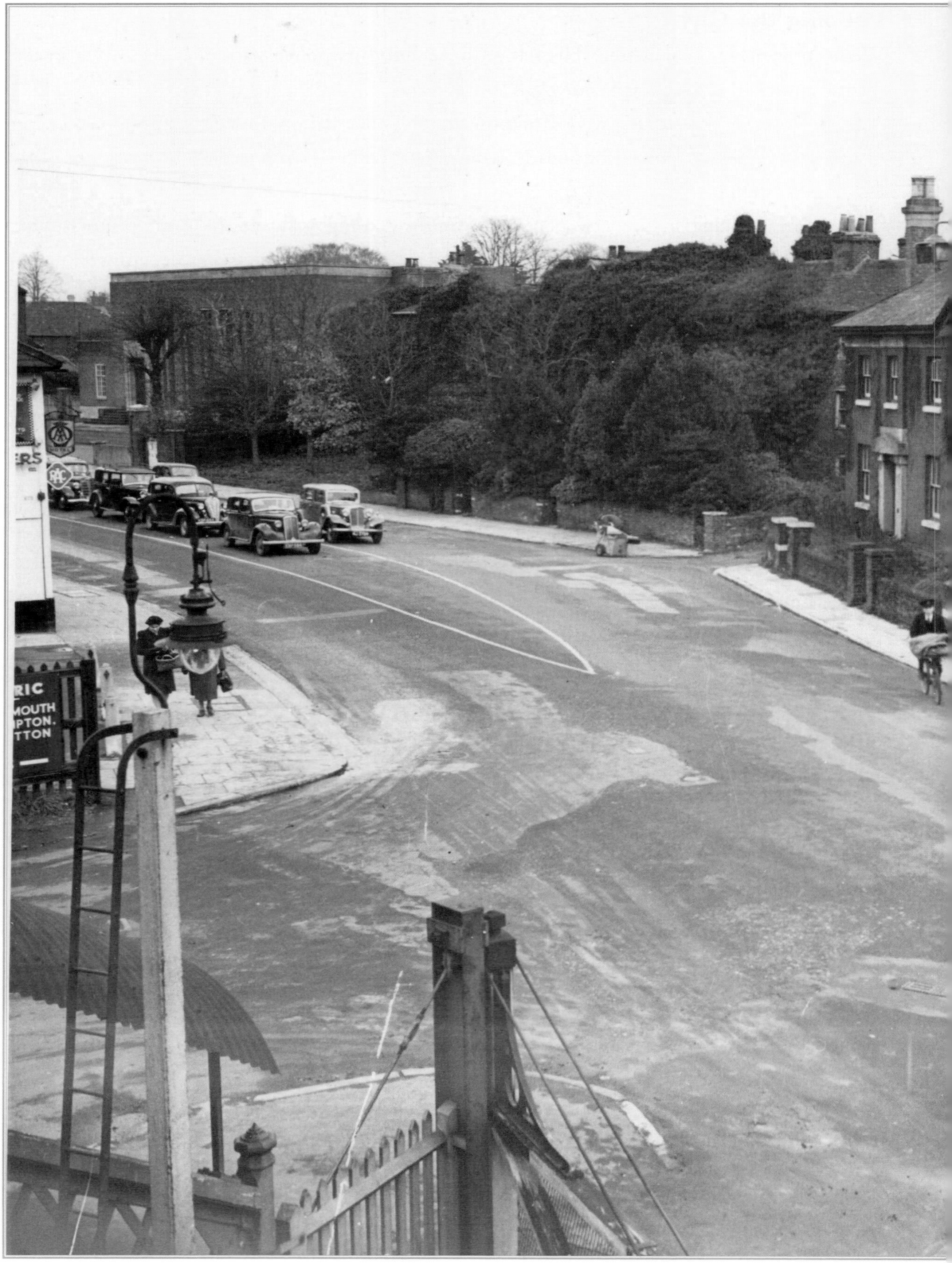
RIC
MOUTH
PTON.
TTON
RAC

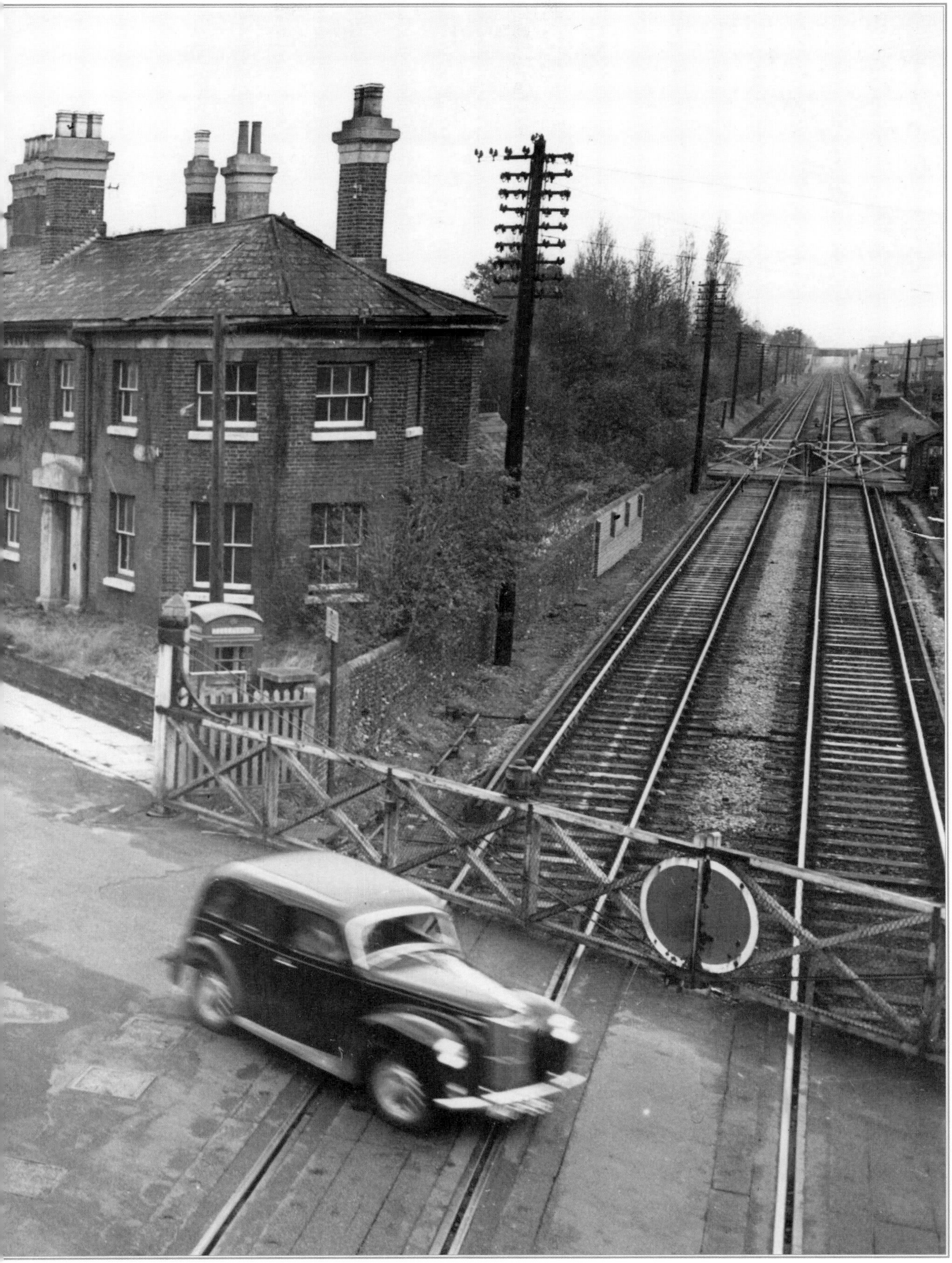

A Problem Unresolved

Now here is a view which has changed little. The older picture, dating from around 1960, shows Chichester railway station with gates, footbridge and newly completed platform.

However, all around it things have changed considerably, and not for the better. The Stockbridge Road level crossing is one of the more pressing problems now facing modern Chichester.

It is impossible to head north or south through Chichester without being forced to sit and fume amid the car exhausts in the daily gridlock the crossing creates.

Aside from the sheer inconvenience, the traffic chaos is reckoned to inflict a huge cost on city shops and the local economy generally – an issue which was thrashed out again in the summer of 2008 when it emerged that the cost of putting a road bridge over the crossing would be £10 million, a price likely to rule it out as an option. It also emerged that the cost of the alternative – an underpass – would be even higher.

District councillors decided to invite a senior Network Rail representative to speak at a future meeting and answer questions about why delays at the railway gates are often so prolonged. They also urged consideration of new technology to resolve the worsening problems.

The gates are closed to the road for 35 minutes in every hour, causing long delays, considerable pollution, greater costs to businesses and frustration to tourists, not to mention the aggravation to local residents.

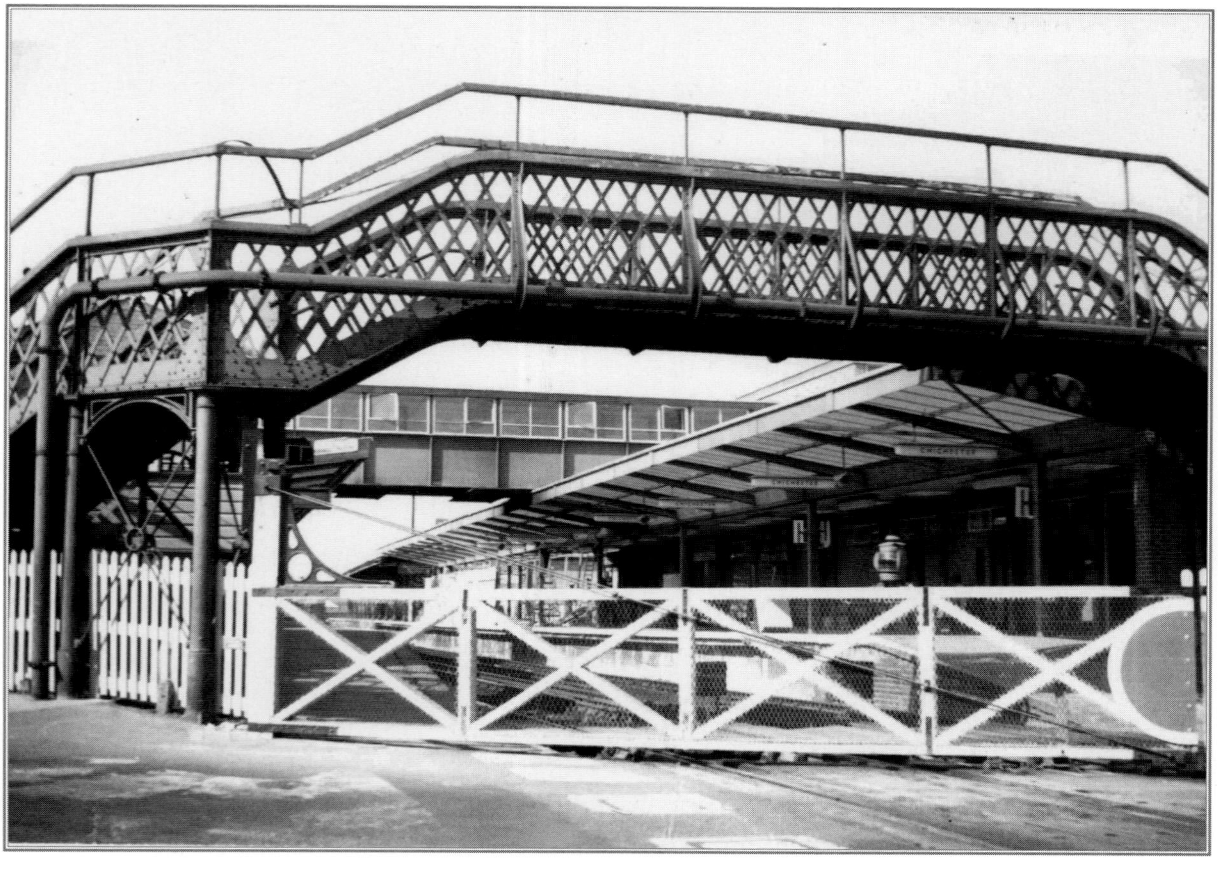

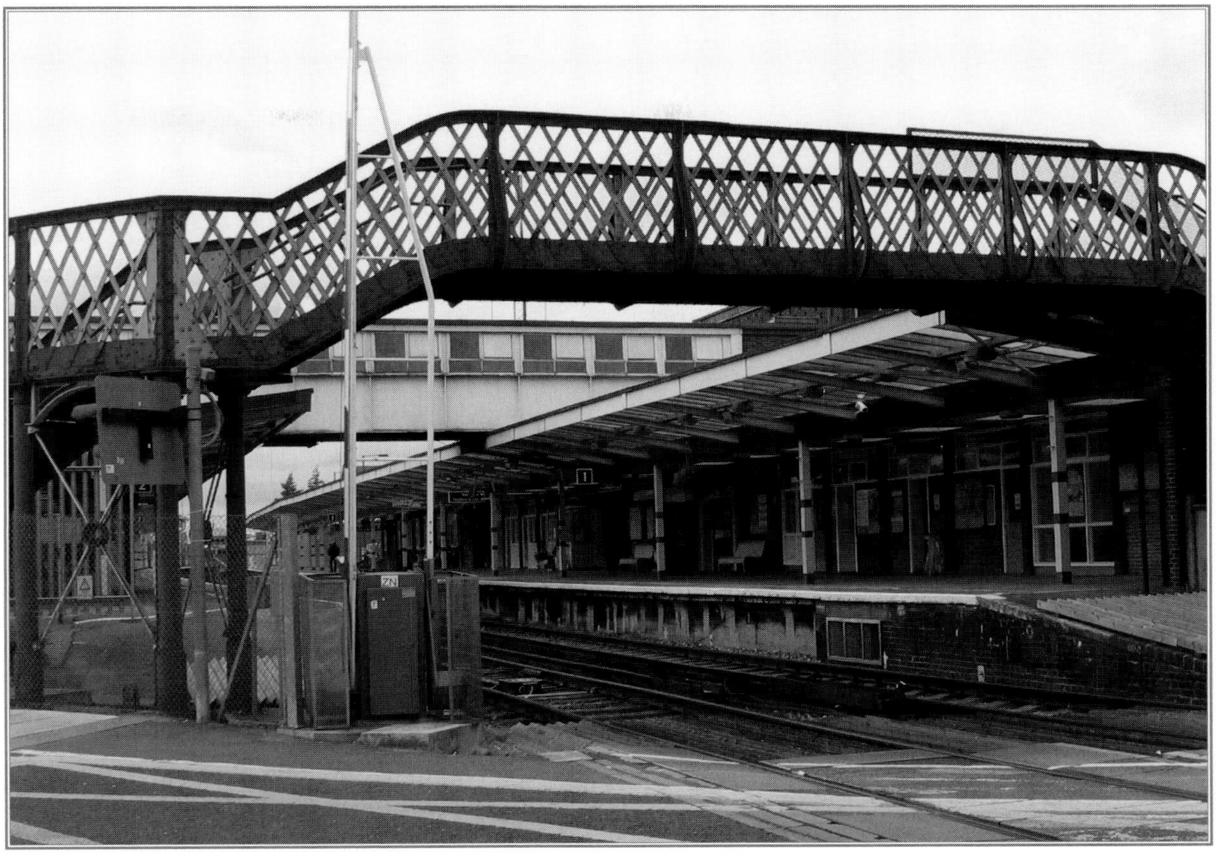

However, even if the cash could be found for a bridge, some councillors voiced worries about its likely visual impact. We can only speculate what another photograph in 50 years time will show.

The First Industrial Estates

An important early post-war change in Chichester came with the creation of the Terminus Road industrial estate just to the south of the city's railway station.

The older photograph overleaf shows the construction of the industrial estate approach road in February 1950. To the right is Canal Place.

Terminus Road offers a very different view today. The road is a busy stretch, home to a wide range of businesses, many relating to cars. Here can be found the Chichester base for Renault, Ford and Aston Martin, plus Chichester Car Auctions. Also in Terminus Road are the Wrenford Centre, which provides a day service for people with learning difficulties, and the Cathedral Works Organisation.

The creation of the Terminus Road industrial estate – and nearby Quarry Lane industrial estate on the site of a former quarry – can be seen as the city reorganising itself for the 20th century.

In Victorian days pretty much everything happened within the city walls. Here you could find shops, factories, slaughterhouses and houses all jumbled together.

Terminus Road looking west.

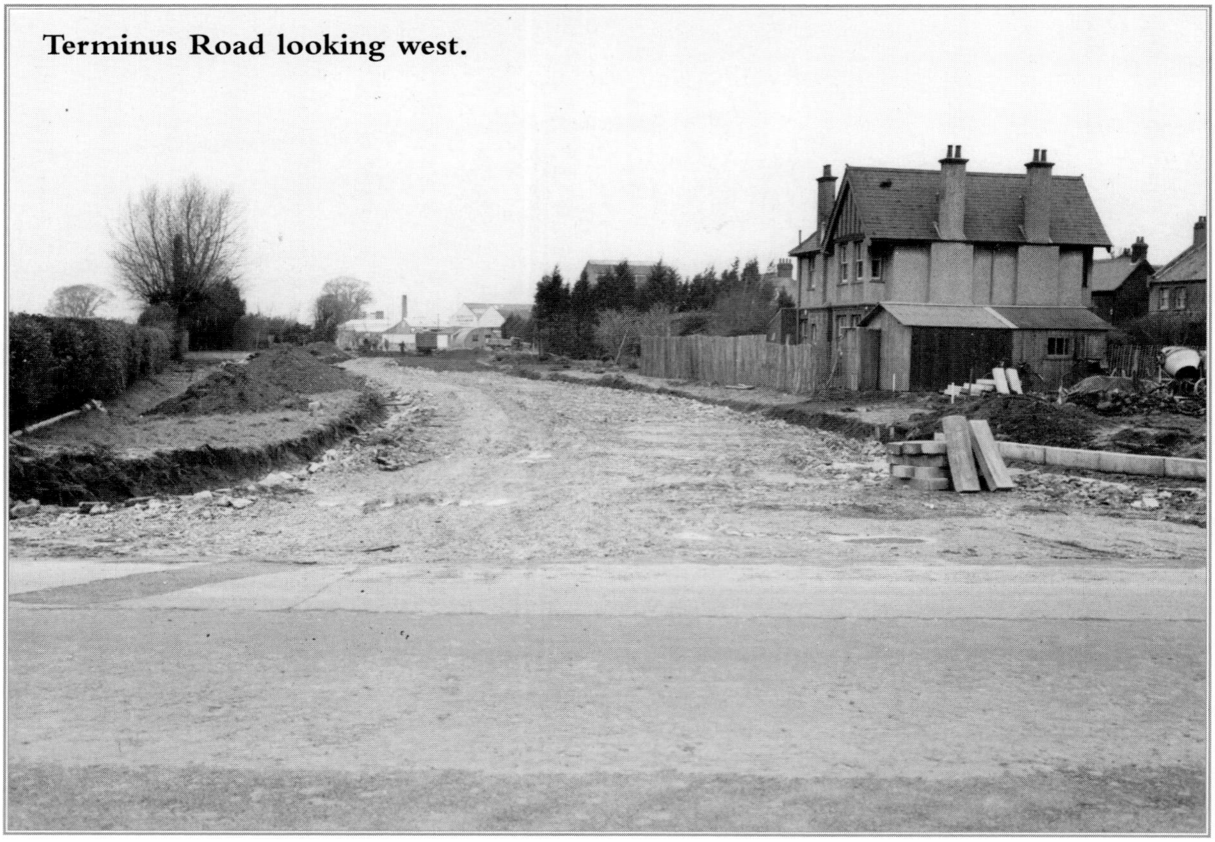

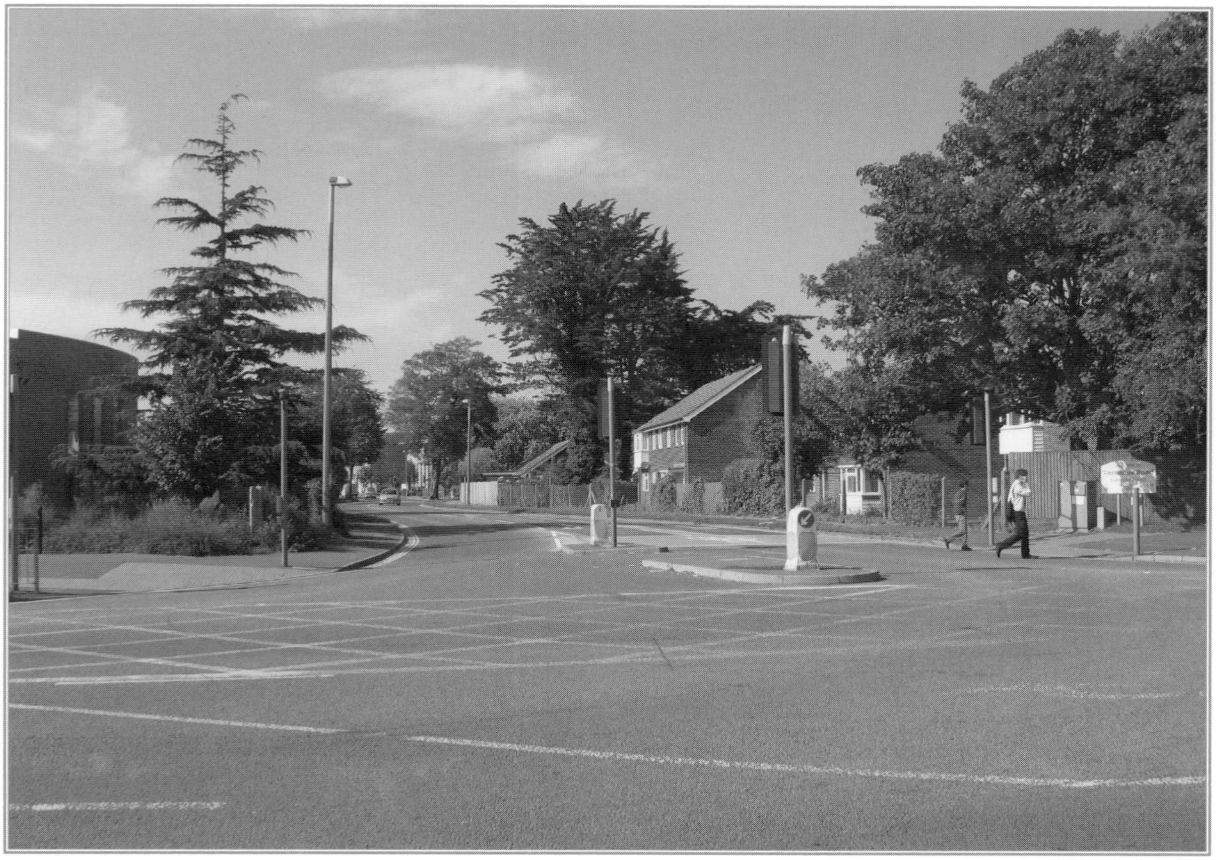

The archetypal building would have been a shopfront with a workshop to the rear and living quarters above. The 20th century saw the separation of these three elements. Terminus Road was very much part of that process, the first time that industry moved out of Chichester city centre en masse.

Industry has been followed by some of the city's leisure facilities, with the creation of the Chichester Gate development to the south of the eastern entrance to Terminus Road.

The development is home to a number of restaurants and a bowling alley. It is also home to Cineworld, Chichester, the city's first multiplex cinema. Chichester's first four cinemas, all long since gone, were situated in the city centre.

Landmarks Disappear

Terminus Road is worth looking at again from a different angle. The previous photograph showed the creation of the main industrial estate approach road looking west.

The top photograph overleaf, taken in 1946, shows the creation of the road looking east – and offers a fascinating glimpse at a collection of lost Chichester landmarks.

Chichester's first purpose-built post office was in South Street. The post office service moved to West Street in the 1930s, but the sorting office remained in South Street until 1967 when new premises were built opposite the canal basin, replacing the gasworks seen here.

Also in the older photograph is the site of R.J. Acford's, the company which used to print *The Chichester Observer.*

The tall building is Sadler's Mill, part of another important Chichester company. In 1886 Fred Sadler's father bought him a small shop and store in East Street, along with a horse and van and one employee. By 1936 Fred Sadler had built up Sadler & Co., a large business supplying seeds and agricultural supplies to the farming community.

Sadler & Co. imported artificial fertiliser and coal and exported locally grown wheat and sugar beet through Dell Quay. The business comprised a fleet of delivery vehicles, a flour mill at Westhampnett, a large store and a mill in Terminus Road and a brickyard at Chidham, though many of these activities dwindled in the years following World War Two.

Sadler & Co. maintained a city centre presence at No. 40–41 East Street until 1953 and then moved to No. 44. The site was turned into a shopping arcade in 1979. The present-day arcade, Sadler's Walk, retains the family business name. Fred Sadler died in 1961, aged 95.

Terminus Road looking east.

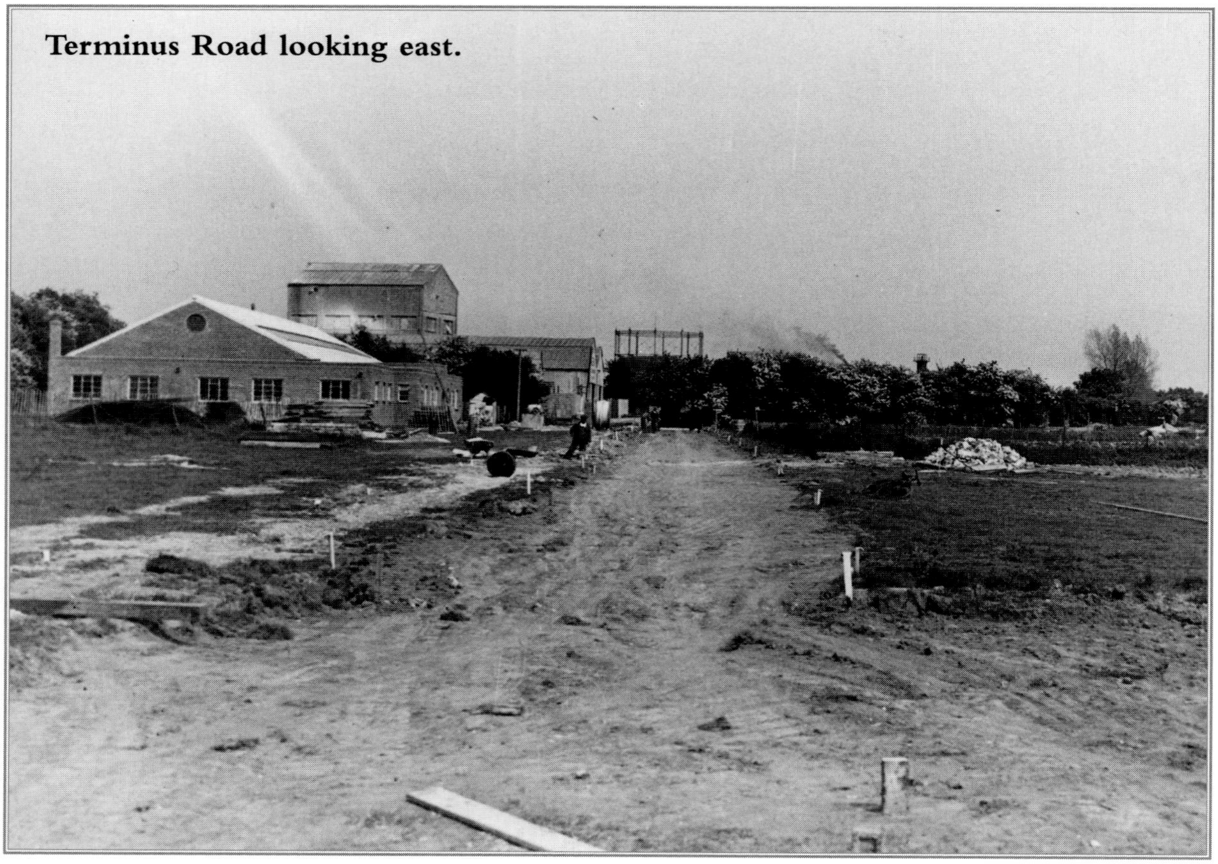

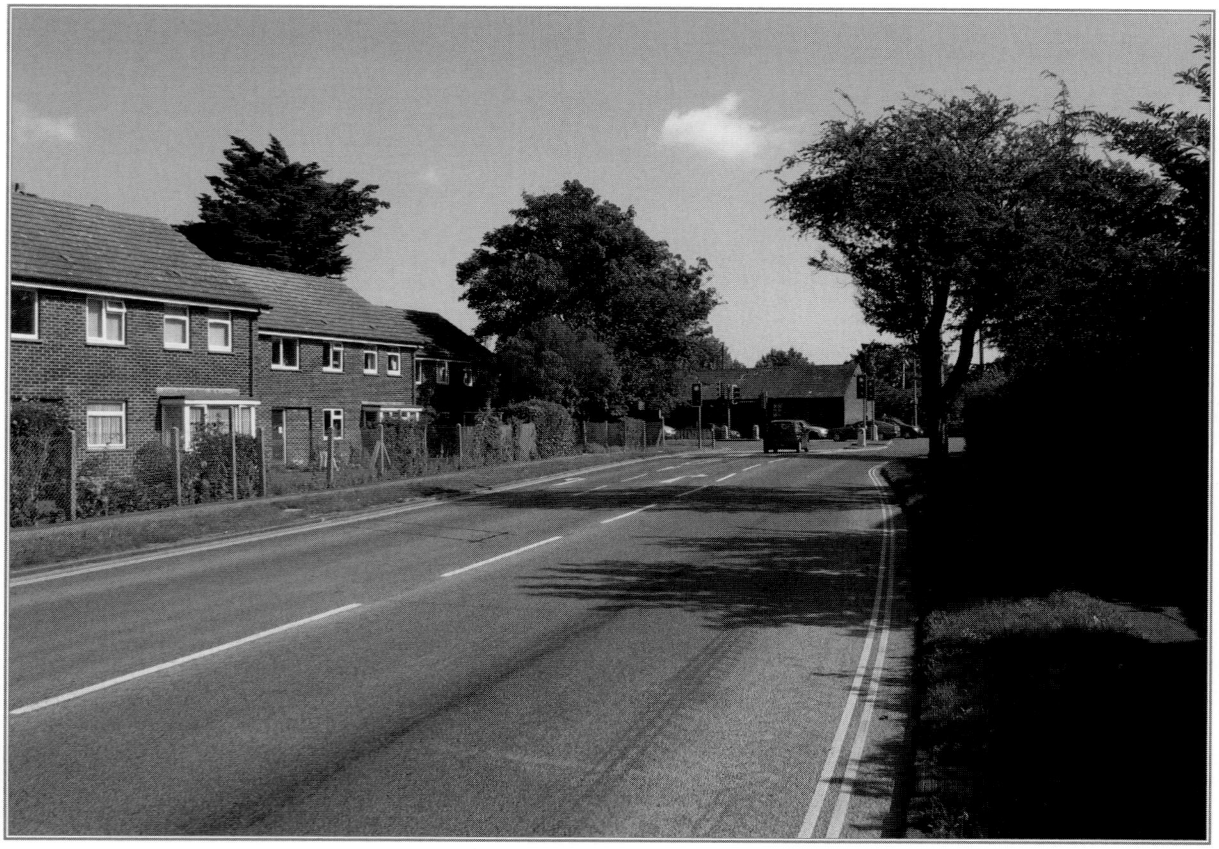

Chapter 8
Northgate

Georgian Influence

North Street's shops dwindle as you head north towards a section with its origins much more in the realms of the impressively domestic. The houses are principally 18th century.

The street embodies the brick town which Chichester became in the Georgian era. Timber-framed buildings would have been the norm in the Middle Ages, but with the dawning of the 18th century Chichester began to change dramatically, gaining many of the buildings which are so familiar now. By the end of the 18th century Chichester had largely been rebuilt, or, at the very least, refronted.

However, once you move outside the city walls, as you can see in this image, the extensions to the city are considerably more modern – as is the roundabout which now stands at the very top of North Street.

Beyond this are some of the city's institutions, including the former Royal West Sussex Hospital and, just across the road from it, Chichester Festival Theatre.

The development of the area north-west of the old North Gate is mostly 19th and 20th century. People were attracted to the area and consequently the church of St Paul was built in

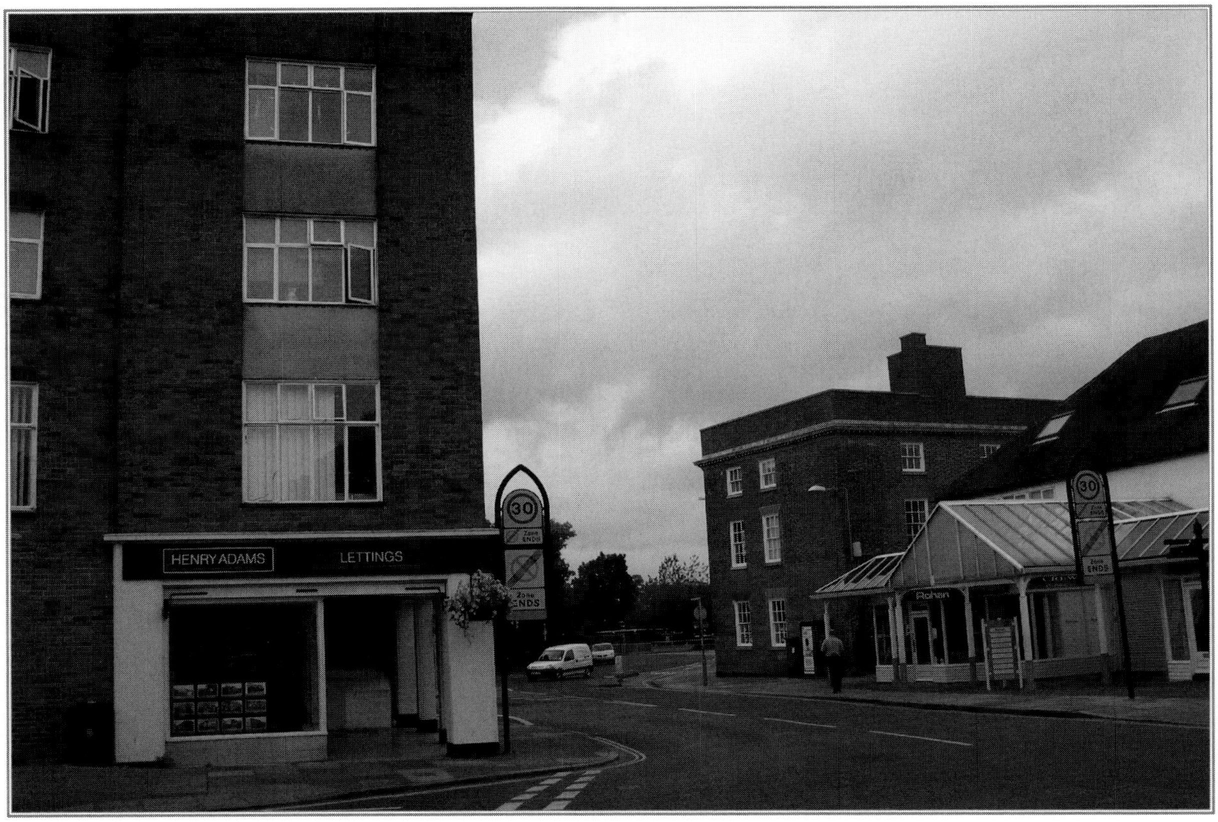

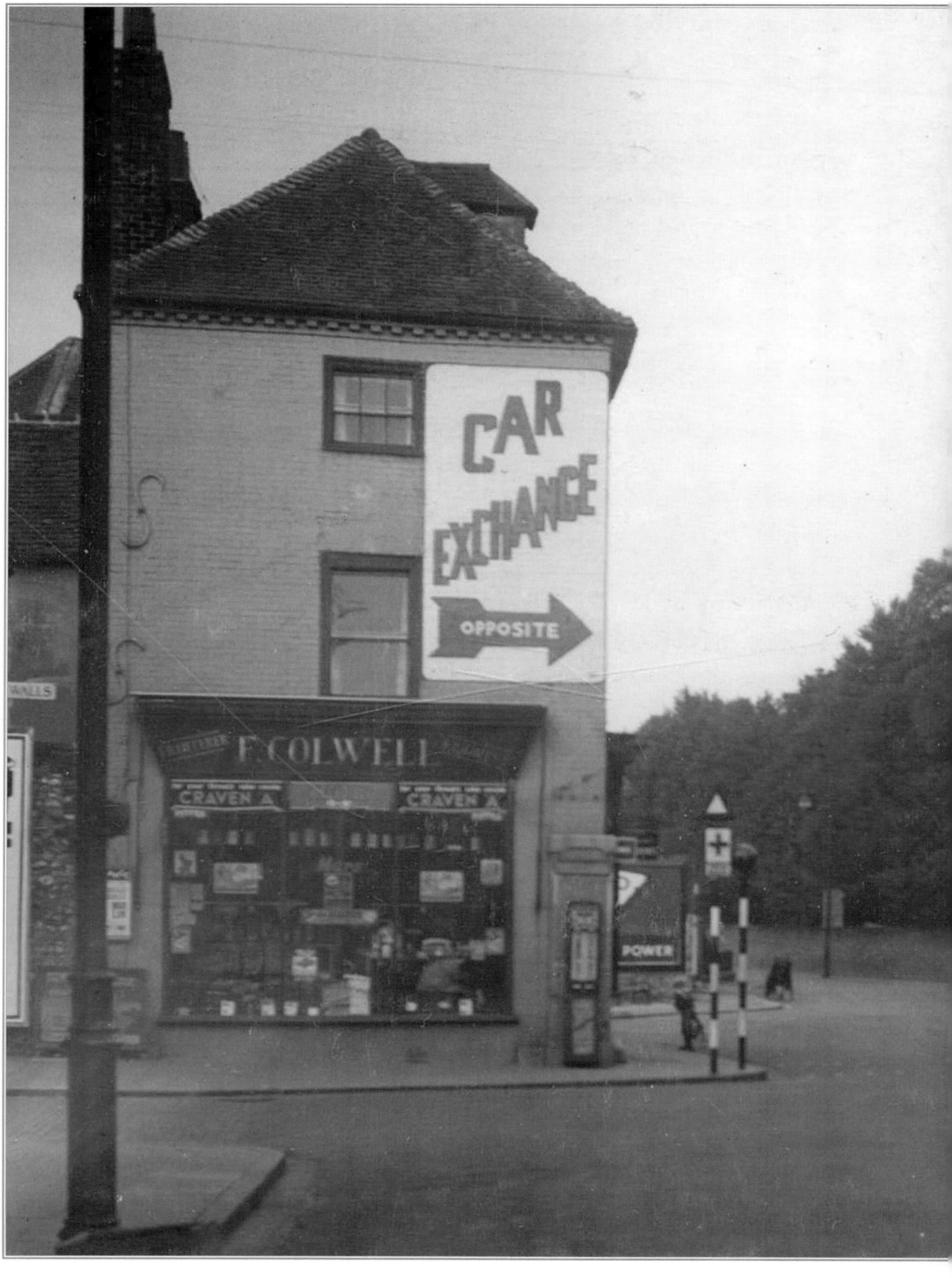
CAR
EXCHANGE
OPPOSITE
F. COLWELL
CRAVEN A
CRAVEN A
POWER

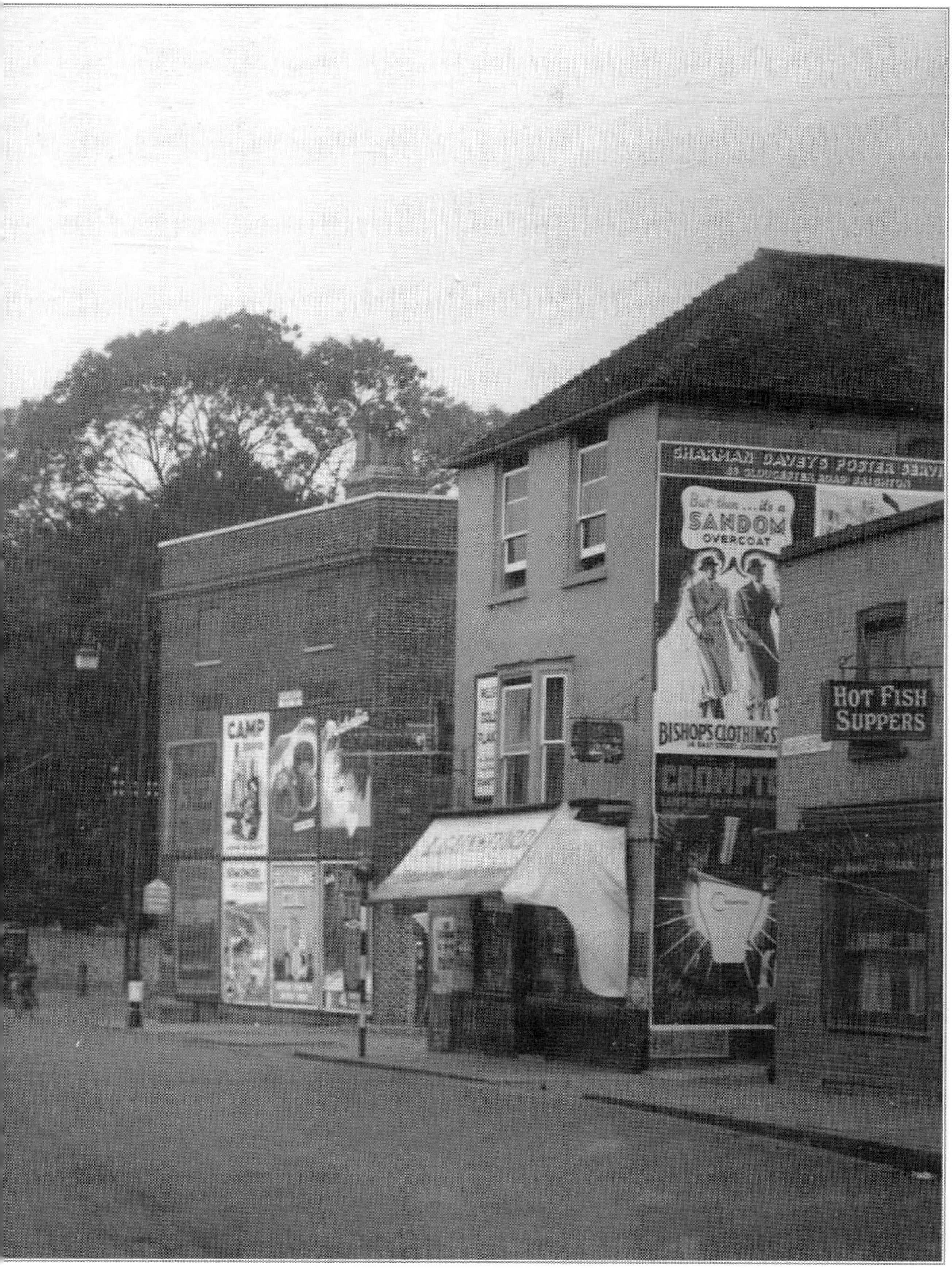
SHARMAN DAVEY'S POSTER SERVI
But then ... it's a
SANDOM
OVERCOAT
BISHOP'S CLOTHING S
CROMPT
CAMP
HOT FISH
SUPPERS

1836 on the west side of Broyle Road to accommodate the increasing population. The church now finds itself on the far side of the Northgate roundabout. A little to the north, on the opposite side of the road, was the workhouse, originally built as the Hospital of St Bartholomew, or the Cawley Almshouses.

The fish and chip restaurant seen on the right of the older picture closed in 1985. The building that housed Colwell's, on the corner of North Walls, was replaced in 1961. On the left today can be seen Henry Adams estate agents. On the right there is now a shopping arcade.

Before the Roundabout

Chichester's Northgate roundabout is one of the city's busiest, not least because it is home to the city's fire station, which opened on 4 November 1965. There is little sign, however, of things to come in this image of where the city's fire station would one day stand, just north of the site of the city's long-gone mediaeval North Gate.

Part of Chichester's pleasing symmetry is that North Street, East Street, South Street and West Street each had their own gate. However, historians are forced to admit that little is known about these four ancient entrances to the city.

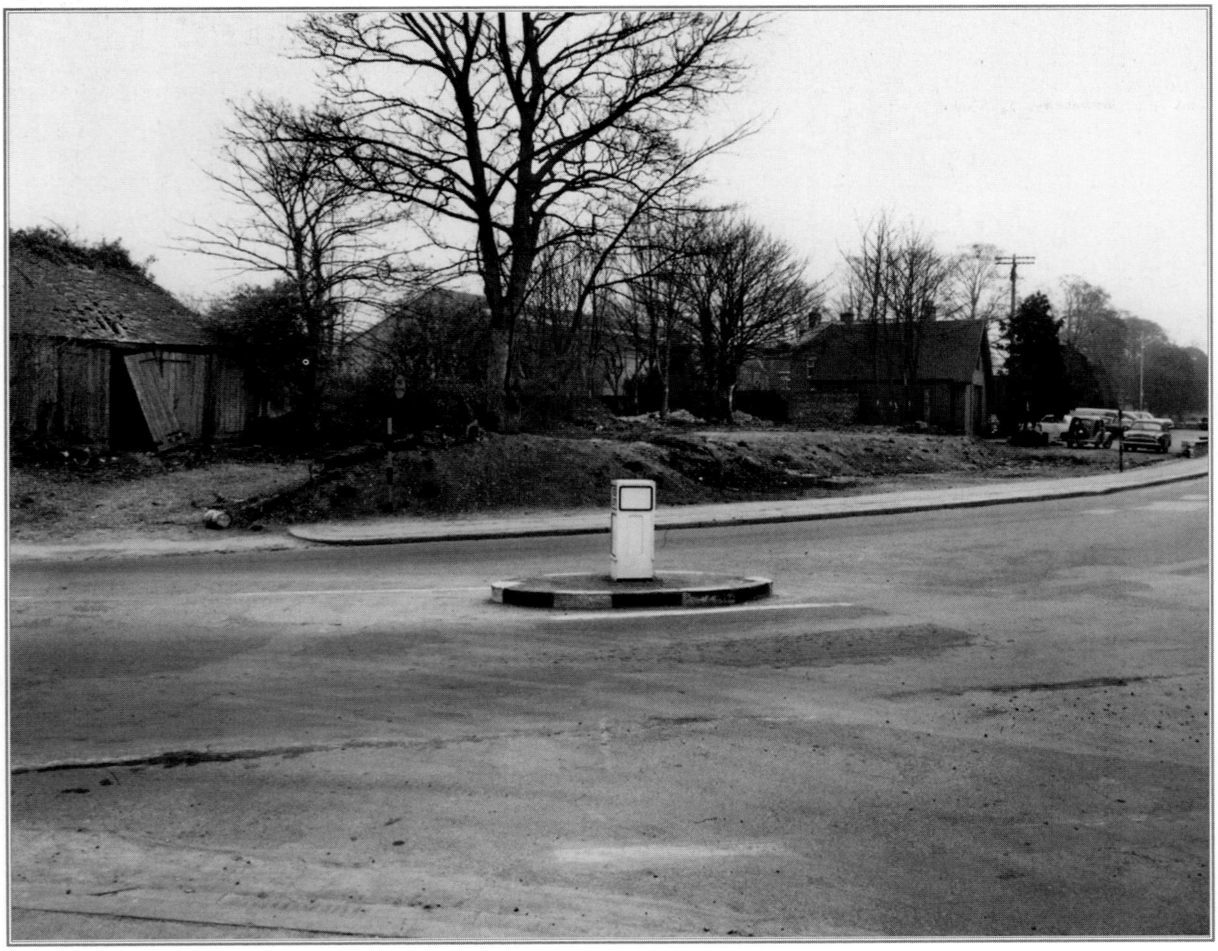

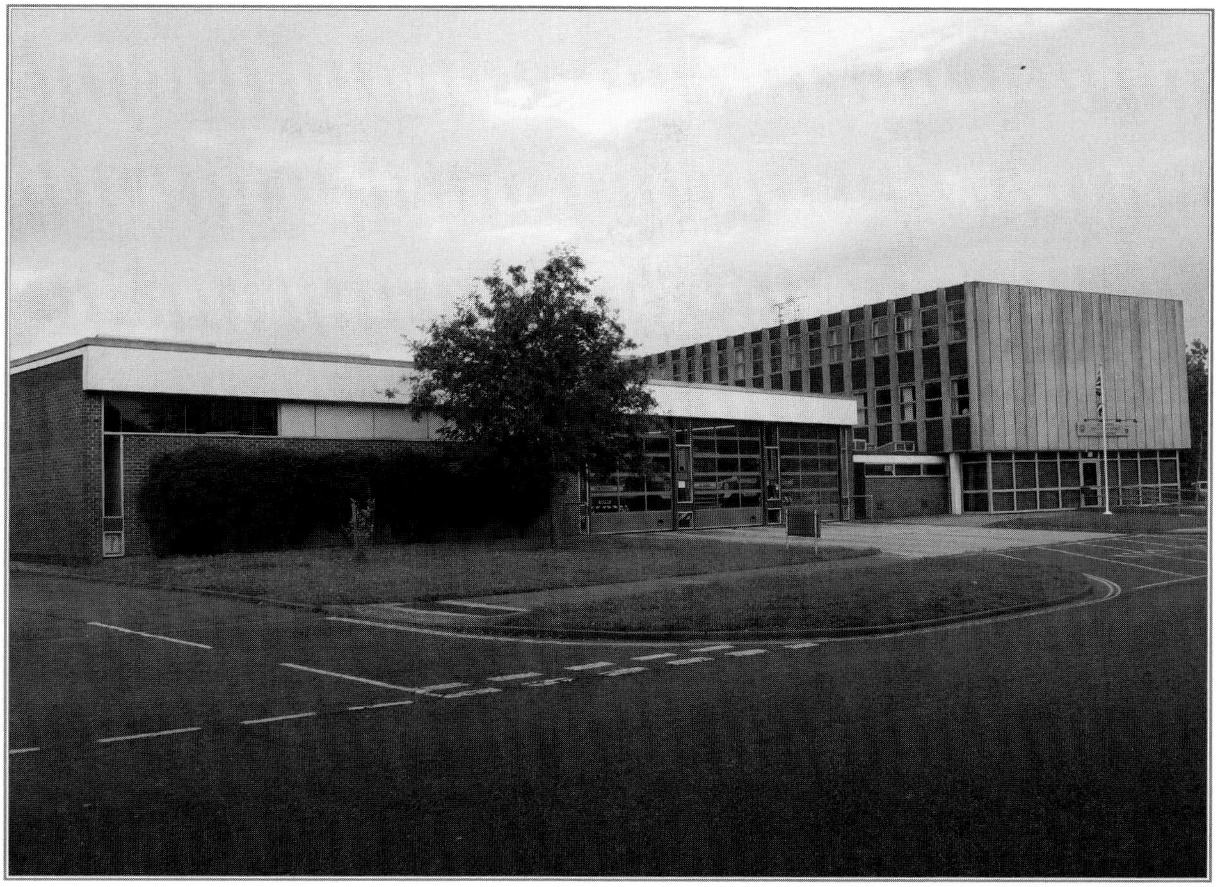

The North, West and South Gates were taken down in 1772–73, it seems, but the East Gate lived on a little longer, coming down in 1783. It supported the city gaol which was then rebuilt on the south side of it.

Over the centuries, for various landmark royal occasions, imitation gates have been erected as part of the fun but the stories behind the real gates largely elude us. In the case of North Gate, it seems the structure boasted the Chapel of Our Lady upon the North Gate in its upper storey.

One thing is for sure though, and that is if you passed through North Gate it would not have been long before you reached woodland. This area was the last to be developed. The Broyle, just beyond it, was farmland belonging to the king.

The Royal West Sussex Hospital

Standing back from the road in its own attractive green grounds is another Chichester gem, the former Royal West Sussex Hospital. Now offering elegant living accommodation, the building is set on the leafy west side of Broyle Road and is positively steeped in history. Some people say that it was here that the stethoscope was first used in this country.

The hospital began as a dispensary for the sick and the poor in 1784 before becoming the West Sussex Infirmary. Extensive additions followed and it was reopened by King George V in 1913 as the Royal West Sussex Hospital, a memorial to King Edward VII.

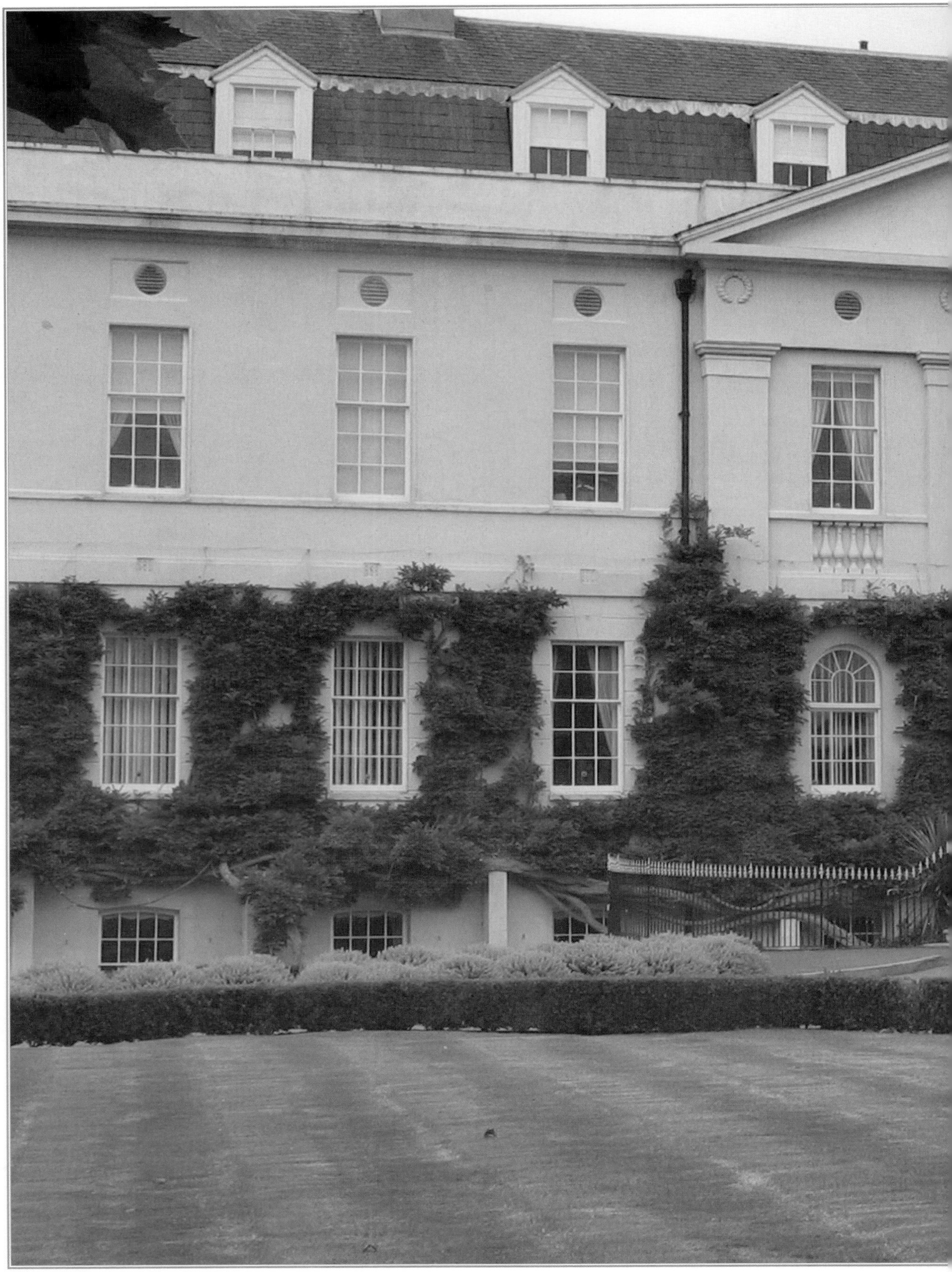

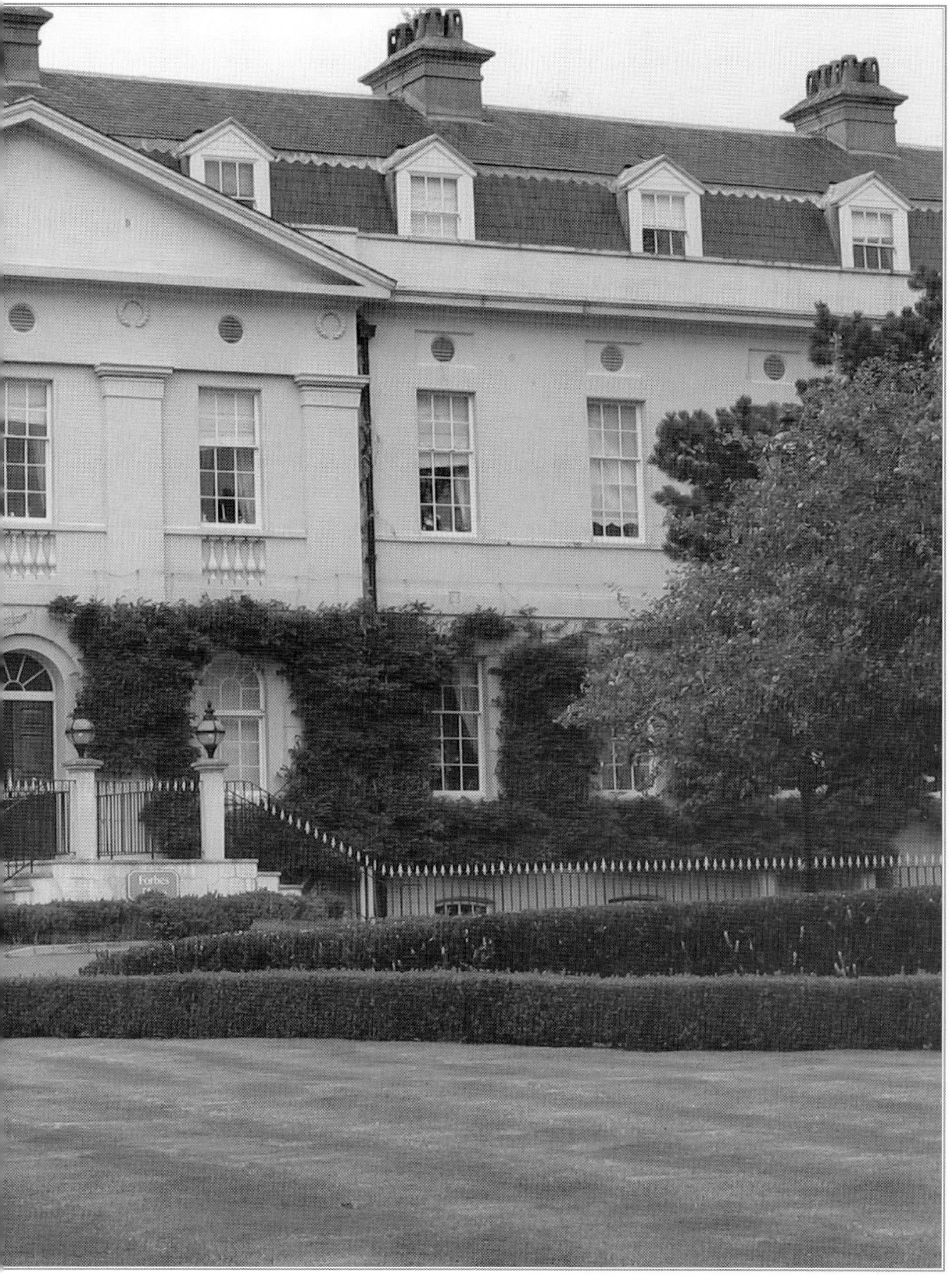

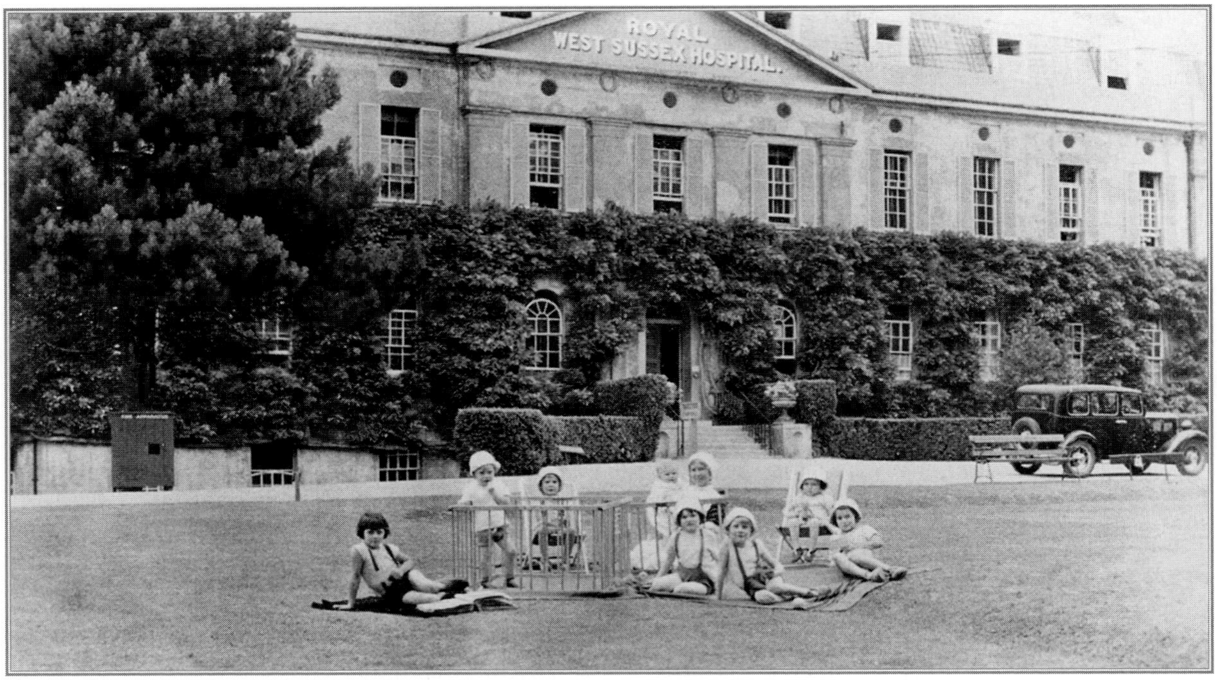

The present building of stuccoed brick with a slate mansard roof was originally begun in 1825, offering a main façade of two storeys with a basement and an attic lit by dormers. For years it functioned alongside the current St Richard's Hospital half a mile away.

The Royal West Sussex at Chichester was the district general hospital for West Sussex, formed from the amalgamation of the Royal West Sussex Hospital with St Richard's Hospital, and it was opened in the mid-1930s as a long-stay hospital by the old West Sussex County Council.

Gradually St Richard's took over and the Royal West Sussex closed down. Having royally served the community, the Royal West Sussex Hospital was converted into accommodation.

Chichester Festival Theatre

For nearly 50 years Chichester Festival Theatre has been at the heart of our country's theatrical life – a remarkable building with a remarkable history.

Over the years there has barely been an actor of note who has not trodden the boards here. Alan Bates, Julie Christie, Alan Bennett and Kenneth Branagh have been lured to the CFT stage; so too have Joan Collins, Ingrid Bergman, Judi Dench, Edith Evans, Alec Guinness, John Gielgud and Anthony Hopkins.

Add to the list Derek Jacobi, Joan Plowright, Diana Rigg, Harry Secombe and Maggie Smith, and you have yet to scratch the surface – a fact which is in itself a tribute to the singular man who put Chichester on the theatrical map.

The theatre's founder and driving force was the late Leslie Evershed-Martin, a man who made the impossible happen – a story he told in *The Impossible Theatre*, an account of the CFT's earliest days which he wrote to mark the theatre's 10th anniversary.

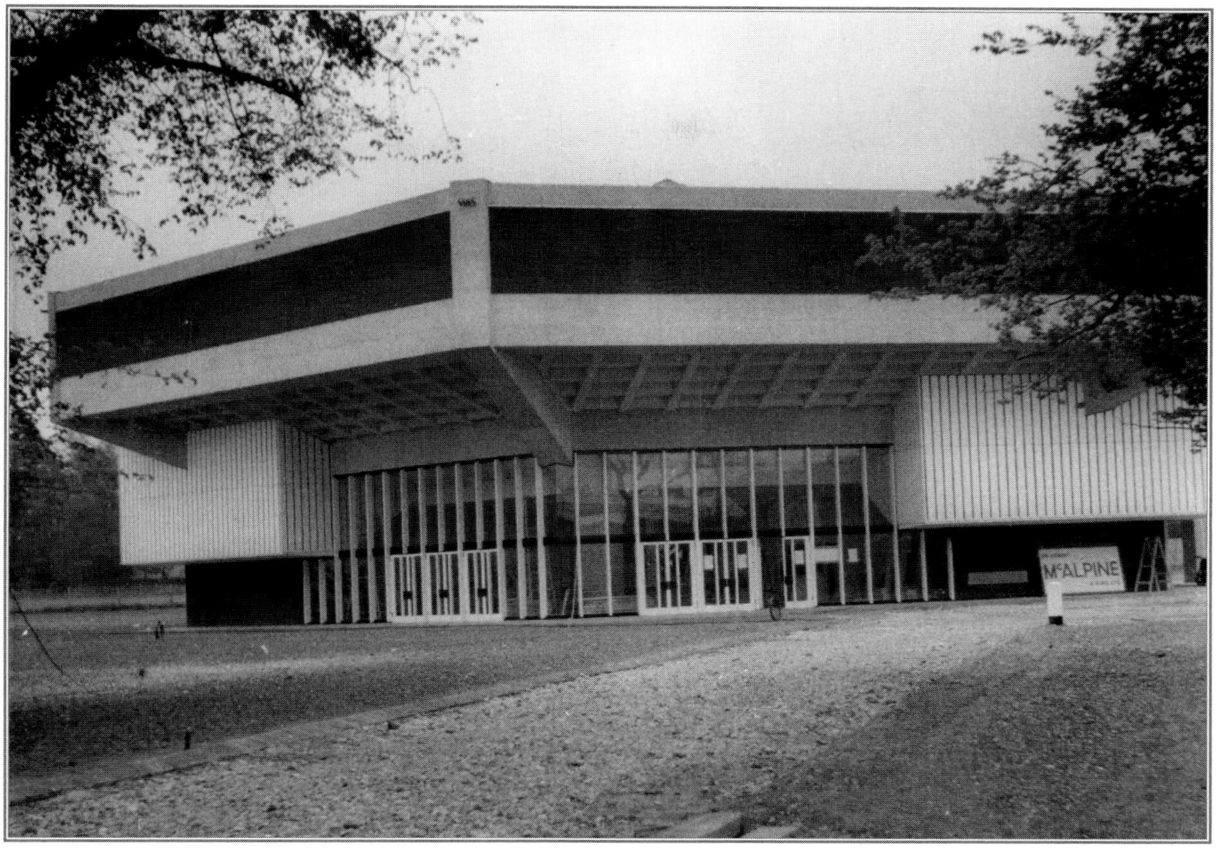
McALPINE

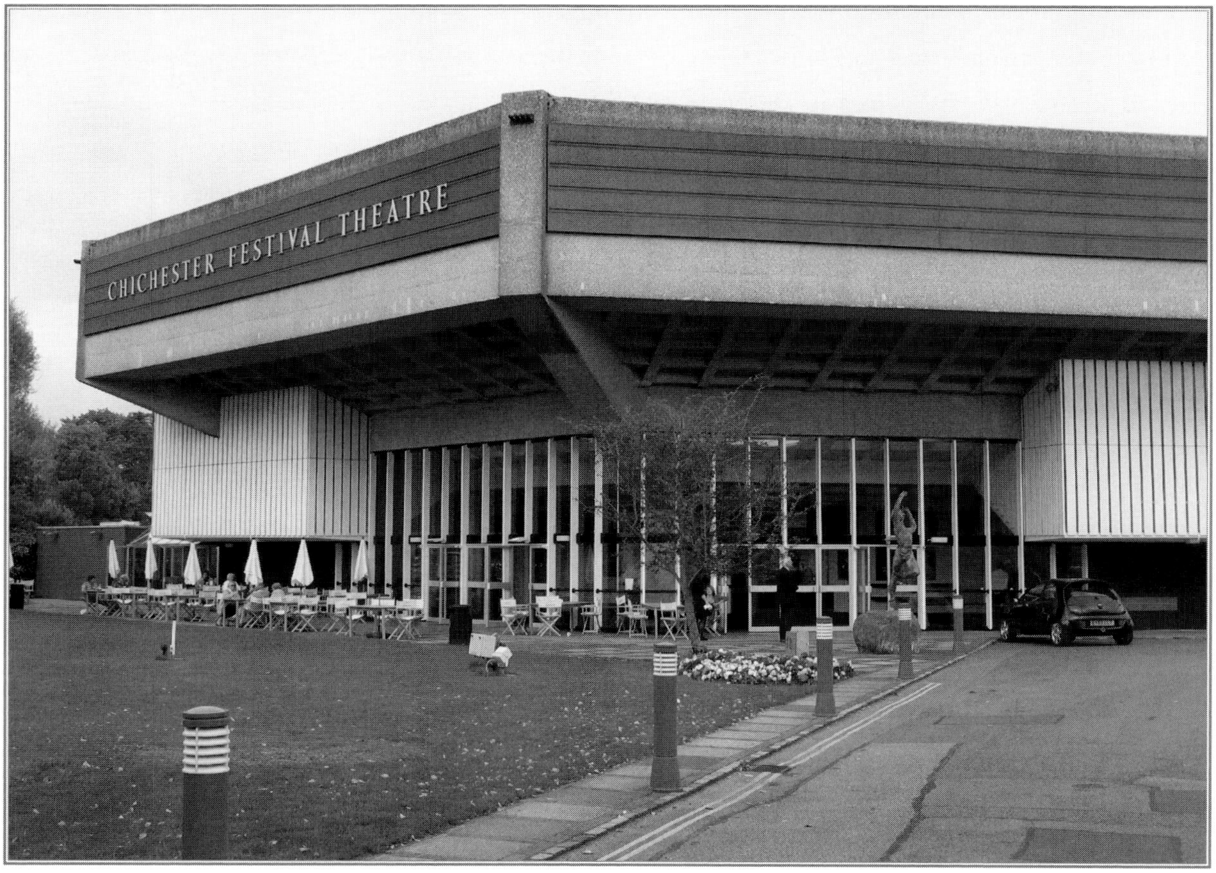
CHICHESTER FESTIVAL THEATRE

Hugely determined, Evershed-Martin galvanised an entire community to raise more than £100,000. Inspired by the Stratford Ontario Shakespeare Memorial Theatre in Canada, he created the first modern theatre in this country to have an open thrust stage.

Evershed-Martin was an opthalmist who saw the stars and brought them to Chichester. His masterstroke was to approach Sir Laurence Olivier as the venue's first artistic director. 'The Sussex Downs will shout with joy to welcome you', he told him. And they did.

The building was finished on 3 May 1962, and on 4 June Olivier welcomed the actors to Chichester for the venue's very first season – a nine-week festival featuring performers including Sir Lewis Casson, Fay Compton, Joan Greenwood, Keith Michell, John Neville, Joan Plowright, Sir Michael Redgrave, Athene Seyler and Dame Sybil Thorndike, with Olivier himself directing three plays and appearing in the last two.

It was the most glittering of starts.

The older image on page 119 shows the Chichester Festival Theatre shortly before its opening in 1962. Since then the CFT has suffered difficult moments at various times in its history, but it is currently enjoying a new golden age under the present artistic director Jonathan Church.

The 2008 season saw a highly acclaimed revival of *The Music Man* and the premiere of the stage version of *Calendar Girls*.

A Military Past

An important chapter in Chichester's history came to an end in 2005 when the Royal Military Police marched through these doors for the last time.

A barracks no longer, the site now awaits redevelopment. It is seen here in the older photograph in 1959.

For well over 200 years Chichester Barracks had been a military site. Since 1964 it had been the home of the Royal Military Police.

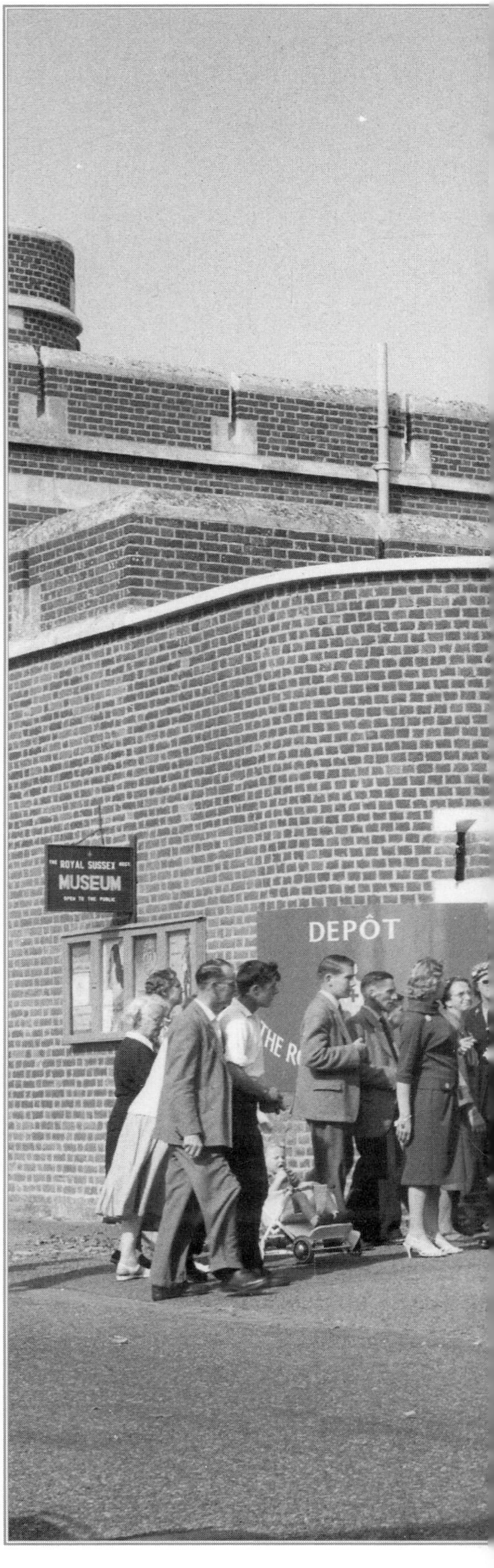

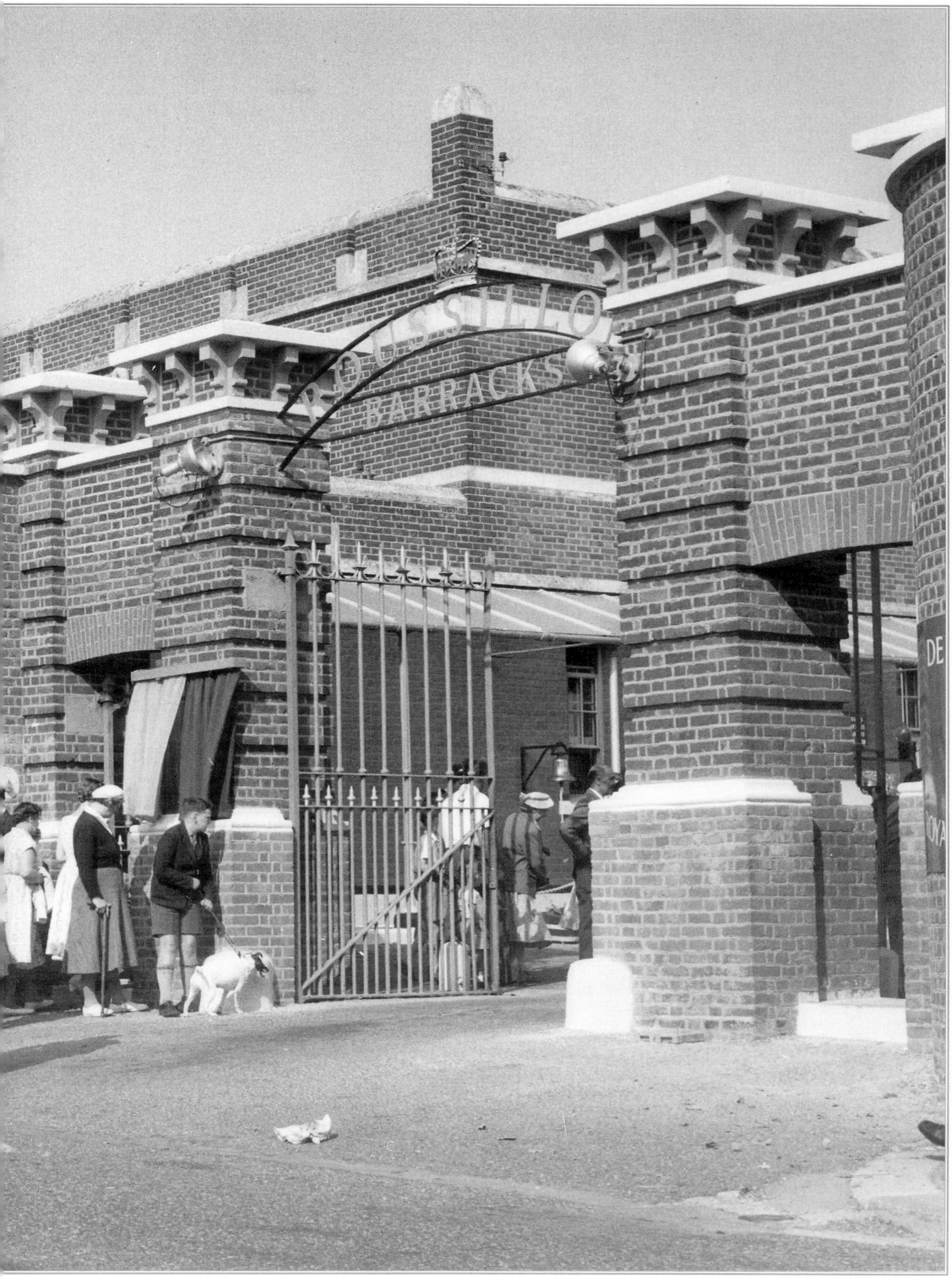
ROUSSILLON
BARRACKS

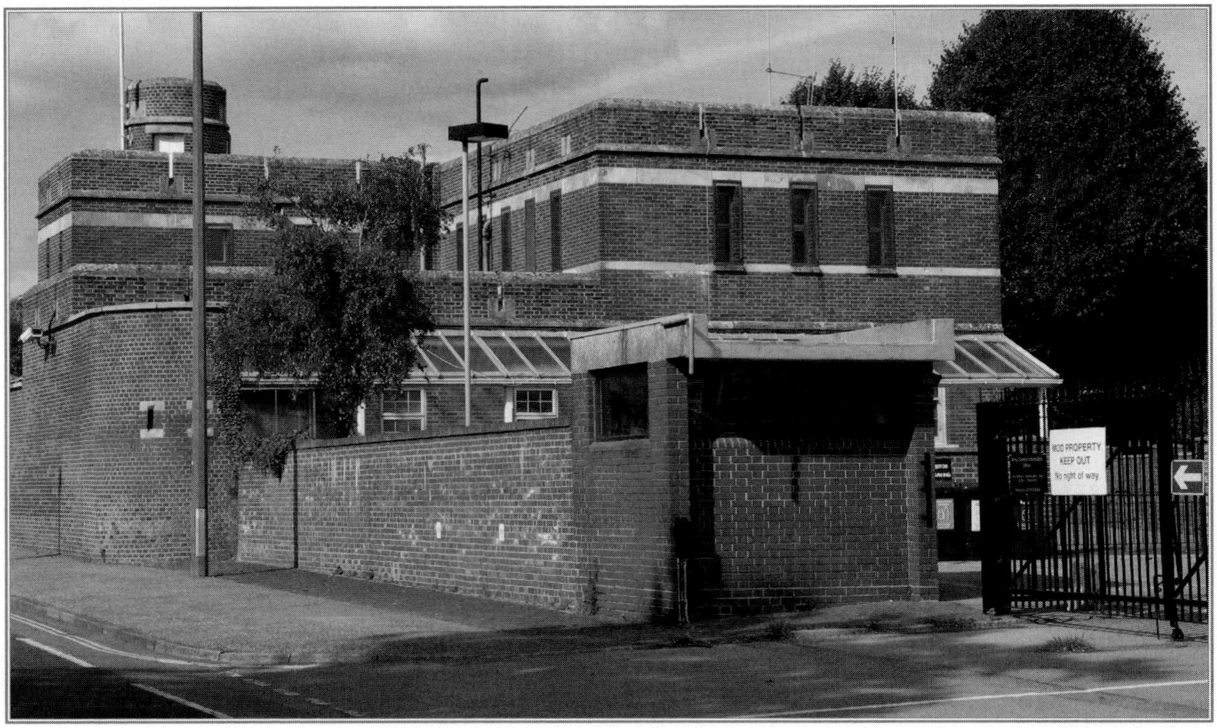

The barracks was named Roussillon barracks in 1958, a name taken from the Royal Roussillon Regiment of France which was overwhelmed by the 35th Regiment at Quebec in 1759 and whose white plume was later incorporated into the badge of the Royal Sussex Regiment (35th of Foot). The Royal Sussex vacated the barracks in 1960.

The barracks occupied an important location in Chichester, strategically situated on a piece of high ground to the north of the city.

During the Civil War, General Sir William Waller used the same ground to form his troops prior to the siege of Chichester in 1642. It was here that he set up his artillery. The cannon fell short and so he moved his men round to just outside Westgate to attack the royalists within the city walls. Later, he attacked from the east, causing severe damage to the Eastgate area.

Various records show that the barracks were built between 1795 and 1813 at a total cost of £76,167, on land bought from the Bishop of Chichester. Church marriage registers show that the military were active on site from the mid-1700s. The barrack accommodation at this time was tented but the story goes that French POWs were employed on the construction of some of the first and more permanent wooden huts in 1803.

However, it was not until 1875 that the main building took place, which included several brick buildings and numerous new wooden huts to serve as accommodation and offices.

The only remaining buildings from this period are the keep, the regimental headquarters, and the RMP chapel, originally built as a schoolhouse. Parts of the original barracks wall still survive. The remnants of the original stables were removed in 1994.

Chapter 9
Priory Park

Chichester at Play

It cannot have been easy playing tennis wearing a hat and with skirts down to your ankles, but these ladies are elegance personified in this richly evocative image of Chichester at play a century ago.

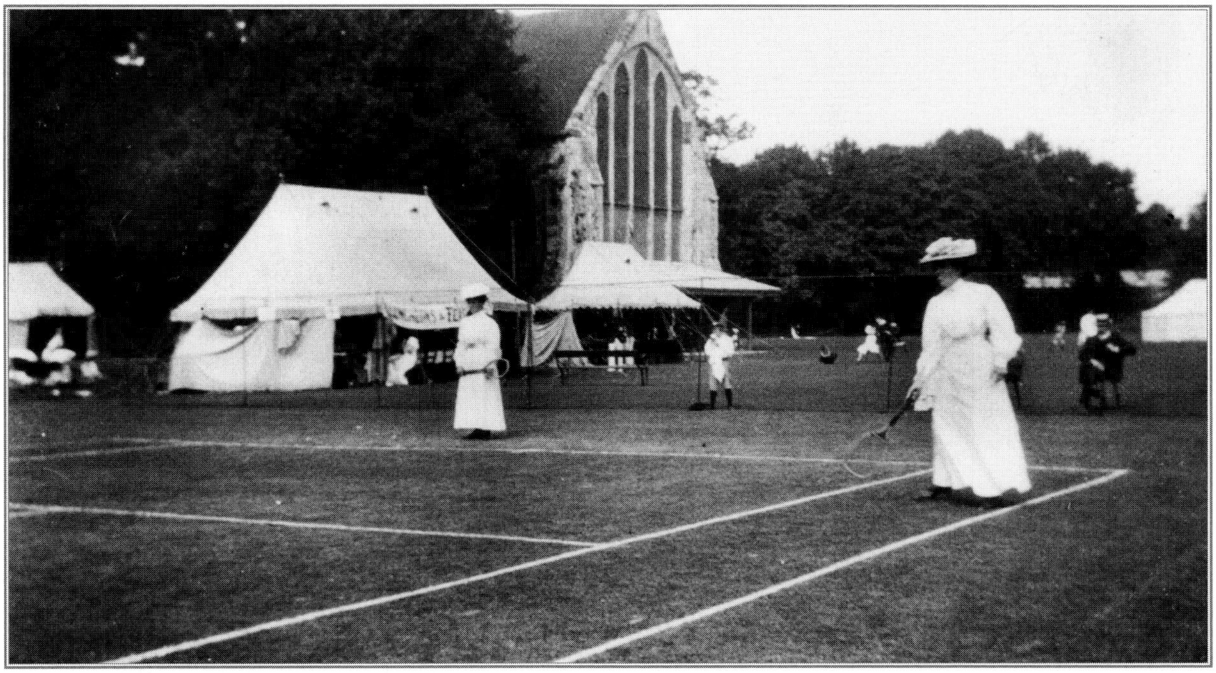

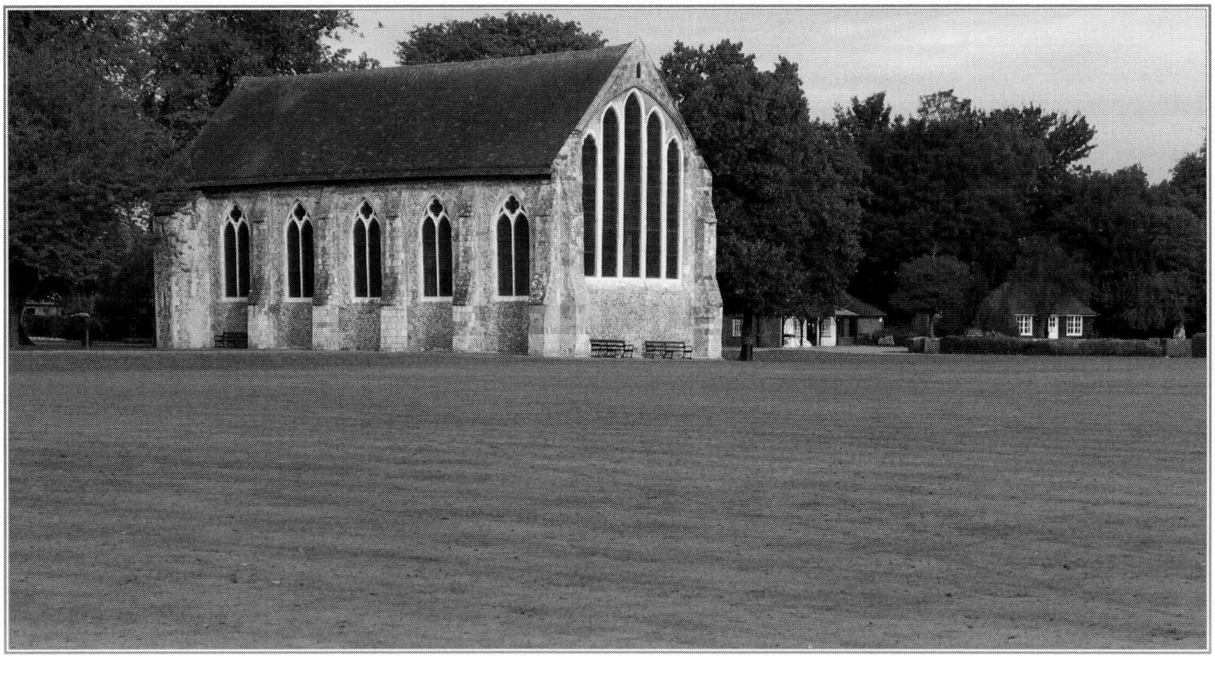

Late Victorian or perhaps early Edwardian, the image was taken in Priory Park in the city's north-east quadrant.

Priory Park remains a place of leisure still but all the old formalities have long since gone. It is a great place to kick a ball, throw a frisbee, exhaust your friends at rounders or simply chill out over a sandwich as you snatch 20 minutes of peace away from the office.

Bounded on the north and east by the city walls and their rampart, Priory Park is a place where Chichester unwinds. It is also home to no fewer than three scheduled monuments – the walls, the Guildhall and the remains of a Norman motte.

The property was acquired in 1824 by the Duke of Richmond and in 1851 was held in trust as a Public Recreation Ground. In 1918 the seventh duke presented it to the city for a pleasure ground called Priory Park.

It is now managed by Chichester District Council and, like the Market Cross, it is invariably at the heart of Chichester's big community celebrations. Coronations and jubilees have been celebrated here, and in more recent times it has become the home to Chichester's hugely popular Real Ale and Jazz Festival.

Every July an impressive marquee is erected, real ale served and the park rocks to some of the biggest names in the music business. Recent years have seen The Pretenders, James Brown, 10cc, Simple Minds, Blondie and Squeeze among the performers.

A Poet Accused

It was in this building (right) that Chichester put arguably one of the nation's greatest poets in the dock – and then sensibly acquitted him.

The Guildhall in Priory Park was home to the county court of quarter sessions, the court before which William Blake was brought in January 1804 on a charge of sedition.

Then living in Sussex, the man who wrote 'And did those feet in ancient time, walk upon England's mountains green,' was accused of saying rather more treasonable words in the Fox Inn at Felpham.

The case was dismissed but provides an interesting footnote to the rich history of one of Chichester's ancient monuments.

The Franciscans came to Chichester in the early 13th century. Their first friary was in St Martin's, but in 1269 they moved to the site of the old castle in Priory Park.

The church would probably have consisted of the existing chancel, possibly a small central tower and a great preaching nave with aisles. To the north of the nave would have been the cloisters and around these would have been the friars' living quarters.

In October 1538 the monastery was dissolved by King Henry VIII who then gave the site to the mayor and citizens of Chichester. Henry then sold the friary church to the city, which became the town hall or Guildhall.

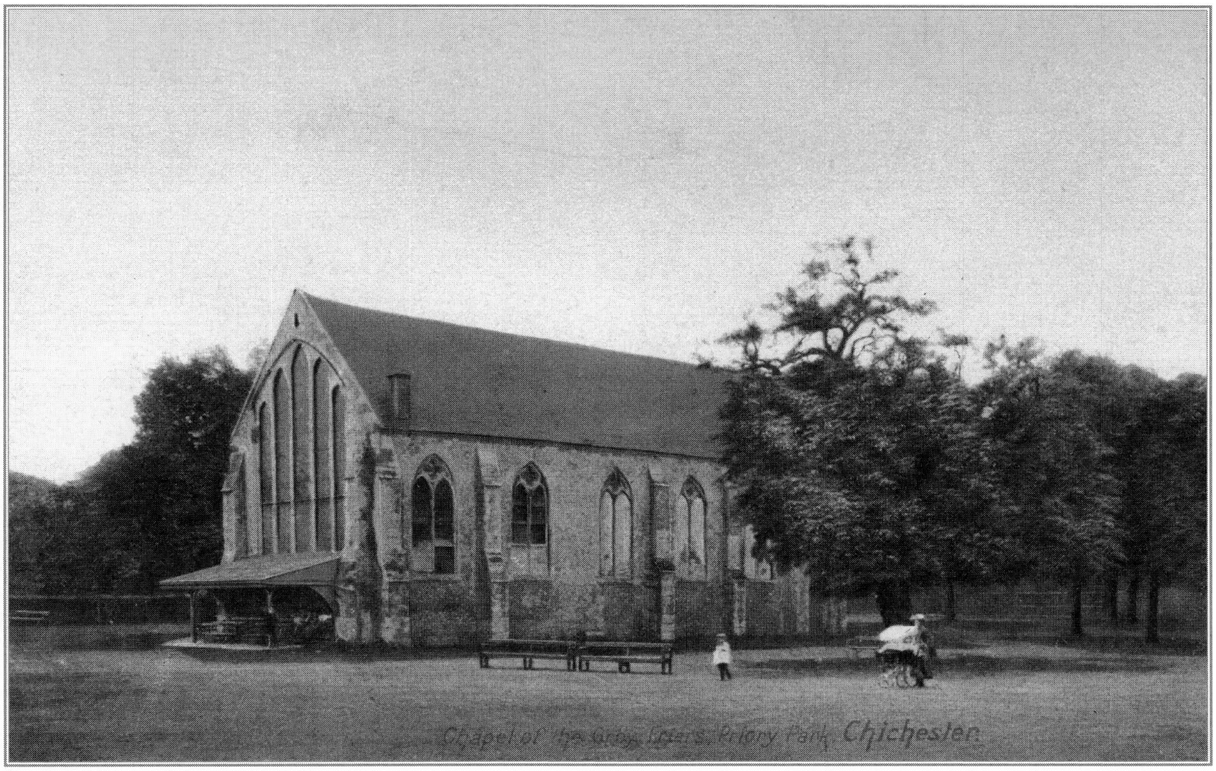

The building housed Chichester's museum from the mid-1940s until 1963 when the current museum was opened in Little London. The Guildhall remains part of the district museum service and is open to the public on Saturdays during the summer.

The older image shows the Guildhall probably some time between 1890 and 1910.

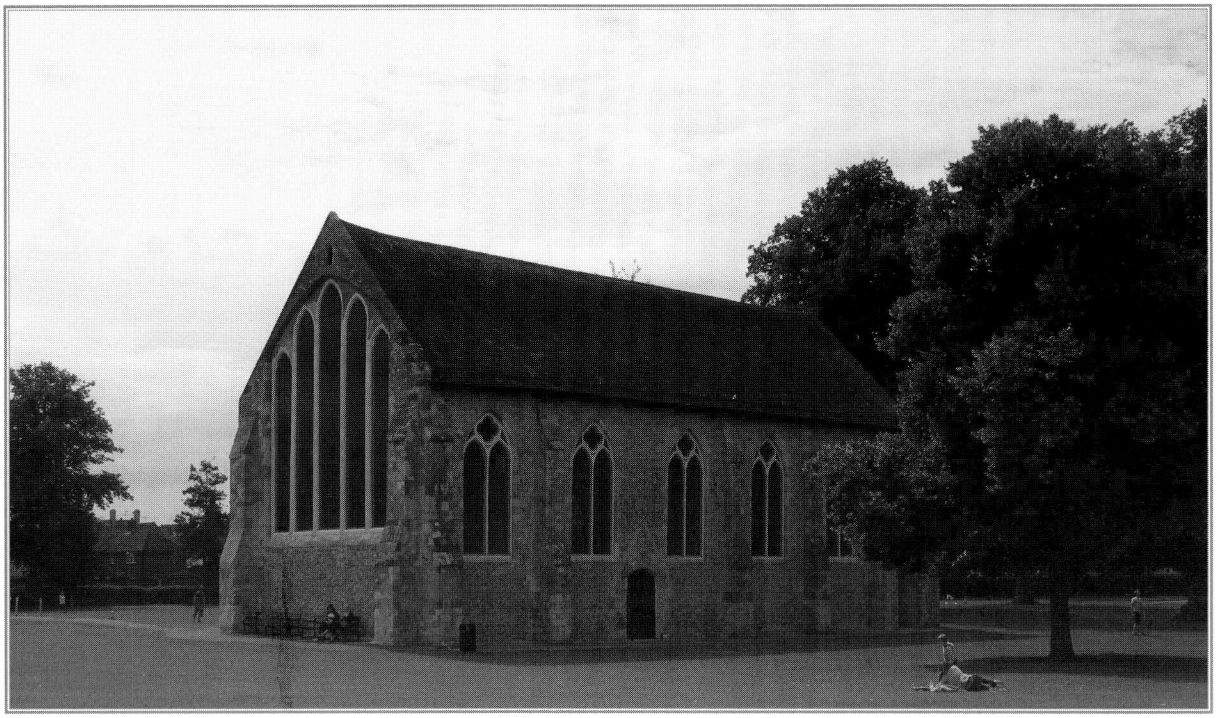

Owzat!

Sussex is a county steeped in cricket, and for many years Chichester's Priory Park was one of the grounds used by the county cricket club.

However, declining attendances in the years immediately following World War Two spelt the end for a proud tradition.

The county games played in Priory Park in 1950 proved to be Chichester's final county cricket week. The last opponents were Glamorgan and Oxford University. Neither of the games was exciting enough to rescue county cricket in Chichester.

Cox scored a century in the first innings for Sussex against Oxford in a total of 384. The students were dismissed for 206 in their first innings, but second time round their openers piled on 231 for the first wicket, as the team rallied to declare at 394–7. Sussex then stumbled to 136–5 as the match petered out into a draw.

The older photograph here shows first-class cricket in the city in 1949, a year before the end.

Cricket is still played in Priory Park, albeit at a lower level. Chichester Priory Park CC celebrated its 150th anniversary in 2001.

Cricket became established in Sussex during the 17th century. The earliest village matches pre-date the English Civil War.

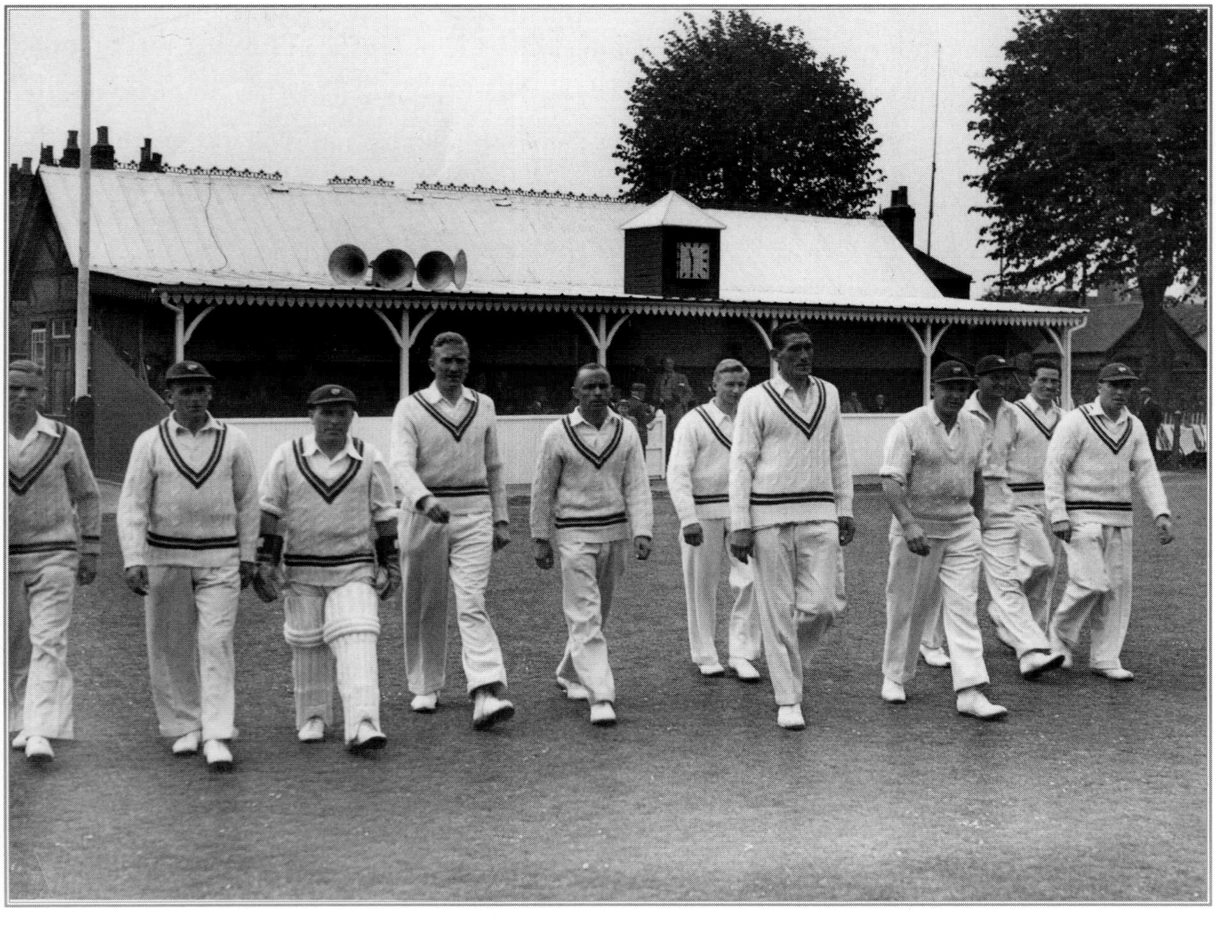

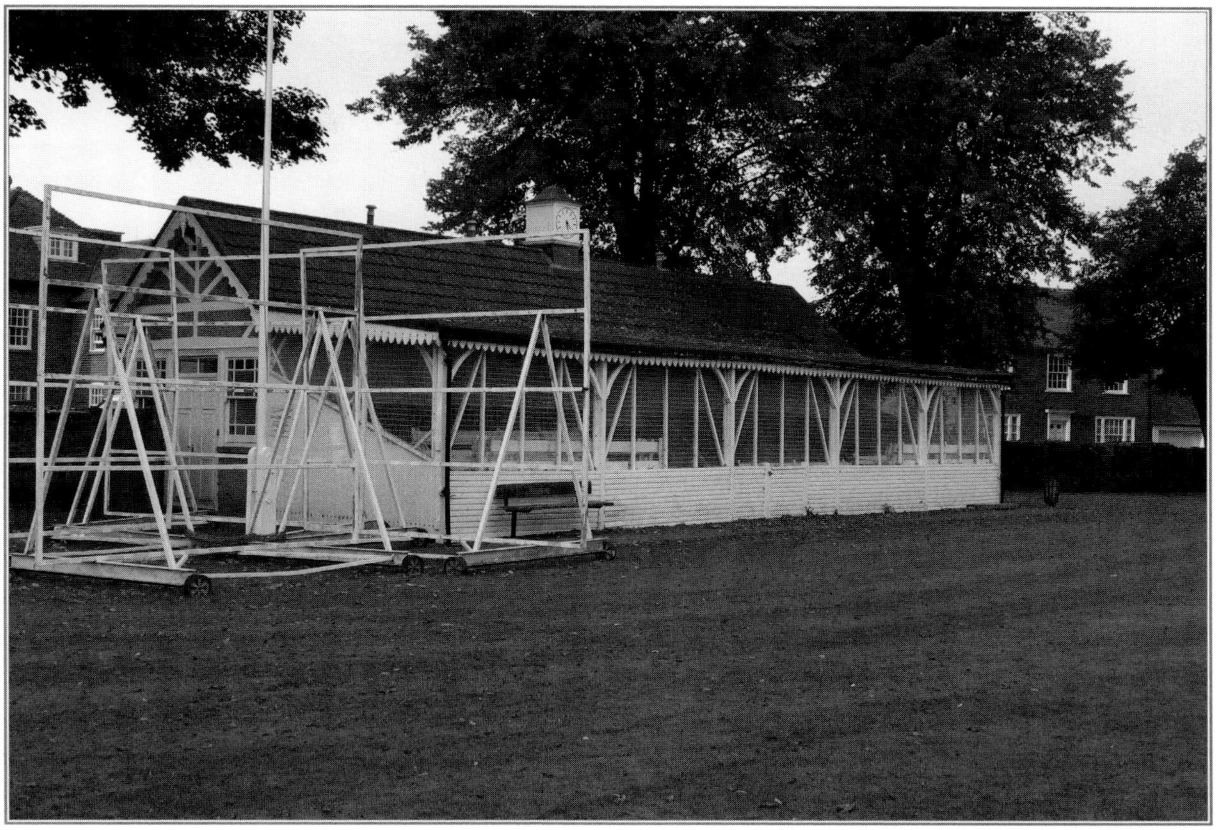

Matches involving the two great Sussex patrons Charles Lennox, second Duke of Richmond, and Sir William Gage, seventh Baronet, were first recorded in 1725, with the earliest use of Sussex in a match title occurring in 1729 – after which there was a long wait for cricketing glory.

It was not until 2003, after more than 100 years of trying, that Sussex won its first ever official County Championship, a feat which inspired the county squad to make up for lost time. They repeated their success in 2006 and 2007.

CHAPTER 10
CINEMAS

The Olympia Electric Theatre

One of the saddest then and now comparisons you will find in Chichester is the former Olympia cinema, the building the city forgot.

Imagine the excitement when the Olympia Electric Theatre opened its doors in 1910. Imagine the buzz which the cinema generated, alongside the roller-skating rink next door.

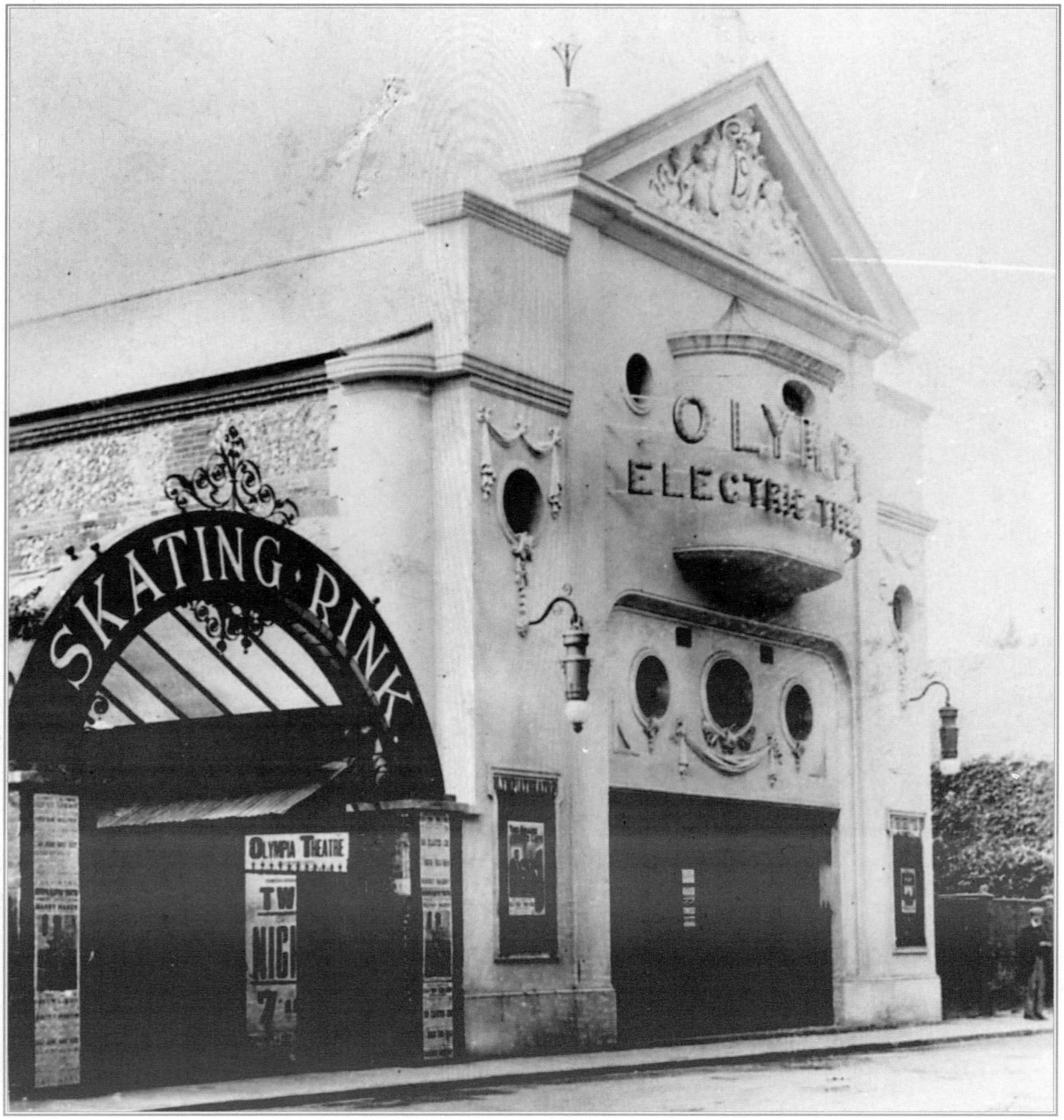

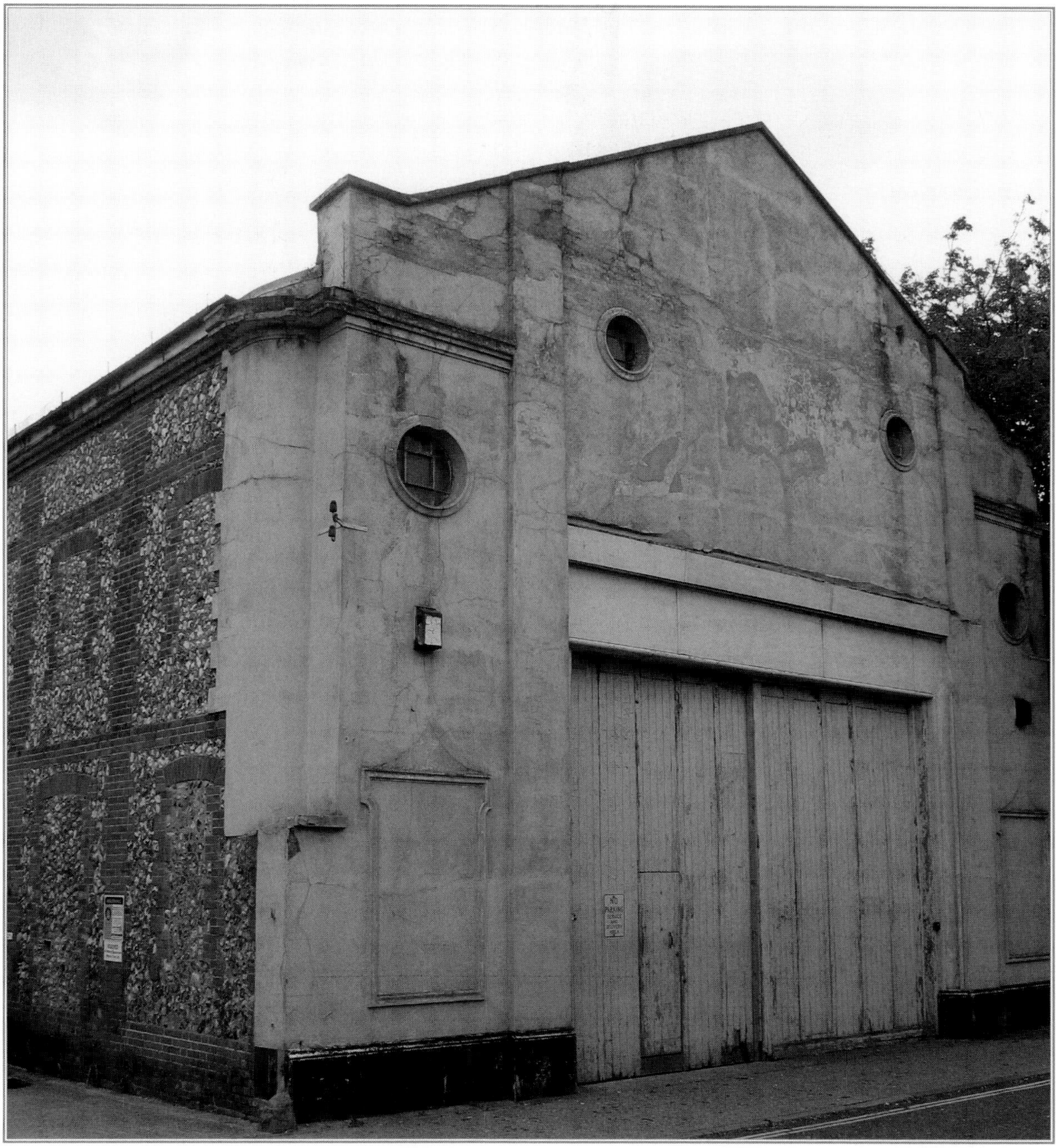

Look at it now, stranded on the Northgate roundabout, cut off from the city it served so well, neglected and forlorn, relegated to a mundane role as a storehouse.

Britain's first cinema opened in Islington, north London, in 1901. The Olympia Electric Theatre in Chichester was not far behind. A hundred years ago it was ornately decorated as the photograph on the left shows, a proud building and a first for Chichester. There is little evidence of its elegance in the way it looks now.

Advertisements lauded it 'the most comfortable and up-to-date Electric Palace in the neighbourhood', but in truth the decline set in not much more than a decade after it opened when a fire ripped through it. Arguably it never recovered, closing for good in around 1926.

For a while it was the Southdown bus garage. More recently storage seems to have been its main use amid a general air of dilapidation. Crowds used to queue for their seats at 3d and 4d. Now it barely gets a glance as thousands of cars pour past each day just yards away.

The Granada

The Corn Exchange is now the clothing store Next. Before that it was a McDonald's. However, for many Cicestrians, it will always be the Granada cinema.

With all the hype and all the computer-generated effects we get these days, it is all too easy to take things for granted.

Chichester did not. When the big films came its way in the Granada's heydays Chichester turned out in force – and sometimes needed a little looking after.

Bonnie And Clyde, starring Warren Beatty and Faye Dunaway, certainly would not raise too many eyebrows now, but things were different in 1967. Its violent reputation preceded it and the cinema staff made sure there was someone on hand to watch out for the faint and the overwhelmed.

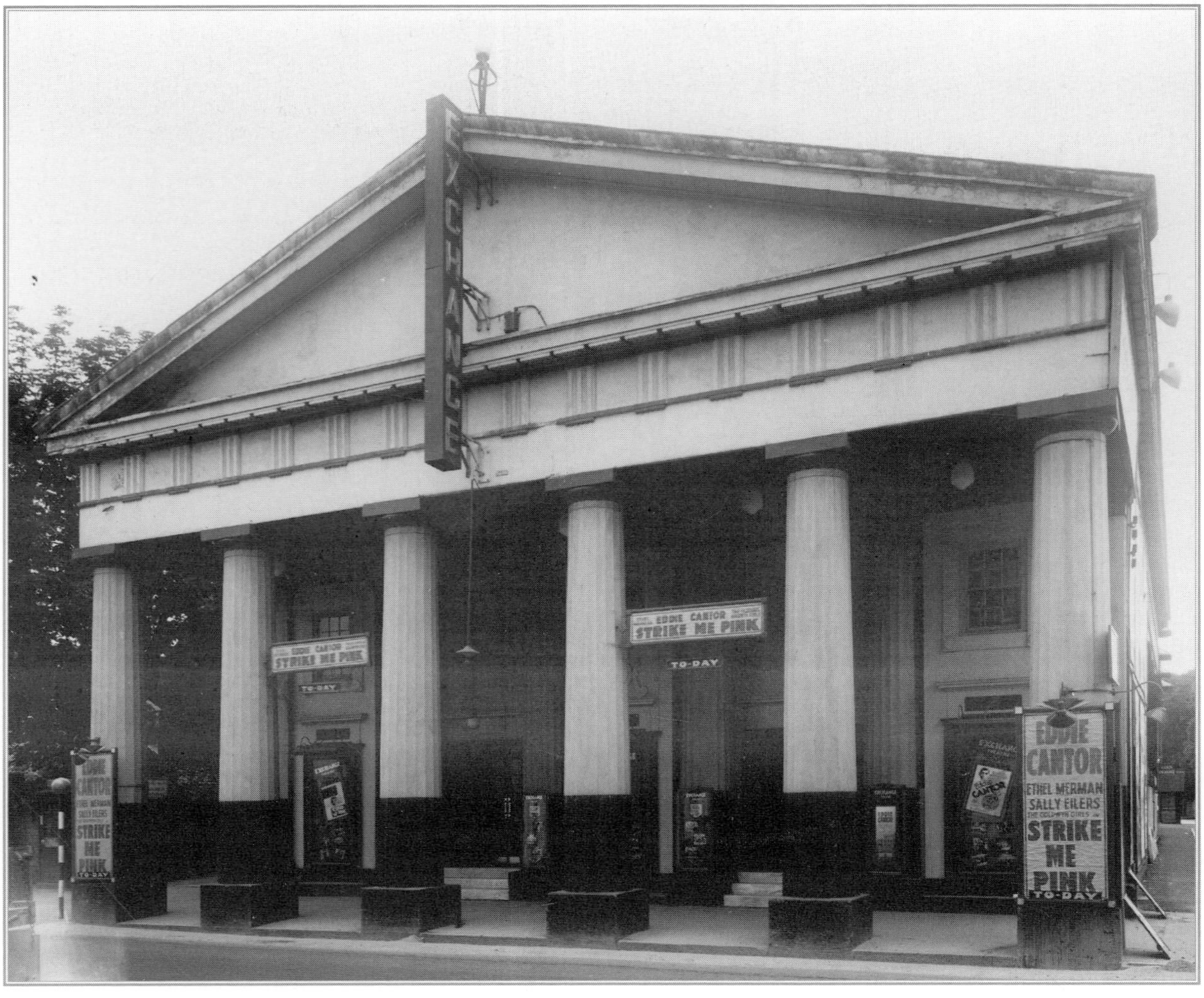

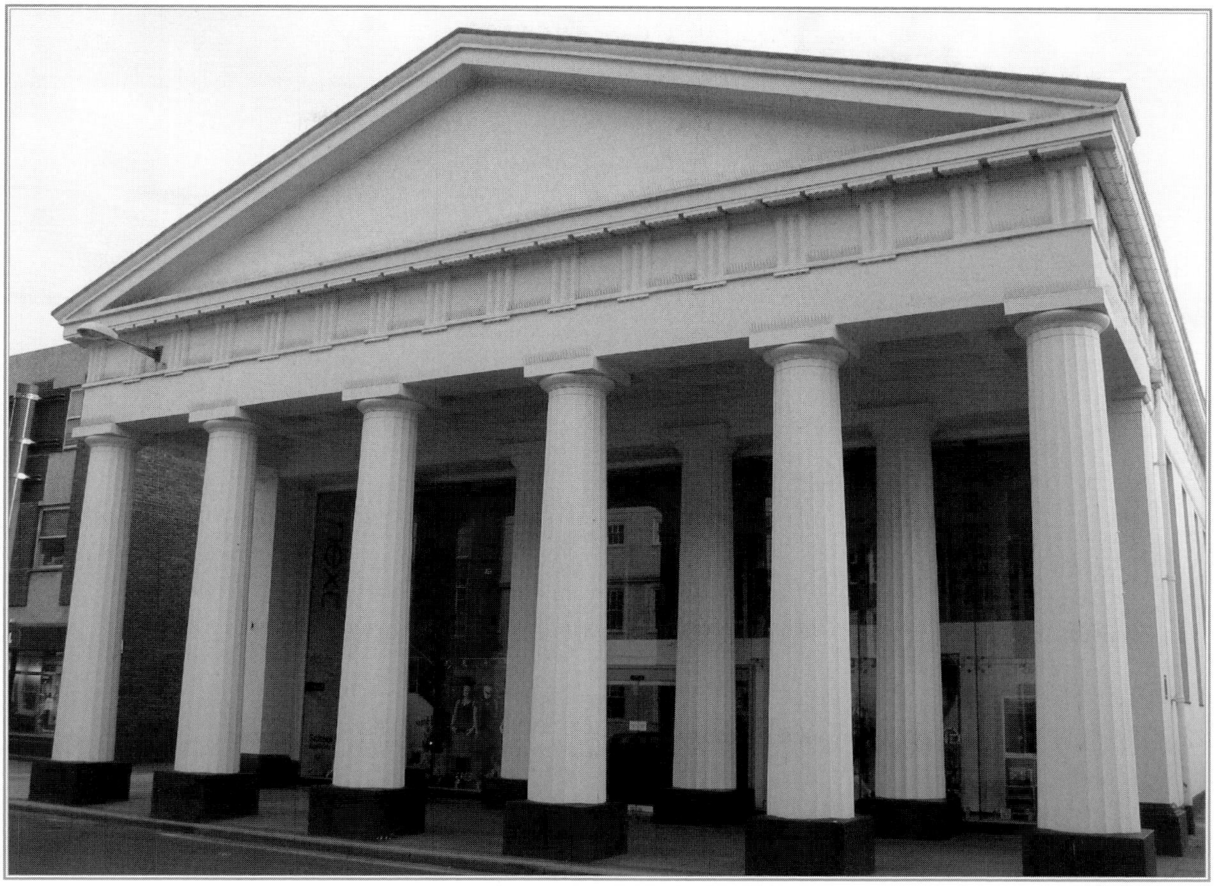

The screening of *The Good, The Bad And The Ugly* (1966) was a momentous event; so too was the arrival in Chichester of Richard Attenborough's *Oh What A Lovely War* (1969), with its memorable closing sequence panning out over a field of crosses set up on Brighton racecourse.

Another film Granada was particularly proud of was *Up The Junction* (1968) starring Dennis Waterman and Suzy Kendall. The world premiere was screened at the Granada in Clapham Junction, but Chichester had its slice of the action, with a large board on display in the foyer showing the stars arriving for the premiere.

Saturday was generally the most important day for the Granada in Chichester. In the morning the cinema hosted the Grenadiers show, the Saturday morning children's club which offered special films produced by the CFF, the Children's Film Foundation. These shows came to an end up and down the country with the arrival of Saturday morning children's television. The cinema itself closed in 1980.

The Gaumont

It is just a building site now, part of the Eastgate Square redevelopment (see overleaf), but for years this is where the city's Gaumont cinema stood – part of the city's cinema-going heyday.

The Gaumont-British Film Corporation bought the site in 1936 and the cinema opened its doors to great fanfare on 20 September 1937, a gala event crowned by the screening of *King*

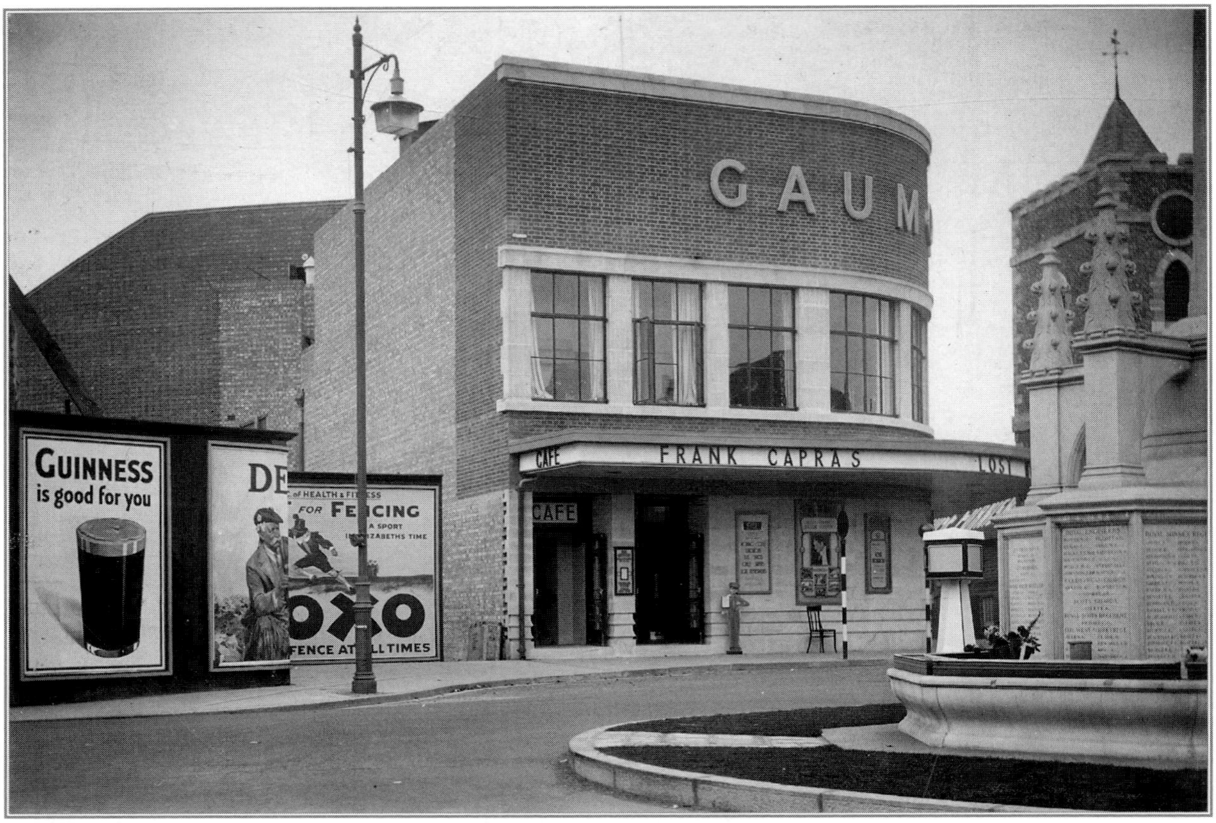
GAUM
FRANK CAPRAS
LOST
CAFE
CAFE
GUINNESS
is good for you
DE
FOR FENCING
OXO
FENCE AT ALL TIMES

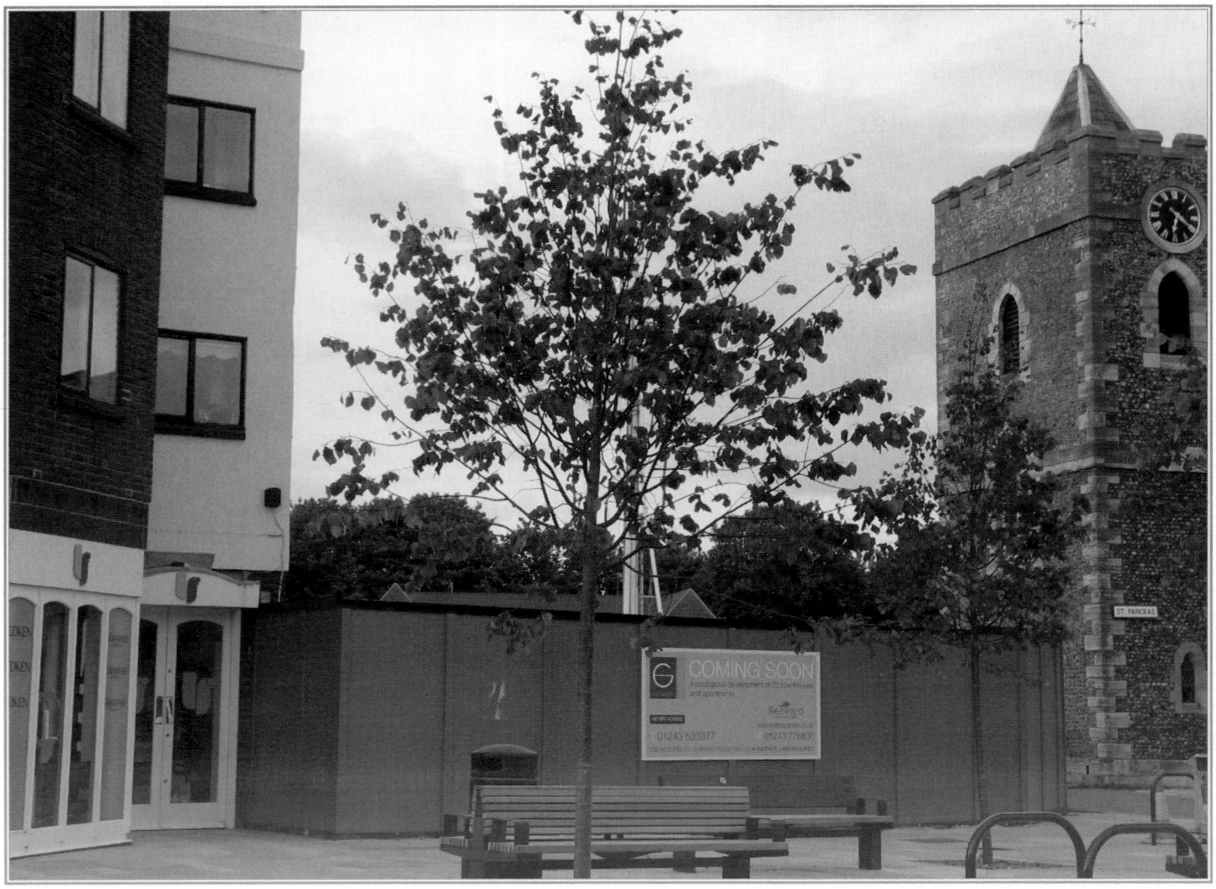
COMING SOON
ST. PANCRAS

Solomon's Mines, starring screen idol Sir Cedric Hardwicke whose son Edward was later to make his home in the city.

The Olympia Electric Theatre at Northgate had closed more than 10 years before, but even so the opening of the Gaumont meant that within a few hundred yards of each other Chichester had three busy cinemas.

Sadly, though, the audiences were not quite there and numbers fell away. The Gaumont closed its doors in October 1960.

However, that was not quite the end of the story for the building, as the focus switched towards securing the city a public swimming pool. Fund-raising began in earnest, and the gutted cinema began a new, watery life, officially opened by the Duke of Richmond on 29 April 1967.

Throughout the 1970s a couple of thousand pupils a week took their swimming lessons there. The pool lived on into the 1980s, surviving until 1987 when the Westgate Centre opened.

Into the 1990s it had a fairly chequered existence. An Indian restaurant occupied the upper floor for a good number of years. Downstairs, the area adjoining the street served a number of uses, including a drop-in centre for the homeless and an advice and counselling centre for those in need.

Whatever the use, the air of neglect deepened. Demolition was inevitable – and ultimately a relief.

The transformation of the site will see 19 four and five-bedroom, three-storey town houses and 53 one and two-bedroom apartments built, together with 11,000sq ft of commercial and retail space.

The Odeon

South Street was home to Chichester's third cinema, which opened in about 1920 on a site now occupied by the frozen food store Iceland (see pages 134–36).

Initially it was called the Picturedrome, but this was demolished. The Plaza was built in its place, later relaunched as the Odeon, the name by which most people still remember it.

Founded in 1930 by Oscar Deutsch, Odeon was acquired in 1941 by J. Arthur Rank who had interests in film production and distribution. Odeon remained a part of The Rank Organisation for a further 58 years.

The apocryphal story goes that Deutsch derived the Odeon name from his motto 'Oscar Deutsch Entertains Our Nation' – a story too good to be true and one rather dented by pre-existing Odeons elsewhere.

However, it was certainly thanks to Deutsch that during the 1930s the word Odeon was a household name. His cinemas became nationally known for their trademark, maritime-inspired Art Deco architecture.

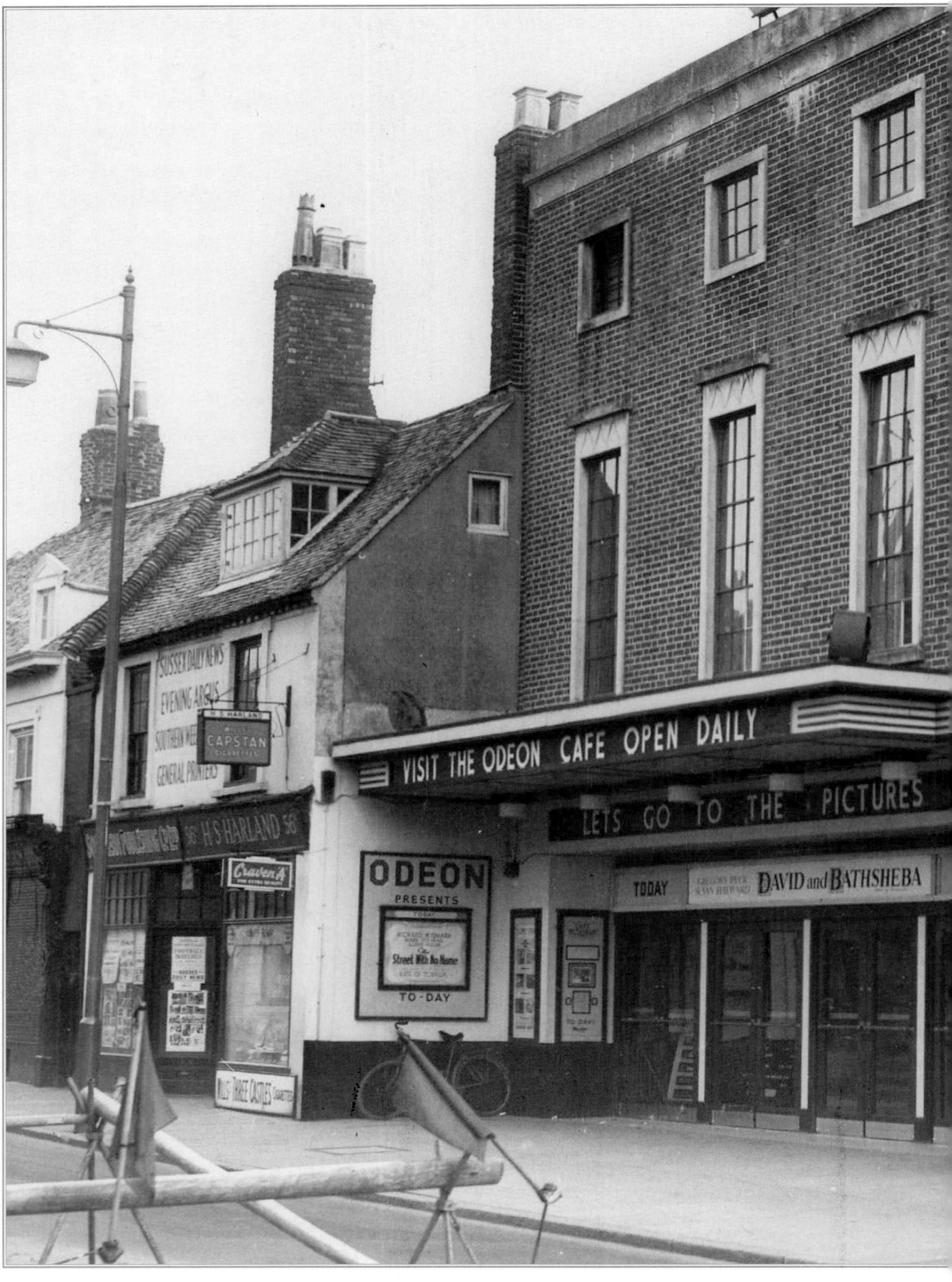
SUSSEX DAILY NEWS
EVENING ARGUS
GENERAL PRINTERS
CAPSTAN
56 H·S·HARLAND 56
Craven 'A'
THREE CASTLES
ODEON
PRESENTS
TO-DAY
VISIT THE ODEON CAFE OPEN DAILY
LETS GO TO THE PICTURES
TODAY
DAVID and BATHSHEBA

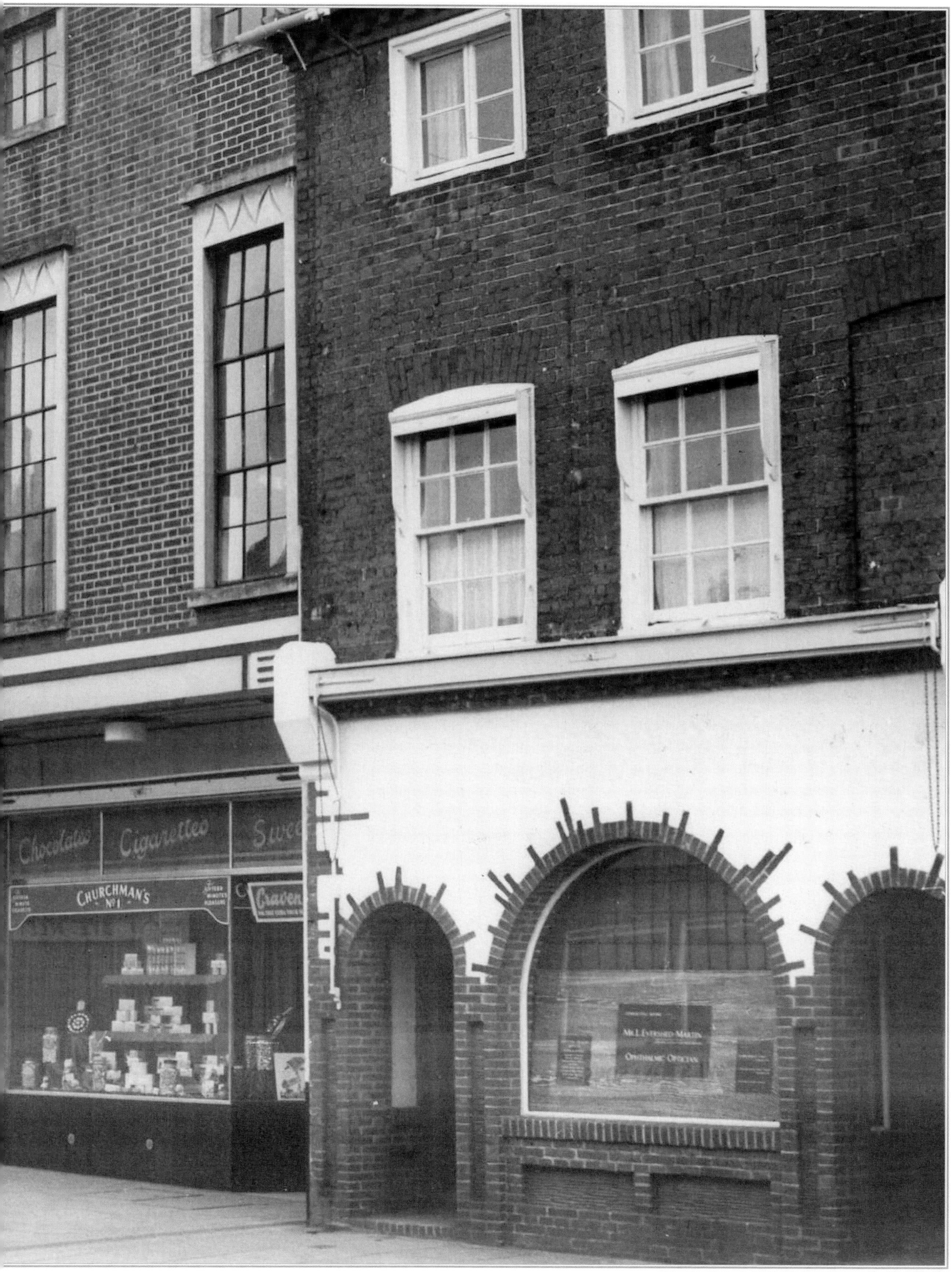
Chocolates
Cigarettes
CHURCHMAN'S No 1
Craven

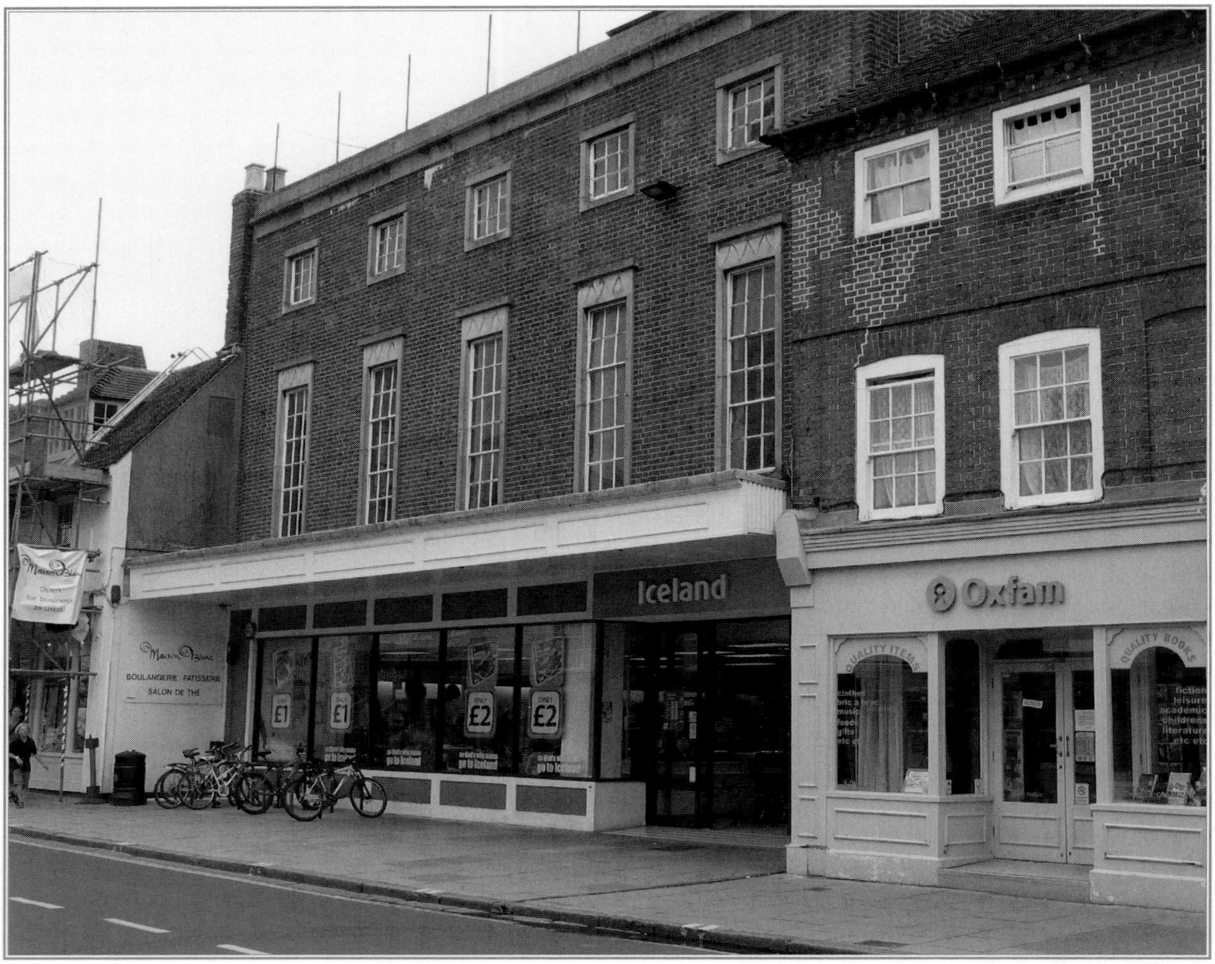

Chichester's Odeon certainly proved popular. Plenty of people still recall their favourite weekend jaunt was a trip to the Odeon, handing over their 1s 9d for seats to watch the latest Gregory Peck, Alan Ladd or Gary Cooper movie.

Sadly, three city centre cinemas were not sustainable for long, particularly with the advent of television. The Odeon closed down in February 1960 and was converted for supermarket use. The Odeon brand, however, still goes from strength to strength. The group is the largest cinema chain in the UK.

Chapter 11
Churches

The Church of St Andrew, Oxmarket

Chichester's thriving Oxmarket Centre of Arts still retains the outward appearance of the church it once was – the Church of St Andrew, Oxmarket, seen overleaf in a photograph dating probably from the mid-1960s.

The building was converted into an arts centre in 1975 and has been used for temporary exhibitions ever since, raising its profile particularly in the past few years under the chairmanship of Leon Bluestone, who was much mourned on his death in November 2007.

Mr Bluestone worked tirelessly to put the centre on a firmer business footing. He always spoke with great enthusiasm about the increasing calibre of artists the centre was starting to attract – and he delighted in the way it had gone from photocopies to colour brochures, all part of the professionalism he brought.

The former church dates back to the 13th century and stands on the north side of East Street, tucked behind the shops. The area has associations with several notable historical figures.

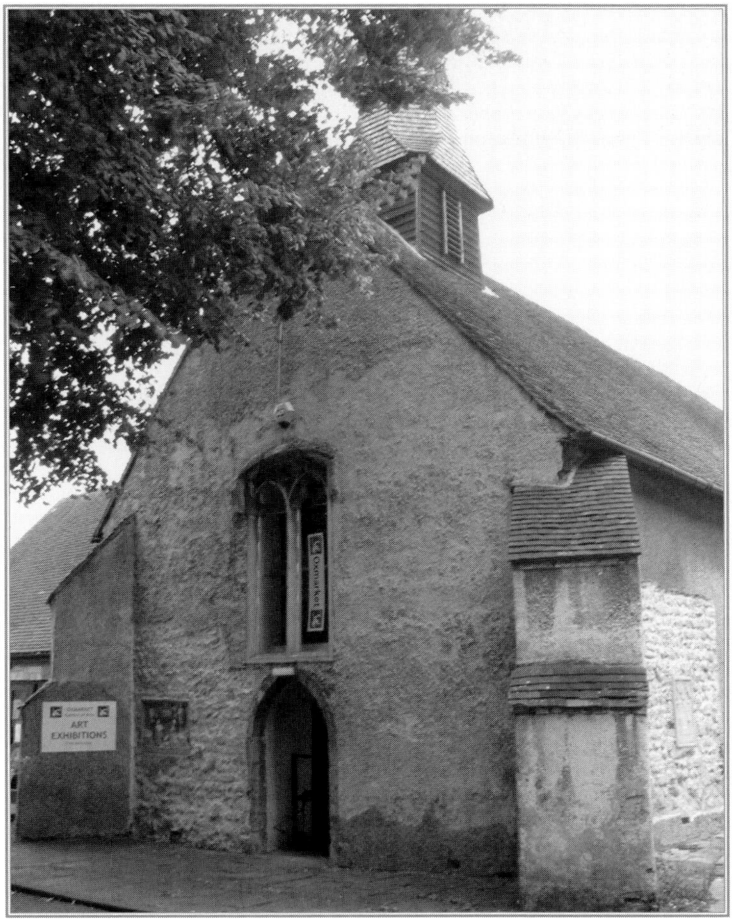

William Cawley, one of the signatories of Charles I's death warrant, was born in the parish in 1602.

The poet William Collins was also born in the parish, in 1721, the son of a hatmaker. Educated at Winchester and Oxford, Collins moved to London in the 1740s before returning to Chichester for the last years of his life. He sank into melancholy and died a broken man, disappointed at the way his writings had been received. He was buried in St Andrew's churchyard in 1759. More recent reconsideration of his work has revealed his true importance in our literary heritage.

The church suffered bomb damage in 1943 and was never again used for services. When it

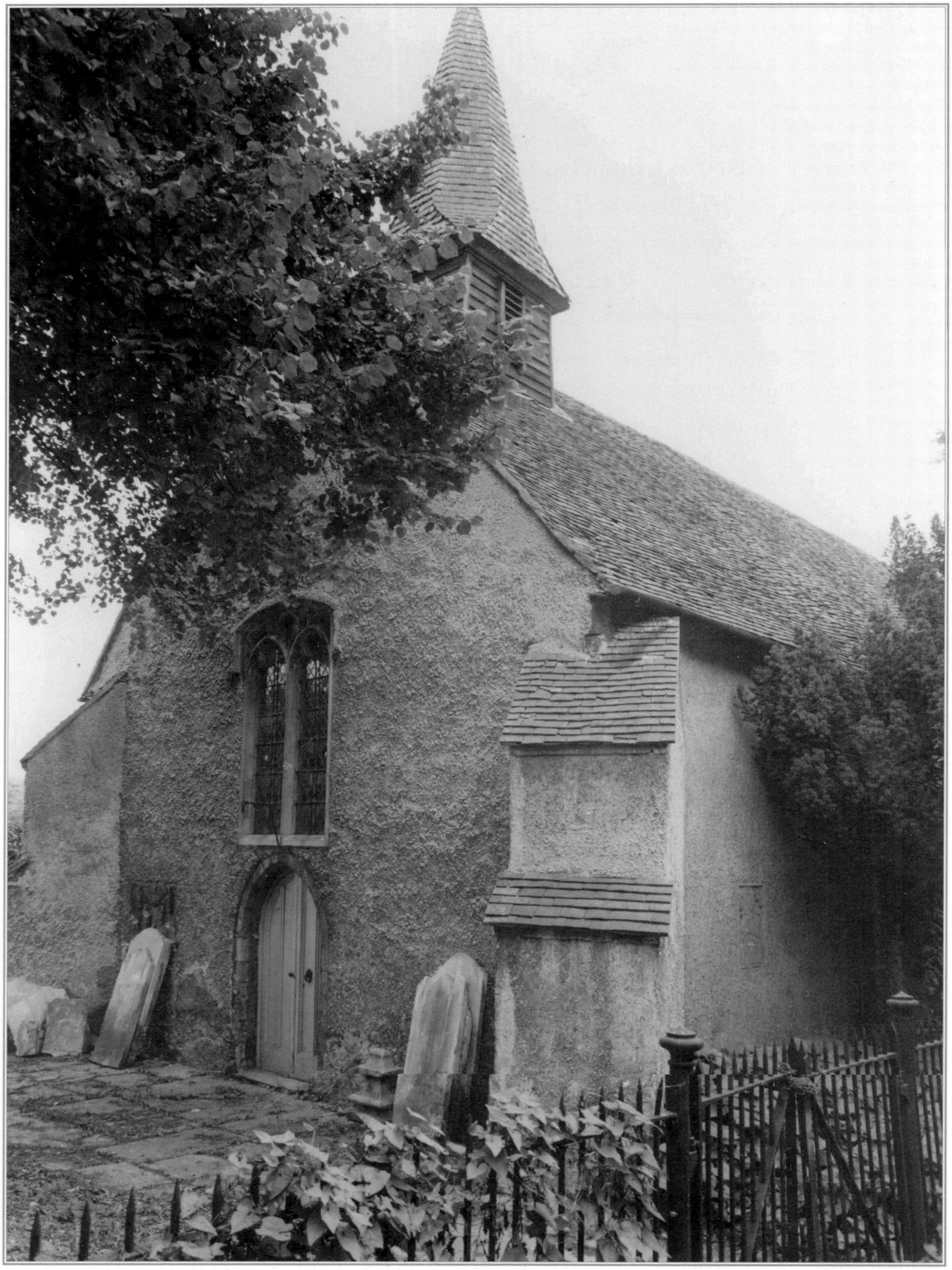

became redundant in the mid-1950s it was deconsecrated and became derelict until its resurrection as an arts centre.

All Saints in the Pallant

Tucked away off East Street is another of Chichester's ancient churches, All Saints in the Pallant. Built in the first half of the 13th century, it was stripped and deconsecrated after the war.

For many years, the church building served as the centre for the British Red Cross in the area, a use that has now ceased. It is sad to see a church door threatening 'strictly no admittance', but the other sign on the building promises a brighter future as a 'prestige office development'.

Located in West Pallant, the building is essentially a rectangular room. A point of interest is the fact that there is no structural division between the chancel and the nave except for a six-inch step and two more steps to the altar rails.

A vestry at the east end of the north side was added in the 19th century as part of extensive restoration.

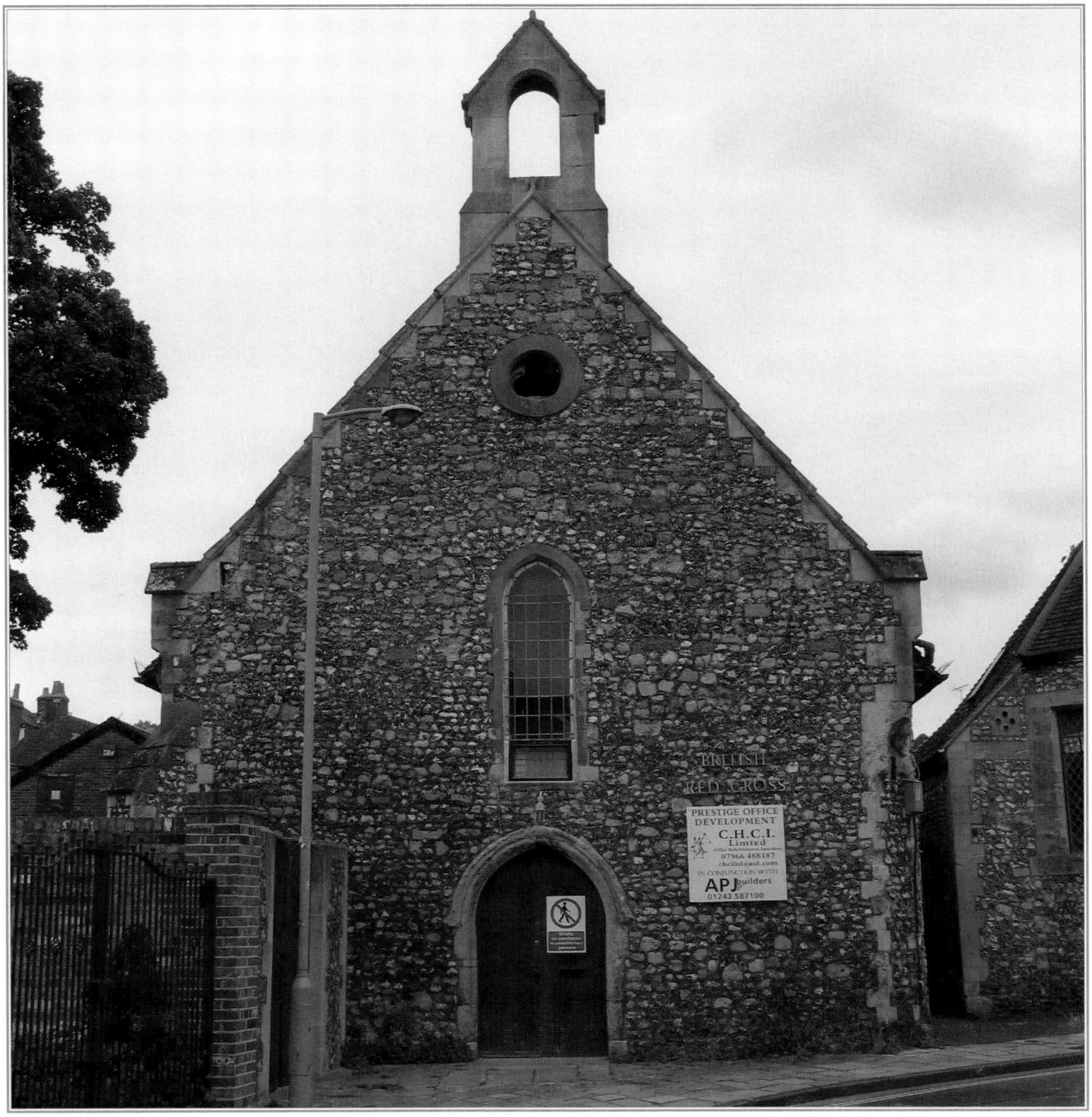

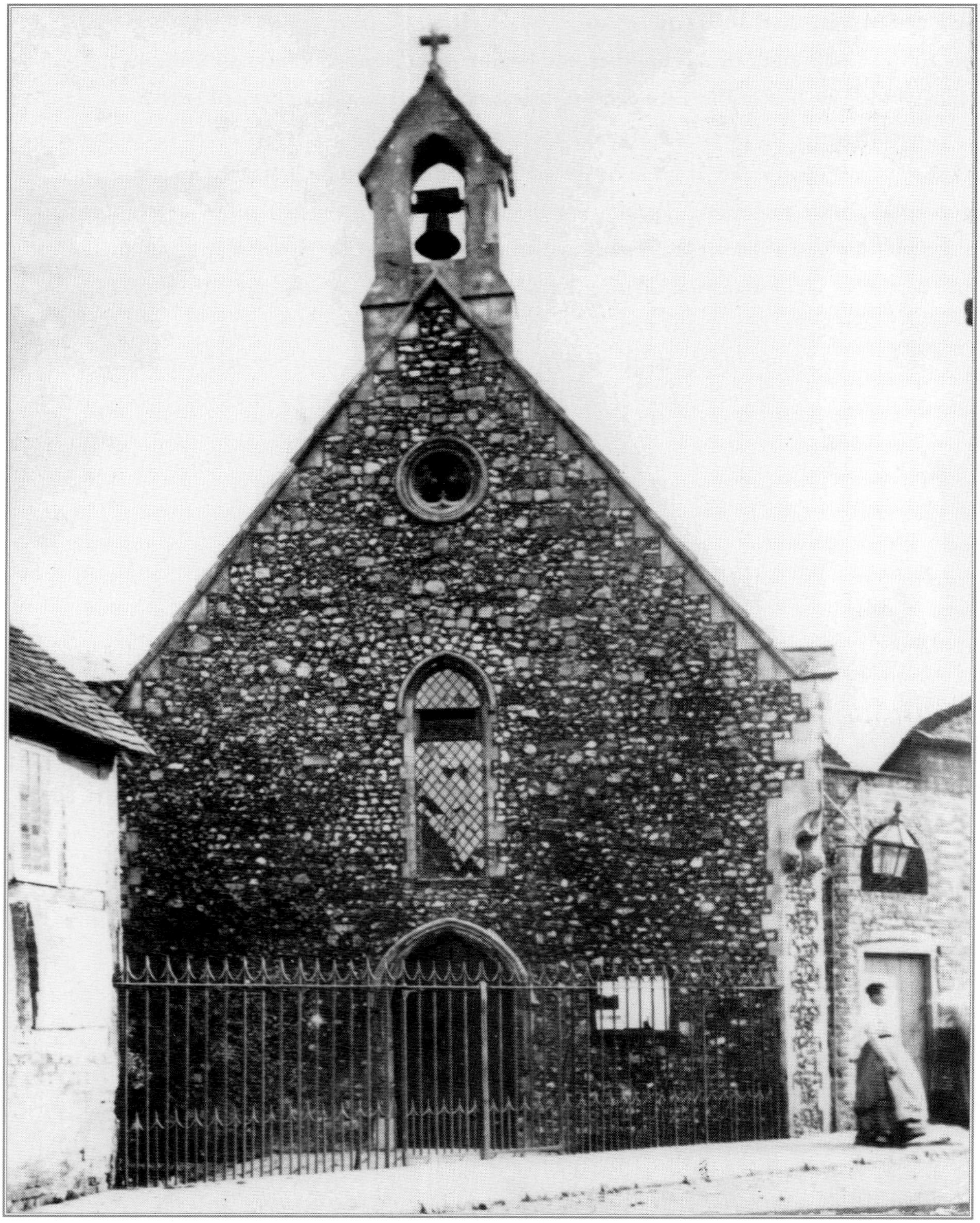

In keeping with Chichester's other ancient churches, the walls are of flint with stone dressings and the roof is tiled. In the east wall is a 13th-century triple lancet window under a hooded arch. The principal features of the south wall are six of these 13th-century lancet windows. There is also a blocked 13th-century doorway at the west end.

The west wall, visible in both the old and new photographs, features a 13th-century single-light window above the doorway. Over the west window is a further window, small and circular.

The older photograph of All Saints in the Pallant probably dates from 1900–10.

St Peter the Less

A sad addendum to Lindsay Fleming's booklet on *The Little Churches of Chichester* notes 'The regrettable demolition of St Peter the Less has commenced while this brief record is in the press.'

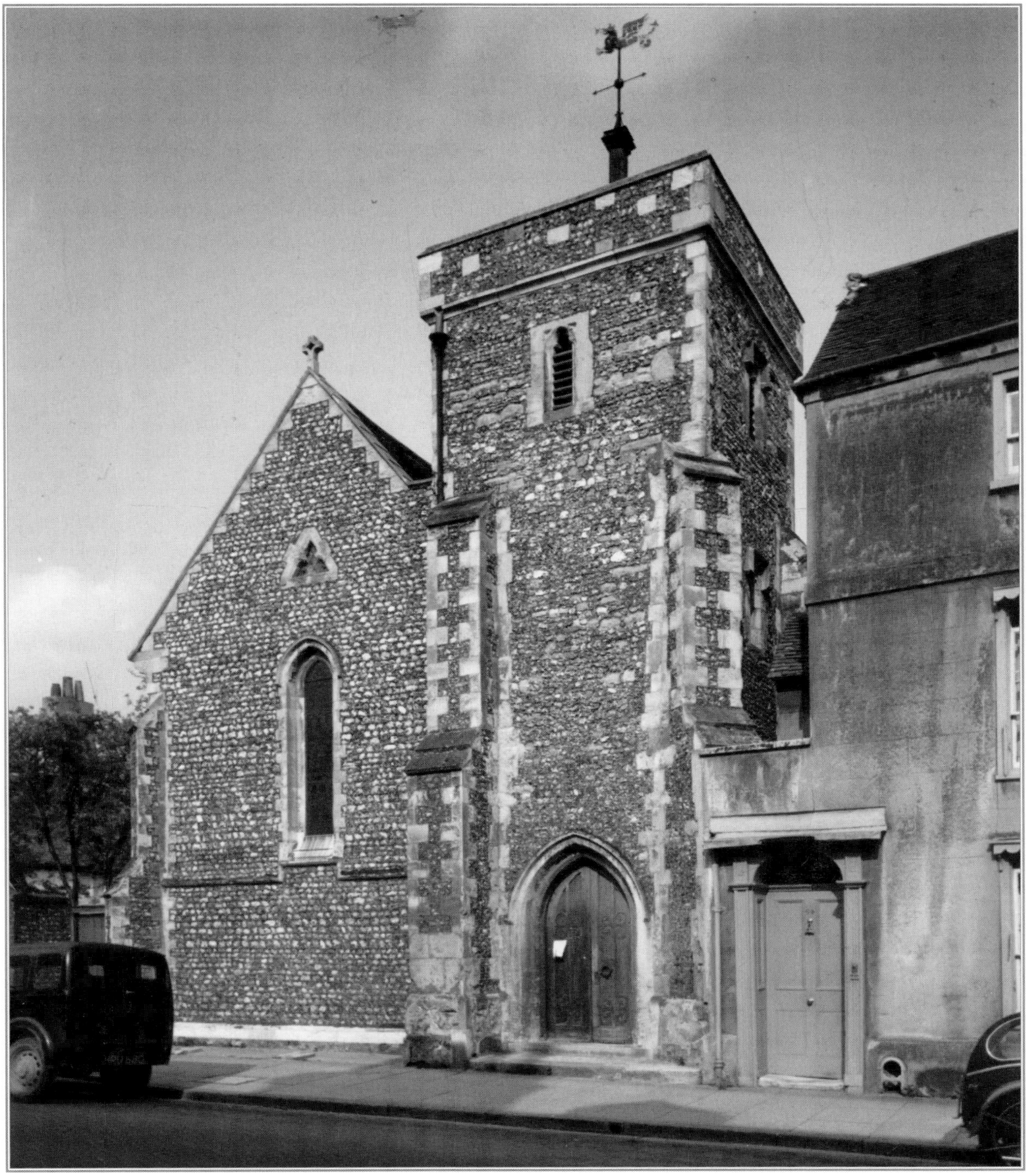

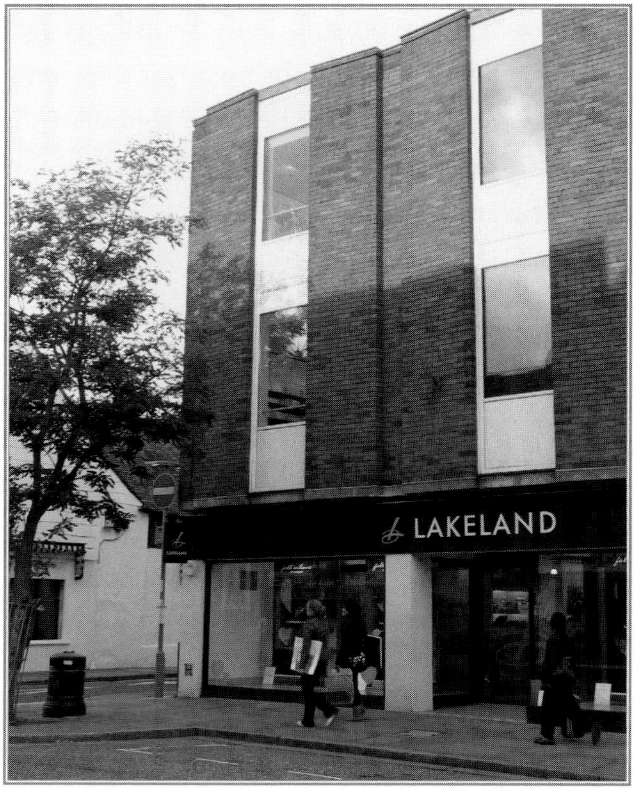

Half a century on it beggars belief that it could possibly have been allowed to happen. The largest of Chichester's mediaeval churches, St Peter the Less became even less when it was bulldozed in April 1957.

The indignity had begun the previous year when the North Street site was auctioned for a paltry sounding £3,000 – a small price for a church dating back to the middle of the 13th century. Some people believe it was actually Saxon in origin, which would make it even older than Chichester Cathedral.

Still remembered by many Cicestrians, the Church of St Peter the Less had flint walls with stone dressings and a tiled roof.

When it was first built it probably comprised the nave and a small chancel. It was enlarged early in the 14th century by the addition of the south aisle and tower. The whole church was restored in the 19th century when the chancel was rebuilt.

Perched on the tower was an iron weathervane representing a seahorse. Inside the tower were three bells, one modern, the second a mid-14th-century bell with the inscription 'Ave Maria', and the third a bell bearing the inscription 'Praysed be thy name o Lord'.

However, none of these features was enough to save St Peter the Less from destruction.

Part of the site is now St Peter's Road, next to Lakeland, which was cut through from Priory Road to form part of the traffic system at the top of the pedestrian precinct. Where the road is now, there used to be the Parsonage Garden. Stretching behind the church, it contained a barn – just memories now.

St Peter the Great

Many are the uses to which Chichester has put its ancient churches. One of the saddest was when the the Church of St Peter the Great became The Slurping Toad pub, a name completely disrespectful of the building's origins. Fortunately, the toad has now slurped off into the distance. The former church has become the rather more decorously named Wests bar and lounge.

Opposite the cathedral the Subdeaneary church was once the mother church of the city. It remains among West Street's most impressive buildings and was constructed in the 14th-century style. Work began on it in 1850, and the church was consecrated in 1852.

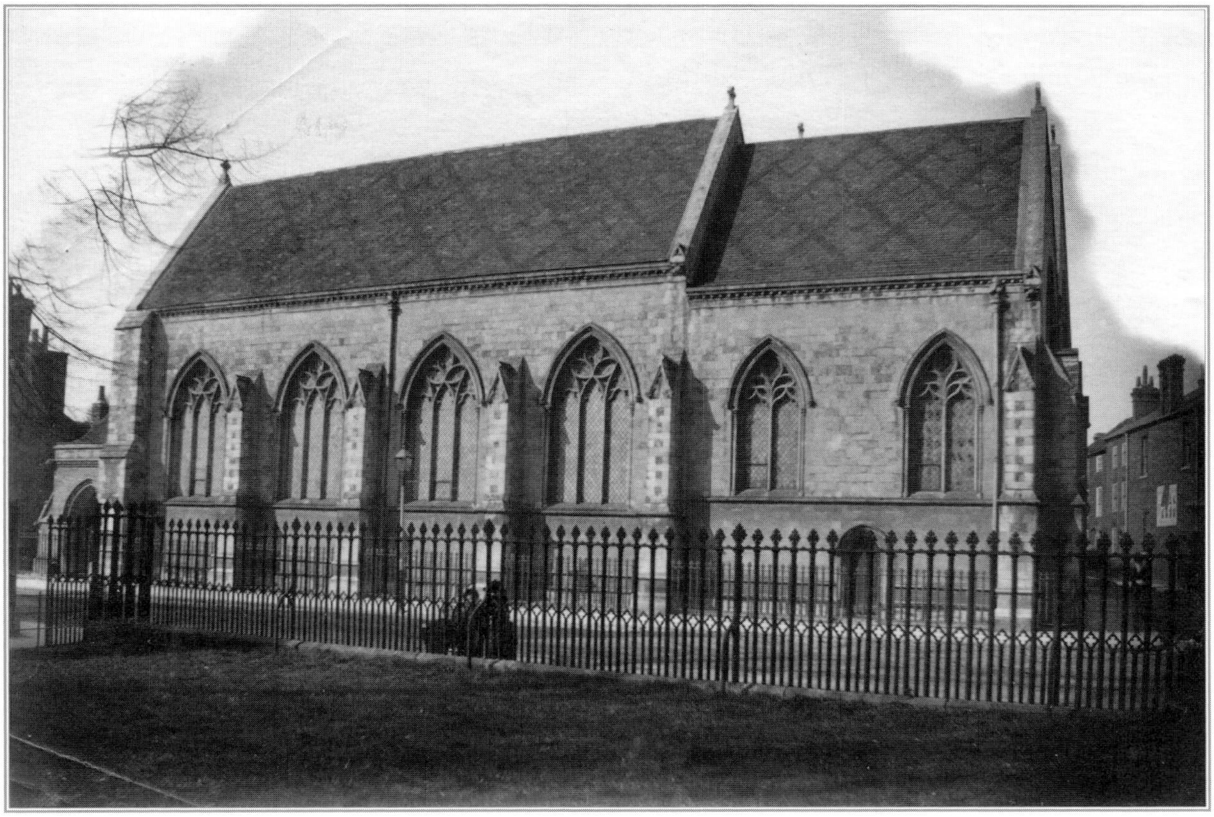

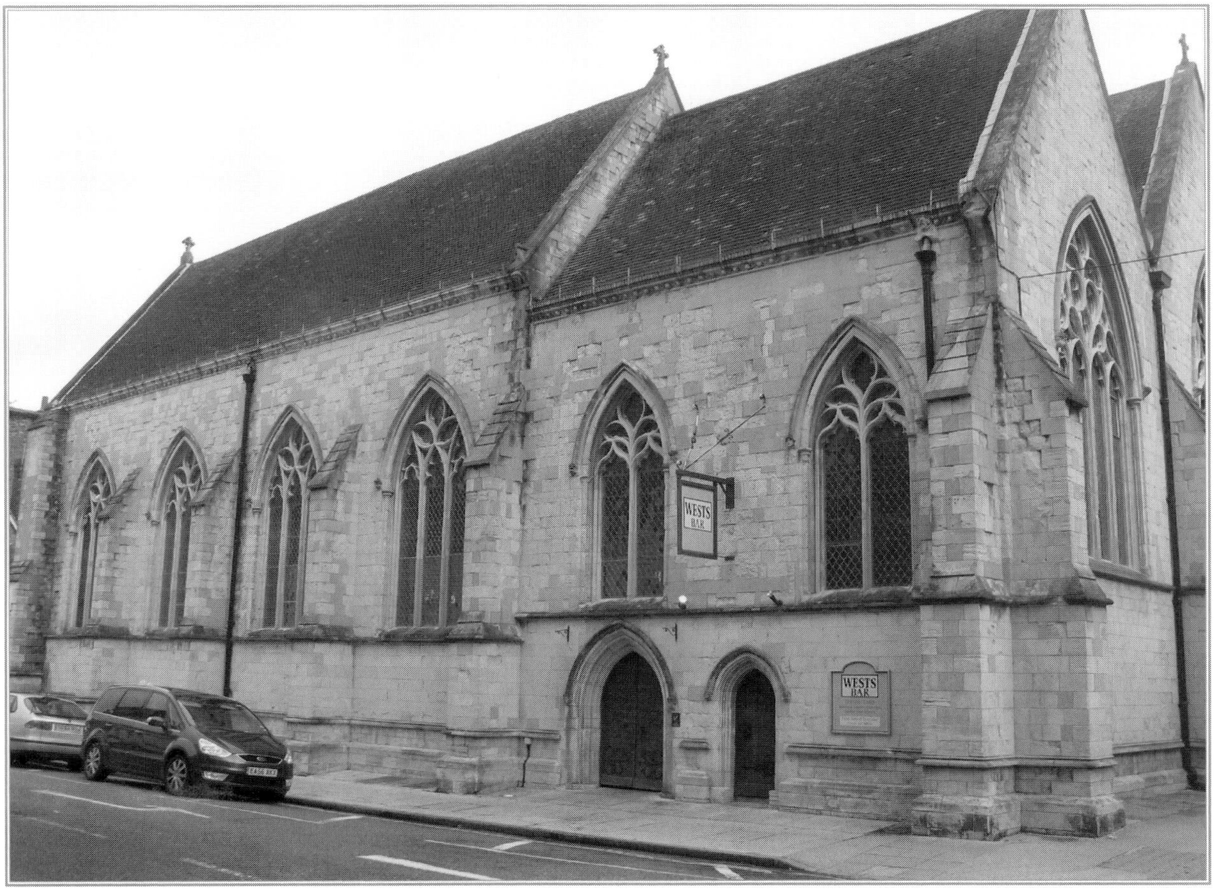
WESTS
BAR
WESTS
BAR

The church was built of stone with a tiled roof and consisted of a nave of four bays with aisles and a chancel of two bays. Its fittings were contemporary, except the font which was apparently 15th century and was probably removed from the cathedral.

The church was designed by Richard Carpenter (1812–1855), consulting architect of the cathedral. Of the eight ancient parish churches within the walls of Chichester, the Church of St Peter the Great was the only one in the western half of the city. Of the other seven, five were in the north-east quarter.

Before becoming a pub, the church served as a shopping arcade until 1997.

St John's Chapel

One of the favourite venues for speaker events during the Chichester Festivities every July is St John's Chapel, a place of worship which grew out of the late-Georgian development of Chichester's New Town in the city's south-east quadrant.

Within the city walls and bordered by East Street and Friary Lane, New Town was the last area of the city to be developed in Georgian times.

Increased population meant a church accommodation crisis in Chichester. The six parish churches within the city walls did not have enough accommodation for all those wishing to attend church, so the solution was to build what was known as a proprietary chapel.

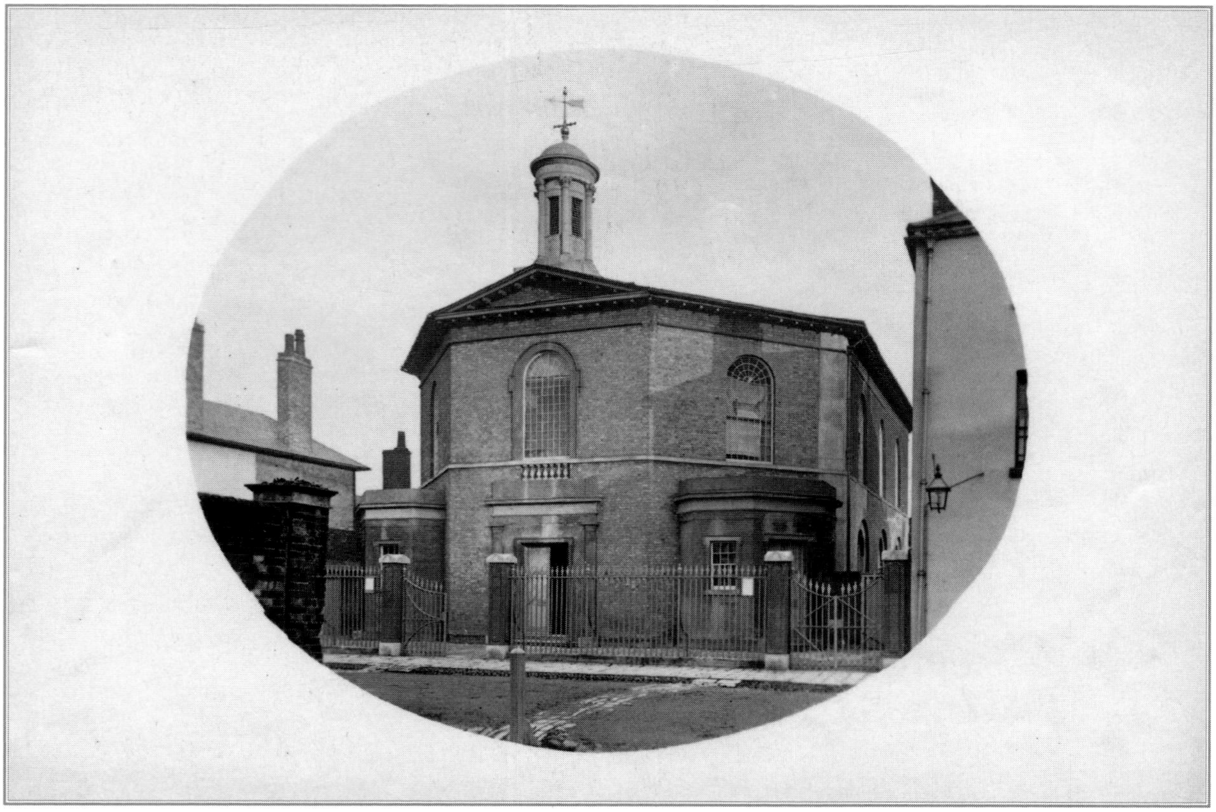

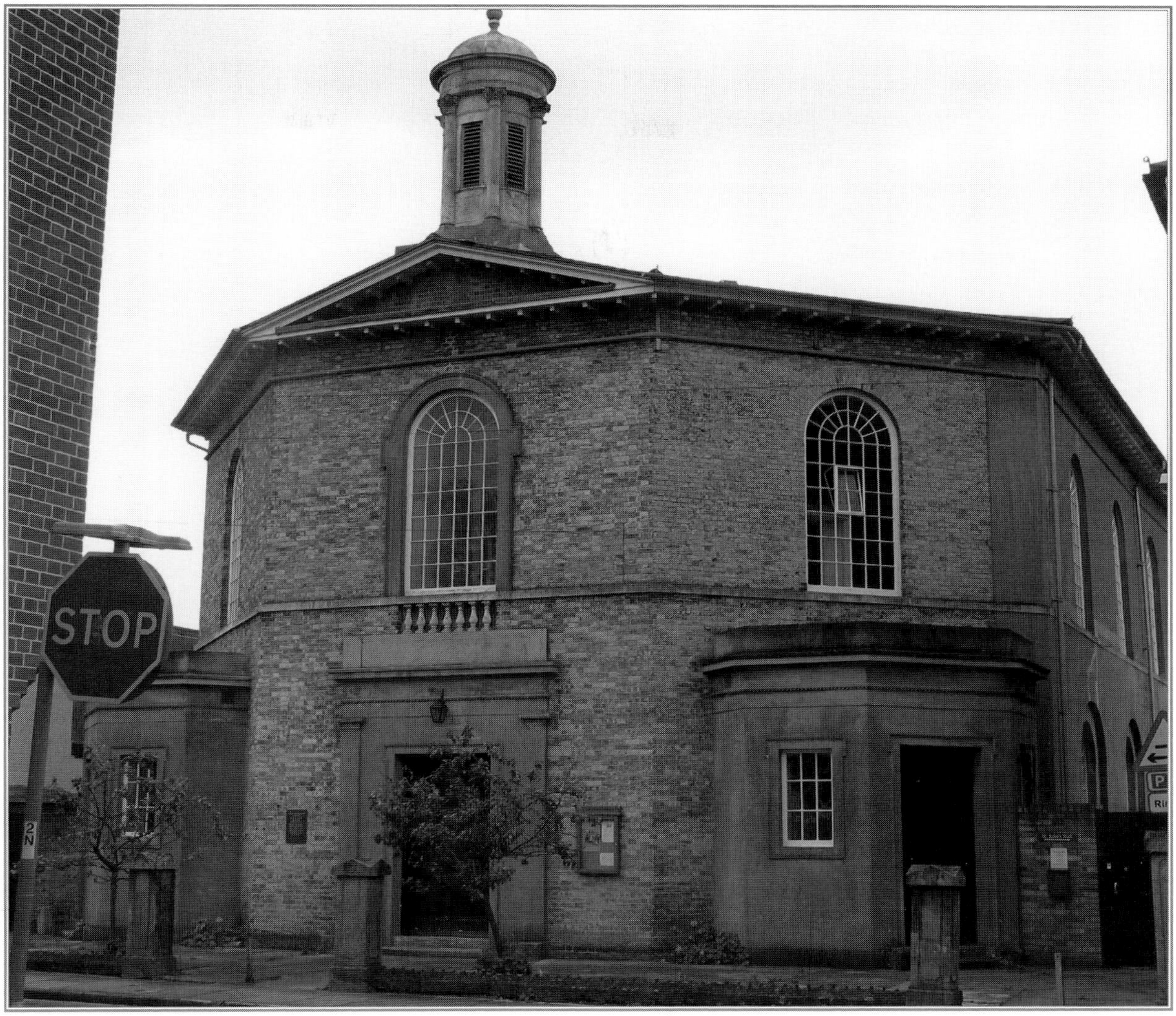

Still part of the Church of England, a proprietary chapel had no parish but was built and run as a commercial venture. The money for its construction came from share issues, and the money to run it came from the sale or rent of private pews.

Thus emerged St John's Chapel in St John's Street, built out of brick in 1812 at a cost of £7,000 and designed by the noted architect James Elmes in a distinctive octagonal shape.

The building is symmetrical with galleries round three sides, reached by staircases north and south of the entrance vestibule. Behind the altar at the east end are the vestries.

The first minister was Stephen Barbut, and there was soon a waiting list for pews. However, hard times were to follow. By the 1950s Chichester had too many churches and St John's was amalgamated with St Pancras. For a while the congregations met separately but they too were eventually amalgamated and in 1973 the chapel was closed, remaining so for nearly 20 years. It is now owned by the Churches Conservation Trust.

It was revived in 1992, largely under the influence of the Duke of Richmond, and is now a popular extra venue for the Festivities.

St Bartholomew's

Tucked away off Westgate is another fascinating church, St Bartholomew's, which stands on the site of a much older place of worship destroyed during the Civil War siege of Chichester in 1642.

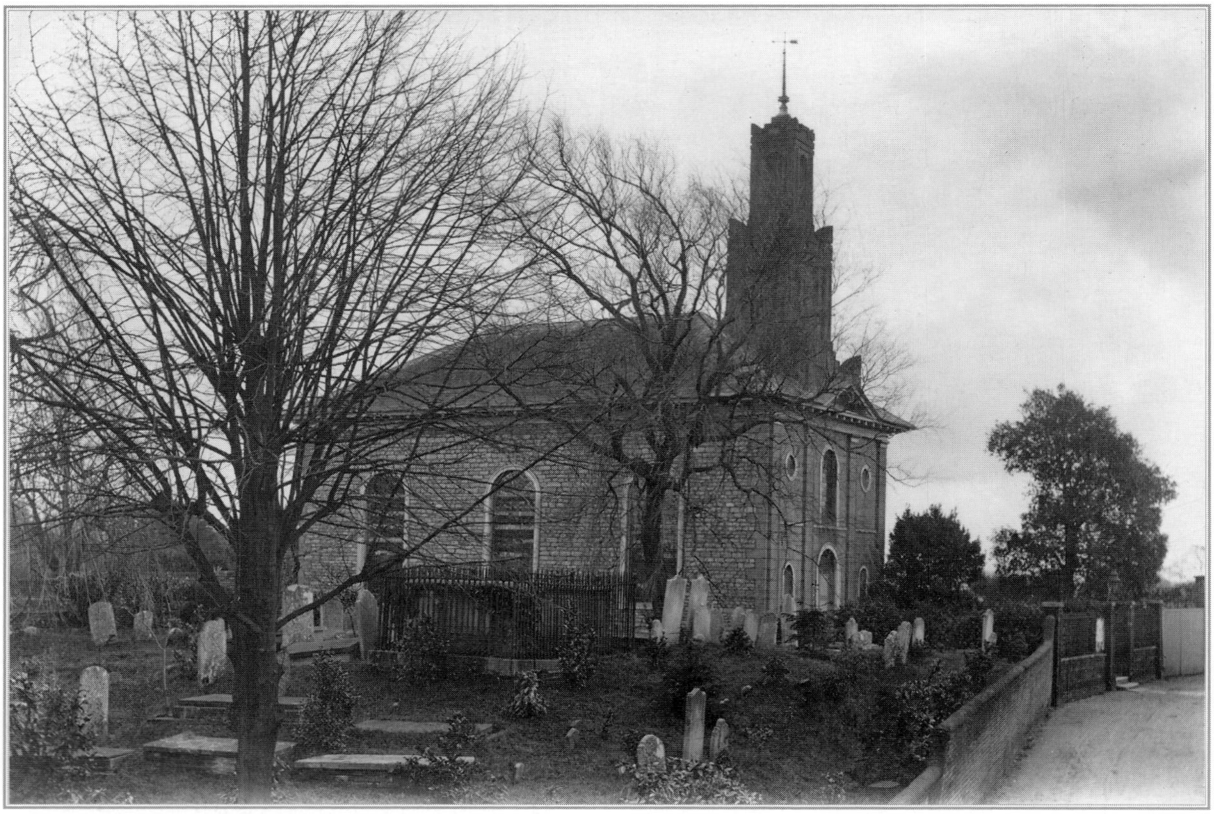

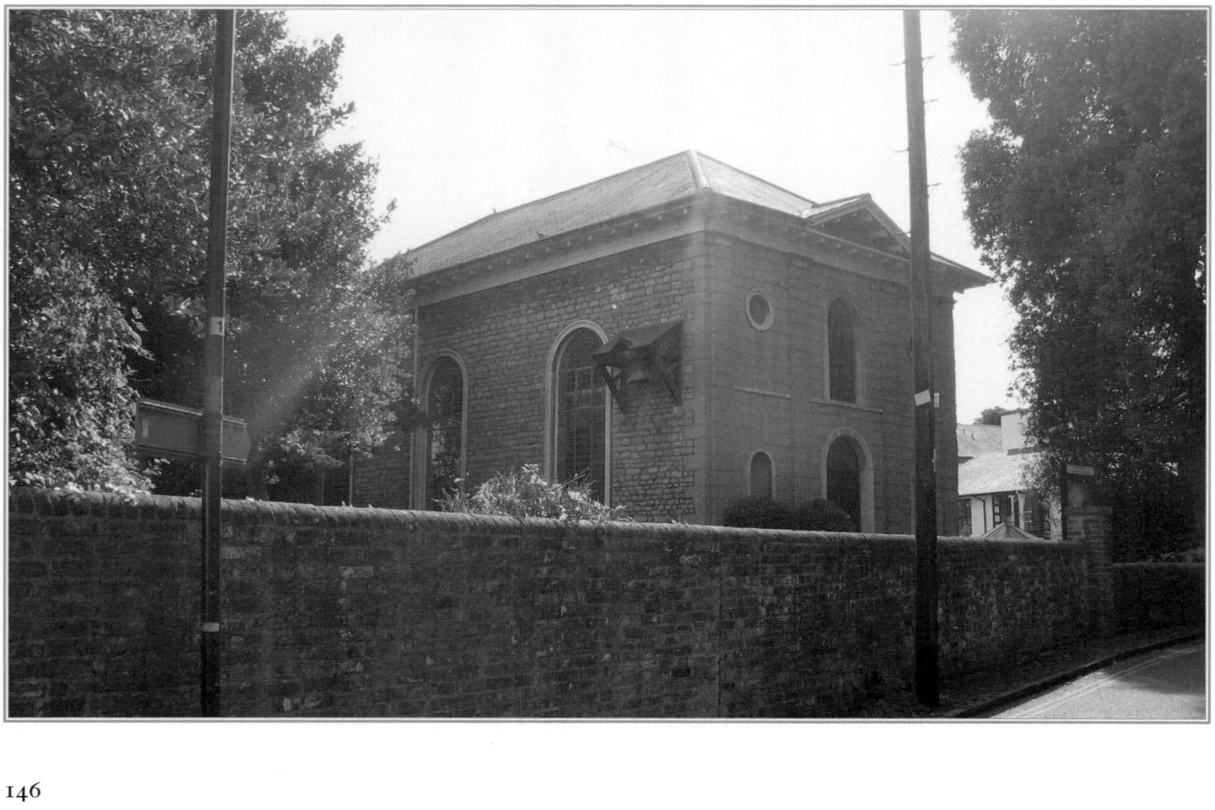

The original church was one of the few round churches in England, built in the circular style of the Holy Sepulchre in Jerusalem. The church was consequently often referred to as St Sepulchre's.

In mediaeval times it was one of no fewer than 16 places of worship in Chichester, including the cathedral.

St Sepulchre's classical replacement is a Renaissance building of grey brick with stone dressings and a low-pitched slate roof. The chancel, which is low and gabled, has been lengthened. The doorway is flanked by statue niches and above it are an arched window and two circular windows. A small tower over the west end was taken down in 1929. The vestry was added in the same style on the north-east corner.

A modern church by Chichester's standards, it later became the chapel to Chichester Theological College which was founded in 1839.

The college did not survive into the 21st century. A report advising the process of regionalisation for the country's providers of theological education was issued for debate in 1981. A further report proposed a radical reappraisal of the country's parochial system, raising questions about the sort of training needed in the nation's theological colleges.

After much debate, further reports and lobbying, Chichester Theological College was closed in 1994 followed by Salisbury, Wells and Lincoln in 1995. The church itself is now Chichester College Chaplaincy Centre and Classroom.

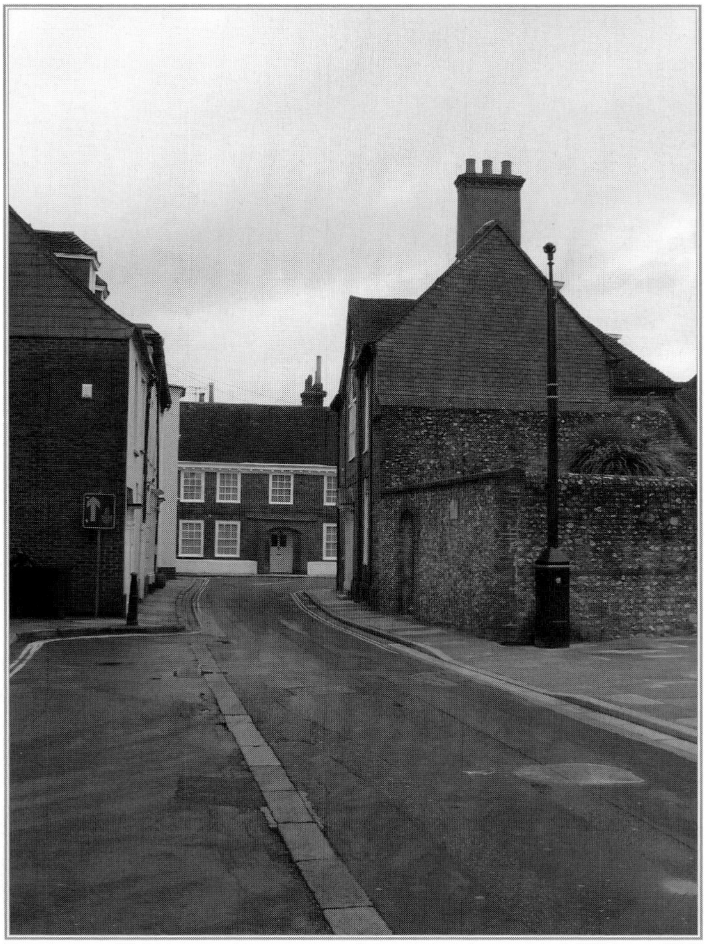

St Martin's

Another lost Chichester church is St Martin's in St Martin's Street (see page 148), just a few hundred yards from where St Peter the Less stood.

It seems likely that it dated from the 10th century, by which time, under the reign of Aethelstan, Chichester was well established as an important commercial town. The church was largely rebuilt in 1802–03.

St Olave's Church in North Street, which probably dates from much the

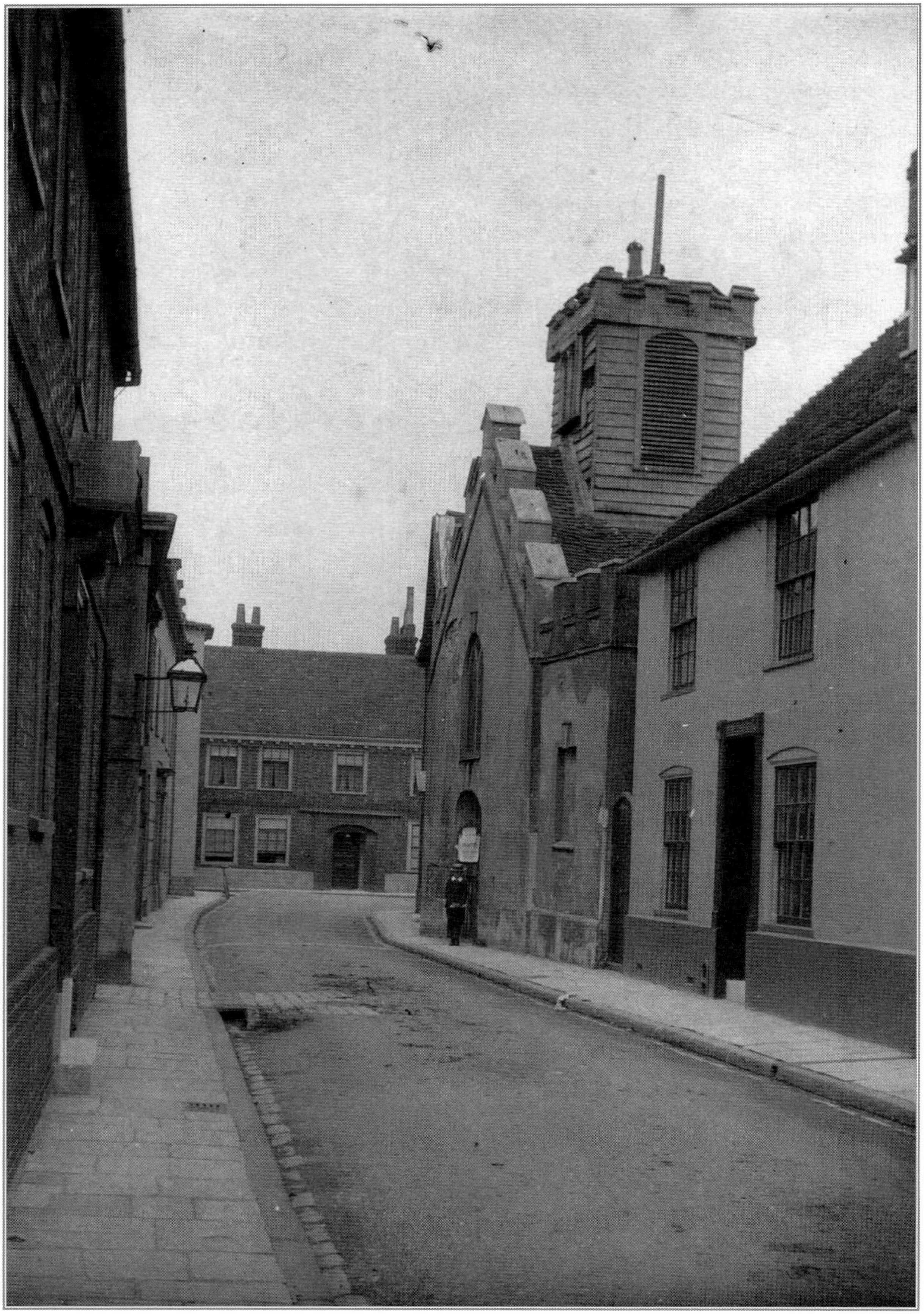

same era, was the recipient of a number of St Martin's monuments following its demolition in 1904. St Martin's had been united with St Olave's in 1899 and had fallen into disrepair.

A public garden now occupies part of the site where St Martin's once stood. A plaque advises 'Service for the united parishes now held in the Church of St Olave.' St Olave's is now a bookshop.

St Martin's Street has a grim place in Chichester's more recent history as the site of Chichester's worst air raid during World War Two. The St Martin's area suffered extensive damage on 10 February 1943 and a number of lives were lost.

Just to the north of St Martin's Street is St Martin's Square, formerly known as Hog Lane. It was here that the weekly hog market was held.

On the east side of St Martin's Square is St Mary's Hospital which has been on the site since 1269. Originally built as a hospital for the sick of the city, it became an almshouse administered by a trust formed of members of the Chapter of Chichester Cathedral.

The buildings consist of a gatehouse on the street front, an aisled infirmary hall and a chapel at the eastern end.

Chapter 12
Pubs

The Globe

The Globe Hotel in Southgate, seen here in an image dating back to around the 1920s, was very much a product of Chichester's railway age.

Visitors arriving at Chichester railway station could hire horse transport next door at The Globe to take them on to their destinations.

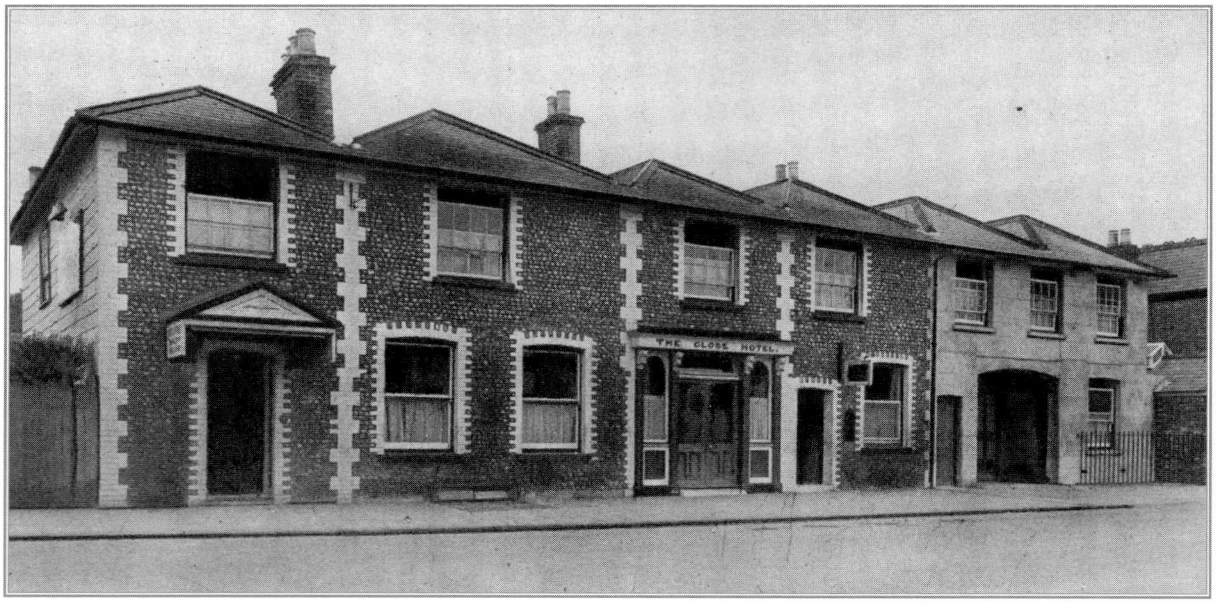

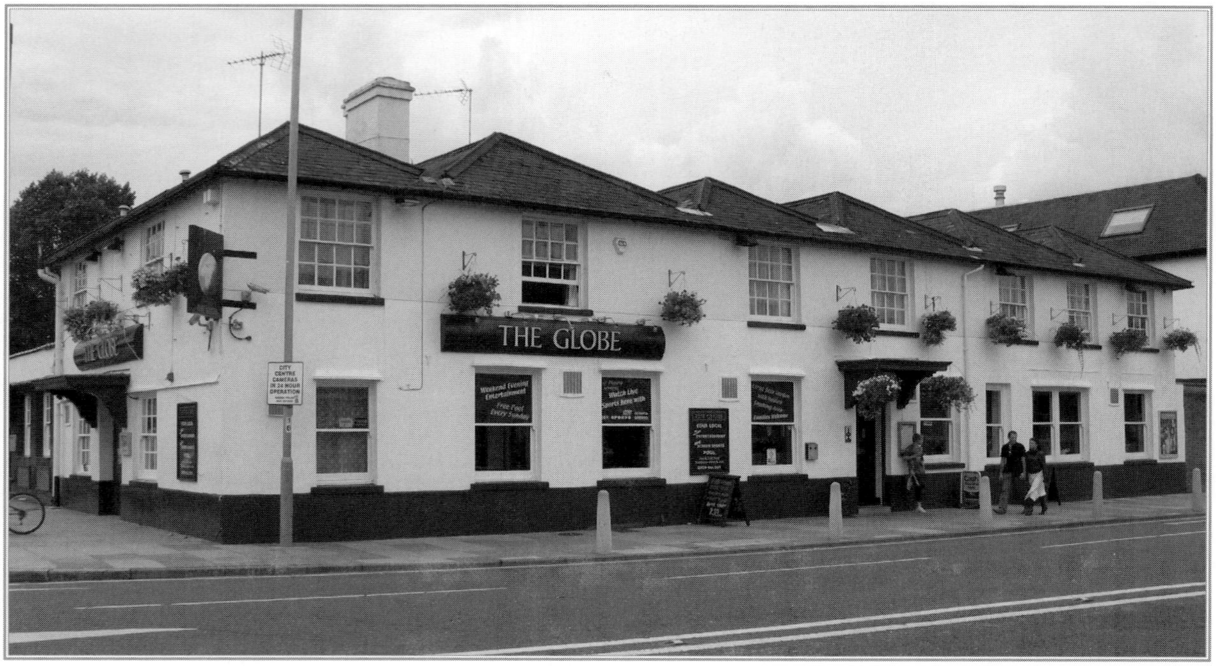

Thomas Purchase (1816–1872), a local brewer, was The Globe's first landlord. Other Victorian landlords at the hostelry included Arthur Purchase in 1878 and John Elias Duncan in 1890.

Entrances have been rearranged and the brickwork has been painted over, but the building seems to have changed remarkably little on the outside at least, and it offers a colourful welcome to Chichester with its range of hanging baskets.

Another significant Southgate inn is The Fountain which dates back to the early 19th century and possibly beyond.

Its most famous landlord is probably George Neal who ran the pub from 1830 to about 1834. In 1855 his daughter Sarah married Joseph Wells, an amateur Kent cricketer and shopkeeper. Their fourth and last child was the author H.G. Wells.

Born at Bromley in Kent, Herbert George Wells (1866–1946) was a prolific writer, most famous today for the science fiction novels he published between 1895 and 1901, most notably *The Time Machine, The Island Of Doctor Moreau, The Invisible Man, The War Of The Worlds* and *When The Sleeper Wakes*.

From 1881 to 1883 Wells had a miserable time as a draper's apprentice at the Southsea Drapery Emporium. His experiences later inspired his novels *The Wheels of Chance* and *Kipps*.

Subsequent landlords at The Fountain have included Mrs F. Foot, J. Stonestreet, George Gladman, Frederick Smart, Arthur Henry Miller and Herbert Edward Evans.

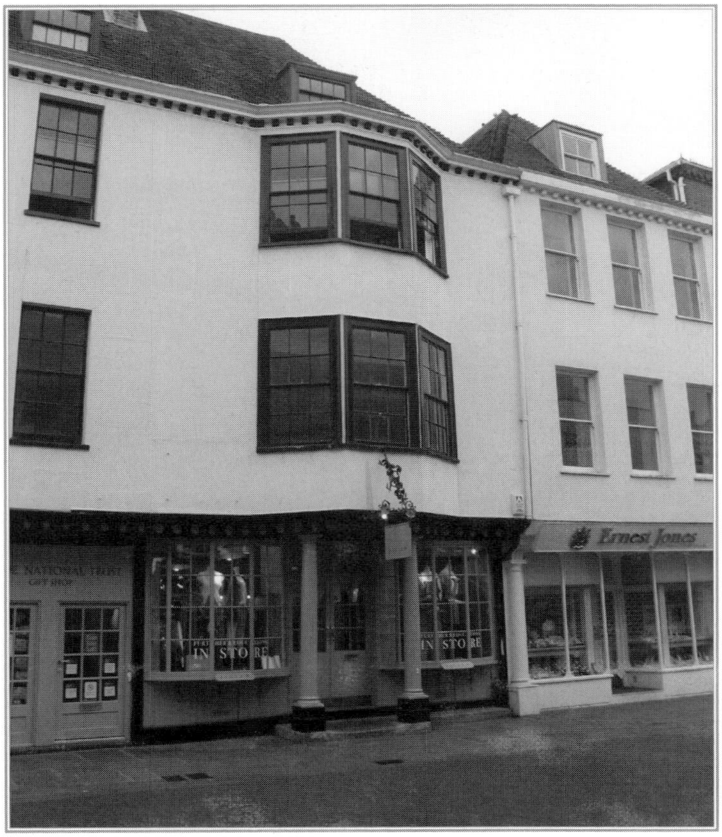

The Old Punch House

Did she or did she not? Let us assume she did. There is something very appealing about the thought that Queen Elizabeth I once visited these buildings in East Street.

On the south side near the Cross stands one of East Street's most important buildings. Formerly known as Scarborough House, it comprises Nos. 92 and 93. In the 1930s, when the older photograph overleaf is believed to have been taken, No. 93, now Ernest Jones jewellers, was Lipton's grocers.

Number 92, recently converted to house Jigsaw clothing store, was The Royal Arms, better known as The

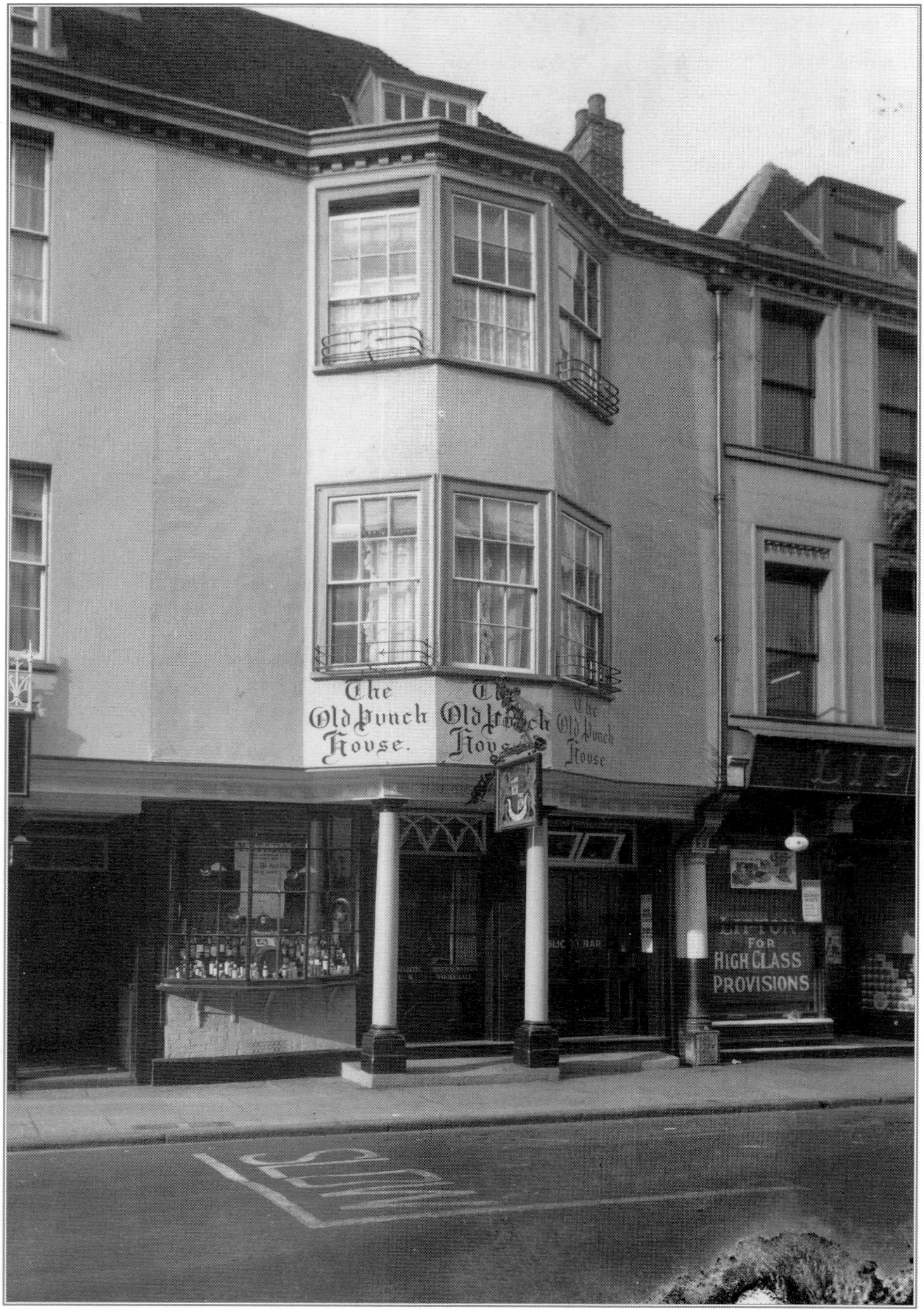
The Old Punch House.
The Old Punch House
The Old Punch House
LIP
FOR
HIGH CLASS
PROVISIONS
SLOW

Old Punch House. It is here, so legend has it, that John Lord Lumley entertained Queen Elizabeth in 1591. It is said that he made elaborate preparations for her visit.

John Lord Lumley was succeeded in 1609 by his kinsman, Sir Richard Lumley, created Lord Lumley of Waterford in 1628, and so the property passed down the generations. In the 19th century Chichester milk punch was made and sold at the site. Hence it became known as The Punch House.

It remains a striking building to this day, with its pleasing symmetry. Its upper storeys offer three-sided bow windows supported on two Roman Doric columns. Two more bow windows are at ground level. Many alterations to the original structure, however, mean that no one can date it with any certainty.

The Fleece Inn

Look up in East Street and you will see the impressive pediment of what was once The Fleece Inn, a hostelry which was also variously called The Golden Fleece, The Bell and The Coach and Horses (see photograph overleaf).

The pediment gives a fair indication as to the importance of the establishment, which dates back to 1641 as an alehouse. The building was refronted in the 18th century, with the Georgians, as they did so often, effectively disguising the much older building behind it.

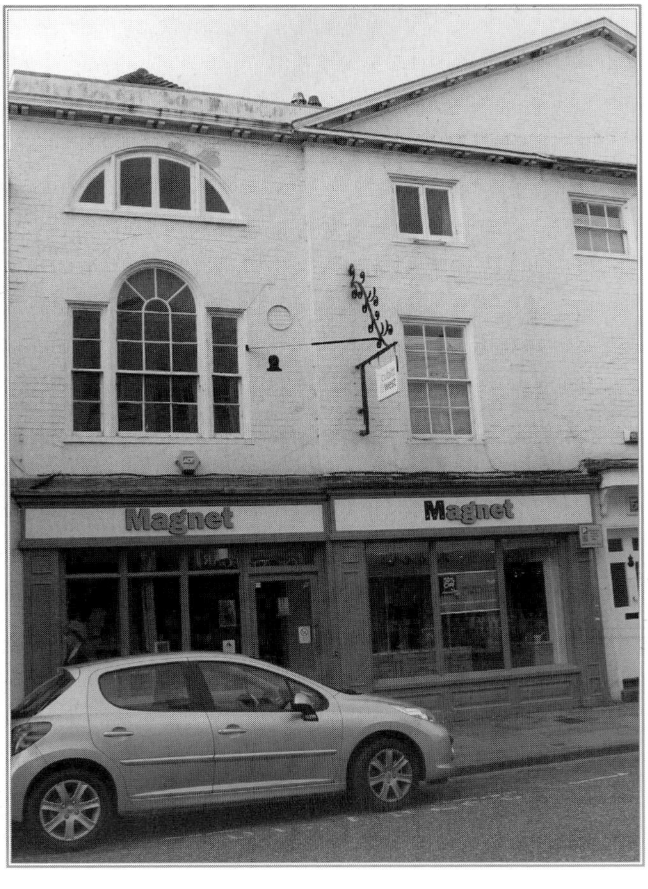

The Fleece stood on the south side of East Street near the junction with Baffins Lane, and as a coaching inn it had stables and outhouses behind it. Embracing Nos. 58 to 60 East Street, it had a significant presence, one of a healthy number of pubs in the immediate area. Other East Street pubs have included The Swan, The Royal Arms, The George and The Rifle or Rifleman.

The spirits stopped flowing at The Fleece in the late 1980s. The pub is featured in *The Historical Directory of Pubs in the South East of England* which gives among its landlords: J.T. Bilson, G. Langley, Charles Morgan, Fanny Morgan, Emma Poole, Charles W. Earwaker, Frances Morgan and Thomas G. Green.

The site of the former Fleece Inn is now occupied by Magnet.

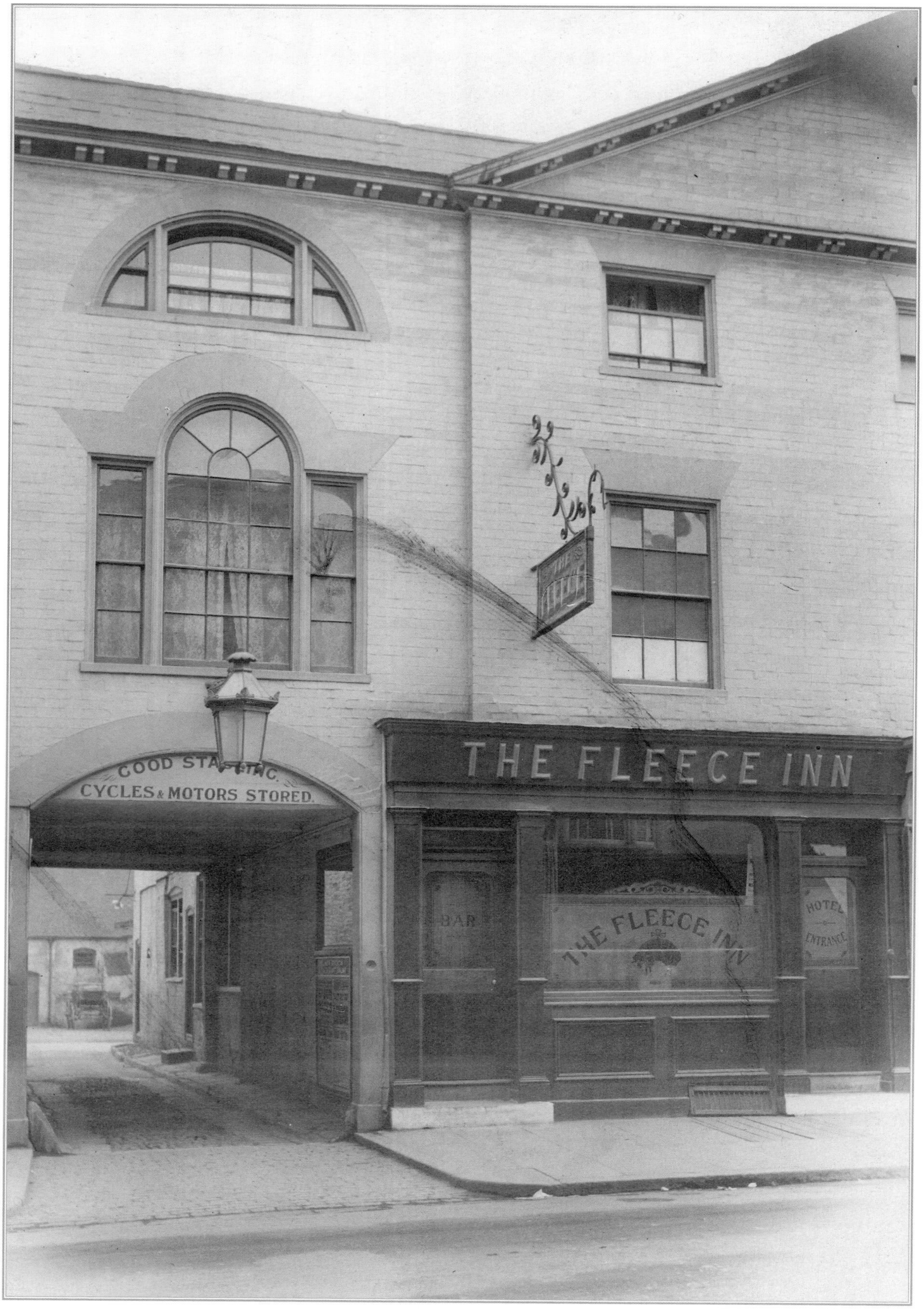
CYCLES & MOTORS STORED.
THE FLEECE INN
BAR
THE FLEECE INN
HOTEL ENTRANCE

The Red Lion

Now a fish and chip shop, The Red Lion in St Pancras was one of a remarkable number of pubs in a comparatively small area of Chichester.

In 1867 there were apparently 17 public houses serving a population of just over a thousand, among them The Golden Lion (possibly a different name for The Red Lion), The Star and Garter, The Hope, The Victoria, The Coach and Horses and The Ship and Lighter.

The suburb of St Pancras outside the East Gate was destroyed at the time of the Civil War siege of 1642 when Chichester's needle-making industry was also wrecked. It was among the slowest of Chichester's suburbs to recover.

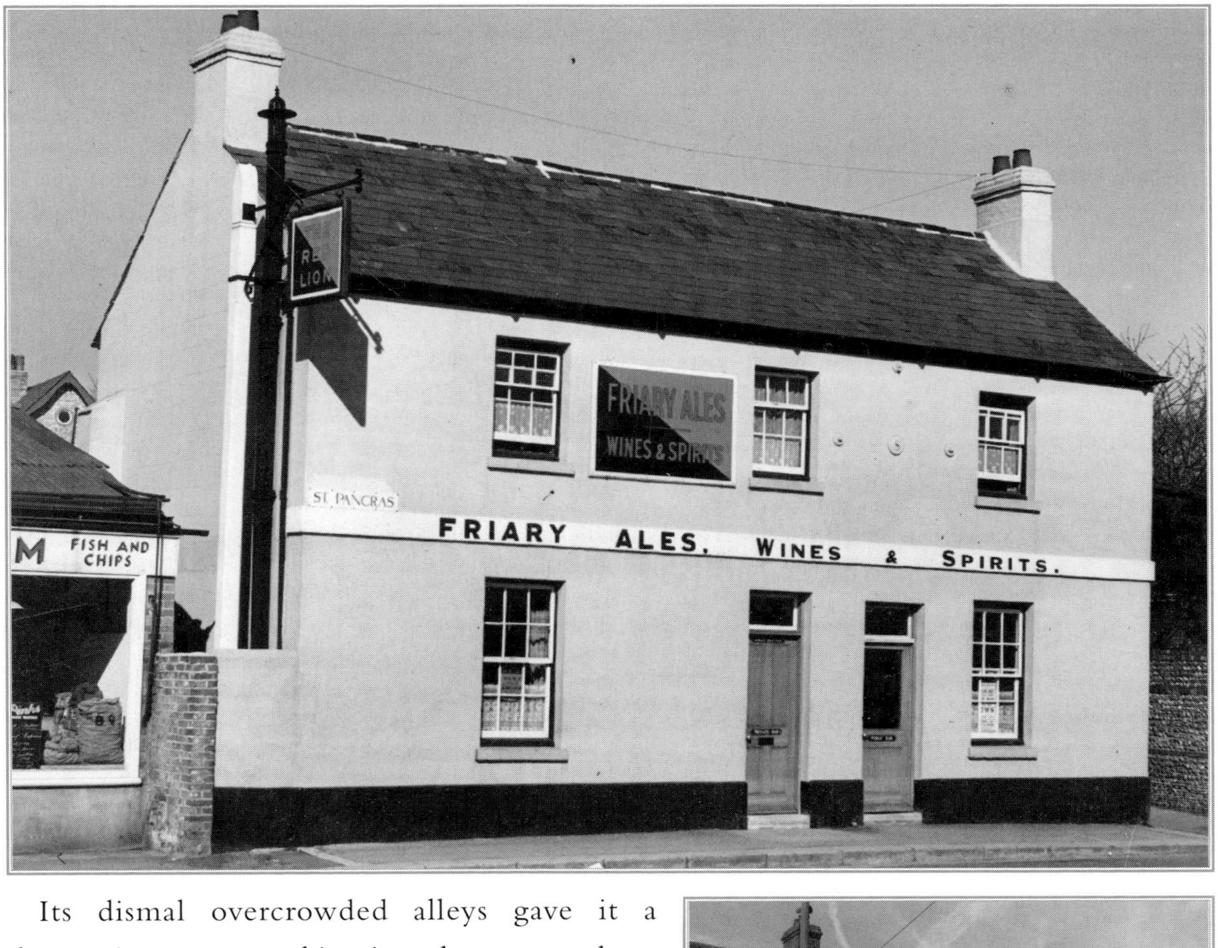

Its dismal overcrowded alleys gave it a threatening aspect, making it a place many chose to avoid. Arguably, it was not until the rebuilding of St Pancras' Church in 1750–51 – destroyed during the siege – that things began at last to look up in this particular part of Chichester. However, even in the 19th century the rebuilt area was among the less salubrious parts of Chichester.

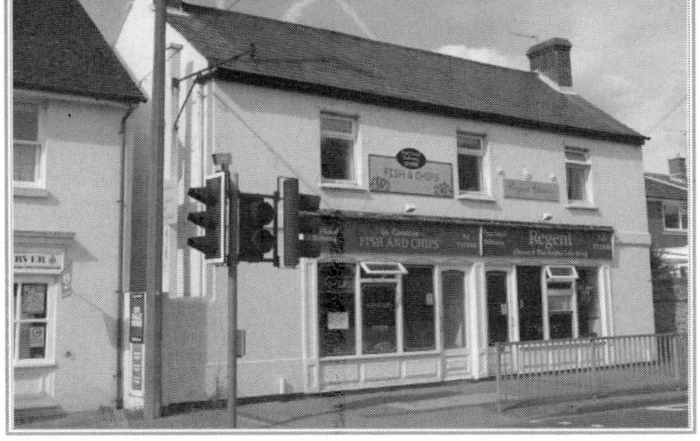

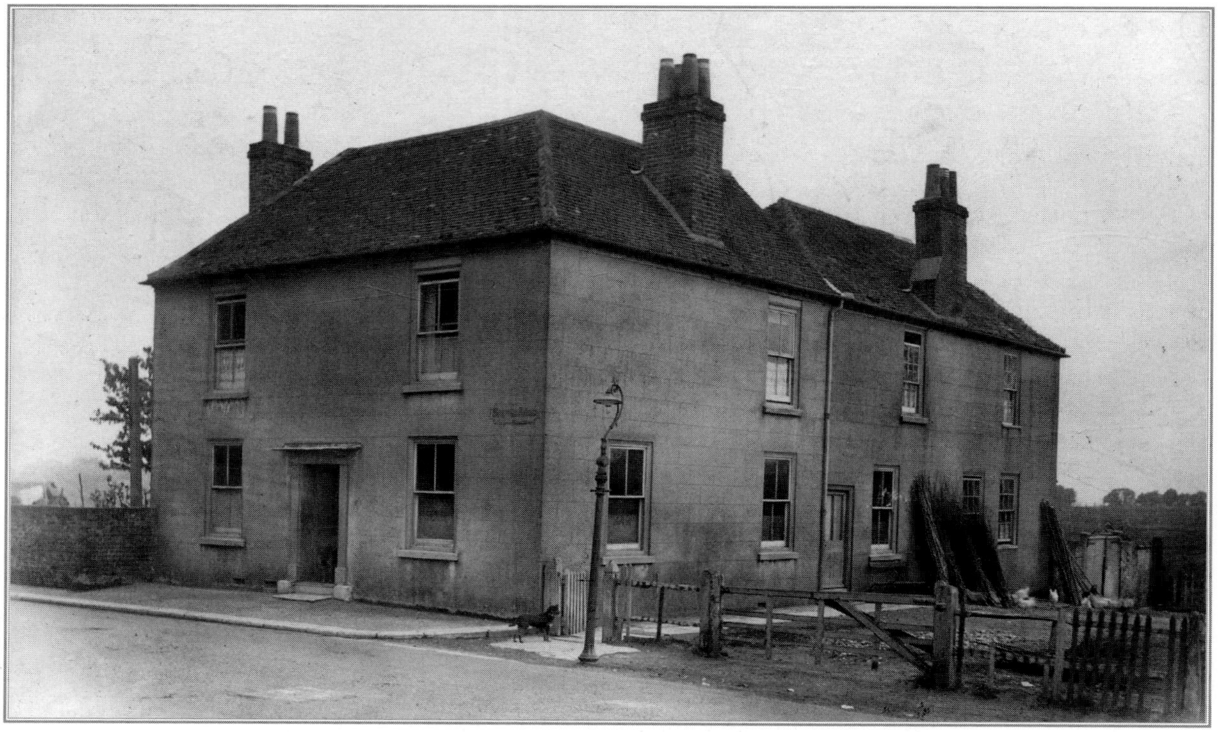

The Broyle

Now the French restaurant Comme Ça, this building was once the Broyle public house, a name which occupies its very own slice of Chichester history.

Broyle or Broil means a forest enclosure containing animals for hunting enclosed by a wall or a hedge – which is exactly what the Broyle was. It was also a highly strategic location on high ground to the north of the city – which is why the barracks were situated here.

The Broyle abounds in grim associations. It was here that the executions were carried out at the city's gallows. One of the last and most memorable executions was that of the Hawkhurst Gang, a gang of nine smugglers and murderers executed in January 1749 with two, Richard Mills the Elder and Richard Mills the Younger, being buried at the side of the gallows on the Broil.

Two of the remaining seven, William Carter and Henry Sheerman, were then displayed in chains along the Portsmouth Road, with the others being displayed along several routes to act as a deterrent to anyone else contemplating a career in murder and smuggling.

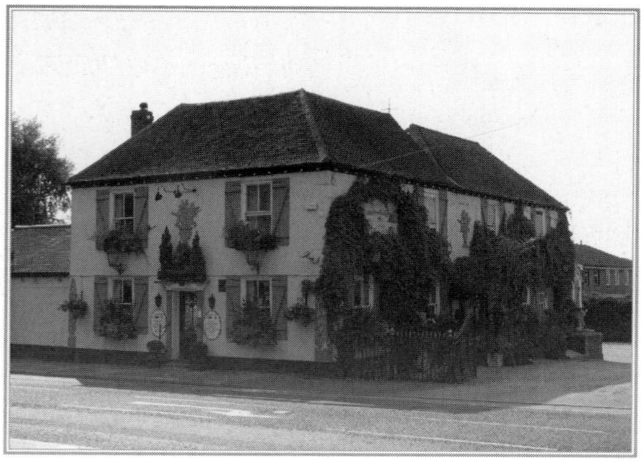

Probably because of the presence of the barracks, Broyle Road has traditionally been an area rich in public houses. The Bell, The Beehive, The Freetraders Hall, The Star, The Duke of Edinburgh, The Wellington, The Inkerman Tavern and The Old House at Home are among those the road has hosted.

CHAPTER 13
WEST SUSSEX RECORD OFFICE AND CHICHESTER DISTRICT MUSEUM

West Sussex Record Office

With its superb collections and professional, ever helpful staff, West Sussex Record Office is the first port of call for anyone engaged in historical research in the county.

Like the District Museum, the County Record Office exists to bring history to life – and the support both have shown in the preparation of this book is typical of two institutions who do not just preserve the past but also, just as importantly, make it available to us in the present.

Established in 1946, the Record Office was situated for a time in what is now Edes House before moving to its present purpose-built accommodation in nearby Orchard Street in 1989. Since then it has continued to collect and preserve the documentary and recorded heritage of the county of West Sussex.

These recent internet-fuelled years have seen a massive increase in interest in family history – a challenge the Record Office has risen to as the major centre for family history research in the county.

Its collections include records of local government from the 16th century, the diocese of Chichester and its parishes and those of courts, businesses, families, estates, societies and schools.

It also holds records of West Sussex hospitals and the West Sussex Constabulary. West Sussex Record Office is also the repository and conservation centre of the regional film archive, Screen Archive South East.

Just as importantly, the Record Office is the official archive for the Royal Sussex Regiment. The archives deposited in the West Sussex Record Office since 1979 consist of documents, photographs, audio-visual records and printed works covering the history of the regiment from its establishment in 1701 as the 35th Regiment of Foot, to its amalgamation in The Queen's Regiment in 1966.

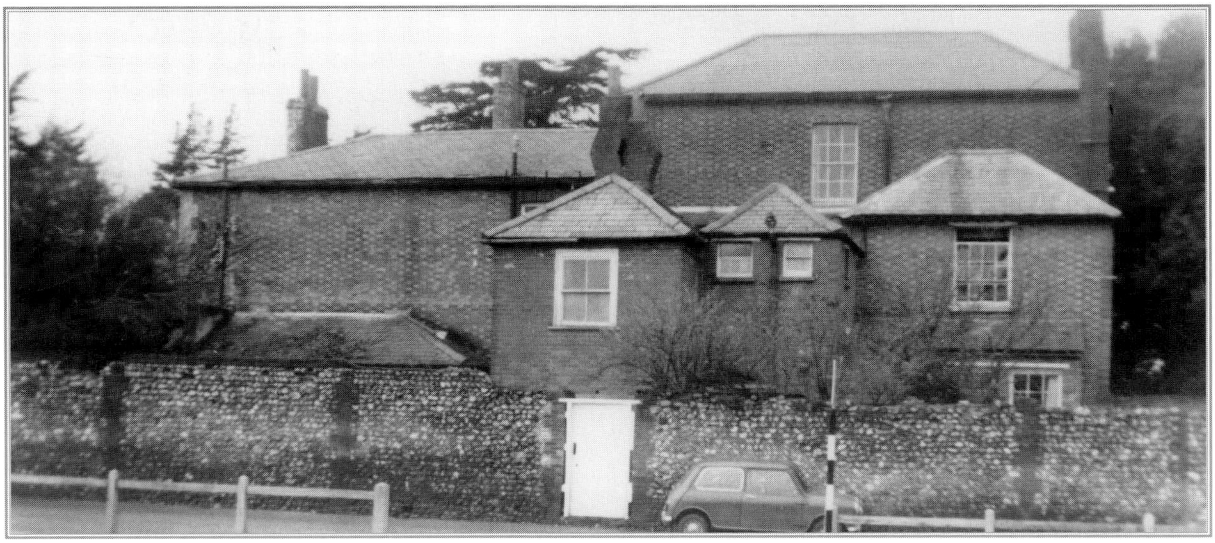

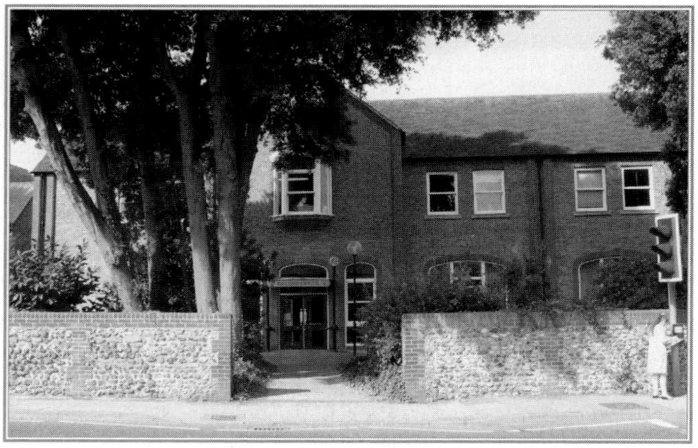

As the Diocesan Record Office, it also holds the official records of the bishops of Chichester, the dean and chapter of Chichester Cathedral and the property they owned. The records include the original parish registers of baptisms, marriages and burials for West Sussex parishes and the bishops' transcripts from every parish in both West and East Sussex.

The Record Office also provides free public access to a wide range of family and local history databases available online and on CD. It is open six days a week and offers a professional research service, document and photographic scanning and an archival conservation service.

Chichester District Museum

Exciting times lie ahead for Chichester District Museum, a key collaborator in the preparation of this book.

The District Museum is currently situated in Little London, a site already rich in history.

However, plans are progressing well for a move to an even more historic site in Tower Street, where the museum will be able to incorporate remains of Roman baths which were first discovered in the 1970s by Chichester archaeologist Alec Down and his team of volunteers.

Plans for the new District Museum include the re-excavation of the baths, allowing the remains to go on permanent display. The idea is that the new museum will tell the story of the whole district, becoming a hub for the area's heritage.

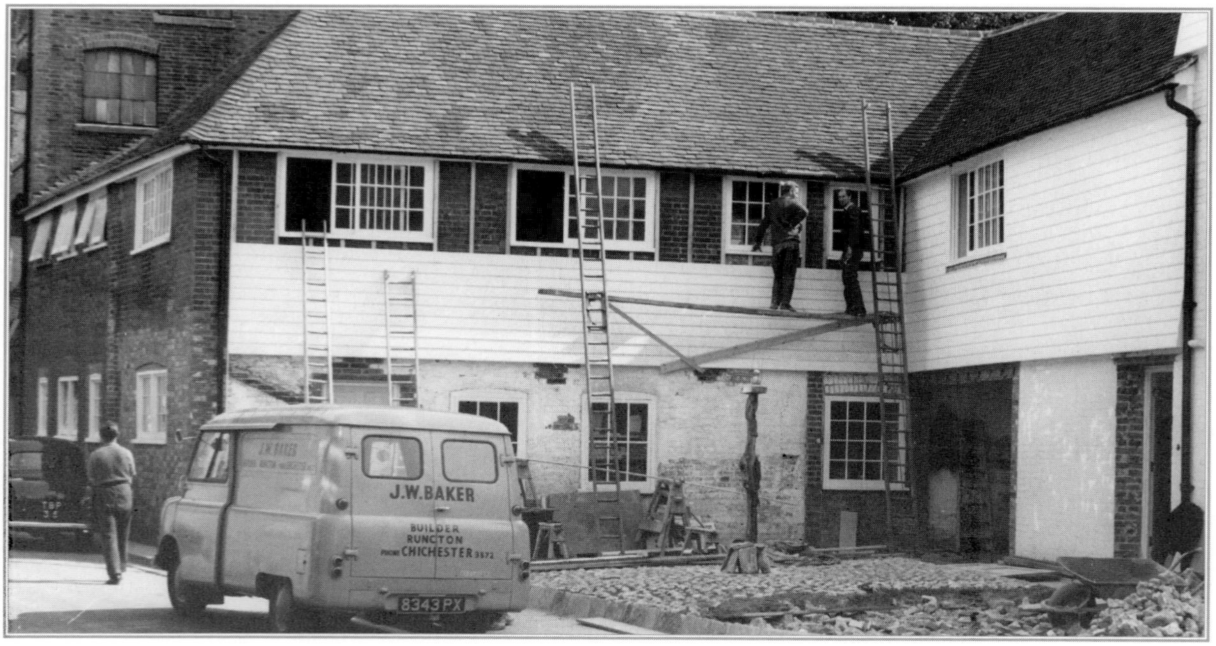

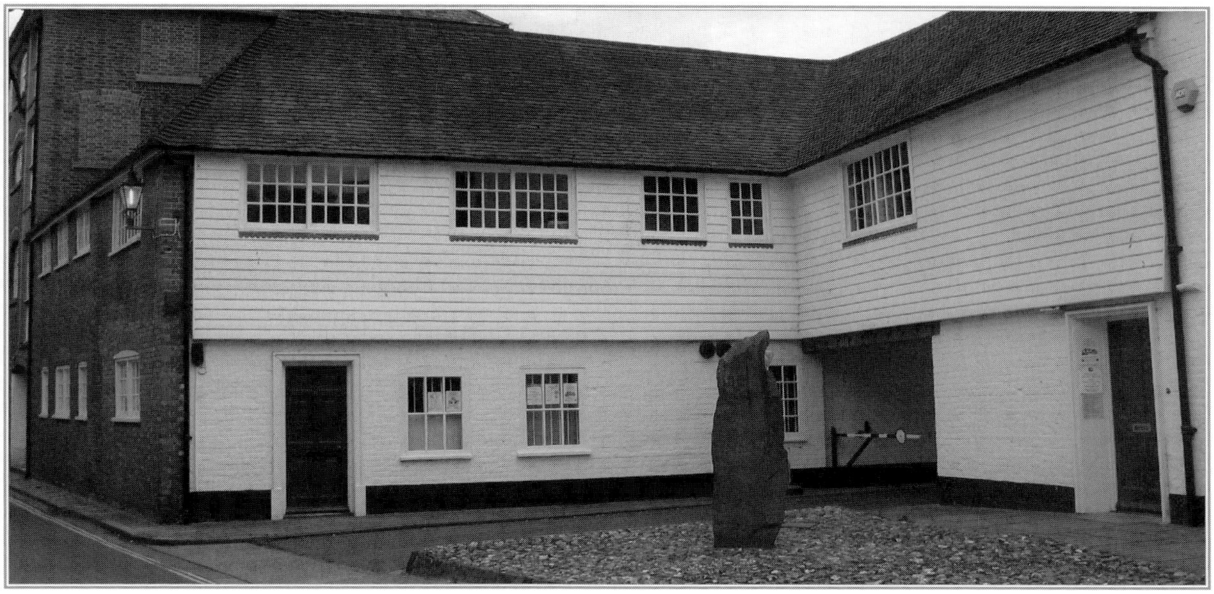

The development will be an exciting new chapter for the city's museum service, which dates back to the beginning of the 19th century. The museum was founded in 1831, a reflection of the thirst for knowledge the Industrial Revolution had sparked.

Number 45 South Street was an early location. However, the 1890s were a period of decline, and during World War One the army commandeered the museum.

In 1936 a two-week exhibition was set up in the Guildhall in Priory Park, and from the mid-1940s the Guildhall was the museum's permanent home.

In 1961 an exhibition on Changing Chichester was held in the Assembly Rooms, provoking widespread interest, as a result of which Chichester architect Stanley Roth bought Sadler's disused corn store in Little London.

Roth suggested the council should lease it from him for a museum, and in 1963 the former corn store became Chichester Museum. The older picture (see page 159) shows the work on No. 29, Little London, during its conversion.

In 1974, under local government reorganisation, the Chichester Museum became Chichester District Museum with a remit to provide museum services throughout the district.

Thanks to its dedicated staff, Chichester District Museum, like the Record Office, is doing a wonderful job of preserving the past, which has helped to make this book possible.

Many of the originals of the older photographs I have used are in the Museum and Record Office collections. I am sincerely grateful for the help, advice and encouragement I received from both institutions in the preparation of this book. Both are huge assets to the city. It is their collections which will make a future edition of this book possible, perhaps in another 50 years. Who knows what will have transformed by then and what will have stayed the same. Let's hope Chichester will once again be able to present the unique blend of change and continuity which makes it the vibrant city it is today.

Roll of Honour

John Farmer
Mrs Angela Stanley
Mr Gerald Kissock
Mr Vic Kissock
Mr Gerald Smith
Mr Desmond Burton
Mrs Mary Barnes
Barry & Rachel Fletcher
Christopher Hatch
Robert Hatch
Margaret Bond-Webster
Mrs J. Fairbrother
Mrs H. Gough
Tony Wingham
Anne Scicluna
Doris Gilbert
Miriam Norris
Ann Tice
L. & A. Sykes
Mike Jennings
Mr I. H. Cross
Philip Storer
Lionel F. Matthews
Mr Brian Trinder
Julie Peverett
Gilbert Dash
Dr Peter Sole
Pam Smith
Sheila Brading
Maureen Martin
Barrie Morgans
Winifrid Brown
Beverly Englesman
Brian Westrop
Peter J. White
Mrs Pat Gibson
Victor Billinghurst
Val Timlin
John Manning
Wendy Mae Knowles
Harold S. Taylor
Ruth Twiss
David Booth
Maureen Stenning
Sheila and John Phillips
Connie Westbrook
Eric John Westbrook
Laurie Cullingford
Tom Holden
Mr Alfie Marsh
John Graham Owen
Sharon Strong
Alan Chapman
Brenda Coombes
Colin Shield
Fiona Wiggins
Jake Wright
Sheila Scutt

Mike Goodchild
Marjorie Hoare Née Dahcer
Yvonne Sutters
Mrs Catherine Corderoy
William Styles
Shirley Fogg
David Gaitt
Gwen Mouncher
Roger Mouncher
Gwendoline Rawes Née Turner
Christine Rosewarn
Ted Liddle B.E.M.
N. A. Hermon-Taylor
Bernard and Peggy Hammond
Cecil Pelling
Iain Pelling
Mark Mundy
Sara Pelling
Trilby Mills
Yvonne Nobes
William Wilson
Ronald Walker
Robert E. C. Woodhead
The Selsey Society
Betty Williams
Frank Hellyer
Mrs Irene Worral
Mr Alan Trevor Gilbert
Mrs Trisha Blackmore
John Pollock
Sandra Jayne Cripps
Elaine Rowe
Ron Peacock
Mrs I. Triggs
R. M. Stenning
Mrs J. Barratt
S. P. D. Hanwell
Mary E. Ramsay (Mrs)
Brian Douglas Knight
Barry Phillip Newell
The Westacott Family
Nick Neal
Mr James Stillman
Derek Nevill Bond
Margaret Ann Knight
Robert Rice
Andrée Harding
Brenda B. Clark (Née Nash)
Tony French
Rachael Osborne
Penny Ladell Marshall
Colin Clark
Toby Palmer
Alan F. Budd
Dorothy Henly
Mrs Rosemary Page
Dr John Lonergan
John Richard Lonergan

Iris Coleman
Mike Darby
Simon D. Field
John Templeton
Valerie Stenning
Philip Tobutt
Gwendoline Mackett
Phyllis Kirk
The Richard Tildesley Practice
Peter Doust
Mrs Rosamund J. Champ
Sue Price
Andrew Berriman
Mrs Tracey Sharp
Therese Brook
Jean Frances
Pamela Cooper
Mr Dennis N. Dean
David M. Morgan
Maureen Lamdin
Richard Ware
Peter Fogden
Joyce Cotterell
Mr A. D. Matthews
Alan North
The Family of Dr and Mrs Gough
Mrs Julia P. W. Baker
James Ayling
Peter Turner
Garry Robert Langridge
Graham Rodney Langridge
Peter Sochall
Tom Creedy
Fredrick Pearce
John Percy 169 WSFB RTD
Ruth Sullivan
Brian J. Tamplin
Barbara Perry
John Holloway
Richard Doman
Ian Fuller
Sheila Castillo
Roger Tadd
K. D. Smith
Mrs K. J. Bosley
Mrs Freda Tucker
Rodney Duggua
Roland Brackley
Christopher New
Sylvia R. Olliver
Mike Apps
Deanna Apps
M. J. Penfold Penfold Butchers
Brenda Ward
Bridget Hoare Fielding
Philip Boxall
Jim Tolley

Barry and Vie Beckett
Margaret Rudderham
Mrs M. A. King
Mrs Jean Ubsdell
Bev Faulks
Sheila Goddings
Brenda Cox
Val Brocklebank
Jill Cosens Shipp
Jackie Tandy
Jeannette Cavalier
J. K. Cross
Kim Leslie
D. J. Robinson
Anne Wadey
Lesley E. Howarth
Betty Down
Malcolm Parvin
Patrick D. Coombes
John Leslie James Faldo
Chris Lindsay
Mr Kenneth Barber
Ron Shippam
Alan Murphy
Montague Griss
Dorothy May Vincent
John Wood
Peter Wilson
Roger Keyworth
Maureen Muir
Mrs I. Fry
Jennifer Chatfield
Rita Charlotte Rook
Pearl Stewart
Sarah Haines
Elizabeth Shone
John Kynaston
M. Simmonds
Richard Bramley
Mrs Mary Briggs
Rodney Wing
Athalie Maskell
Brenda Sharpe
Jonathan Carver
David Carver
Barbara Holloway
Brenda Billings
Adam Long
Pamela Debenham
Raymond Debenham
Miss Lucilla Walker
David Swaffield
John Fitzmaurice
Clifford Funnell
Mrs Margaret Hall
Jessie on her 90th Birthday
Pamela J. M. Moore Née Radford
John Richard Moore